A POLITICAL ECONOMY OF THE AFRICAN CRISIS

Bade Onimode

Institute for African Alternatives
Zed Books Ltd.
London and New Jersey

A Political Economy of the African Crisis was first published in 1988 by
Zed Books Ltd., 57 Caledonian Road, London N1 9BU and
171 First Avenue, Atlantic Highlands, New Jersey 07716 with
The Institute for African Alternatives, 23 Bevenden Street, London N1 6BH

Typeset by EMS Photosetters, Rochford, Essex
Cover design by Andrew Corbett
Printed and bound in Great Britain by
Biddles Ltd, Guildford and King's Lynn

British Library Cataloguing in Publication Data

Onimode, Bade
A political economy of the African crisis.
1. Africa. Economic conditions. Political
aspects
I. Title
330.96'0328

ISBN 0-86232-373-8
ISBN 0-86232-374-6 Pbk

Library of Congress Cataloging-in-Publication Data

Onimode, Bade.
A political economy of the African crisis / Bade Onimode.
p. cm.
Bibliography: p.
Includes index.
ISBN 0-86232-373-8. ISBN 0-86232-374-6 (pbk.)
1. Africa—Economic conditions—1960– 2. Africa—Social
conditions—1960– I. Title.
HC800.055 1988
330.96'0328—dc19

A POLITICAL ECONOMY OF THE AFRICAN CRISIS

Other Titles by the Author

Economic Development in Nigeria: The Socialist Alternative (Ibadan: Nigerian Academy of Art, Sciences & Technology, 1975)

Basic Mathematics for Economists (London: Allen & Unwin, 1980)

Mathematics for Economics and Business (London: Allen & Unwin, forthcoming)

Imperialism and Underdevelopment in Nigeria: The Dialectics of Mass Poverty (London: Zed Books, 1982)

An Introduction to Marxist Political Economy (London: Zed Books, 1985)

Contents

Tables

Figures

1 The Crisis of Underdevelopment in Africa

> The African continent, in addition to being faced with the rapidly deteriorating food situation and increasing dependence on food aid and food imports, continues to face ominous accentuation of mass poverty, the risk of natural resources depletion and of environmental degradation. Life expectancy at birth remains low, while nutritional deficiency and the danger of physical disintegration remain serious. The continent is plagued with large-scale unemployment and inflation, and continues to labour under the crushing burden of inherited alien socio-economic structures and patterns. Little wonder that Africa is the least developed of the world's major regions (harbouring twenty of the world's thirty-one least developed among the underdeveloped countries).[1]
> **Adebayo Adedeji**, Executive Secretary, Economic Commission for Africa.

The bleak scenario depicted in this quotation attests to the grave and deteriorating crisis in Africa. Indeed, to one observer, the situation is so critical that the title of a book on contemporary Africa poses the question: *Can Africa Survive?*.[2] Though the hysteria is justified, it is important to perceive the myriad problems threatening Africa in an epistemological perspective that emphasises the essential crisis character of these conditions within the framework of the historiography of the continent and its role in world economy.

The nature of the African crisis

The African crisis is not merely an economic crisis in the bourgeois or Marxian sense. It is much deeper than a bourgeois economic crisis of threatened starvation, massive unemployment, growing deficits and debts, disequilibria in different markets and sluggish economic growth. These are merely the surface manifestations of the crisis. Neither is the deepening crisis in Africa just a Marxian crisis arising from underconsumption, disproportionality and related factors, which are commonly associated with the contradictions of industrial capitalism. This is because most African countries are either pre-industrial or semi-industrial, their capitalist contradictions are still muted and mediated by their dependence on metropolitan capitalism, so that much of the symptoms of Marxian crises they exhibit are essential spill-overs from the industrialised countries.

Fundamentally, the African crisis is one of underdevelopment, the central problematic of the African continent and the Third World generally. This makes the crisis basically structural and historical. But though underdevelopment is largely an economic phenomenon, the African crisis is also accentuated by serious social and political problems as well as an intellectual crisis. The intensification of the contradictions of underdevelopment are visible in the food crisis, deplorable mass poverty, decimating disease, pervasive illiteracy, technological backwardness, prostrate external dependence and mounting foreign debts. The social trauma is exhibited in the sharpening social divisions arising from widening distributional inequalities, ethno-religious primordiality, rising crime and cultural degradation. Correspondingly, Africa's political contour is disturbed, with widespread and growing repression, resulting in a massive refugee problem, coups and counter-coups, apartheid oppression and external subversion. Then, too, there is the intellectual crisis, which results not merely from the lingering colonial mentality and foreign intellectual domination, but from the dominant bourgeois scholarship's fundamental irrelevance to African social reality, especially in the imported social services.

The structural roots of these contradictions of the African crisis are anchored primarily to the relations of exploitation, domestic class structures, prostrate external dependence and the distortions of the dominant neocolonial social formations in Africa. The pliant class structures, production relations and forms of exploitation that sustain neocolonialism, and the nature of the client post-colonial states that these class structures have developed, also operate to intensify the crisis. These structural deformities of the African milieu are inexorably bound up with the continent's historiography. As this history is an integral part of the global history of imperialism, a clear understanding of the major historical epochs in Africa is essential to the correct appreciation of the idiom of the African crisis.

By contrast, Basil Davidson perceives the African crisis as a "continental crisis of institutions".

> Africa's real problems are those of a period of major transition from systems of development viable in the pre-colonial past to other systems, similarly viable, which can face the challenges of the future . . .
>
> The crisis which thus arises is, therefore, one of institutions. Those of the past have lost their containing power. Those of the present offer little save confusion. Those of the future have yet to appear. And it is this that gives all these societies . . . their essential unity of situation.[3]

He is right that this is a crisis of system and structure, and that the profound institutional failure is beyond the remedial power of any mere modification or reform, since the system or systems as they stand simply do not work and cannot be made to work.

But even for 1974, this perception of the Africa crisis needs modification. It is, indeed, possible that Basil Davidson has revised his view of the crisis since it has been unfolding more clearly and more deeply in the 1970s and 1980s. For example, the predominant transition to neocolonial capitalism has not been viable. Similarly, some of the present institutions, such as liberation movements, mass organisations, public ownership, democratic rule, workers' control of enterprises, etc. offer some real hope of grappling with the complex problems of the continent. For these reasons it is more appropriate to emphasise the analysis of systems and structures than of their derivative institutions.

The paradox of continental wealth and mass poverty

The paradox of the deepening crisis of mass poverty in Africa and the enormous wealth of the continent is very painful.[4] Yet this cynical asymmetry is an integral part of the perverse logic of capitalism and imperialism. Marx and Engels were compelled by the force of the irony to devote considerable attention in the *Communist Manifesto* to the fact that just as capitalism has created more massive wealth than all previous modes of production, it has also generated more incredible squalor than any previous epoch in human history. This is one of the central contradictions of bourgeois society.

In contrast to the cynicism of the vicious-circle-of-poverty theorists that "a country is poor because it is poor", Africa is poor because she is rich. Indeed, one of the keys to the resolution of the African crisis is the explanation of how the enormous wealth of Africa is also the basis of the relationships that have generated the profound misery of the vast majority of Africans. The following confession by a representative of Africa's predators is instructive.

> To the crowded Europe, Africa holds the promise of a frontier land still susceptible of great expansion, both as a market and as a source of unexplored industrial potential. Its riches in strategic and other minerals are impressive. In industrial diamonds, columbium, cobalt, chromium and beryllium Africa either heads the list of world producers or stands close to the top. It is a significant producer of tin,manganese, copper, antimony; and its reserves of iron ore and bauxite are just beginning to be tapped. The uranium of the Congo and South Africa has contributed to the unfolding of the atomic age. The French discovery of oil in the Sahara has enhanced the importance of Algeria, and Libya has also come into new riches. To this mineral wealth, Africa adds through its agriculture a variety of foodstuffs and industrial materials such as cocoa, coffee, tea, vegetable oil, cotton and pyrethrum. The United States has a direct interest in many of these products, but it is probably of less importance to assure its own access to Africa's resources and markets than to make sure that its European allies are not cut off from them.

Another dimension of Africa's colossal riches in minerals is summarised in Table 1.1.

The critical significance of this huge mineral wealth lies in the fact that the basic structure of contemporary civilisation worldwide is dependent on minerals. They are required for the production of tractors, cars, railways, ships, planes, steel,

Table 1.1
Africa's mineral production: 1973

Mineral	*Total African production (inc. South Africa)*	*% of world production*	*Major producer in Africa*
Steel industry metals (metric tons):			
Iron ore	47.8m	4.9	Liberia
Nickel	31,626	2.8	South Africa
Manganese	3m	14.9	South Africa
Chromium	1.1m	22.0	South Africa
Cobalt	18,374	68.9	Zaire
Vanadium	8,900	42.4	South Africa
Tungsten	1,100	0.9	Rwanda
Columbium	1,300	4.0	Nigeria
Older major metals (metric tons):			
Copper	1.4m	9.9	Zambia
Tin	15,800	3.2	Nigeria
Lead	212,000	3.0	Morocco
Zinc	290,400	2.1	Zaire
Light metals (metric tons):			
Bauxite	4.1m	4.5	Guinea
Precious metals:			
Gold	899,000 kilos	75.4	South Africa
Platinum	1.8m ozs	36.8	South Africa
Fuel minerals:			
Coal (metric tons)	67.9m	2.8	South Africa
Crude oil (metric tons)	286.5m	3.8	Libya, Nigeria, Algeria
Natural gas (cu m)	16.3m	0.9	Liberia, Nigeria, Algeria
Gem stones, abrasives & insulators:			
Diamonds (carats)	33.5m	29.3	Zaire
Asbestos (metric tons)	452,000	6.7	South Africa
Nuclear & chemical (metric tons):			
Uranium	4,000	13.7	South Africa
Phosphates	28.5m	17.3	Morocco
Antimony	16,800	22.3	South Africa
Fluorspar	357,300	4.7	South Africa

Source: G. Lanning with M. Mueller (1979) *Africa Undermined – Mining Companies and the Under-development of Africa* (Harmondsworth; Penguin), pp. 100–1.

etc. The USA, Western Europe and Japan depend on Africa for more than 50% of their imports of bauxite, natural gas, phosphates, cobalt, uranium ore, alumina, chromium, manganese, etc.[5] Yet, most of Africa's mineral wealth remains untapped and unknown.

Africa produces virtually every agricultural and sylvicultural raw material, such as rubber, cotton, paper, timber, oils, fruits and so on, plus a rich variety of foodstuffs including meat, as well as fish. The continent is blessed with rich alluvial and sandy soils in numerous, large river valleys and undulating terrains, and over 50% of this vast arable land is still uncultivated, despite the waste of shift-cultivation. This huge wealth is supported with a virile population of approximately 492 million in 1982 in a land area of more than 10 million square miles. Though the per capita income for the continent is still under $US200, this large population constitutes a relatively extensive market for many products. In addition, Africa possesses excellent transport potentials in numerous navigable rivers and highly accessible plains and lowlands.

Collectively, therefore, Africa has an excellent resource base that could have supported a much higher standard of living for the people than their current squalor. This enormous resource base is still an impressive potential for the genuine future development of the continent under the appropriate socio-economic transformation. This is without prejudice to the objective fact that the imperialist balkanisation of the continent into mini-states has limited the availability of these resources within each country. But relative to countries such as Japan with virtually no minerals, which have nevertheless industrialised, the resource base of African countries could have supported, and can still sustain, a very healthy level of development.

Yet, in spite of this enormous wealth, Africa remains the poorest continent in the world, and is sinking into deeper crisis. The main reason for this is that for centuries, Africa's huge wealth has been plundered for the benefit of non-Africans. The visible tragedies of this long foreign depredation of Africa, which constitute the empirical manifestations of the continental crisis, bear summarising.

Some facts about the African crisis

The surface manifestations of the crisis of underdevelopment in Africa presented here are merely the economic evidence. They are the effects of the crisis on the economic plane and, therefore, they cannot also be regarded as the only causes of the disaster, as in bourgeois theorising on underdevelopment. One feature of the crisis is that 21 of the 30 countries classified by the UN as least-developed in the world are in Africa.[6] With respect to Gross Domestic Product (GDP), while 12 African countries had negative annual growth rates of GDP per capita (that is, per head of population) during 1960/70, 20 countries had negative annual growth rates in 1970/76. For 1960/79, the per capita income growth rate was negative in eight countries, 0 to 1% in another ten countries and 1 to 2% in five others.[7] The annual real growth of GNP (Gross National Product) and GNP per capita for Africa and other regions during 1966/80 are shown in Table 1.2.

Table 1.2
Global growth levels of GNP and per capita income, 1966/80

Region	*GNP*					*GNP per capita*				
	1966/76	*1977*	*1978*	*1979*	*1980*[a]	*1966/76*	*1977*	*1978*	*1979*	*1980*
All developing regions	6.1	5.8	5.2	5.2	4.6	3.6	3.5	2.8	2.7	2.3
Africa South of the Sahara	5.0	2.9	3.4	3.3	2.3	2.3	0.3	0.7	0.6	–0.4
Industrial Countries	4.2	3.8	4.0	3.5	1.3	3.3	3.2	3.3	2.8	0.6

[a] Preliminary.

Source: World Bank: World Development Report, 1981 (Washington), p. 19.

The corresponding per capita income of selected African countries from the highest to the lowest in 1979 and 1982 is shown in Table 1.3.

Table 1.3
GNP per capita in selected African countries: 1979/82 (US$)

	1979	*1982*
Gabon		4,000
Ivory Coast	1040	950
Mauritius	1030	1,240
Botswana	720	900
Nigeria	670	860
Congo	630	1,180
Cameroon	560	890
Zambia	500	640
Rwanda & Malawi	200	210 (Malawi)
Burundi & Burkina Faso (Upper Volta)	180	210 (B.Faso)
Guinea Bissau	170	170
Mali	140	180
Ethiopia	130	140
Chad (lowest)	110	80

Source: World Bank, *World Development Report*, 1981 and 1984 (Washington), pp. 31, 37, 218.

The per capita income in Africa rose from an average of $US133 in 1960 to $US170 in 1970. By 1979, it fluctuated between $US110 and $US370 for the whole continent, except South Africa. By contrast, the average per capita income in the industrialised capitalist countries (ICC's) was $US1,500 in 1960 and $US2,980 in 1970: eleven times the average income for Africa in 1960 and 18 times in 1970 – a measure of widening global inequality.

In agriculture, 29 out of 45 African countries had negative annual growth rates of per capita food production during 1970/76, while in the 1960/70 period only 17 of the 45 countries had such negative growth rates. In 1980, taking 1969/71 as base (that is, 1969/71 = 100), the per capita food production index was below 100 in 16 countries. This declining production has resulted in massive food imports into what is a primarily agricultural continent. Thus, by 1980, each African country had an average food import bill of $US102 million for cereals and livestock. For all non-oil producing African countries, the total food import bill which in 1973 was $US1.9 billion rose to $US6 billion in 1980; or, from being 19.4% of total export earnings in 1973, by 1980 the food import bill was 23.7% of these exports.[8]

In manufacturing, in the 1970/80 period, the annual real growth rate of manufacturing value-added (mva) was negative in six countries, but in 1975/80 it was negative in 13 countries and 0 to 3% in 14 other countries. In 1980 constant prices, mva per capita averaged $US21.1 for all Africa, but less than that for 37 countries. The corresponding mva in GDP at factor cost in constant 1980 was 9.8% for all Africa, and less than that in 34 countries.[9] During 1950/60 and 1960/70, Africa's share in world manufacturing output remained stagnant at 0.6%. The per capita manufacturing output in Africa rose from $US11 to $US16 or by $US5 in 1960/70, by $US220 in the industrialised capitalist countries (ICCs) and by $US430 in the socialist countries.

Africa's foreign debts have also been piling up; rising from $US7 billion in 1965 to $US28 billion in 1974, or from $US9.02 billion in 1970 to $US49.6 billion in 1978, with total debt servicing increasing from $US0.85 billion in 1970 to $US5.6 billion in 1978. Debt servicing has thus been rising by $2 billion annually for non-oil exporting African countries. Debt servicing as a proportion of export earnings was 10 to 20% in 15 countries in 1970 and more than 20% in eight countries by 1978/79.[10]

Africa's consolidated balance of foreign trade payments in billions of US dollars is shown in Table 1.4.[11]

Table 1.4
Africa's trade balances, 1970/79

Item	*1970*	*1979*
Trade balance	+0.6	−3.7
Current account balance	−1.8	−10.3
General balance	+0.6	−1.4

The associated net exports of Africa as a percentage of GDP at current market prices are shown in Table 1.5.[12]

These data imply that a rising proportion of GDP is needed to offset trade deficit. The associated terms of trade (ratio of export to import prices) and purchasing power of exports (PPE) for Africa are shown in Table 1.6.

Similarly, non-oil producing Africa's current account balances and long-term external debt for 1967/82 are shown in Table 1.7.

Table 1.5
Africa's net exports as percentage of GDP, 1970/80

African sub-region	*1970*	*1971*	*1972*	*1973*	*1974*	*1975*	*1976*	*1977*	*1978*	*1979*	*1980*
Main oil exporters	4.7	5.9	5.2	5.1	16.2	0.4	2.1	2.6	−3.4	6.8	14.8
Least developed 21 countries	4.2	−5.3	−3.7	−4.5	−9.6	−10.4	−7.0	−7.3	−10.0	−9.3	−10.4
Other African countries	−0.8	−3.7	−2.0	−0.8	−2.3	−8.2	−7.0	−6.7	−8.2	−8.9	−8.0

Source: UNIDO, op. cit., p. 135.

Table 1.6
The purchasing power of Africa's export earnings

Africa (excluding South Africa)	*Change from Preceding Year*										
	1972	*1973*	*1974*	*1975*	*1976*	*1977*	*1978*	*1979*	*1980*	*1981*	*1982*
Terms of trade	−1.8	8.5	4.7	−12.7	6.7	17.1	−7.2	0.1	−9.1	−4.9	−3.1
PPE[a]	4.7	11.9	3.7	−17.5	13.6	11.3	−5.6	8.1	−8.2	−8.6	3.4
Balance on current account = exports minus imports ($ billion)	—	−2.1	−3.5	−6.9	−6.1	−6.6	−9.0	−9.7	−12.7	−13.3	−13.0
Overall balance of payments	—	0.5	0.2	−0.7	−0.2	0.6	−0.4	−0.2	−1.1	−2.2	−1.3

[a] PPE = export earnings deflated by import prices; all figures with minus sign are unfavourable.

Source: IMF, *World Economic Outlook*, 1982, pp. 156, 158, 162, 164.

Socio-political aspects of the crisis

The social, political and cultural aspects of the African crisis also exhibit some graphic symptoms. These socio-political data are in most cases reflections and spill-over effects of the syndrome of underdevelopment. For example, superficially, political instability and cultural degradation may appear to be unrelated to underdevelopment but they are often the by-products of some of its mechanisms such as dependency, imperialist penetration, illiteracy and the grinding poverty that

Table 1.7
Non-oil producing Africa's trade and foreign debts

Item	*1967/72*	*1973*	*1974*	*1975*	*1976*	*1977*	*1978*	*1979*	*1980*	*1981*	*1982*
Balance on current account as % of exports (weighted for non-oil exporting countries)	−16.9	−10.6	−17.9	−34.2	−27.0	−17.7	−19.0	−12.6	−14.8	−32.2	−29.5
Long-term external debt (non-oil exporting countries) (US$ billion)	—	13.1	15.9	19.9	24.2	31.7	38.7	44.7	49.2	56.0	66.0

Source: IMF, *World Economic Outlook*, 1982, pp. 156, 158, 162, 164.

Other indicators of Africa's crisis are summarised in Table 1.8.[13]

Table 1.8
General indicators of Africa's crisis

Item	*African average*	*Average ICC*	*Latin America*	*Asia*
Industrial sector as % of economy[a] (1978)	23	44.2	—	—
Industrial labour force as % of active population (15–64 years, 1979)	11.4	40.9	—	—
Literacy rate (1980)	29.8	99.0	—	—
Inhabitants per physician (Sub-Saharan Africa)	53,407 (1960) 21,234 (1980)	3,600 (1960)	—	—
Scientists & engineers per 10,000 population	5.8	112	69	22
Scientists & engineers in R & D per 10,000 population	0.35	10.4	1.15	1.6
R & D expenditure as % of GNP	0.6	1.2	0.2	0.6

[a] Industrial sector is larger than manufacturing.

Source: Haile Woldemikael (1981) "Issues in Social and Economic Development in Africa" (mimeo.).

define the character of backwardness on the continent. Though this is not so in all cases, there is some fundamental, causal unity stemming from underdevelopment between the economic and socio-political data of the African crisis.

To start with the indicators of Africa's social trauma, we find these to be reflected in wide and growing structural inequalities, primordiality and crime. The structural disparities are visible in inter- and intra-class inequalities, rural–urban dichotomy and sectoral disparities. Though there are as yet no comprehensive and reliable data for the whole continent, it is quite clear that in most African countries the development of neocolonial capitalism has been associated with very wide and growing inequalities in power, wealth, income and social opportunities with regard to educational, health and related facilities.[14] The problems here are so basic and serious that they are taken up separately in a later chapter. While the African bourgeoisie contains multimillionaires like Mobutu and the "mandarin millionaires" of Nigeria and elsewhere, the vast majority of Africans in each country languish in almost inhuman misery with open starvation, malnutrition and massive unemployment. The associated rural–urban cleavages are closely tied up with the sectoral disparities between a largely rural agricultural sector and the urbanised modern sector. These have produced Africa's massive rural–urban migration with decaying villages and stinking, sprawling urban slums.

Urban slums and massive unemployment, together with yawning inequalities, have bred a rapidly escalating wave of crimes, especially in African cities. Armed robbery has made many cities and highways extremely dangerous, especially in such countries as Nigeria, Zaire, Kenya and so on. These dens of crime are also creeping with drug abuse and prostitution, especially among young, female school-leavers. The extent of the human decay from these crimes can only be imagined.

Primordiality in the form of the colonial survival of semi-feudal, ethnic and religious relations is another major form of social trauma in Africa.[15] The arbitrariness of colonial boundaries in lumping together different nationalities within and between national borders, the divide-and-rule tactic of encouraging rural reaction in the form of traditional oligarchies as local support for imperial power (as in Lugard's "dual mandate" in Nigeria) and regionalism based on ethno-religious divisions have all planted the seeds of parochialism in Africa. Post-colonial ruling groups in Africa have manipulated and reinforced these primordialities in their often myopic and selfish bid to retain power. This has led to ethno-religious animosities, cultural irredentism and conflicts involving open civil wars as in the Congo, Sudan, Nigeria, Ethiopia and so on. Apartheid in Southern Africa is the worst manifestation of this social trauma.

The economic disabilities and growing social divisions of Africa have resulted in widespread political instability and pervasive political repression. Perhaps the most notable examples of these are the spate of military coups and counter-coups across the continent. By 1968, barely a decade after flag independence around 1960, there were 30 major military operations with 19 successful coups.[16] These have been associated with fascist police states involving large-scale murder, torture, terror and detention, as in Idi Amin's Uganda,[17] Mobutu's Zaire, Bokassa's Central African Republic and Nguema's Equatorial Guinea. Then neo-fascist one-party states under neocolonial capitalism, massive curtailment of civil liberties and oppressive harassment of the press have also featured in the political repression that keeps Africa's leaders in power for 20 or more years – even when they have no clue to their country's deepening crisis.

One gruesome consequence of Africa's political repression, primordial conflicts and natural disasters is a massive and growing refugee problem. By July 1985, there was a total of about 5.7 million refugees on the continent, with some one million political, and an estimated 4.7 million economic refugees.[18] While political refugees are those fleeing from territories considered to be areas of political persecution, economic refugees are the socially marooned who have lost their means of livelihood and shelter through such natural disasters as drought, flood and the like. These refugees are spread across the entire continent in countries such as Sudan, Ethiopia, Somalia, Djibouti, Kenya and Uganda in North-East Africa; Ghana and Chad in West Africa; Zaire, Namibia, Angola, Mozambique, Zimbabwe and South Africa in South-Central Africa. With the refugee population growing at about 2.7% annually, UN sources have estimated that more than one million metric tons of food are needed to cope with the requirements of these refugees, while Africa will need a total investment of over $US2.9 billion by 1986 to offset the refugee and food problems. These requirements are clearly beyond the current internal resources of the continent, with the implication of growing external dependence or massive disaster. Such is the eloquent testimony of Africa's growing "mobile referendum on the march" for the crisis of underdevelopment.

Finally, the cultural degradation in Africa is a critical aspect of the continental crisis. This has resulted from the cultural penetration or the cultural imperialism associated with the post-colonial survival of "colonial mentality" and the cultural aspects of the activities of multinational corporations on the continent. Both are reflected not only in the pervasive and growing use of foreign languages, dress, music (of which America's Motown for disco is the best example) and religion but more seriously in foreign intellectual domination. The widespread retention of the colonial educational system, which has left curricula and syllabi largely unchanged since independence and basically irrelevant to Africa's needs, is reinforced by foreign intellectual domination through foreign publishing, research funding, educational exchange programmes and so on. As ideas and theories must be the basis of any sustained social action, including policies and programmes for dealing with the African crisis, this increasing cultural penetration of the continent is one of the most dangerous threats to Africa.

Towards a theory of the African crisis

According to Basil Davidson, Africa has had an "inherent crisis", which assumed immense proportions in the last years of colonialism, and gave the wrong impression of a new crisis. The later decades of colonial rule only deepened the crisis of growth that already existed, through such processes as the population increase owing to the introduction of preventive medicine; the increasing numbers of slum-dwellers on the outskirts of cities owing to the dismantling of traditional structures, customs and beliefs, as well as institutionalised subjection within the general economic system. On account of his great influence in Africanist circles, Davidson bears quoting at length on this fundamental question. He stated:

> Any attentive reading of the historical evidence, it seems to me, displays a *latent institutional breakdown started even before the colonial period began*. Its origins, on this view, will be found in Late Iron Age structures of society and systems of

> production whose capacity for further expansion, or growth, was nearing its possible limit even by the early part of the nineteenth century.
>
> . . . The early systems grew and spread and diversified in a thousand cultural contrasts. *But progress came from the modification of what existed rather than from any departure in system or in structure.* It came, in short *from growth rather than development.*
>
> *By the early or middle nineteenth century, however, this steady growth had begun to break through its containing institutions.* Harried here and there by external factors of disintegration, such as the inland slave trade from the Zanzibari Coast, or the consequences of the much older and much larger Atlantic slave trade, the ancient checks and balances of traditional society began to give way to royal autocracies, to vast reorganisations of power, to a general increase of interstate rivalry and warfare.[19]

Davidson's account of an "inherent crisis" in Africa is a feature of any part of the international capitalist system. The scenario he paints for Africa before the mid-19th century is generally applicable to most pre-capitalist societies. The "latent institutional breakdown" corresponds to periods of transition from one mode of production, or from one social formation, to another (for example, from the feudal to the petty-commodity producing mode of production in Europe); the progress through "growth rather than development" is reminiscent of the slow development of productive forces under pre-capitalist social formations; while the breaking of growth through its institutional constraints is the change in the superstructure concomitant on the transition from, say, feudalism to petty-commodity production in the last pre-capitalist epoch. In varying degrees these different phases are identifiable in the history of all industrialised countries, as economic history shows very abundantly.[20]

Furthermore, societies have typically transcended this inherent crisis over time through their own internal dynamics – provided their transition is not blocked by external forces. Thus, after such debacles as the autocratic monarchies, interstate warfare (of which the Franco-Prussian wars in Europe are very reminiscent), and the revolutions in Europe, the American Civil War, the Tokugawa restoration in Japan, to mention a few, these regions successfully liquidated underdevelopment; they were not underdeveloped like the Third World. Yet, Third World countries, and Africa in particular, have remained trapped in the crisis. The fundamental non-linearity of historical experiences between the industrialised and the underdeveloped countries is rooted in the critical role of imperialism and its contemporary neocolonialism. Africa suffered a triple tragedy in this respect: slavery, colonialism and the last escape from colonial subjugation into neocolonialism as elaborated below. This is why Davidson's statement that Africa's innate crisis "assumed tumultuous proportions in the last years of colonialism" underlines this neocolonial contradiction.

The crucial significance of this dominant external constraint on Africa is that it forestalled or delayed the global diffusion of the Industrial Revolution to the continent. It is instructive in this regard that although the USA was a former British colony, she gained independence in 1776 before the critical mid-19th century when industrialisation began to spread around the world. China, which was also partly colonised by Japan, needed a socialist revolution to terminate the abuses of underdevelopment, while Japan, far from being colonised, exploited colonies in parts of China and the Pacific Islands for her early industrialisation. From the 1830s, post-colonial Latin America was a veritable American neocolony, while South-East Asia and Africa remained dominated by colonialism up to the mid-20th century. It was an integral part of the logic of the colonial system to keep the colonies under primary production, technologically backward and underdeveloped. These facts demonstrate the need to develop a theory of the African crisis.

First, it should be emphasised that the African crisis is neither a crisis of institutions *per se* nor a bourgeois business cycle. Bourgeois economic theory, whether Keynesian or neo-classical, is also useless for understanding the crisis. The Marxist theories of crisis such as the falling rate of profit, under-consumption or over-production and disproportionality do not explain the African crisis either, though the Marxist method of analysis contains the basic tools for theorising the crisis. For example, in spite of the crisis, multinational corporations have been hauling huge super-profits from the continent, so that in Nigeria, during the crisis of the 1980s, many enterprises were doubling their profits annually since 1983. The African crisis is also associated with acute shortages of many essential commodities, which is indicative of excess demand or under-production, rather than under-consumption or over-production. Only the theory of disproportionality, especially between agriculture and other sectors of the economy, is marginally relevant to the crisis. Orthodox crisis theories, both bourgeois and Marxian, are not adequate for comprehending the African crisis, and the crisis of the Third World generally, because its basic generating causes essentially postdate the elaboration of these theories, which were developed for the industrialised capitalist countries.

Basically, the African crisis is a composite of underdevelopment and cyclical fluctuations. Underdevelopment in its contemporary form in Africa and the rest of the Third World is also a phenomenon of neocolonialism (or imperialism), therefore, this composite crisis of underdevelopment is also a crisis of neocolonial capitalism, or simply a crisis of neocolonialism.[21] Cyclical fluctuations are merely superimposed on the underlying crisis of underdevelopment. So whether the affected countries are in cyclical boom or depression (or the milder recession), they are still trapped in the crisis of underdevelopment, represented by disarticulation, structural distortions, external dependence, low productive capacity, technological backwardness and mass squalor.

Since both underdevelopment and neocolonialism are integral aspects of global capitalism, the African crisis is a derivative of the growing crisis of global capitalism. The peculiar nature that the disarticulation of the individual African countries takes with respect to the distortions of the economy, and the character of the post-colonial state, also affect the specific manifestations of the crisis in Africa generally, and in individual African countries. It is thus not possible to explain the crisis within the closed-economy model (that is, excluding international economic relations) of the orthodox theories of crisis. The interplay of broad and inter-related internal and external factors lies at the root of the African crisis.

In individual African countries the largely internal factors that generate the crisis are the structural distortions inherited from the perverse international division of labour under colonialism, the resulting prostrate external dependency of the economy, unequal exchange with international capitalism, the external debt crisis, the further distortion and external drain of economic surplus by multinational corporations through foreign direct investment and loans, and the superstructure of these countries as represented by their lop-sided class structures and pliant post-colonial states. These internal class formations and the post-colonial states they control then become the ideological link between the internal and external factors in the crisis. The succeeding chapters will analyse these complex internal factors.

The leading external factors in the industrialised capitalist countries that propel the African crisis are the increasing concentration and transnationalisation of power, capital and production; the new technological revolution that has been displacing many of the exports of the poor countries, and increasing foreign technological control over their economies; the rising scarcity of basic raw materials; the diversion of trade and investment from the poor countries; and changing capitalist cycles, which have been getting shorter and with weaker recovery.[22] Thus the advanced capitalist countries currently control about 50% of world trade and some 85% of the main exports of the Third World. Similarly, there has been increasing privatisation of international monetary and financial relations represented by the rapid growth of the Eurodollar market. Thus, between 1970 and 1979, foreign direct investment fell from 56% to 28% of all private capital flows, while by 1979, private loans and credits that were virtually non-existent in 1970 rose steeply to 44% of these private capital flows. It is in these circumstances that the current crisis started with a sharp fall in the growth rates in the Gross National Product of these advanced capitalist countries from 3.7% in 1979 to barely 1% in 1980/81 and –0.5% in 1982. All these external developments have been aggravating the impact of the historical roots of underdevelopment in Africa.

The roles of slavery, colonialism and neocolonialism in Africa's underdevelopment

Any serious account of the historical origins of African underdevelopment must transcend any inherent crisis of African societies and grapple with the central roles of slavery, colonialism and contemporary neocolonialism in the context of world imperialism. The basic reason for this is that researches have clearly demonstrated that up to the 17th century (i.e., under mercantilist imperialism), Africa was not generally inferior to the rest of the world.[23] Indeed, it was because Africa's mining technology was superior to that of southern Europe that skilled African miners were taken into slavery by Europeans to operate the gold and silver mines of South America.[24] But the transitional conjunctures produced by the Euro-American[25] slave trade – colonialism and neocolonialism – deeply intensified and transformed any innate crisis in Africa, and thereby laid the basic structural foundation for the systematic underdevelopment of the continent as summarised by Walter Rodney's *How Europe Underdeveloped Africa*. Under mercantilist and free trade imperialism and for about 350 years from 1451 (when the first slaves were on sale in Lisbon, Portugal) to the effective abolition of slavery after the 1833 Abolition Act,[26] Africa lost between 30 and 160 million people due to depopulation caused by the slave trade. Most of these were the productively most virile members of the population.

Their loss constituted a drain on direct human labour and skilled miners, on the invested capital in the development of their productive power and on the physical capital structures burnt down in slave raids. The loss also included the disruption of productive activities because of the slave raids and the resultant low population density and small internal markets, which persist in many parts of Africa to this day (see Table 1.9).

Table 1.9
European slave trade – exports by region 1701–1800 (totals of British, French and Portuguese slave exports)

	1701–20	*1721–40*	*1741–60*	*1761–80*	*1781–1800*
West Africa:					
Number in '000	497.6	594.2	619.1	654.1	648.7
% of total	77.6	67.6	61.0	63.2	45.9
West, Central & Southern Africa:					
Number in '000	144.0	278.5	379.3	379.3	758.9
% of total	22.4	31.7	37.4	36.7	53.7
Other & unknown					
Number in '000	—	6.3	16.2	0.8	6.5
% of total	—	0.7	1.6	0.1	0.4
Total ('000)	*641.9*	*879.0*	*1,014.6*	*1,034.2*	*1,414.1*

Grand total, 1701–1800 = 4,983,000

Source: P. D. Curtin (1969) *The Atlantic Slave Trade* (London), p. 211.

Thus the estimated population of Africa south of the Sahara was as in Table 1.10 (in millions):

Table 1.10
Africa's estimated population in millions, 1750/1960

	1750	*1800*	*1850*	*1900*	*1950*	*1960*
Variant A	135	124	124	124	180	207
Variant B	54	61	69	89	160	207

Source: J. F. Monroe (1976) *Africa and the International Economy, 1800–1960* (London; Dent & Sons), p. 20.

Variant A's stagnation between 1800 and 1900 was attributed by the author to the forced migration and high mortality owing to the Euro-American slave trade; variant B's modest growth rate of 0.25% during 1750/1850 was also due to the demographic impact of the slave trade in that era.[27]

Conversely, the gains of the European, American and Arab slave traders included the enormous super-profits from the extraction of surplus from the production by African slaves of tobacco, cotton, sugar and coffee in Central, South and North America as well as the Arab West Indies (Southern Arabia and Lower Iraq). In addition, profits accrued to Britain for the manufacture of textiles and guns exported to Africa. The use-values derived by these foreign regions from the consumption of the commodities produced by slave labour (that is, the implicit saving from not having to purchase those commodities) were part of the gains as well as physical structures such as roads, bridges, canals, and so on, also constructed by slave labour. David and Alexander Barclay used their slaving loot to establish Barclays Bank (now Union Bank in Nigeria) and slave profits helped James Watt to produce his steam engine. The Great Western Railway in Britain was also built with slave profit from Bristol slave merchants, while several iron, textile and other infrastructures were built with money from slave proceeds. In these different ways, while slavery accelerated any inherent crisis of disintegration in African communities and destroyed traditional technologies by the forced export of their practitioners, it vastly retarded primitive capital accumulation by destroying existing forms of capital and inhibiting additional accumulation over centuries of human exploitation. This drastic annihilation of productive capacity through the intergenerational destruction of human and material productive forces[28] operated everywhere in Africa to stultify technological development and intensify the contradictions of the initial "undevelopment". By contrast, slave looting provided an important part of the primitive capital accumulation of North America and Europe for launching their agricultural and industrial revolutions from the mid-18th century. It supplied those continents with the material precondition of the accumulation and concentration of money capital for the transition from feudal and petty-commodity producing social formations to industrial capitalism.[29] As Karl Marx summarised these dialectics of slavery under mercantilist and free-trade imperialism:

> The discovery of gold and silver in America, the extirpation, enslavement and entombment in mines of the indigenous population of that continent, the beginnings of the conquest and plunder of India, and the conversion of Africa into a preserve for the commercial hunting of blackskins, are all things which characterise the dawn of the era of capitalist production. These idyllic proceedings are the chief moments of primitive accumulation.[30]

Colonialism under free-trade and corporate imperialism, intensified the crisis initiated by slavery. The two phases of colonialism correspond to the "empire of outposts" from 1598 to 1763 under free-trade imperialism, and the era of formal colonialism with direct political control after 1763 under corporate or monopolistic imperialism.[31] In the first phase, the strategy was based on capitalist production at home and free trade overseas. By this time, the emergence of industrial capitalism in Britain during the Industrial Revolution required free, mobile labour against the indenture of slavery, and Britain's status as "the workshop of the world" dictated her leadership role in the anti-slavery campaign and free trade – to the point where the "Little Englanders", or liberal free traders among the industrial bourgeoisie, advocated the dissolution of white settler colonies.[32]

But with the spread of the new industrial technology and the emergence of Germany, France and the United States as strong capitalist rivals to Britain, competition for foreign markets sharpened. Formal colonisation for lucrative monopoly markets and cheap sources of industrial raw materials and labour thus emerged. The domestic transition in the metropoles from competitive to industrial capitalism also led to the transition from free-trade imperialism to the monopolistic imperialism styled "constructive imperialism".[33] The era witnessed the scramble for Africa and her avaricious partition among the imperial powers at the Berlin Conference of 1885.

This colonial system rested on a new capitalist international division of labour, based on Ricardo's comparative advantage, in which the imperial countries specialised in manufacturing activities and the export of manufactures and capital to the colonies, which were *forced* to specialise in the primary production of agricultural and mineral raw materials for the colonialists' factories. Local manufacturing in the colonies was effectively banned in order to preserve their raw materials and markets for Europe, while their traditional technology, which had been under attack since the slave era, now atrophied through the disappearance of its raw materials and local markets (taken over by Europe), and the non-absorption of the displaced indigenous craftspeople into new industries – as happened earlier in Europe during the Industrial Revolution.

To facilitate the exploitation of the colonies through the extraction of both absolute surplus value and value transfer (through the consumption of use value for the reproduction of the African communities' local labour), the *political instance* (i.e., coercion) superseded the *economic instance* in surplus extraction.[34] The colonial state became a *coercive interventionist state* with two dominant functions: 1) the wholesale destruction of the simple reproduction cycle of pre-capitalist social formations through peasant dispossession; and 2) the reproduction of distorted forms of pre-capitalist social relations of production under capitalist hegemony in the forms of agrarian capitalism, capitalist mining and colonial import–export trade. These were the sources of the critical *disarticulation* of the colonial social formation. It was based on violence and the use of force for the extraction of surplus labour; the reproduction of pre-capitalist ideological and political divisions; the cheap administration of the colonial state through the mediation of pre-capitalist superstructures articulated to it in the mutual support of imperial authority and traditional power; and on racism as an ideological justification for the savagery of colonial exploitation.

In these processes, three broad colonial zones have been identified in Africa, corresponding to "Africa of the colonial trade economy", the zone of the "concession-owning companies" and "Africa of the labour reserves".[35] The colonial trade economy embraced traditional West Africa (Ghana, Nigeria, Sierra Leone, Gambia, Liberia, Guinea-Bissau, Togo and former French West Africa), Cameroon, Chad, Sudan and North Africa, organised largely for colonial import–export trade anchored to agrarian capitalism in the colonies. Africa of the concessionary companies consisted of the traditional Congo River basin, embracing Congo-Brazzaville, Gabon and the Central African Republic. While the ecology protected this zone from slavery, its low population density and insufficient

African hierarchies made the colonial trade model unviable. Industrial plantations for oil palm, rubber and so on were, therefore, established there, especially after World War I. Thus Lever Brothers was welcomed to this region by the Belgians after the company's failure in Ghana (then Gold Coast). The region of labour reserves spanned eastern and southern Africa (Kenya, Uganda, Tanzania, Rwanda, Burundi, Malawi, Angola, Mozambique, Zimbabwe, Botswana, Lesotho, Swaziland and South Africa), and was subjected to Enclosure Acts for the supply of temporary and semi-permanent labour migrants on a vast scale for mines and farms, and later for the manufacturing industries of South Africa, Zimbabwe (then Southern Rhodesia) and Kenya.

These regions clearly overlapped because the concessionary companies operated all over the continent. Labour reserves were created for colonial mining, plantation agriculture, industrial processing and public works, while the colonial trade model was established extensively in eastern and southern Africa for export crops such as tea, coffee, cotton, etc. All over the continent, the creation of the colonial proletariat involved the extensive imposition of taxation, dispossession of the peasantry and forced labour.[36]

One fundamental consequence of the colonial moment in African history was the capitalist penetration of the continent. This was the point Marx made about British colonialism in India, when he suggested that colonialism was both destructive and regenerative in creating a new capitalist mode of production on the ashes of the liquidated pre-capitalist modes.[37] But he was mistaken about the regeneration, as the greedy logic of colonial exploitation blocked the capitalist transformation of the colonies. Rather, colonialism produced *disarticulation* on the ruins of pre-capitalist colonial societies, by reproducing deformed and truncated forms of these pre-capitalist social relations under the hegemony of colonial capital. Yet it is the transformation of these social relations of production, rather than Adam Smith's trade or market expansion, that produces capitalism. Thus, the emergence of new social relations of production or new social classes, which intensified the exploitation of the rest of the society (dispossessed peasants and artisans) via the economic instance, produced capitalism in Europe, North America and Japan, but this did not happen in the colonies. The authoritarian colonial state imposed coercion on the political instance (rather than the economic instance) as the dominant source of exploitation, transferred the economic surplus whose reinvestment constitutes the accumulation of money, and permitted the survival of petty peasant production and its pre-capitalist social relations of production, thus subverting the basic preconditions for capitalist transformation. By imposing the systematic transfer of the economic surplus of these colonies to the metropoles through various devices (unequal import–export trade, taxation, foreign investment and theft) and directly prohibiting manufacturing in the colonies, colonialism everywhere retarded the development of productive forces, sustained technological backwardness, decapitalised the exploited societies, inhibited the flourishing of capitalist relations of production, and in these ways blocked capitalist development in the colonies.

For the development of *neocolonialism*, colonial regimes everywhere carefully cultivated a domestic, rabidly reactionary *petit-bourgeois class* of comprador merchants in import–export trade: traditional rulers, feudal landlords, civil and uniformed professionals and politicians. These not only provided local support for imperial authority, but more importantly constituted the nucleus of the post-colonial ruling group (not yet a class in the early post-colonial era). This *petit-bourgeois* class not only constituted the leadership of the anti-colonial nationalist struggle, who compromised the objective of the struggle to mere political freedom; except where they were relatively weak, and colonialism involved settler racism, when the nationalist struggle became liberation wars leading to popular revolution, as in Algeria and the Portuguese African colonies. More seriously, this pro-imperialist colonial elite retained the post-colonial state as a satellite of the former colonial power by ensuring the survival and intensification of colonial-type mechanisms of domination and exploitation.

Hence such neo-colonies usually achieved only flag or nominal (political) independence without achieving *national economic independence*. The basic strategy is the forging of symbiotic collaboration between the reactionary domestic *petit-bourgeoisie* and the imperialist bourgeoisie for the joint, if unequal, domination and exploitation of the post-colonial state. As economic methods replace old political control in this age of multilateral imperialism since 1945, the multinational corporations in different economic sectors become the dominant agents of imperialism in the neo-colony. It then claims to be pursuing the capitalist path of development that is really only the development of underdevelopment.[38]

Imperialism, uneven development and the crisis

On account of their central role in the crisis, it is important to deal with two issues here: 1) the nature of imperialism; and 2) the erroneous idea or myth that in the post-colonial era, imperialism has ended. First, *imperialism* is basically a system of domination and exploitation of one country by another, or of one group of countries by another group of countries.[39] So the industrialised capitalist countries of Western Europe, North America and Japan have been maintaining imperialist relationships of foreign control and plunder over Africa and the rest of the Third World; in the past, even the USA and China were colonised. The fundamental goal of imperialism or the imperial system is to acquire economic surplus from abroad. Other objectives are to maintain political, economic, technological and cultural domination of foreign countries in order to achieve territorial expansion, foreign markets, sources of cheap raw materials, outlets for capital export and even a safety valve for surplus domestic population. The main source of imperialism is inequality among countries, as a result of differences in military might or national fire-power, technological development, level of national economic development and size.

As a historical process that has been changing over the years, imperialism has been employing different methods that depend on its pressing objectives, internal contradictions and the global environment. Thus the earliest and best known method of imperialism is violence through the military conquest of weaker states. This violence was the basis of slavery and colonialism as imperialist strategies. The first and second World Wars were thus imperialist wars of division and redivision of the world. Trade has also been such a major strategy of imperialism that we talk of free-trade imperialism and the imperialism of foreign trade. In the post-colonial era, and with respect to Canada (which did not experience direct colonisation), neocolonialism has also been the dominant method or form of modern imperialism. The common mechanisms of neocolonialism are foreign direct investment, loans and credits (by private foreign banks, the IMF and the World Bank), foreign "aid" (economic, technical and military), unequal trade, technology and cultural ties. Historically, imperialism has thus passed through different stages, which caused it to employ different methods. These main stages of imperialist development are mercantilist, free-trade, corporate or monopolistic, and contemporary, neocolonial or multilateral imperialism. Correspondingly, imperialism's most profound effects on a world scale are the familiar wars and arms race, and the more pervasive but less familiar generation of unequal development.

It is important to emphasise that the gap between Africa and the industrialised capitalist countries (ICCs), which started in the 17th century, is the fundamental by-product of world imperialism or the international capitalist system.[40] It is this same organic system, which produced the development of the ICCs, that simultaneously generated the deepening crisis of underdevelopment in Africa. The concurrence of both development and underdevelopment on a global scale is the direct and systematic consequence of the differing effects of slavery, colonialism and neocolonialism on the ICCs, which reaped the advantages of these processes, and on Africa, which paid the price and bore the losses.

The basic reason for this is that throughout its history, imperialism in its different phases has been consistently addressed to the domination, plunder and exploitation of the Third World in order to advance capital accumulation in the ICCs.[41] Thus, under commercial capitalism, we had mercantilist imperialism, which used slavery and so-called legitimate trade as its strategies of plunder and exploitation of Africa for the primitive accumulation of capital. With the emergence of industrial or competitive capitalism towards the end of the 18th century, imperialism changed its character to free-trade imperialism, using colonisation and unequal exchange for the exploitation of the periphery of world capitalism in the Third World. In the era of monopoly capitalism, when the giant monopolies and multinational corporations (MNCs) emerged from the 1880s, Rudolf Hilferding's "finance capital" used the colonial vehicle for foreign exploitation by employing imperial power and MNCs' capital. After this phase of imperialism led to the war to redivide the world among the imperial powers during 1939/45, the emergence of USA (which had had no formal colonies thus far) hegemony in world imperialism, dictated the need for multilateral imperialism. This opened up the erstwhile monopolised colonies (under the slogans of "self-determination" and "open door policy") to global imperial exploitation, using MNCs as the main catalysts of this neocolonial strategy.

Consequently, it is false to suggest, as do bourgeois scholars, that development is a process while underdevelopment is an original state — both are concurrent products of world imperialism.[42] Underdeveloped countries are, therefore, not merely at a lower stage of the development of the ICCs — this historical linearity is false, because even though ICCs were *un*developed in their earlier history, they were not *under*developed by any conscious imperialist policies of exploitation. Similarly, the bourgeois causes of underdevelopment in terms of resource scarcity, archaic culture and institutions, population explosion, vicious circle of poverty, "ideal types" and such racist theories, are all apologetic nonsense in the service of imperialism. By implication, the "trickle down" or diffusion notion, according to which technology and development will trickle down to underdeveloped countries in the fullness of time, is a pathetic delusion — after 150 years of Latin America's flag independence, this trickle down has not occurred in those distorted and mercilessly exploited "banana republics".

Equally false and misleading are the claims that the underdeveloped countries are dual societies with non-capitalist segments, and that, therefore, they have a possibility of independent capitalist development. The fact is, that though the peripheral societies, as predominantly neocolonial social formations, embrace a dominant capitalist mode of production and subsidiary pre-capitalist modes, these social formations as *structured* articulations of different modes of production, are all integrated and not distinct modes. Correspondingly, no independent capitalist development outside the orbit of the international capitalist system is possible, as the manufacturing imperialism in so-called newly industrialised countries (NICs) in South-East Asia and Latin America (Taiwan, Hong Kong, Philippines, Argentina and Brazil) clearly demonstrates.

For these reasons, the deepening crisis of underdevelopment in Africa cannot be understood outside the logic of world imperialism. To say this does not absolve the peoples of these countries from responsibility for their predicament. From what has been explained about neocolonialism, it is clear that the domestic *petit-bourgeois* classes in these countries are an integral part of the problem. It is from these perspectives that the dialectics of the nature and resolution of the African crisis derive critical imperatives.

This makes it necessary to debunk the myth that in the post-colonial era, imperialism has come to an end in Africa or elsewhere. As indicated in the discussion of the stages of imperialism, what is true is that in the post-colonial era, imperialism has changed its appearance (but not its substance), and replaced direct colonialism with *neocolonialism*. This involves the use of indirect methods of domination and plunder of Africa and the other post-colonial regions. Foreign direct investment by multinational corporations, increasing foreign loans and credits by imperialist banks, unequal trade, monopoly of technology, so-called foreign aid and cultural ties have become the new mechanisms of foreign domination and exploitation in modern Africa and the rest of the post-colonial world. The dominant agents of post-colonial imperialism are the multinational corporations that manage the transnationalisation of monopoly capital and production: the IMF and the World Bank. They work closely with the imperialist countries to systematically transfer huge amounts of economic surplus from Africa to the metropolitan countries, decapitalise the poor countries, sustain their technological backwardness and intensify their mass poverty. This is how unequal development and the underdevelopment of Africa and the rest of the Third World are nurtured in the post-colonial era. This neocolonialism is precisely the heart of the African crisis.

Besides its changed methods, another difference between imperialism in the post-colonial and earlier periods is the role of dominant local classes in the Third

World. Before the post-independence era, imperialism was basically imposed unilaterally from abroad, whereas in the post-colonial era, imperialism involves the symbiotic collusion or collaboration of the local *petit-bourgeoisie* (which controls the post-colonial state) with the imperialists. The gains from the domination and plunder of the post-colonial countries are then shared (unequally of course) between the imperialist bourgeoisie and the local *petit-bourgeoisie*. It is because of this mutual advantage that the domestic bureaucratic bourgeoisie in Africa and the rest of the Third World assist in formulating and implementing neocolonial policies that intensify the underdevelopment and crises of their countries.[43] Hence, the African crisis has both foreign and local agents that must be combated.

Notes

1. Adebayo Adedeji (1981), parentheses mine.
2. Basil Davidson (1974).
3. Ibid., p. 6.
4. See F. Robson and D. Lury (eds.) (1969).
5. Ibid., pp. 112–3.
6. These least developed countries in Africa are: Benin, Botswana, Burundi, Chad, Cape Verde, Central African Republic, Comoros, Ethiopia, Gambia, Guinea, Guinea-Bissau, Lesotho, Mali, Malawi, Nigeria, Rwanda, Somalia, Sudan, Uganda, Tanzania and Upper Volta; others in Asia and Oceania are Afghanistan, Bhutan, Laos, Maldives, Nepal, Sikkim, Western Samoa and Yemen; in Latin America, Haiti.
7. See World Bank, *World Development Report, 1982.*
8. Economic Commission for Africa (ECA), Statistics Division, Addis Ababa.
9. UNIDO, *Africa Development*, vol. VII, no. 1/2, 1982.
10. IMF, *World Economic Outlook, 1980.*
11. Ibid.
12. These net exports are exports less imports.
13. See World Bank, *World Development Report, 1980*; and F. Stewart (1977) p. 120.
14. See, for example, J. F. Rweyemamu (1980).
15. For the colonial origin of primordiality, see R. Zahara (1974).
16. W. F. Gutheridge (1976).
17. See M. Mamdani (1983).
18. For data on Africa's refugee problems, see the UN Commission for Refugees publications and *New Nigerian*, 28 April 1983, p. 5.
19. B. Davidson (1974), pp. 15–16; emphasis mine.
20. On this issue, see the economic history of Europe in M. M. Knight et al. (1928).
21. This crisis of neocolonial capitalism is reported in detail in B. Onimode (1987).
22. See Fidel Castro (1983), chs. 1 and 2.
23. See S. Amin (1981) in D. L. Cohen and J. Daniel (eds.) ch. 2.
24. Mai Palmberg (ed.) (1983) p. 7.
25. The so-called "triangular trade" or "Atlantic slave trade" was really a

Euro-American slave trade because the demand, the actual transactions in humans and the surplus appropriation from it involved both Europeans and Americans with their African middlemen, who were merchants, traditional nobility and chiefs.

26. The 1833 Act that abolished slavery in British colonies exempted India, Ceylon and St. Helena, and did not cover such slaving non-British colonies as Zanzibar, Mozambique and Angola — and, of course, the Act took years to enforce even in British colonies.

27. On account of the impossibility of estimating the total population losses from those killed in slave raids, those captured into slavery and those who died from post-slave-raid famines, and the cumulative growth effect of these losses over the years, Africa's demographic loss from slavery is incalculable.

28. See also J. D. Durand (1967) in *Proceedings of the American Philosophical Society*, 11, 138.

29. Eric Williams (1972).

30. Karl Marx (1977) *Capital* vol. I, ch. 31.

31. See D. Nabudere (1981) vol. I, ch. 1.

32. See Jeremy Bentham (1793).

33. See A. Temu and B. Swai (1981), ch. 2.

34. See L. Althusser (1969).

35. S. Amin (1981) pp. 28–9 and 38–42.

36. See T. Nzula et al. (1979).

37. K. Marx and F. Engels (1978) *On Colonialism*.

38. See A. G. Frank (1970).

39. Dan Nabudere (1978).

40. S. Amin (1974).

41. See Dan Nabudere (1978).

42. On these distortions of underdevelopment, see A. G. Frank (1970) chs. 2–7.

43. This is the theme of A. G. Frank (1972).

2 Bourgeois Social Science and the African Crisis

In a continent-wide tragedy of the magnitude of the African crisis, which affects major aspects of the economy, state and society, it is only logical to look into the role played by the sciences of society. Without even *a priori* presumptions, it is imperative to examine the possible connections between the crisis and the predominant social sciences in Africa, as indeed in the Third World generally. Specifically, we should investigate the role of social sciences in generating, preventing, ameliorating or sustaining the crisis; in explaining the structural character of the crisis; and, therefore, in proposing remedies for eliminating or containing the disaster at present and in the future.

Bourgeois social science: its contribution to the African crisis

The predominant social sciences in Africa were imposed initially under colonialism and imported subsequently under post-colonial neocolonialism as the intellectual core of the cultural offensive of imperialism against Africa and the rest of the Third World. This common historical and contemporary origin of the social sciences in Africa from the capitalist and imperialist countries of Western Europe and North America is what constitutes these imported disciplines as bourgeois and imperialist. To balance the perception of their role in the African crisis, it is perhaps best to start with the perspective of their practitioners and defenders on the continent: the African *petit-bourgeois* social scientists.[1]

Most African social scientists recognise the unsatisfactory state of their disciplines in failing to cope with the crisis, but there are some recalcitrants among these *petit-bourgeois* scholars who feel differently. They are surprised by any suggestion that their disciplines have failed, or that they have any connection with the tragedy. From their own point of view, social sciences have done very well in terms of quantitative criteria, such as increasing the number of professionals, student enrolment, and expansion of institutions, publications, etc. And, they would ask, is knowledge not to be pursued for its own sake as an objective, positive and neutral affair? But their position is trivial and unacceptable.

The majority of African social scientists who are disturbed by the role of their disciplines in African societies insist that their paradigms are relevant, and that with the exception of specific aberrations, their theories and policies are correct. What is wrong, they argue, is the poor implementation of their blueprints and recommendations by incorrigible politicians and technocrats.[2] Thus, in bourgeois economics, while accepting the neoclassical and Keynesian paradigms as valid for Africa, or seeking a revival of bourgeois classical political economy, these social scientists quibble about the theory of income distribution and inequality, planning models and similar defects in their discipline. In bourgeois political science, the perceived defects are the absence of modernising elites, of the correct type of government, the number of political parties, pluralism and the like, while sociologists tinker with mobility theory and role specificity, leaving psychologists to tackle need-achievement motivation, aggressive individualism and so on.

In spite of these aberrations, most African social scientists insist that the basic problem with the performance of their disciplines lies with wayward and ineffective policy makers and policy executors. In one Nigerian version of this self-congratulatory rhetoric, some economists claim that the problem with the Nigerian economy is that government has not allowed sufficient capitalism.[3] Other social scientists claim that they are ineffective because government functionaries routinely ignore their research findings and distort the implementation of their policy prescriptions.

Without denying the veracity of these allegations, we must insist, however, that at best they are symptoms rather than the real causes of bourgeois social science's failure in Africa. Yes, Africa has more than her share of theatrical clowns, state gangsters and incompetent politicians and technocrats as the Idi Amins, Bokassas, Mobutus and others demonstrate. But there is more to it than that, for several reasons. For example, 1) even when such *petit-bourgeois* African social scientists as professors and doctors serve in government at cabinet level and as professional advisers, they are often failures, or at least set no consistent examples of competence, vision and integrity; 2) in spite of policy-makers' alleged incorrigibility, these social scientists continue to hob-nob with them, neither resigning their advisory and other positions, nor publicly criticising them. Governments also tend to recruit the more reactionary elements among social scientists; and 3) as for the quality of bourgeois research findings and policies, it is on record that even those that are faithfully implemented, such as export promotion, import-substitution industrialisation, foreign aid and investment, Green Revolution and agricultural modernisation (new seed varieties, fertilisers and mechanisation), tax reforms, etc. have resulted in such disasters as starvation, massive unemployment, pernicious inflation, balance-of-payments crises and rising external debts under the rhetoric of "under-borrowing", as in Nigeria during 1982/83.

Policy-makers correctly ignore many of the theories and policies of bourgeois social science in Africa because past and comparative experiences show them to be quite useless. The claim by *petit-bourgeois* African social scientists that their theories and policies are disregarded or distorted by government presupposes that these bourgeois principles are socially relevant to start with. That this claim is false, and that the *paradigms*, *theories* and *policy prescriptions* of bourgeois social science in Africa are basically socially irrelevant to the African and Third World situation, is the crux of the matter.

The major defects of bourgeois social science

The deepening character of the African crisis, widening global inequality, growing alienation of the elite from the masses, political instability and massive social trauma, all reflect, in part, the professional failure and futility of bourgeois social science in Africa. The major defects of this imported discipline are fivefold.

One: the paradigms or conceptions of reality are fundamentally incongruous with observable reality.[4] In the different forms of neoclassicism and Keynesianism in bourgeois economics, Lockean empiricism and the cultural secularisation of the theory of political development, Parsonian functionalism in sociology, Freudian psychology and the "continuity and change" of Africanist historiography, bourgeois social sciences posit false pictures of the real world. The common elements of this false conception of reality consist in the search for equilibrium in a basically disequilibrious world; for harmony of interests and cooperation rather than observed pervasive conflicts; the insistence on gradual change (Alfred Marshall's economics insisted that *natura non facit saltum*, that is, nature makes no leaps, whereas we observe *natura facit salta*, that is, nature makes leaps, for example, in revolutions);[5] and the demand for universalism in a divided world. Together with their common origin in British empiricist philosophy and its piecemeal approach to social phenomena,[6] the false premises of these paradigms predicate the social irrelevance of bourgeois social science.

Two: bourgeois social science is basically imperialistic, ideological, and apologetic on behalf of capitalism; and, as an integral part of bourgeois ideology, it has been imported into the Third World, including Africa, as the intellectual handmaiden of imperialism. This explains why the value premises of this social science emphasise private property, the competitive liberalism of free market forces of supply and demand, aggressive individualism and escapist commitment to the social values of capitalism in the name of scientific universalism.

Thus neoclassical economics portrays *social Darwinism*. In this ideology, wealth accumulation is considered as a *de facto* proof of evolutionary superiority, and poverty is evidence of evolutionary inferiority. "Competition in economics is the same as the law of . . . 'natural selection' in nature. Thus placing reliance upon neoclassical economic theory is a matter of *faith*. I personally have the faith; but at present the best I can do to convince others is to invoke the weight of Samuelson's authority . . ."[7] Unfortunately, Samuelson, other neoclassical and bourgeois economists have no answer to the American and global capitalist crises, and their authority has been seriously questioned. As an integral part of the status quo, bourgeois social science is necessarily an apologetic ideology, largely because its modern theories have been elaborated in deliberate defence of the property relations of industrial capitalism since the 1840s.

Thus, neoclassical economics was fashioned in the 1870s by William Stanley Jevons, Wilfred Pareto, Leon Walras and others as an ideological alternative to classical political economy and its labour theory of value, which was accused of asking too many questions and becoming a danger to private property.[8] The new neoclassical economics has since been made increasingly narrow, more mathematical, trivial and abstract in order to conceal the property relations and irrationality of capitalism. The other social sciences have been growing more mathematical for similar reasons. For example, the marginal productivity theory of distribution in neoclassical economics explains away inequality in terms of differences in the technical marginal contributions to social wealth by different individuals. So poverty and unemployment are due to inadequate competition or evolutionary inferiority.

Three: for these ideological reasons, bourgeois social science poses false problems and proffers bogus, pro-imperialist solutions, especially in the Third World; *The Journal of Economic Theory* offers classic examples of these. Other common examples of these false problems are the advocacy of sophisticated and automated technology, optimal growth and much of the rest of mathematical economics, general equilibrium analysis, game-theoretic and consensus politics, social mobility, need-achievement analysis (so-called n-achievement motivation in psychology which is even analysed through dreams), and so on. As false problems beget false solutions, these bogus preoccupations divert serious attention from genuine and urgent problems and constitute an epistemological barrier against the rational understanding of the African world.

Four: for these reaons, bourgeois social science also foists an irrelevant capitalist model of development and growth strategies on Africa and the rest of the Third World. The basic orientation is to attempt to reproduce, in these poor countries, the decaying societies of Western Europe and North America through the capitalist path of development. This is a logical consequence of the false universalism and unilinear conception of history claimed for the imported social sciences, and the reason why these abstract and mathematical models of growth fail disastrously to cope with the legitimate aspirations of the majority of the population of these poor Third World countries. The egregious example here is the import-substitution industrialisation strategy imposed on these countries, which rests basically on import-intensive industries based on inappropriate foreign technology to meet the perverted foreign consumption habits imported by imperialism.

Finally, the Third World's hapless dependence on bourgeois social science is the collective consequence of the persistence of colonial mentality in scientific endeavours, and foreign intellectual domination in teaching and research with respect to curricula, publication and academic funding which underscore this external intellectual dependence. It leads to teaching and researching according to the preferences of imperialist mentors, rather than according to the social requirements of African and other poor societies. This is an additional source of the praxiological failure of bourgeois social science in Africa.

Social science as an apologetic ideology

Both the ideological and apologetic characteristics of bourgeois social science are interrelated in one critical sense: its apologetic aspect is necessary in order to rationalise its capitalist–imperialist ideology and whitewash its irrationalities and perverse functioning. As it has been observed, the insistence on equilibrium, harmony and gradualism "was dictated not by the scientific requirement of fidelity to reality, but by the bourgeois need to prettify and justify a system which was [is] anything but harmonious, equilibrated and gradualistic".[9]

Bourgeois social science is ideological both in *scope* as "symbolic universes" or comprehensive world-views of specific rationalisations of broad political programmes and social arrangements, and in *function* in the Marxist interest theory as false consciousness that distorts the picture of social reality and serves dominant class interests, thus leading to three basic features of its ideological character:[10]

1) it promotes such capitalist values as materialism, individualism, acquisitive aggression, and so on; fosters capitalist institutions such as market exchange and private property, and promotes capitalist development;

2) it promotes the class domination or dictatorship of the African and Third World *petit-bourgeoisie*, and provides intellectual justification for their perverse activities, thus fostering the social acceptance of their class oppression; and,

3) by these means, bourgeois social science fails scientific tests of validity through fidelity to reality and the canon of social usefulness.

The philosophical origin, historical development and theoretical preoccupations of bourgeois social science demonstrate its ideological character. Historically, it evolved from philosophy (ancient religion, metaphysics, Aristotle's writings, etc.), which in Western Europe was dominated initially by the philosophy of the enlightenment and British empiricism;[11] this empiricist philosophy is the philosophical origin of bourgeois ideology. It is the source of the sharp distinction between the empiricist tradition in bourgeois thought and, for example, the Marxian materialist tradition.

The historical development of bourgeois social science should be analysed from the perspective of the sociology of knowledge and its social construction of reality.[12] The two relevant points here are that the development of ideas and theories typically reflects the material development of society, and that people's particular thought reflects their status and role in the social organisation of production. Thus, the transformation from feudalism to capitalism, which started with the Industrial Revolution in Britain, and the emergence of the new industrial property class under industrial capitalism, was also associated with the bourgeois transformation of the social sciences. In political science, the divine right of kings was challenged by the democratic principles of popular sovereignty, universal franchise and electoral government. In economics – the so-called science of wealth – the bourgeois reorientation was more obvious and thorough. Classical political economy and its robust labour theory of value encouraged socialist criticism of the then emerging capitalist order of the mid-19th century; the machine-smashing riots of the Luddite movement which ended in 1813 were also attributed to the same labour theory of value. These anti-property revolts led to deliberate attempts to shift the focus of economic enquiry to a safer and pro-capitalist plane. This led to the replacement of classical political economy and its labour theory of value by marginalist neoclassical economics with its metaphysical utility theory of value.[13] Bourgeois economics has since concealed capitalist social relations of production behind the technical sophistry of production functions; class conflicts were replaced by the alleged co-operation of factors of production in input-output conceptions of the business and of production functions. Exploitative property incomes were then mystified as the technical properties of things, as the marginal products of productive factors, corresponding to the rewards for their alleged sacrifices. Weberian sociology then rationalised the bureaucratic principle for the new capitalist organisations, with psychology chipping in with achievement motivation, industrial and social psychology. In these ways, the emergence of capitalism also witnessed the transformation of the social sciences into the intellectual ideology of corporate capitalism and imperialism.

The major intellectual preoccupations of bourgeois social science also demonstrate its corporate ideological character.[14] For example, its treatment of revolution shows that "the drift of much bourgeois social theory is to undermine the idea that men [people] can ever transform society – its function is to induce a morbid paralysis of social will".[15] Bourgeois social science understands revolutions only when they fail, and since it claims that revolutions change very little, they are to be averted, for example, by courses in counter-insurgency and the attempted suppression of revolutionary potentiality by applying the concept to common social phenomena, as with "green revolution", technological revolution and so on.

Similarly, to distort the differences between capitalist and socialist industrialisation strategies, bourgeois social theory links industrial society with technological determinism, as in J. K. Galbraith's *New Industrial State*. The technological determinism here is the suggestion that the industrial nature of technology dominates social organisation as a whole. By deducing social organisation from industrial technology, as with the nuclear family, bureaucratic organisation and the like as in Talcott Parsons' "evolutionary universals" (bureaucracy, money market, etc.), imperialist social science trivialises the major differences between capitalist and socialist societies, and magnifies the minor similarities (money, bureaucracy, etc.). The ideological objective is to portray capitalism as devoid of contradictions and, therefore, ultimate. This falsely suggests that only by abandoning modern technology can capitalist social relations of production be rejected and transcended.

The treatment of bureaucracy in bourgeois social theory deriving from Max Weber also has ideological and fatalistic overtones as an institutionalisation of the imperatives of capitalist society and its consequent alienations. This theory suggests that the style of work in the bureaucratic enterprise or firm will generalise itself inevitably through society in all institutions. Yet, the formal abstract efficiency of bureaucracy serves only the powers that be – its formal rationality thus depends on the rationality of the capitalist system of which it is part.

Charisma is another ideological factor in bourgeois social science. Here, Weber identified social creativity and innovation with the irrational, and subsumed it under charisma. This denies such rational factors as the dynamics of social forces, potency of ideas, imaginative programmes that propel leaders and movements. As charisma is derived from the medieval doctrine of essences, this means that unless societies are accidentally endowed with charismatic leaders, it is futile trying to transform them through social programmes – a classic celebration of inertia and the impossibility of planned social change.

The apologetic use of capitalist social science as ideology, on the other hand, consists of two elements. On a more visible plane, this apologetic theorising involves the rationalisation of the malfunctioning of capitalism and the posing of false and diversionary problems in an attempt to dodge awkward social issues including the use of euphemisms to deny the social realities which they obscure. Thus, instead of exploitation, one bourgeois social scientist prefers "reciprocity imbalance"; instead of dominant and antagonistic social classes, we hear of elite groups; rather than class analysis, we have social stratification and mobility; and underdeveloped countries become developing countries. In place of an analysis of sharp class conflicts, we read of consensus politics; and the growing polarisation between rich and poor countries is camouflaged as "partners in progress" (between exploiting and exploited countries!). Bourgeois economics rationalises poverty and widening income inequalities as differences in the marginal products of factors of production and as imperfect competition. The idea is to suggest that these fundamental capitalist irrationalities are temporary aberrations which time will correct, and that there is nothing basically wrong with the economic system that generates them. The growing mathematical sophistry of bourgeois social science, especially neoclassical and Keynesian economics, has been designed for this apologetic use, to provide such facile rationalisations and obscure the structural problems of capitalism.

The apologetic use of imperialist social science also involves its preoccupation with appearances rather than reality. These appearances of bourgeois society are taken for granted and the relations between them become the subject of study. Thus, bourgeois economics is predicated on the appearances of exchange, so it studies markets, wages, profits, interest rate and general commodity fetishism. In the process, the relations of production, distribution and exchange are stripped of their social significance. The fundamentally antagonistic character of the capital–labour relation in capitalist production is also reduced to the appearances of wages and labour-market competition. Similarly, vulgar economy, as Marx disdainfully called bourgeois economics, is trapped into the atomisation of the economy by Adam Smith, so it analyses the economy in terms of the behaviour of individual economic agents. Society is then analysed by bourgeois social theory in terms of individuals, rather than vice versa. The idea, of course, is to abstract from the social relations and class positions of individuals since, as Marx stated, individuals are merely the bearers of definite social relations. In its method of analysis, this apologetic social theory uses the "axiomatic deductive method" for establishing its claim to consistency. But the unilinear causation implied by this method cannot deal with the dilemmas posed by the appearances of atomisation and social categories. The successive approximation for building more and more realistic models by this social theory also implies that facts can be constructed atheoretically, or that theories can be tested by a knowledge of the real world separate from theory.

In these different ways, the most important assumptions of bourgeois social science are metaphysical, like utility maximization, perfect competition, future certainty, and so on; this is to prettify the irrational and perverse reality of bourgeois society. In order to deal with the inevitable crises of this asocial theorising, much of the bourgeois social sciences have been reduced to practical disciplines for managing the contradictions of capitalism. The egregious example of this is in economics where the managerial revolution has sprouted practical fields such as management science – which is anything but scientific, as it lacks any grand vision of society – business administration, accounting, operations research, and so on. All of them are poised towards intervention or non-intervention in the allegedly free market capitalism, and for social engineering at micro and macro levels. This is not to deny the practical usefulness of these disciplines, but to underline their ideological role under capitalism. They are built around capitalist categories like the primacy of money, profit, market, competition, etc. In socialist countries, these practical disciplines are not used in this way.

A more subtle, apologetic use of bourgeois social theory is in treating social phenomena as equalities in quantitative models, and giving apologetic interpretations to the technical properties of things in such models. Thus, in general equilibrium theory, the capitalist economy is stylised as attaining equilibrium or full employment in which,

> the postponement of consumption is described as a *sacrifice* to be measured by the relevant subjective rate of time preference, the receipt of extra commodities is described as a *reward* to be measured by the relevant rate of interest, and finally, marginal products are described as the *marginal contribution to production* of capital in the particular form it happens to take.[16]

In these ways,

> neoclassical theory . . . [and bourgeois social theory generally] represents the capitalist world as a Kibbutz [Israeli cooperative] operated in a perfectly enlightened manner to maximize the welfare of all its members.[17]

Women in development is also the latest element in this ideology of imperialist social science. Here, the urgent need for women's liberation from centuries of mindless oppression under patriarchy and capitalism is not disputed, as it is already an integral component of the struggles of all progressive humanity. What has to be exposed and combated is the imperialist attempt to:

1) make it a separate ideology of development in opposition to the anti-imperialist ideology in the Third World;

2) de-class the women's question so that women have only gender and no class;

3) separate the women's question from the general problems of oppression and exploitation in society.

Having failed to provide a consistent theory of underdevelopment and to formulate effective development policies, imperialist social science has been trying to find a refuge under the rubric of women in development. The progressive women's struggle is thus being converted into a reactionary ideology for getting women to endorse the discredited capitalist path of development. So the question must be constantly posed: *women in which kind of development?* The answer of bourgeois social science is women in capitalist development, and this should be rejected, as capitalism is one of the strongest bastions of women's oppression and exploitation.

Ideology and curricula

If the bourgeois social sciences are ideological, the curricula for teaching these disciplines must be equally ideological.[18] This arises from the nature of ideological relations and the social character of educational institutions. Ideological relations exist as a precondition for the formation of individual consciousness. These ideological relations are embodied in specific ideological institutions such as the factory, market mechanism, legal system and educational institution. This is why ideological struggle is waged on two levels – 1) the ideological relations themselves, as in the struggle for freedom of education and speech, and 2) the control of ideological institutions through which ideological relations materialise as ideologies.[19]

Educational institutions as ideological structures are unique combinations of elite and popular culture, and critical mechanisms for the social distribution of culture. This leads to the problem of determining the "reality" which schools select, preserve and distribute – why certain social and cultural meanings and not others are distributed through schools. This is connected with the relation between the (ideological) economic structure and school knowledge or curriculum. This relationship implies that the culture (ideas and values) preserved and distributed by educational institutions is not neutral. Educational institutions serve the dominant social classes very well and the less privileged classes less well. This is why Marx stated that the class that owns and controls the means of material production also dominates the mechanisms of mental production. Hence, there is an organic link between control and the meaning or content of curricula in educational institutions. For the same reason, there is a relation between high status and knowledge on the one hand and their economic and cultural effects in society on the other.

In respect of bourgeois social science in Africa, this means that we have to pay close attention to schools and their curricula as critical mechanisms of economic and cultural reproduction. This is both with respect to the credentials conferred by and the socialising functions of educational institutions by which societies stabilise themselves. In the African context, the colonial and missionary origins of educational institutions and their curricula were structured after imperialist public schools in Britain and elsewhere abroad; the persistent failure to decolonise them must imply the operation of educational systems whose curricula are loaded with ideological preoccupations for preserving imperialist Western Europe and North America, rather than for stabilising Africa and the Third World in general. Furthermore, as these educational systems expand and Africa totters in crises, the imperialist countries develop faster from the continuing exploitation of the Third World.

All this bears on the relationship between hegemony and the "hidden curriculum". Hegemony, in the context of educational institutions, corresponds to ideological stability or the control and maintenance of particular forms of ideology. Correspondingly, while curricula knowledge relates to "legitimate culture" or the stuff taught, "hidden curriculum" concerns the social relations of classroom life with respect to such issues as obedience, the negative conception of topics like conflict, exploitation, social justice, and so on, and the neglect of the study of such topics. The hidden curriculum of bourgeois social science in Africa reinforces the ideological hegemony of its oppressors and their capitalist–imperialist system. This ideological role of curricula is essential for the reproduction of bourgeois social science in Africa as discussed below. All this underlines the urgent need for the radical overhauling of educational curricula at all levels of schooling in Africa.

Imperialism and the imported social science

The imperialist character of the dominant bourgeois social science in the Third World will be analysed here with respect to its ideological orientation, historical development, contemporary preoccupations and collective consequences. It is important to note that if bourgeois social science is an integral part of bourgeois ideology, this bourgeois ideology is the ideology or world-view of international capitalism or imperialism. By serving the interests of capitalism, even in the Third World and African periphery, bourgeois social science is equally serving the interest of imperialism, because both the imported imperialist bourgeoisie and its *petit-bourgeois* collaborators in the Third World are allies of world capitalism or imperialism. The consolidation of the dictatorship of these bourgeois classes world-wide is one of the major preoccupations of bourgeois social science.

Historically also, bourgeois social science was initially imported into Africa and the rest of the Third World as the core of the cultural offensive of imperialism in its colonial phase. The subsequent reproduction of this reactionary social science in the capitalist periphery has been an integral part of the neocolonial mechanisms of imperialism in its contemporary multilateral phase. Thus colonial educational institutions, including university colleges (as in the former British colonies) and universities in other former colonies, were developed by imperialist missionaries and colonial administrations. By designing peripheral educational institutions along metropolitan models both the colonial church and state introduced imperialist social science into the Third World countries; the peripheral and metropolitan curricula, books and even teachers were (and largely still are) the same, or drawn from the same imperialist sources; the values, institutions and development model promoted in these imperialist schools in Africa and elsewhere in the periphery were (and still are) basically the same; the colonial schools also aimed to cultivate dominant classes to provide local support for imperialism.[20] As the persistence of colonial mentality in modes of thought clearly demonstrates, the imperialist character of education and social science in the periphery has changed very little in the post-colonial era.

The mystification of underdevelopment

The imperialist preoccupation of the contents of the imported social science in the Third World has been well documented by A. G. Frank, Samir Amin, Claude Ake and others.[21] The vast literature on bourgeois development economics, sociology of development and political development has been intensively scorched for their basic commitment to the promotion of imperialist values, by insisting that capitalist development is the only model of development for the Third World in a vain proclamation of "the end of ideology", attempting to reproduce decadent Western society in the periphery and generally mystifying the tragic reality of these regions in the service of imperialism. Thus orthodox economics propagates a false harmony of interests between the imperialist and Third World countries through slogans like "partners in progress", mutually advantageous trade through comparative advantage, "aid", technology transfer, and so on. Bourgeois development economics mystifies underdevelopment as lack of economic growth in its GDP number-game or growthmanship, preaches a false "vicious circle" theory of underdevelopment – "a country is poor because it is poor" – and incarnates interminable missing factors of development, such as capital, management, skilled labour, technology, etc., as if their presence (or absence) is fortuitous and ahistorical. The reformist solutions for underdevelopment such as import-substitution, export promotion, tax reform, and so on, from the technical nostrums of bourgeois economics have been a fiasco. Their eclectic GDP planning, rooted in discredited Keynesian economics, has succeeded only too well in fostering neocolonial dependence, promoting kleptocratic accumulation by a predatory minority, exacerbating mass squalor and intensifying food crises and structural inequalities.

For its part, the bourgeois sociology of development has formulated the "ideal type" index approach to development.[22] This approach consists of first, defining the alleged features of underdeveloped countries, such as role diffusion, ascriptive status, particularism and collectivism. For successful development, these characteristics are supposed to be replaced with the corresponding ideal indices of Western society, which are said to be role specificity, achieved status, universalism and individualism. The so-called theory of political development in its eclectic imitation of neoclassical economics conceives of development falsely as a technical input–output process with the objective of maximising such nebulous variables as structural differentiation, cultural secularisation, formal equality (of the market place as opposed to concrete social equality), and Weberian bureaucracy.[23] Bourgeois psychology then posits inertia, lack of foresight, low need-achievement motivation and similar banalities as the causes of underdevelopment.[24] Apart from the racist character of some of these prescriptions on underdevelopment, they are all united in mystifying and distorting its historical and social nature by denying its fundamentally imperialist root cause and imposing a false unilinear conception of history, according to which all societies must traverse the Western Rostovian stages of development.[25]

The collective consequences of this imperialist social science throughout the Third World are basically twofold. One is the entrenchment of capitalist values and development models in these regions in a futile attempt to reproduce Western capitalist economy and society there. Fanon's "mimic intellectuals" of these countries and their frenetic reproduction of this reactionary and imperialist social science is, perhaps, the most visible symbol of this morbid attempt to replicate decadent Western development in these poor countries. One fundamental flaw in the intellectual nostalgia of imperialist social science for reproducing Western development in the Third World is its refusal to recommend the adoption by underdeveloped countries of the Western model of capital accumulation by expropriation – because capitalist accumulation in Western Europe, North America and Japan was achieved through inhuman slavery, the exploitation of American plantations and mines, the sale of opium to China and the expropriation of the grazing lands of American Indians (and their genocidal annihilation) and of the common lands of the European peasantry in the violently imposed enclosure movement.[26]

The other more tragic consequence of imperialist social science is the unmitigated disaster so eloquently manifested in the deepening crisis of underdevelopment in Africa and elsewhere in the periphery of world capitalism. Far from being epiphenomenal to this crisis, bourgeois social science is fundamental to the legitimation of the capitalist class dictatorship that nurtured and sustains this mass poverty, and to the bankrupt theories and policies that generate and rationalise it for social acceptance by the pauperised majority in the poor countries.

The reproduction of imperialist social science in Africa

The mechanisms of reproduction and the criteria of irrelevance of imperialist social science in Africa and throughout the Third World, which the foregoing analysis has implied, must be discussed explicitly. This is important for the elaboration of appropriate strategies for intellectual liberation in Africa. In this regard, though the uncritical reproduction of imperialist social science is familiarly a function of teaching and research, it is in fact possible to identify several other mechanisms involved. They include the control of educational institutions, curriculum development, publication, funding and educational exchange programmes, all of which determine the character of teaching and research.[27]

The significance of *control over resource allocation and decision-making* in educational institutions for the puerile reproduction of bourgeois social science in the periphery is bound up with the basic issue of dominant *petit-bourgeois* class control of the state in these countries, and the fact that educational institutions, as critical ideological institutions bearing ideological relations, are major arenas of class struggle in bourgeois society. This explains why Africa's educational institutions, especially at tertiary and university levels, have their boards of governors or councils dominated by appointed (rather than popularly elected) *petit-bourgeois* representatives of the dominant classes, drawn from such conservative strata of society as the feudal traditional elite of chiefs, comprador chambers of commerce, pro-imperialist bar associations, capitalist-oriented bureaucrats and conservative professionals. These are precisely imperialism's local allies in the Third World whose predatory class interests are so well served by the predominant imperialist social science in these countries.

For the same reasons, these pro-imperialist elements provide the political and ideological support for *petit-bourgeois* social science academics as professors, vice-chancellors or presidents, provosts, deans, departmental heads or chairmen, directors and lecturers, to devise reactionary curricula for their educational and research establishments. As direct products of colonial and metropolitan educational institutions, these scholars invoke an asocial and obtuse universalism of knowledge, international standards and even "knowledge for its own sake" to replicate imperialist curricula in Africa with various reactionary and socially irrelevant courses and programmes. In the process, the pressing problems of their societies receive scant attention, and even perverted treatment.

The imperialist intellectual domination of the Third World is then forcibly demonstrated with the foreign publishing of textbooks and research findings. In virtually all disciplines, in peripheral educational institutions, especially in Africa, major textbooks are written by imperialist scholars (with few by their local protégés) and mostly published by such imperialist publishing houses as Praeger, McGraw Hill, John Wiley, Addison-Wesley, Prentice-Hall, Macmillan, Longman, Oxford University Press (now University Press Ltd., UPL, in Nigeria), etc.[28] Research findings by Third World scholars are also usually sent for publication in such journals as *World Politics, Economic Development and Cultural Change* (EDCC), etc. some of which have notorious records of imperialist patronage.[29] The basic problem with publishing in the imperialist press is that apart from subordinating Third World scholars, it imposes an overt or covert capitalist ideological standard on the writings and research of peripheral scholars.

The imperialist funding of social science teaching, research and staff development in the Third World also imposes the same ideological and imperialist orientation and surveillance on peripheral social science scholarship. The issue here is more obvious: "who pays the piper, calls the tune". This is how the valuable energies of Third World scholars are diverted into the pursuit of false problems, the mystifications of the realities of their countries, and the whims and caprices of imperialist foundations and other research grant donors. True enough, the recipient institutions and scholars should be able to define their own academic priorities, but the problems are that some of the foreign grants are like project-tied "aid" (in reality subsidies for the donor country's exports), while the pro-imperialist orientation of peripheral social scientists ensures that their most irrelevant and obscurantist projects may be funded from abroad in this symbiotic relationship between comprador scholars and imperialist donors. This is how the system of imperialist intermediary in the larger neocolonial economy and society is reproduced in the intellectual sphere.

Educational exchange programmes involving students and scholars of Third World educational and research institutions and their imperialist counterparts, and the foreign training of academic staff also encourage the reproduction of imperialist and irrelevant social science in a more obvious way. But the major problems of both sets of countries differ, and the preoccupations of their academic institutions and personnel should also differ. So, in unequal exchange and collaborative programmes between institutions in peripheral and metropolitan countries, it is most likely that the teaching and research agenda as well as the ideological orientation of the imperialist countries will be imposed, directly or indirectly, on the dominated countries. Any sharing of costs (for travel, equipment, etc.) in such programmes may even mean that the meagre resources of the poor countries are being diverted, not only from their myriad pressing problems, but to promote the academic interests of the imperialist countries. Even the exposure to advanced research methods and equipment by Third World scholars under such arrangements may not be of the best advantage in terms of the priorities of the poor countries – because such advanced equipment and methods are neither available nor usable in poor countries, and where they are, the problems which they address are not Third World priorities. The training of social science academic staff abroad should be more selective, with closer monitoring of research programmes.

In these different ways, the contents of social science teaching and research in the Third World tend uncritically to reproduce imperialist social science. By being preoccupied with the same paradigms, such as neoclassical and Keynesian economics, the Weberian theory of the state, consensus politics, Parsonian functionalism and Freudian psyschology, peripheral social science produces graduates and academics with the same ideological and imperialist orientations as their imperialist mentors. These then perpetuate the same false problems, mystifications and obscurantism in teaching and research that constitute real epistemological barriers to the rational understanding and consequent resolution of the deepening crisis of underdevelopment, through the liberation of the Third World from stifling imperialist domination and exploitation. The basic point of this critique of bourgeois or imperialist social science in Africa is not that some parts of it cannot be found useful. Rather, the point is that, taken collectively, imperialist social science contributes significantly to the African crisis by mystifying, distorting and concealing many critical aspects of the African reality.

The irrelevance of imperialist social science

It is important to underline the social irrelevance of imperialist social science to the Third World in explicit terms. First, on purely *scientific* grounds, bourgeois social science is a failure on two counts. One is that its theories fail the test of correctly reflecting reality, or of providing an accurate explanation of the real world. The conflict between its theories and observed reality has reached such a level as to generate the rupture of consensus in individual social science disciplines and lead to an intellectual crisis. For example, distributional theory and the shifting missing-factor explanation for underdevelopment in bourgeois economics have both collapsed because of growing inequalities and the persistent underdevelopment of such capital-rich OPEC countries as Nigeria. Similarly, in spite of flirtation with consensus politics, inter- and intra-class conflicts as well as irredentism have been generating political instability in the Third World. The second reason for the scientific failure of bourgeois social science is that many of its basic theories are meaningless and useless.[30] For example, the vicious circle theory of under-development and the metaphysical utility theory of value with its impregnable circularity, according to which a commodity has utility if it is useful, while this usefulness is derived from its utility in the first instance! Other useless bourgeois social theories are general equilibrium theory, which insists that everything depends on everything else, capital theory and the aggregate production function, the theory of political development and functionalist sociology.

Furthermore, imperialist social science poses bogus problems for the Third World and thus constitutes a barrier to the scientific understanding of the true reality of these countries. Examples of such diversionary problems in the different social science disciplines are: the search for metaphysical utility maximisation; general equilibrium; aggregate production function; optimal growth; the insistence on "technology transfer" and GDP planning in bourgeois economics; consensus politics; cultural secularisation and greater bureaucratisation for alleged social efficiency, which mars democratic political participation; the social contract theory of the state; abstract stability and harmony of interests in political science; social mobility; role specificity; and the attributes of sociological functionalism, as well as the problem of need-achievement motivation and the search for innovative personalities (as if they were a special genre of humans) in imperialist psychology. African countries are already being invited internationally to study environmental pollution – when they have no clue to the problem of human pollution manifested principally by the naked starvation of millions, not to mention malnutrition! In bourgeois economics, talented African scholars are also being diverted into developing a model of global capitalism – for the more effective domination and exploitation of their countries – when they do not even have basic data for budgeting, let alone for planning.

Imperialist social science is also irrelevant in the sense that it has no answer to a whole range of pressing problems of Third World countries – and even of the imperialist countries. Its theories either cannot explain or the policies distilled from such theories cannot solve these urgent problems. Among these are growing inequalities, which neoclassical theory cannot explain and reformist redistributive taxation of Kaldor and others cannot resolve. Indeed, bourgeois economics simply has no consistent theory of distribution. On this score, Lipsey confesses:

> We conclude by raising the interesting question of the share of profits in the national income. We have no satisfactory theory of the share of national income going as profits and we can do little to explain (the) past behaviour of this share, nor do we have a body of predictions about the effect on this share of occurrences like the rise of unions, wage freezes, profits taxes, tax controls, etc.[31]

Similarly, orthodox economics has no consistent theory of value, capital, the firm, multinational corporations or monopoly capital and long-run development. These are precisely the critical problems plaguing the poor countries. The bureaucratic failures, political militarisation, pervasive instability and separatist irredentism of the periphery also have no adequate theories in bourgeois political science, just as functionalist sociology has no satifactory explanations for the rising crime, leadership failure, class polarisation, social decay and related manifestations of the traumatised social milieu and social disintegration of the periphery. Likewise, bourgeois psychology has no credible theories to explain the growing alienation of the masses, their deep disenchantment and paranoia.

Finally, we must insist against the protestations of right-wing apologists that many of the solutions and policies of imperialist social science for the major problems of the Third World, and Africa in particular, have resulted in disastrous calamity with tragic human cost. The deteriorating food crisis and widespread starvation in spite of years of so-called internally consistent planning is the most visible expression of this disaster in Africa. Agricultural and tax reforms, "green revolution", foreign "aid" and investment, "technology transfer", bureaucratic modernisation, social mobility programmes and policies for achievement motivation have featured in these solutions. They have succeeded only too well in generating agricultural stagnation, rural decay, massive and rising unemployment, multinational pillage, balance of payments crises, technological backwardness, hypertrophic administrative spending and the fiscal crisis of the state, sharpening social divisions and producing mass psychological paralysis across the entire African continent. In the face of this tragic record, the apostles of imperialist social science raise the mantle of Africanity.

The opium of Africanity

With mounting criticism of bourgeois social science and the growing demand for a more socially relevant social theory, the apologists of imperialist social science falsely charge that the new orthodoxy demanded implies,

> that there is an African political [social] science, one that is *sui generis*, simply because it is decolonised . . . Only on the assumption that "Western" political [social] science has exhausted all possibilities, . . . could one begin to wonder if the time had not come for a separate discipline called African political [social] science . . . the discipline throughout its history has been persistently concerned with the reconceptualisation of significant variables, with the continuing search for adequate units of analysis.[32]

Another version of this position insists that to concentrate on the study of African societies is "ethnic replicative scholarship" – whatever that means!

We reject this defence of imperialist social science in the guise of false intellectual universalism. The objective of the legitimate critique of bourgeois social science by the "new orthodoxy" and the valid demand for greater intellectual concentration on African societies is not the creation of an African social science. And, after over a century of maturity with industrial capitalism since the 1840s, what possibilities, what new vistas within its dominant paradigms, short of ongoing eclecticism, sophistry and the sprouting of "practical disciplines", have bourgeois social science or any of its components not exhausted? After half a century of fulminating since two global holocausts and a world depression, after the sterile marginalist, Keynesian, functionalist and Freudian intellectual revolutions with the barren neoclassical synthesis, what new vistas of imperialist social science are being canvassed? We also maintain that the alleged "reconceptualisation of significant variables" and "search for adequate units of analysis" have not prevented the tragic irrelevance and disastrous consequences of imperialist social science in Africa and the rest of the Third World.

It is for these reasons that both those who wrongly condemn the requirement for a "new orthodoxy" as a demand for African social science, and those who insist on a separate African social science, like their *petit-bourgeois* counterparts who insist on a separate African ideology, are being diversionary, evasive and obscurantist. They pervert a scientific argument into a parochial obsession. They do so in a veiled opposition to the scientific alternative to bourgeois economy and society, and the imperialist social science that defends and promotes them. This veiled opposition, moreover, is nothing but the oblique defence of vested interests in terms of the privileges of *petit-bourgeois* membership of a predatory and minority dominant class. The prerequisites of elite status and corporate ambition generally slumber deep beneath these oblique objections to the elaboration of a scientific alternative to the bankrupt imperialist social science in Africa.

Marxist social science as the scientific alternative to imperialist social science

Just as "imperialism is the eve of the socialist revolution", Marxist social science is the only scientific alternative to the bankruptcy and social irrelevance of imperialist social science. Why, on epistemological, political and other grounds should Marxist social science be the scientific alternative to the tragic failure of bourgeois social science in the Third World? There are six reasons.

1) the theory of historical development or historical materialism demonstrates that just as the capitalist mode of production and social formation succeeded its feudal predecessor, so the socialist transitional phase and social formation is the logical, historical higher level of development into which capitalism is transformed. Correspondingly, just as the sociology of knowledge shows how capitalism necessarily develops bourgeois and imperialist social science, through the process of the social construction of reality, the socialist society into which capitalist society has to be transformed demands Marxist social science. As soon as bourgeois social science has reached a stage in any society when it cannot adequately explain and resolve the problems of that society, it is into an intellectual crisis, which is the signal that it is due for replacement by the higher power of Marxist social science. The deepening crisis of the Third World and its imperialist social science amply demonstrate that neocolonial capitalism and its imperialist social science are ripe for transformation into scientific socialism and Marxist social science, respectively.

2) on the purely epistemic canons of scientific validity, Marxist social science is superior to imperialist social science, especially with respect to the Third World. This is in the sense that Marxist social theory, in general, corresponds more to objective social reality than does bourgeois social science. And this does not rest on the dramatised trite point that all of Marx's predictions have not been fulfilled. Nobody denies that Marx as a human being made mistakes. What we contend, however, are (a) that Marxist social theory is more than Marx's social science, even though Marx first systematically elaborated the former; and (b) in spite of its shortcomings, Marxist social science is more congruent with observed social phenomena and, therefore, has greater explanatory power, especially for the Third World milieu, than has imperialist social science. Perhaps the best proof of this is not only the proliferation of Marxist literature, but the growing abandonment of imperialist social science and the increasing eclectic incorporation of the Marxist tradition by many of its adherents – even though they often class-consciously reject the unpalatable political implications of Marxist theory.

3) the basic goal of liberation in Marxist social theory and the exploited Third World countries is essentially the same, whereas the basic exploitative and domination objective of imperialist social science conflict with that of the poor

countries. In laying bare the laws of motion of modern bourgeois society, Marxist social theory is fundamentally addressed to the rapid change of society. As Marx put it, "philosophers have been explaining the world in various ways; the point, however, is to change it." Lenin also insisted that "the liberation of the people is the measure of all intellectual work". The liberation of the Third World from its imperialist domination and exploitation is thus consonant with the revolutionary preoccupations of Marxism – hence the militant and growing popularity of Marxist social theory and the corresponding decline of bourgeois paradigms in these countries.

4) the major preoccupations of Marxist social science also correspond to the critical and urgent problems of the periphery. These are alienation, exploitation, mass poverty, class domination, oppression and conflict, monopoly capital and imperialist contradictions, multinational pillage, racism, the features of technological development, economic crises and so on. These are precisely the dominant problems on the social agenda of African and other Third World countries. By contrast, the obsessions of imperialist social science with equilibrium, harmony, gradualism, consensus, mobility, individualism, acquisitive aggression, achievement motivation and so on are diversions from Third World priorities.

5) the long-term and structuralist emphasis in the Marxist tradition accords more closely with the persistent and systemic nature of underdevelopment in the Third World than the short-term and myopic predilections of bourgeois social theory. This also explains why the solutions from the short-term theories of imperialist social science perform so disastrously when applied to the long-term problems of the poor countries. While bourgeois social science is preoccupied with economic growth, periodic cycles and the efficient management of wealth for the imperialist countries, the Third World is addressing the longer-term questions of generating development, achieving structural transformation, coping with permanent economic, political and social crises, and liquidating mass poverty. This is why short-term Keynesian prescriptions are useless, and even counter-productive, when applied to planning and other structural development problems in the poor countries.

Finally, the empirical performance of Marxist social theory is not comparable with the tragedy wrought by imperialist social science, especially in the Third World. Thus while the application of Marxist theory since 1917 has generated the economic, technological and social miracles in the USSR, China, Cuba and other socialist countries, the application of imperialist theories to the poor countries since the 1930s (when Latin American countries started gaining nominal independence) has been a tragedy.[33] Not a single underdeveloped country operating bourgeois social theory since 1900 has achieved successful transformation. The Japanese development is atypical, because Japan was never colonised like the rest of the Third World, and she colonised parts of China and islands in the Pacific. The North American transformation was also an imperialist experiment rooted in slavery, internal expropriation of Indians and Blacks and the exploitation of the entire Third World. The contrasting fortunes of China and India based on the opposing social theories is also instructive here. Indeed, the superiority and desirability of Marxist social theory is so obvious at this historical juncture that, if anything, it is imperialist social theory, and not Marxist social science, which should now justify its practice, especially in Africa and the Third World in general.

In this regard, the misguided and class-inspired selfish opposition to Marxist social science by imperialist apologists like René Dumont is basically the veiled defence of vested interests in the bankrupt capitalist and imperialist order. Their quibbles about different social conditions in Africa and the rest of the Third World are more a caution against imperialist social science, which is alien to the Third World, than against the socialist alternative. All that is implied scientifically by their criticisms is that we have to be *creative* in the practice and application of Marxist social science in the Third World. The specific theories and policies have to be rooted in the concrete social reality of each poor society. This is even part of the requirements of the Marxist tradition – hence the insistence on the historical specificity of all scientific theories.

Maximising social science contribution

Besides the elimination of the contribution of bourgeois social science to the generation of the African crisis, the foregoing analysis has another critical objective. This is to maximise the contribution of social science to African development. The important requirements for this have been itemised as follows:[34]

(1) Social relevance of social science research – this depends on the African (and other Third World) governments, public and other agencies that fund them and the social scientists themselves. The de-trivialisation of social science research is also critical.

(2) Effective communication of social science research results – this requires research reporting to government, business, the public, other social scientists, etc.

(3) Mass education and the political consciousness of the broad masses – which will raise the demand for socially relevant social science research and lead to a desirable change in the distribution of politico-economic power.

(4) Funding radical social science research – if the demand for radical and socially relevant social science research is not backed up by adequate funding, little result can be achieved.

(5) Political participation of social scientists – it is important that African social scientists should become more involved and participate actively in political processes and decision-making in order to sensitise them, widen their perspectives and sharpen their analytical apparatus.

(6) National liberation through the achievement of national economic independence is critical to all these. This is essential in order to eliminate false and diversionary problems, and the distortion of national priorities by vested foreign interests like those of the multinationals.

Notes

1. These African social scientists are *petit-bourgeois* in the etymological sense,

like the rest of the African *petit-bourgeoisie* because, like them, they are dependent and lacking in the resources for constituting an autonomous national bourgeoisie as Frantz Fanon suggested (1965), ch. 4.

2. See, for example, Y. Barongo (ed.) (1982).

3. See the proceedings and communiqué of *The Punch Seminar on the Nigerian Economy*, Lagos, 7 & 8 December 1983.

4. On the paradigms of bourgeois social science, see P. M. Sweezy (1972), ch. 4.

5. Ibid., pp. 53–4.

6. On the empiricist origin of bourgeois social science, see G. Novack (1971).

7. Richard R. Bowker in S. Fine (1964) p. 100.

8. On this, see E. K. Hunt (1975).

9. P. M. Sweezy (1972) p. 54.

10. See G. Novack (1971).

11. For a specific discussion of the ideological character of the bourgeois theory of political development, see Claude Ake (1979), ch. 3, pp. 60–98.

12. See Karl Mannheim (1936); and P. L. Berger & T. Luckman (1967).

13. For these developments, see E. K. Hunt (1975), chs. 4–8.

14. On the ideological preoccupations of bourgeois social science, see R. Blackburn in R. C. Edwards et al. (eds.) (1972), pp. 36–46; N. Chomsky (1969) especially "Objectivity and Liberal Scholarship" and "The Responsibility of Intellectuals".

15. R. Blackburn, op. cit. p. 44.

16. Bob Rowthorn (1980), p. 20.

17. Joan Robinson (1971), p. 144.

18. See M. W. Apple (1979), chs. 1–3 & 8.

19. Ben Fine (1980), ch. 1.

20. On these, see Kwame Nkrumah (1973), chs. 4 and 5.

21. For detailed critiques of the bourgeois theories of underdevelopment, see A. G. Frank (1970), and Samir Amin (1974) (2 volumes).

22. For a critique of bourgeois sociology of development and the "ideal type" index approach, see A. G. Frank (1970), ch. 2.

23. For the mystification of underdevelopment by bourgeois sociologists, see B. F. Hoslitz (1960); Talcott Parsons (1960).

24. D. C. McClelland (1964) in *Economic Development and Cultural Change*, vol. 12, no. 3, and his book *The Achieving Society*.

25. For this backward perception of historical development, see W. W. Rostow (1962).

26. On these expropriatory methods of Western capitalist accumulation, see Eric Williams (1972).

27. For the discussion of the issues involved in the reproduction of imperialist social science in Africa, see UNESCO, Expert Meeting on the Formulation of Social Science Policies in Africa South of the Sahara, Kinshasa, Zaire, 8–12 October 1979, Declaration and Recommendations.

28. Macmillan, McGraw-Hill and John Wiley & Sons are reported to have subsidiaries in South Africa, See *Newsletter of URPE* (Union for Radical Political Economic), vol. 16, no. 4, Summer 1985, p. 7.

29. See discussions of the reactionary orientation of EDCC in A. G. Frank (1970), ch. 2.

30. On the scientific failure of imperialist social science, see Alvin Gouldner (1972).

31. R. G. Lipsey (1971), p. 481.

32. Yolamu Barongo (ed.) (1982), p. 58.
33. On the tragedy of Latin America, see E. Galeano (1974).
34. See UNESCO (1979) "Declarations and Recommendations" of the Expert Meeting on the Formulation of Social Science Policies in Africa South of the Sahara, Kinshasa, Zaire, 8–12 October.

3 Multinational Corporations and the Underdevelopment of Africa

Multinational corporations have played, and continue to play, a critical role in the generation and intensification of the contradictions of underdevelopment in Africa and throughout the Third World. Bourgeois economics' misleading conception that multinationals are partners in development because they convey foreign capital to poor countries, transfer technology, create jobs, pay wages and taxes, and promote industrialisation conceals the stark reality: the pillage of natural resources, superexploitation of labour, net capital transfer *from* the poor countries, technological retardation, structural distortions, political instability, cultural degradation and other abuses imposed by multinationals on Third World countries. In generating these contradictions, foreign direct investment (FDI), the transnationalisation of capital and production, multinational corporations (MNCs) or transnational corporations (TNCs), neocolonialism and multilateral imperialism all mean basically the same thing.

Multinational corporations as agents of imperialism

It is important to analyse the multinational corporations (MNCs) in the context of world imperialism in order to gain a correct appreciation of their role in the intensifying drama of underdevelopment in the Third World. In this regard, World War II marked the watershed of bilateral imperialism as colonial domination and exploitation; the anti-colonial defeat of France in Indo-China at Dien Bien Phu in 1954 sounded the death knell of bilateral imperialism. The transition from a strategy of bilateral to a strategy of multilateral imperialism was dictated by some basic factors in imperialism's adjustment to its structural crises.[1]

One factor was the weakening of the European imperialist powers during World War II. This led to the collapse of direct colonisation and ultimately forced Britain, France, Germany and the other imperialist countries to change their strategy of domination.

Another factor was the US imperialist motive after emerging from World War II as the strongest capitalist country. While Britain sold over \$6 billion in overseas investment, used up \$0.8 billion in gold reserves and incurred private capital losses of over \$8 billion, in the US, GNP rose by 100% during 1939/44, gold reserves increased from \$4 billion in 1932 to \$20.6 billion in 1958, and world capital exports rose from 35.3% in 1930 to 59.1% in 1960. This US hegemony nurtured expansionist ambition as reflected in the paradox of an isolationist state with an aggressive foreign policy. The US's previous lack of colonies and need for vast trade and investment outlets as the strongest post-war economic power with surplus goods and capital, propelled the launching of the Marshall Plan and the transition to multilateral imperialism. European imperialist powers, in their weakened post-war position, had their own motive in the emergence of multilateralism: they needed to retain their interests and to contain the anti-imperialist nationalism in their colonies. This required the "unity" of all imperialist powers under US domination and a change in the strategy of colonial exploitation.

Given these motives, the US elaborated the new imperialist strategy around a demand for a "new world order": a neocolonial order under her domination. It was to this end, that the first Marshall Plan was launched to rescue and dominate European capitalism. Then, despite the effective colonisation of the US's own black population, propaganda was mounted for the "self-determination" of all colonised peoples (similar to the recent hypocritical human rights campaign in the US) plus a demand for an "open door policy" in order to achieve colonial dissolution and penetration. In the proposals for the Atlantic Charter at the end of World War II, the US Under-Secretary of State declared: "The age of (bilateral) imperialism is ended. The right of all peoples to their freedom must be recognised . . . The principles of the Atlantic Charter must be guaranteed to the world as a whole – in all oceans and in all continents."[3] "Aid" was launched – both military and economic – to fight communism and to capture the comprador bourgeoisie of the poor countries and to soften and contain their post-colonial nationalism and prevent the consolidation of national independence in these countries. This "aid" was also (and still is) an indirect subsidy for US exports (e.g. as tied-purchase aid) and the development of the US's military–industrial complex as well as a form of military assistance for building new neocolonial armies and police.[4]

Under US leadership, all the imperialist powers also fashioned two strategies for multilateral imperialism. One was the establishment of multilateral institutions, the International Bank for Reconstruction and Development (IBRD), the International Finance Corporation (IFC), the International Development Association (IDA), the International Monetary Fund (IMF) and the General Agreement on Tariffs and Trade (GATT) within the framework of the post-war international monetary system, styled the Bretton Woods System, which was launched in 1944.[5] While the World Bank looked after imperialist investment, the unequal GATT treaties policed free trade and the IMF imposed currency convertibility. The second component of the joint imperialist post-war strategies consisted of the elaboration of a new international division of labour centred around the new corporate structure of the MNC, which first emerged in the US from the growth of monopoly capitalism and from Hilferding's finance capital, which started in the 1880s. This was the strategy of global accumulation of capital anchored to the internationalisation of capital and production across the entire non-socialist world. The basic idea of these two joint imperialist strategies and the US inspired neocolonial mechanism was to replace direct bilateral imperialism, which had come under nationalist, socialist bloc and US attacks, with indirect economic mechanisms of domination and exploitation.

The MNCs, on account of their diversity of activities, enormous resources and rapid growth, soon became the core of the new multilateral imperialist strategies. "These firms' motive, whatever their nationality, is rationally to exploit all existing inequalities, including human ones, purely and simply for their own gain. The more liberalisation there is, the more these companies will grow."[6] Hence they demand the abolition of customs barriers (through GATT) and the elimination of restrictions on foreign investment (through the IMF and the World Bank) for their internationalisation of accumulation. For these reasons, the MNCs develop highly centralised organisations; monopolistic competition; the insertion of representatives in the "host" state itself; investment at a loss for protecting markets and sources of raw materials; and joint ventures. The joint ventures in particular offer the MNCs several advantages such as insurance against nationalisation and other risk minimisation through short pay-back periods of three to five years; easy profit repatriation; a docile labour force; such incentives as local loans; and importation of raw materials and spare parts, as well as first claim to local raw materials, markets, management, skilled labour, and distributive outlets, including state networks.

In addition, MNCs also perform three critical roles for multilateral imperialism. The first is to blur the visibility of the imperialist strategy of domination by shifting it to the ostensibly objective economic plane. This facilitates imperialism's quiet penetration of "host" countries, and enables the MNCs to advance the foreign policy objectives of their home countries. The second is the development of a new international division of labour through the internationalisation of capital and production. While serving to offset a tendency to the falling rate of profit, and advancing the global accumulation of capital, this strategy accentuates the centre–periphery dichotomy and Third World countries' dependence on the industrialised home countries of the MNCs. Thirdly, this system is functional for world imperialism because it ensures that the MNCs not only become the dominant purveyors of monopoly capital and technology, but the critical actors in the dialectics of development in the centre (the imperialist countries) and underdevelopment in the periphery. This ensures the survival of imperialism by guaranteeing it a region of the world that can be used as the extensive margin of imperialist exploitation for resolving its basic contradictions in the advanced countries.

The scope of MNCs in Africa

Though the first foreign production subsidiary in the world has been traced to the Belgian firm, Cockrill, in Prussia, the multinational phenomenon in Africa started with the activities of old colonial mercantile houses, such as the Royal Niger Company, United Africa Company (UAC), Chandaria in Kenya, Lever Brothers and so on.[7] With the growth of monopoly capitalism from the 1880s and the emergence of multilateral imperialism after 1945, these mercantile houses gradually diverted their investment portfolio into plantation agriculture, mining and manufacturing. The stiff tariff protection of early post-colonial nationalism also encouraged the establishment of multinational affiliates as "tariff factories" in Third World countries.

The motives of these MNCs have historically been analysed, by Lenin, Hobson and others, around the falling rate of profit from shrinking home markets.[8] Apart from the search for profitable investment outlets for surplus capital and for protected foreign markets, control over sources of such raw materials as oil, copper, rubber, etc. has remained a major motive of multinational activity. The exploitation of cheap labour in low-wage countries is also an important source of the super-profits of the MNCs as Table 3.1, providing comparative data on compensation per hour (CPH), shows.[9]

Table 3.1
Hourly wages of multinational corporations

Region	*Average Hourly Compensation* $	%
US parent MNC	8.76	100
Developed countries' affiliates	6.34	72
Foreign affiliates, all countries	4.92	56
Developing countries' affiliates	1.74	(20% of US rate)
Indian affiliates	1.27	(About 15% of US rate)
Sub-Saharan African affiliates	1.16	(13.3% of US rate)
Philippines' affiliates	0.57	(About 6.7% of US rate)

The other advantages sought by the MNCs include risk minimisation through geographical spread, checking competitors globally or at home (which makes Alcan and Alcoa control over 50% of world production of bauxite–aluminium at all levels and price leaders in the industry), exploitation of the monopoly advantage of a new product as market leaders, and reaping economies of scale.

For the whole world, UN estimates show that in 1971, the total value-added of all MNCs was $500 billion or 20% of the GNP of all the non-socialist countries. The worldwide investment stock of these MNCs rose from $104 billion in 1967 to $650 billion in 1982. The annual sales of some of the multinational juggernauts like Exxon, Shell-BP, ITT and so on, is also more than $26 billion from over 200 subsidiaries in more than 100 countries. For the underdeveloped countries (UDCs) alone, the annual flow of foreign direct investment (FDI) to them rose from $1.8 billion in 1960 to $13.5 billion in 1979. The US investment (total stock) in these countries also increased from $5.7 billion in 1950 to $52.7 billion in 1980, while for the past two decades, US MNCs have accounted for over 50% of the total flow of FDI to the poor countries.[10]

Correspondingly, FDI as a percentage of total capital exports to the UDCs by OECD countries was 21.6% in 1960/61 and 23.5% in 1970/71. But the significance of this direct investment exceeds its quantitative magnitude as it grows over time, corresponds to permanent productive structure with penetration and control in the "host" countries, and is aimed at the maximisation of global accumulation. Export credits, loans, public aid, portfolio investment (share ownership) and so on, also seek to maximise accumulation but do not represent the same degree of control of resources and opportunities as foreign direct investment. Thus it has been argued that the UN study of MNCs errs by failing to see FDI as a tool of the corporate headquarters and not as a type of financial flow analytically distinguishable from the corporation itself.[11]

The sources or origins of foreign direct investment to Africa and the rest of the Third World show a high degree of concentration. Thus eight countries – USA, West Germany, Britain, France, Italy, Japan, Canada and the Netherlands – account for over 90% of the total flow of FDI to the poor countries.[12] In 1979, the US share of the total flow was 59%. In spite of the dissolution of bilateral colonial links, most of the multinational stock in each African country is still held by the erstwhile colonial predators. Thus Britain, France, the Netherlands and the US dominate most of the multinational capital in the continent (see Table 3.2).

Table 3.2
Total DAC[a] FDI by country of origin, 1967, 1971, 1976 ($ billion and %)

Country of origin	*1974–1979*	*1967*		*1971*		*1976*	
	%	*Amount*	%	*Amount*	%	*Amount*	%
USA	29.3	56.6	53.8	82.8	52.3	137.2	47.6
Britain	9.2	17.5	16.6	23.7	15.0	32.1	11.2
W. Germany	17.0	3.0	2.8	7.3	4.6	19.9	6.9
Japan	13.0	1.5	1.4	4.4	2.8	19.4	6.7
Switzerland	—	5.0	4.8	9.5	6.0	18.6	6.5
France	7.8	6.0	5.7	7.3	4.6	11.9	4.1
Canada	6.2	3.7	3.5	6.5	4.1	11.1	3.9
Netherlands	9.6[b]	2.2	2.1	4.0	2.5	9.8	3.4
Sweden	3.7[c]	1.7	1.6	2.4	1.5	5.0	1.7
Belgium-Luxembourg	2.5	2.0	1.9	2.4	1.5	3.6	1.2
Italy	2.0	2.1	2.0	3.0	1.9	2.9	1.0
Sub-Total	—	101.3	96.2	153.3	96.8	271.5	94.2
All others (estimate)	—	4.0	3.8	5.1	3.2	16.8	5.8
Grand Total	—	*105.3*	*100.0*	*158.4*	*100.0*	*288.3*	*100.0*

[a] The DAC Countries include the above countries plus Australia, Denmark, Finland, New Zealand, Austria and Norway;
[b] from 1974 to 1978;
[c] from 1974 to 1977.

Source: H. S. Marcussen and J. E. Torp (1982) *Internationalisation of Capital – Prospects for the Third World* (London: Zed Press), pp. 166 & 168.

Between the advanced and underdeveloped countries (UDCs) about 30% of foreign direct investment went to the latter. But although the volume of foreign direct investment to these poor countries increased over this period, their share in total FDI decreased, according to the United Nations Commission on Transnational Corporations (UNCTC). For the US alone, investment in UDCs increased from $5.7 billion in 1950 to $52.7 billion in 1980. But the share of US multinational investment of total FDI in UDCs *declined* from 48.7% in 1950 to 24.7% in 1980.

Table 3.3
US FDI in Africa and the Middle East
(Cumulative book value at year end, in $ million)

Location	*1957*	*1964*	*1967*	*1970*
Total all areas	25,394	44,386	59,267	78,090
Total in Africa	664	1,769	2,277	3,476
South Africa	301	467	667	864
Rhodesia & Nyasaland (Zimbabwe, Zambia & Malawi)	59	83	—	—
Libya	24	402	456	1,009
Liberia	72	189	173	201
Others	208	628	982	1,404
Middle East	1,138	1,332	1,748	1,645

Source: S. Smith (1974) *US Neocolonialism in Africa* (New York; International Publishers).

Regionally, in 1978 the share of FDI stock in UDCs declined in Africa to 12.6% of the total – with 10.4% fall south of the Sahara and 2.2% fall north of it. Correspondingly, South-East Asia's share fell to 26.3% of the total while Latin America's share increased to 57.2%. The remaining 3.9% of FDI in the poor countries was lodged in Western Asia.

Size and distribution of multinational activities in Africa

For Africa, excluding South Africa, total FDI by OECD countries was $6.6 billion in 1967 and $9.4 billion in 1972 out of a world total of $165 billion in 1972.[13] This shows a relative decline of the African share, which grew by 43% between the two years, while the world total rose by 60%. This decline is attributed to the relative economic decline of the old colonial powers, especially Britain, and the unlikely possibility that accumulated investments in the continent represented sufficient penetration of the African economies, since global accumulation has no regional ceiling. The US is the other major source of FDI in Africa, accounting for 20.8% of all foreign investment there in 1967; 2.3% of US world investments were in Africa.

In terms of national distribution, MNCs tend to concentrate in high per capita income and fast-growing economies, as well as in tax havens. For Africa, this makes Algeria, Ivory Coast, Kenya, Libya, Nigeria, Zaire, Zambia and a few other countries besides South Africa, the main bases of MNCs in the continent (see Table 3.3). Thus, Nigeria which ranks as the fifth most attractive foreign investment (FI)[14] area in the Third World (after Brazil, Venezuela, Mexico and Argentina) almost doubled her stock of FI from 1967 – a 17% share – to 1971, with $2.1 billion in 1972, which represented 22% of Africa's FI. Indigenisation during 1972/77 did not change the situation significantly. Libya also increased her African share, which is mainly in oil, from 9% to 16.5% during 1967/72, while Algeria, which has been the most restrictive, reduced her share by 64% in the same period; Libya has followed the Algerian example since 1970. Since the partial nationalisation of the copper industry in Zaire in 1967 and the Mulungushi declaration in Zambia in 1969, both

Table 3.4
Total DAC private direct investment[a] in UDCs by country, 1978 ($ million)

Country		*Amount*
Africa, North of Sahara		
Algeria		385
Libya		660
Morocco		350
Tunisia		280
Egypt		245
Sub-Total	(2%)	1,920
Sub-Saharan Africa:		
Angola		(100)
Benin		34
Botswana		57
Burundi		26
Cameroun		370
CAR		(70)
Chad		(26)
Congo (P.R.)		170
Ethiopia		(100)
Gabon		780
Gambia		15
Ghana		280
Guinea		200
Guinea (Eq.)		20
Ivory Coast		530
Kenya		520
Lesotho		4
Liberia		1,230
Sub-Saharan Africa (continued):		
Malawi		100
Mali		10
Mauritania		25
Mauritius		24
Mozambique		(100)
Rwanda		25
Senegal		340
Seychelles		12
Sierra Leone		82
Somalia		(100)
Sudan		60
Swaziland		50
Tanzania		170
Djibouti		10
Togo		100
Uganda		(10)
Upper Volta		20
Zaire		(1,250)
Zambia		330
Zimbabwe		(400)
Sub-Total	(5%)	4,668
Less South Africa		

Source: Marcussen and Torp, pp. 170–1.

countries have pursued moderate nationalisation with disinvestment, though they remain major hosts of MNCs. For Kenya, the total estimated book-value of FDI in 1971/72, which originated mostly from Britain and USA, was K£125 million.[15] By policy spread, Nigeria, Kenya and Ivory Coast are most liberal to MNCs; Algeria, Libya, Ethiopia and other socialist countries are most restrictive, with others in between. (Table 3.4.)

The sectoral distribution of foreign direct investment in Africa shows that 30% was lodged in oil in 1967 and about 20% in mining and smelting. Together with agriculture, 56.5% of the FDI in Africa in that year was in raw material extraction; 23.4% in the processing sectors of manufacturing and petroleum refining, with the remaining 20% in service sectors such as import–export trade, banking and insurance, and so on (see Table 3.4). The pattern since then has not changed drastically except that the manufacturing share has risen, while more countries like Nigeria, Gabon, Congo and Cameroon have joined the core extractive countries, comprising Libya, Algeria, Zambia, Zaire, Liberia, Senegal and Sierra Leone. The comparison of the sectoral distribution of FDI in the Third World shows that in 1967, Africa had the highest share for extractive activities and almost the smallest share for processing activities (see Table 3.6).

In manufacturing, which is the fastest growing sector of most economies, MNCs accounted for over 50% of all foreign investment in Gambia, Swaziland, Chad, Somalia and Burundi, although in these countries both foreign investment and the manufacturing sector are small. Though the proportion of multinational investment in manufacturing in these and other African countries has been rising with import-substitution industrialisation generally, the processing level and value-added are still very low.[16] Thus, most multinational manufacturing in Africa consists of consumer goods and assembly plants for brewery, sugar and flour mills, textiles, matches, assembly of bicycles, motor cycles, transistor radios, refrigerators, cars, etc. with very high import content of over 90% for the turn-key projects like the assembly of completely-knocked-down parts (CKDs). The technological implications of these manufacturing activities are examined later.

In the financial sector, the MNCs' role in Africa is illustrated by the holdings of West Germany's Grossbanken in ten African countries as shown in Table 3.5.

In the mining sector, MNCs' control on Africa is summarised in Table 3.6 with respect to the investments of the major mineral multinationals in 1977.

Ownership, control and dependency

MNCs generally establish financial control over their African operations through majority ownership. Thus 81% of US and 72% of non-US MNCs had over 51% share of the book-value capital of their African subsidiaries in 1971, against a world average of 78% and 71%, respectively. Correspondingly, 50–50 joint ownership of operations was reported for only 6% US and 7% non-US African subsidiaries, with MNCs holding minority interest in only 13% and 20% of cases, respectively.

In addition to stock ownership, market control, especially in manufacturing, is a critical mechanism of the MNCs' leverage, domination and exploitation. This is why market control is an important objective of multinational activity. It has been reported that in 1971 the local "host" country was the main market for 95% of US

Table 3.5
Known holdings of West Germany's Grossbanken in banks in Africa excluding South Africa, 1976

Country	*Bank*	*Holdings (% of shares)* Deutsche Bank	Commerz Bank	Dresdner Bank
Congo	Banque Commerciale Congolaise	3.1		
Morocco	Banque Commerciale de Commerce Morocco	7.1	*	
	Banque Nationale pour le Developpement Economique	0.4	*	*
Chad	Banque Tchadienne de Credits et de Depots	7.5		
Cameroun	Societe Camerounaise de Banque	5.0		
Ivory Coast	Societe Ivoirienne de Banque	12.0		
Gabon	Union Gabonaise de Banque	8.0		
Senegal	Union Senegalaise de Banque pour le Commerce et l'Industrie	1.9		
Togo	Union Togolaise de Bank	18.0		
Zaire	Societe Financiere de Developpement (SOFIDE)	—	†	
Tunisia	Union Internationale de Banques S.A.	—	*	

* unspecified shareholding
† also acts as representative bank

Source: A. Seidman & N. S. Makgetla (1980), p. 215.

and 94% of non-US MNCs in Africa. In Nigeria, the proportion was 100% for 48 multinational subsidiaries sampled; 35% in Zambia; and 38% for 31% of the reporting subsidiaries in French-speaking Africa, which had external markets as their major clients. French multinationals rely mainly on neighbouring African countries or their home countries. Moreover, 93% of the African multinational subsidiaries in 1971 sold their products primarily to customers outside the MNC; the corresponding percentage for the Magreb countries was 73%. These figures imply that the practice of sub-contracting African subsidiaries to produce for other multinational affiliates higher up in the corporate structure (for example under vertical integration of subsidiaries from those involved in raw material extraction to those processing finished products) is small in Africa. This suggests that the pattern of specialisation of multinational subsidiaries in Africa is that of being the last link in the product cycle. This partly explains the relatively low value-added, poor technological impact and weak linkage effects of multinational activities in Africa.

All these have critical implications for the dependency syndrome imposed by multinationals on the African continent. Thus, while in terms of the world total, industrialised capitalist countries' (ICCs) foreign investment in Africa is not high, in terms of penetration and control (that is, the dependency it generates) multinational capital constitutes effective penetration of Africa. This can be gauged from the ratio of FI to GNP (FI/GNP) for five groups of African countries

Table 3.6
Mineral multinationals in Africa, 1977

Home country/ Parent company	*African subsidiaries*	*African "host" countries*	*Minerals*	*% share*
Britain:				
Consolidated Gold Fields	Gold Fields of South Africa, Doornfontein, East Driefontein, West Driefontein, Deelkraal & Waterval Platinum	South Africa	Gold	100 to 10
Rio Tinto Zinc	Palabora Mining Co., Rössing Uranium & Rio Tinto Zimbabwe (Rhodesia)	South Africa	Copper	38.9
		Namibia	Uranium	46.5
		Zimbabwe	Nickel	90.0
Lonrho	Ashanti Gold Fields Corp. Ltd.	Ghana	Gold	45.0
	Inyati Copper	Zimbabwe	Copper	100
	Western Platinum	South Africa	Platinum	50.0
British Petroleum	BP (Nigeria) Ltd. (nationalised in 1979)	Nigeria	Oil	—
Selection Trust	DIMINCO	Sierra Leone	Diamonds	49.0
	Tsumeb Corp.	Namibia	Copper & lead	14.25
British Aluminium	Ghana Bauxite Co.	Ghana	Bauxite	45.0
	Halco	Guinea	Bauxite	61.0
London Tin Corporation	Amalgamated Tin Mines	Nigeria	Tin	83.0 of output
Turner & Newall	Havelock Asbestos	Swaziland	Asbestos	60.0
	Rhodesian & General Asbestos Corp.	Zimbabwe	Asbestos	100
	New Amianthus Mines	South Africa	Asbestos	100
William Baird Ltd.	Sierra Leone Development Corp.	Sierra Leone	Iron Ore	95
USA:	Mobil (Nigeria) Ltd.	Nigeria	Oil	—
	Texaco (Nigeria) Ltd.	Nigeria	Oil	—
	Total (Nigeria) Ltd.	Nigeria	Oil	—
ALCAN	Alcan Aluminium of Nigeria	Nigeria	Aluminium	72.8
	Huletts Aluminium Co.	South Africa	Aluminium	24.0
Reynolds Aluminium	Volta Aluminium Co. (VALCO)	Ghana	Aluminium	10.0
	Ghana Bauxite Co.	Ghana	Bauxite	45.0

Kaiser Aluminium	VALCO	Ghana	Aluminium	90.0
	BASCAL	Ghana	Bauxite	80.0
Amax	Tsumeb Corp.	Namibia	Copper & lead	29.6
	O'Okiep Copper	South Africa	Copper	17.3
	Roan Consolidated Mines	Zambia	Copper	20.4
Martin Marrietta	HALCO (Mining) Inc.	Guinea	Bauxite	20.0
Union Carbide	African Manganese	Ghana	Manganese	45.0
	Rhodesia Chrome Mines	Zimbabwe	Chrome	100
	African Chrome Mines	South Africa	Chrome	100
	Tubatse Ferrochrome	South Africa	Ferro-chrome	49.0
US Steel	COMILOG	Gabon	Manganese	44.0
Bethlehem Steel	Sierra Rutile	Sierra Leone	Rutile	85.0
	LAMCO Joint Venture	Liberia	Iron	35.0
Falconbridge Nickel	Oamites Mining Co.	Namibia	Copper & silver	74.9
	Kilembe Copper	Uganda	Copper	72.8
Phelps Dodge	Tin & Associated Minerals	Nigeria	Columbium	49.0
Kennecott	Richards Bay Minerals	South Africa	Iron & titanium	39.3
Nord Resources	Nord Mining & Exploration	Namibia	Tin & wolfram	100
Foote Minerals	Rhodesian Vanadium Corp.	Zimbabwe	Vanadium	100
France:				
na	FRIGUIA	Guinea	Bauxite	27.0
na	HALCO (Mining) Inc.	Guinea	Bauxite	10.0
na	COMINA	Malagasy	Chrome	70.0
na	SOMAIR	Niger	Uranium	69.1
na	COMUF	Gabon	Uranium	74.5
na	URCA	CAR	Uranium	19.2
na	COMINAK	Niger	Uranium	44.0
na	COMILOG	Gabon	Manganese	50.5
na	Cie Potasses du Congo	Congo	Potash	36.0
na	Phosphates de Taiba	Senegal	Phosphates	na
na	Cameroun (SEBACAU)	Cameroun	Bauxite	25.0

Source: G. Lanning and M. Mueller (1979), pp. 284–5, 289, 291, 294 & 298–300.

classified as "colonies", "independents", "protectorates", "condominia" and "countries on the road to annexation". Where the ratio of FI to GNP is at least 30% (FI/GNP ≥ 30%) such countries are classified as colonies and this implies that in 1967, there were three French "colonies" – Gabon, Congo (Brazzaville) and Mauritania; two British "colonies", Zambia and Swaziland; two US "colonies", Liberia and Libya, and one Belgian "colony" in Zaire. The "independents" are those where the ratio is less than 1%; in 1967 these countries were Lesotho, the United Arab Republic (UAR) with Ethiopia, Sudan and Mali as proximate members.[17] By 1971, the five groups of countries were the same, except Lesotho which was going on the annexation road, Congo becoming a protectorate, Zambia decolonised, Libya also decolonised after 1972, and Zaire reduced in status by Mobutu's blatant neocolonial antics. Algeria moved from being a French protectorate in 1967 with a 17% ratio to a condominium, with 4% ratio in 1971.

In addition to the above dependency groups, there is also the incidence of *national monopoly* associated with the activities of the MNCs in Africa. This occurs where one ICC accounts for most (e.g., 70%) of the foreign investment in a country. In 1967, France had national monopoly in 12 African countries, which constituted two-thirds of her ex-colonies; Britain in nine countries including the former Rhodesia; and the US exercised the monopoly in three countries: Libya, Liberia and the UAR.[18]

By 1983, with the increased integration of most African countries into the imperialist orbit through greater multinational investment in oil and manufacturing (in, for example, Nigeria, Kenya, Ivory Coast, Gabon and Cameroon) the increasing food imports by these countries with their mounting food crisis, and the economic collapse of countries like Zaire, Sudan, Ghana, etc. their dependence had exacerbated. This trend has been mitigated only by the increasing socialist transformation, as Ethiopia, Ghana, Benin, Burkina Faso, Zimbabwe and the former Portuguese colonies show.

The leverage exercised on African countries through the modality of multinational capital also involves carving out "spheres of interest" in foreign investment, trade, aid, military and political policies. Some of these, especially aid, military and political policies involve the MNCs' home governments. Thus, for the US, Britain and France, these spheres of interest with respect to foreign investment are illustrated by 1967 data in Table 3.7.[19]

Table 3.7
World and African shares of foreign investment by country

Country	*Share of total FI in Africa (%)*	*Share of country's world investment in Africa (%)*
US	20.8	2.3
Britain	30.0	11.4
France	26.3	28.8

Table 3.7 shows that FI, as a sphere of interest in Africa, is highest for France, then Britain, then the US.

Finally, the dependency generated in Africa by the multinationals has also been related to their "economic penetration index". This is the turnover of the activity established by foreign investment, and is estimated as equal to the book value of FI, multiplied by a constant factor of 3 or 2.7.[20] This approximates the depth of penetration of the "host" economy by FI and the extent of local accumulation. But the formula for its computation with the 3 or 2 constant factor appears arbitrary. Other more straightforward formulas that readily come to mind are the multinational share in total capital stock, in output, value-added or employment, or an average of all four ratios.

Decapitalisation and displacement of local entrepreneurship by MNCs

The most serious economic consequence of these multinational control mechanisms over African economies is decapitalisation of the region; a related effect is displacement of local entrepreneurship. A similar displacement of domestic capital (both private and state) in addition to the outright transfer of capital from Africa to the ICCs constitutes decapitalisation.[21] Together, this capital drain and local displacement constitute two basic ways in which the MNCs generate and sustain the underdevelopment of the region. Indeed, the magnitude of this export of capital from Africa by MNCs and their unpatriotic class collaborators throughout the Third World is so high, and the associated intensification of the contradictions of mass poverty so serious, that chapter 4 has been devoted to that topic.

Historically, the displacement of local entrepreneurial capacity began in the colonial era. Then, the import of previously locally produced commodities, such as textiles, soap, metal implements, ornaments, etc. simply displaced the local markets for such products. The additional export, as primary products, of such raw materials as tin, cotton, vegetable oil, rubber, etc., previously used for the local production of such displaced products, forced their traditional producers and craftsmen into redundancy. When the Industrial Revolution displaced such artisans and craftsmen who operated 'the putting-out system' in Europe, they were reabsorbed by the expansion of the factory system. But in the case of Africa, the colonial (and even post-colonial) factories were mainly in Europe, so the displaced African skilled labour and entrepreneurs could not be re-engaged in them. The deliberate prohibition of local manufacturing for many decades under colonialism (in order to ensure effective colonial monopoly of local resources and markets) contributed not only to a deterioration of the situation but to the creation of a situation that the MNCs have been exacerbating.

The deliberate, ruinous competition of the larger and better (home government) supported foreign monopoly capital against the much weaker local capital exacerbated the multinational destruction of local enterprises. Some techniques used included the outright exclusion of Africans from certain activities under colonialism, or the imposition of entry barriers (via large capital requirement as in banking), or stiff regulatory conditions beyond the scope of African resources. In colonial Nigeria, banking and shipping witnessed this discriminatory exclusion of Africans.[22] In the post-colonial era, techniques employed to displace local talents were: the artificial lowering of prices to such ruinous levels that local competitors are forced out before higher exploitative prices are charged to recover the MNCs' earlier losses; the multinational monopoly of patents and trade marks: imperialist banks' discriminatory credit policy against local entrepreneurs; political pressure, graft and log-rolling. This is partly why, in the challenging sectors dominated by the MNCs, local entrepreneurs are scarce. The local enterprise capacity therefore remains concentrated in marginal, mainly comprador and speculative activities.

MNCs and Africa's technological lag

Multinationals' depredations in Africa have a serious technological effect. This is with respect to the different concepts of technology such as, embodied and disembodied, neutral and non-neutral, proprietary and non-proprietary, as well as production, product and materials technology.[23] The last three types are usually emphasised in the development context: production technology relates to the method of production (besides the ratios of output per worker and per unit of capital) and the stages of production (material receiving, handling and processing as well as packaging and storage of product); product technology embraces product innovation, adaptation and differentiation; materials technology involves the production of intermediate inputs and the use of different raw materials with the same method of production. In the Third World all these aspects of technology, including research and development (R & D) are dominated by the MNCs and this multinational domination constitutes the dominant source of the technological backwardness of African and other underdeveloped countries. This imperialist retardation of technological development also constitutes an important component of the MNCs' pillage of Africa through the extraction of monopoly technological rents on patents, trade-marks, engineering fees and other charges. This technological domination, exploitation and retardation of Africa will be examined here with respect to the location and expenditure on R & D; ownership; registration and number of industrial or technological property rights, such as patents and trade marks registered in Africa; and Africa's expenditure on the import of technology under the illusion of the so-called "transfer of technology".[24] In these ways, imperialist domination of technology centres on two main processes: separation between production, ownership and use of technology, and monopolisation of the distribution of technology.

Research and development is the most important source of technology in the modern world. Before research in pure and applied science, as well as technological development, can take place, a knowledge of pure science is essential. This makes the geographical location and extent of the MNCs' R & D activities a critical factor for understanding the multinational impact on technological development in Africa. As the MNCs dominate the most important economic sectors of African countries, the scope of their R & D activities in these sectors is decisive for the technological fate of the region. It has been widely documented that multinationals concentrate about 98% of their R & D activities in their home countries,[25] which means that most of their expenditure on R & D for their subsidiaries worldwide is concentrated in the parent headquarters in the metropolitan countries. This has two adverse consequences for the MNCs' Third World "host" countries.

One is that MNCs' R & D expenditure in the poor countries is insignificant. A 1972/73 survey in Nigeria, for instance, found that total R & D expenditure by local and foreign firms was barely ₦22.3 million or 0.31% of the GNP, with only 2,423 scientific personnel engaged in all forms of scientific research (all of which are not R & D). Nearly all the research personnel were in universities and government establishments.[26] The Nigerian Council for Science and Technology Survey of 1971 also indicated that of 309 establishments sampled, only 40 reported any form of annual expenditure on R & D.[27] Kaplinsky also reported that for Kenya in 1978 out of seven British multinational subsidiaries sampled only two engaged in experimental development, none were engaged in basic research, while the small experimental development conducted was tied to quality control. For the US in 1966, it was reported that of the 52% multinational share of R & D expenditure, only 6% occurred abroad – mainly in Canada, Britain and Europe.[28]

The other adverse consequence is that most of the technologies MNCs import into Africa and the rest of the Third World are inappropriate for the resource endowment and other local conditions of these countries. Thus, while the relative abundance of capital in the MNCs' home countries dictates the need for capital-intensive technology, the relative abundance of labour in the poor countries calls for relatively labour-intensive technology. One egregious illustration of this contradiction is the finding that manufacturing enterprises in labour-abundant Nigeria were relatively more capital-intensive than corresponding enterprises in relatively capital-abundant Japan in 1967.[29] A similar survey of the cement industry in East Africa yielded the following high capital-labour ratios:[30] Waso Hill Plant (Dar-es-Salaam, Tanzania): 1.6 or 1.6 units of capital to 1 unit of labour; Tororo Plant (Uganda): 1.15; Bamburi Plant (Mombasa, Kenya): 0.87; Athi River Plant (Nairobi, Kenya): 0.71 (oldest plant).

The domination of R & D in the MNCs' home countries and the ownership of patents and other industrial property rights reflect the associated monopoly of technology by imperialist forces. Thus of the 98% of all R & D activities concentrated in the imperialist metropoles, it has been reported that the four largest multinationals in each country account for 20% of all industrial R & D in the US, 25% in Britain, 21% in France and 46% in Italy.[31] An UNCTAD secretariat study has also shown that of the estimated 3.5 million patents existing in 1972, only 6% (200,000) were granted by the underdeveloped countries, and that more than 83% were owned by foreigners.[32] D. S. Thomas has estimated that only 5% of the modern technology employed in Africa is under indigenous control, with the remainder held by foreigners.[33] Kaplinsky also reported that of the seven British MNCs he sampled in Kenya, property rights over technology generated in the Kenyan subsidiary and the responsibility for registration of patents and brand names in Kenya both belonged to the parent MNC abroad.[34] In Ethiopia, it was estimated that of 29 patents registered in the country, at least 26 were foreign-owned, while 97% of a sample of 760 trademarks also belonged to expatriates.

This tight imperialist domination over technology and the monopoly restriction of its use through the industrial property system (patents, trademarks, etc.) have imposed huge technological costs on Africa for the so-called transfer of technology. It was estimated that of the $2,760 million overseas receipts of royalties and fees for technology transfer by US firms in 1977, 85% to 90% went to MNCs and, of that amount, 75% originated from these MNCs' foreign subsidiaries.[35] A survey of Nigeria's energy sector also revealed that during 1970/78, the country paid a total of ₦1,197 million for 600 contracts for the import of technology, especially to the oil sub-sector. In Ethiopia, where technology import was mainly under the rubric of technical assistance, the country paid 421 million Ethiopian dollars between 1964 and 1969.[36] The UNCTAD secretariat has also reported in a recent study[37] that evidence is,

> most vividly seen in the negligible participation of developing countries in the ownership of patents, reported in an earlier study by the UNCTAD secretariat which shows that only 6 per cent (200,000) of the estimated 3.5 million patents in existence in 1972 were granted by developing countries, and that less than one-sixth of that total was owned by nationals of those countries.

In these different ways, MNCs have inhibited and distorted the development of technology in Africa by separating the production of technology from its use, and restricted its import, adaptation and use through the industrial property system, technological lock-ins (where machines, parts and materials are packaged together) and extortionate technological charges. By the restriction of African employment in imperialist enterprises, through conflicts over Africanisation and multinational insistence on expatriate quota, MNCs have also monopolised the operation of the restricted technology imported into Africa. Their African employees are marginalised into such minor technical jobs as welding, riveting, etc. Thus, in Africa, technology has become an ideological weapon of domination, mystification and underdevelopment in the hands of the MNCs.

The basic cause of these technological problems is that MNCs divorce technology in Africa from local resources and domestic needs by tailoring their imported technology to the elitist and often perverse consumption technology (based on imperialist tastes) imported from abroad. Restructuring African tastes to correspond to the basic needs of the mass majority, and the liberation of African resources from multinational control are, therefore, basic preconditions for the indigenous development of technology in Africa and throughout the Third World.

Other adverse effects of the MNCs

The generation of unemployment; structural distortions and inequalities; perverse import-substitution industrialisation; the promotion of consumerism; corruption of the "host" state through the creation of "fifth columnists"; political destabilisation and cultural decay are other major adverse consequences of MNCs' activities in Africa and the Third World in general. Unemployment is generated in the "host" country because MNCs, like capitalists generally, have a vested interest in the creation of a cheap, docile and exploitable labour force. The "industrial reserve army" of the unemployed is functional for capitalism because it is used to depress the wages of the employed part of the labour force, for imposing otherwise unacceptable working conditions on workers and generally ensuring a compliant labour force by holding its aspirations in check. The MNCs' exploitable interest in cheap labour is demonstrated in Table 3.1. On average, US MNCs pay their African workers only 20% of what they pay workers in their parent companies, and only 36% of the hourly rate of their subsidiaries in all other countries.

The four major sources of the unemployment created by the MNCs are: the initial proletarianisation of the African peasantry by the colonial state through forced labour, oppressive taxes and land alienation;[38] inappropriate capital-intensive technology; the export of investible surplus for expanding job opportunities in the "host" country; and the import of labour into Africa through the expatriate quota. For example, in East Africa, it has been reported that while a capital-intensive cement plant at Waso, Tanzania, with a capacity of 350,000 tonnes annually, employed fewer than 600 workers in 1974, a labour-intensive plant at Tororo, Uganda, with a capacity of less than 200,000 tonnes per annum employed over 1,000 workers in 1972.[39]

The structural distortions imposed on Africa and other poor regions by MNCs are most visible with respect to sectoral and regional imbalances, income, wealth and other structural inequalities and a warped industrialisation programme. In their obsession with quick and high profits, MNCs have concentrated their investments, in such lucrative sectors as commerce, mining, finance, export agriculture, and recently, manufacturing and construction, to the neglect of other vital sectors of the economy, especially agriculture for domestic needs in food and raw materials. The disastrous consequence has been structural anaemia, most eloquently manifested by stagnating agriculture, the collapse of the rural economy and food crisis all over Africa. The fundamental source of this profound distortion, which started with colonialism, has been the imposition of the basic contradiction between resources and needs, whereby MNCs exploit Africa's resources to produce for the needs of imperialism and force Africa to rely on the imperialist countries for her basic needs: Africa mainly produces what the majority of her population do not consume, while she consumes what she does not produce. The associated imbalances and disproportions between sectors of the economy are among the persistent causes of crises in the region. Thus, the expansion of all other sectors outstrips domestic food supply capability for the employed labour force, while the agricultural sector cannot meet the raw material requirements of industry.

The structural inequalities associated with this multinational perversion relate to spatial, class and personal inequalities in the distribution of resources and the benefits of political freedom and whatever modest growth without development has occurred. In Frank's concentric circles of dependency and exploitation, just as the centre of world capitalism dominates and exploits the periphery, the capitals and urban centres of each peripheral country dominate and exploit the hinterland. This is because in the familiar anarchy of capitalism, the MNCs have virtually been allowed a free hand in locational policy, so they concentrate their investments, job, wealth and income opportunities along the coastlines and in southern parts of their "host" countries, in urban centres and among the parasitic elite. Thus most enterprises and other facilities are concentrated in the towns, with, for example,

Lagos alone accounting for over 30% of Nigeria's entire industrial, commercial and financial capacity since 1960.[40] The grossly unequal distribution of income, wealth and opportunities among classes, groups and individuals which reflect this multinational distortion of distribution has unfortunately been documented only with respect to income inequalities.[41] In Kenya, it was reported that in 1972/74, 63% of households received only 18% of total national income, while the top 12% of households got 59% and the top 3% got 29% of total income. In Nigeria in 1971/72, while the poorest 60% got 28% of total national income, the richest 5% got 41.0%; in Liberia during the same period, 73.7% of the poor got 24.6% of total national income while 3.9% of the rich got 60.4%; in Sierra Leone, the bottom 51.6% of the population got 13.6% of total income while the top 1.8% got 16.2%; and in Ghana, while 52% of the population got 35.4% of the total national income, the top 6.1% got 12.9%.[42]

The distortion of Africa's industrialisation by the MNCs is equally serious. The issues involved in import-substitution industrialisation by the multinationals include resource misallocation from the basic needs of the mass majority in favour of the imported consumption tastes of the elite minority; the neglect of capital-goods manufacturing and over-concentration on frivolous semi-luxury consumer manufactures in the "textile-first" strategy of industrialisation; the high import content of multinational manufacturing, which intensifies neocolonial dependence; the inappropriate technology and high urban localisation of the manufacturing enterprises, which accentuate structural inequalities, both of which were discussed earlier.[43] While the neglect of basic-needs manufacturing to meet the legitimate requirements of the majority of the population of the poor countries distorts national priorities in resource allocation, the industrial orientation towards the imported consumption technology of the minority elite is buttressed by the bourgeois tastes nurtured by gross inequalities in the distribution of income. In particular, this elite orientation of multinational manufacturing ensures the limited domestic market and atrophied nature of neocolonial manufacturing, MNCs' refusal to undertake the vitally essential investment in heavy capital-goods manufacturing ensures poor countries' prostrate dependence on imperialism for capital goods and modern technology, and the persistence of the Third World's low productive capacity, which can be broken effectively only through the initiation of capital-goods manufacturing that alone can build a self-expanding compound-growth factor into the economy. While it is true that consumer goods have a higher initial base and a higher growth rate than capital goods, after a while, the capital-goods industries generate a higher and more self-expanding growth rate, than does the production of consumer goods. This is the logic of the superiority of the Feldman–Mahalanobi's planning model over the bourgeois models.[44] Finally, the MNCs typically encourage heavy dependence on the import of raw materials, intermediate inputs, spare parts, technology, skilled labour, etc. in their Third World manufacturing. This is why multinational industrialisation litters the poor countries with all manner of imported foreign gadgets, mainly for the final-stage assembly of completely-knocked-down (CKD) parts. Besides intolerable structural dependence, this import-based manufacturing panders to the massive looting of the poor countries' scarce foreign exchange earnings, especially under suppliers' credit, for the import of foreign resources for local industrialisation. This is particularly crushing for the poor countries as the imported raw materials and intermediate products have to be procured under the usual unequal exchange and the over-invoicing of imports, which characterise multinational trade with such countries.

In spite of these glaring defects, some misguided foreign commentators see capitalist industrialisation as a viable strategy for the poor countries. Some of them, like Bill Warren, even insist mischievously that the internationalisation of capital under the MNCs is so fundamental that it renders the nation state an anachronism.[45] This is quite false and smacks of that pimping for imperialism that is frequently disguised as radical scholarship. The suggestion of foreign take-over implied by such reasoning is unacceptable. The success story of the so-called newly industrialised countries (NICs) is also clearly exaggerated and misleading. Many of these NICs like Taiwan, Singapore, Philippines, Brazil, Argentina, etc. are essentially multinational havens and imperialist show-pieces. The capital stock in most of their enterprises is foreign-owned and many of them, especially in Brazil, Mexico, Argentina and Latin America, have been submerged in debt peonage to imperialism. The South-East Asian members of this so-called newly industrialised club are a particularly sorry case of the super-exploitation of very cheap labour which makes them so attractive to imperialist capital as sources of easy super-profits. Moreover, we must ask how long it has taken these so-called NICs to emerge through capitalist industrialisation – the answer in most cases is more than 100 years. Clearly such a long gestation period cannot be held up as a promise for the traumatic and deepening crisis, as well as the urgent industrial requirements of the poor countries. In these ways, MNCs also encourage an indolent and permissive culture of consumerism.

At the political level, apart from their corrosive effects on the state, MNCs are also imperialist vehicles of subversion and destabilisation. This is the sense in which these profit hyenas are Trojan horses, and partly responsible for the chronic political instability of the Third World, especially in the banana-republics of Latin America and the mini-states of Africa. The nefarious political role played by MNCs is concerned with 1) the destabilisation of nationalistic and progressive regimes; and 2) the support and consolidation of pro-imperialist, repressive and corrupt governments.

Examples of 1) include the Katanga secession and the murder of Patrice Lumumba in the former Congo (now Zaire) involving the MNC, Union Minière, the murderous Idi Amin regime in Uganda which was enthroned by British imperialism against Obote's socialist leaning towards Tanzania; and the role of the oil multinationals both in the Nigerian civil war, the overthrow of Yakubu Gowon and the abortive coup of 1976 in which General Murtala Muhammed was assassinated.[46] MNCs are also behind the repressive stability of the rotten regimes in Mobutu's Zaire, neocolonial Kenya and Ivory Coast, pre-Doe Liberia under the domination of the Firestone Company, etc. This "bribe-block-and-break" politics of the MNCs provides them with a basis to penetrate the state apparatus in their "host" countries in order to secure cheap mineral and other resource concessions; fraudulent contracts and commissions; over-generous fiscal incentives; soft tax laws and easy profit repatriation; repressed cheap labour; and other material advantages. This politics of destabilisation is the leadership target of the MNCs' local class collaboration, which propels them to support reactionary and pro-imperialist leaders, political parties and mass organisations, infiltrate military establishments, intensify problems of national integration and generally meddle in the internal politics of their "host" countries.[47]

The subversive role played by the multinationals is also manifest at the social and cultural levels. The structural inequalities generated by the multinationals nurture social cleavages in that the cultivation of a national identity is inhibited by structural inequalities and the employment of a de-nationalised labour force. More systematically, the multinationals are harbingers of imperialist and capitalist values, institutions and world outlook in their dissemination of an abstract and false universalism. In language, dress, advertisement, literature, attitudes, etc. MNCs cultivate capitalist consciousness by patronising such major cultural and ideological institutions as churches, educational institutions, publishing houses and other media establishments. In such ways have MNCs launched a cultural offensive, which hypocritically patronises indigenous culture as a prelude to undermining it, and generally intensifying the cultural confusion of the post-colonial social milieu. The resulting cultural rootlessness, especially among the elite, facilitates imperialist domination and the exploitation of poor countries by undermining their self-confidence and assailing their collective will.[48]

Class collaboration with MNCs and the neocolonial state

These nefarious activities of MNCs in Africa and elsewhere are facilitated by the active and willing collaboration of the dominant *petit-bourgeoisies*. This symbiotic collusion between the multinationals (representing the imperialist bourgeoisies) and African and other Third World bureaucratic bourgeoisies derives from two main sources. One: the historical cultivation of a "native" dominant class, comprising a traditional or chieftaincy elite, landlords, a comprador fraction, professionals, emergent politicians and service personnel in the armed forces and the police. These provided the main local support for the colonial regime and, in Nigeria, the system was perfected under Lugard's "dual mandate", deriving from the traditional rulers and the colonialists. The more aggressive offspring of these colonial collaborators were socialised into capitalist values and attitudes in imperialist schools, locally and abroad. Later as leaders of the anti-colonial struggle they compromised their nationalism into mere political freedom and have since been sharing economic power with the imperialists. The second source is the bureaucratic bourgeoisie that controls the post-colonial state. The departing colonialists usually handed power to the most reactionary and trusted fractions of the indigenous elite groomed by the colonialists – except where the anti-colonial struggle developed into a revolutionary liberation struggle, in which the most radical groups seized power, as in Algeria, Guinea and the Portuguese former colonies. This compromised flag-independence is the basis of the communardist-type politics of accommodation with imperialism and its MNCs in the post-colonial state; it is the basis of neocolonialism in Africa.[49]

The multinationals and the domestic bureaucratic bourgeoisie share common material advantages and socio-political interests in this class symbiosis; the imperialists hold on to their investments, gain concessions and super-profits, while their local *petit-bourgeois* collaborators, as imperialist intermediaries between their people and imperialism, gain political office and its perquisites such as commissions, fraudulent contracts, lucrative jobs, foreign bank accounts, shareholding and executive posts in MNCs, etc. In one of the most celebrated cases of this symbiotic collusion, *Africa Now* reported in June–July 1982 that Mobutu Sese Seko of Zaire was one of the richest men in the world, with foreign assets estimated at about $5.5 billion while Zaire's external debts were put at about $4.5 billion.

This sinister collusion explains how, in poor countries, imperialism nurtures its "fifth column" of collaborators and *agents provocateurs* and engages in the scandalous corruption of their state officials. It also explains why negotiations between the MNCs and neocolonial states are so regularly concluded in the MNCs' favour, and never go beyond pro-imperialist joint ventures and indigenisation, which strengthens the fragile capital base of the domestic *petit-bourgeoisie* against the mass majority. Additionally, it explains why the MNCs continue their super-exploitation of the labour and other resources of the poor countries with total impunity, and why poor countries' local bourgeoisie elaborate pro-imperialist policies of underdevelopment.

Finally, this relationship between the peripheral bourgeoisie and the multinationals also shows that to insist we should no longer blame imperialism for our domestic failures, or to suggest that the crisis in poor countries is not the sole responsibility of imperialism, is incorrect. The truth of the matter is that imperialism initiated the crisis of underdevelopment through enslavement, subjugation, plunder and the cultivation of a domestic bourgeoisie of fifth columnists, who aid and abet the domination and impoverishment of the poor countries. This demands a dual strategy of struggle: domestic mobilisation of all patriotic forces in a *nationalist* anti-imperialist struggle to win national economic independence from foreign exploitation; and the mobilisation of the exploited class of working people to dislodge the pro-imperialist bourgeoisie. In what sequence the struggle should be waged depends on the specific dialectics of each country, but the same class of working people has a crucial role to play in both struggles.

Multinationals: "flywheel of growth"?

Despite all that has been discussed in this chapter, it might still be argued that MNCs constitute the "flywheel of growth" in underdeveloped countries. This is the burden of the capitalist industrialisation thesis, which maintains that the capitalist road to development through relying on MNCs for industrialisation is a viable strategy as shown by the experiences of the newly industrialised countries (NICs) of Latin America, South-East Asia, Israel and South Africa. Multinational activities in Kenya, Ivory Coast and Nigeria can also be cited as examples of this alleged "success story" of multinational industrialisation. If the MNCs can achieve these results, so the argument goes, then they must be effective and reliable agents for the industrialisation and development of Africa.

Yet, this apparently seductive case is facile and untenable for several reasons. First, Africa's basic need is development, not growth, so even if MNCs have been growth catalysts, they have not generated development. This is because in addition to increased income, development requires the structural transformation of the entire economy, the capacity to meet the basic needs of the majority of the population and a general increase in the economy's erstwhile low productive capacity, all of which must imply a drastic reduction in external dependence.

Furthermore, a country's resource base is a factor in its development. This is why the MNCs have crowded into the potentially rich countries, which would have recorded a success story, or a better success story, without the intervention of imperialism and its multinational agents. Most African countries do not fit the model of multinational success because they lack rich resources, large internal markets, and so on, which would make them attractive candidates for multinational transformation.

As for the NICs, most of them achieved political independence in the 1830s and it has taken them about one-and-a-half centuries to attain their present levels of development. At that rate, Africa would have to wait till the 22nd century for industrialisation and development – hardly a feasible timetable for a continent threatened with mass hunger and rapid deterioration.

In any case, because characteristically, multinational industrialisation in the NICs is associated with massive export of national economic surplus, prostrate dependency, structural distortions and gross inequalities in the distribution of income, wealth and the other benefits of development, it is undesirable. Thus, southern Brazil is still in the 18th century, submerged in massive squalor and racism, India is riddled with mass poverty, while many parts of South-East Asia are regarded as an imperialist brothel. The huge external debts of many of these countries have been part of the consequences of multinational intervention. The so-called successes in Israel and South Africa do not provide models of humane societies.

The point should also be stressed that by incorporating their client states in the global capitalist system, multinational industrialisation has a built-in commitment to crises because of its external dependence. Nigeria, since 1981, is a good example, along with the rest of Africa and the Third World, in the crisis of the 1980s. Lack of adequate foreign exchange to import raw materials, spare parts and capital goods has led to massive factory closures, unemployment and other dislocations due to the heavy import dependence of multinational industries. In many cases, because neocolonial industries depend on imports to the tune of about 90% of their total investment, their domestic value-added is barely 10%, and any foreign capitalist crisis quickly engulfs them as well.

Hence, these perverse multinational activities in Africa should be phased out as soon as possible – by socialisation, which is nationalisation plus installing workers' control of the nationalised enterprises. Domestic resource-based needs of the national majority should then guide the collective self-reliant development of African countries.

Notes

1. Nabudere (1978), pp. 144–5.
2. This US paradox is discussed in Harry Magdoff (1968).
3. Nabudere (1978), p. 146.
4. On "aid" as an imperialist mechanism, see T. Hayter (1971).
5. For the structure of the post-war international capitalist system, see Y. Fitt et al. (1980).
6. Ibid., p. 31.
7. Widstrand (1975).
8. See V. I. Lenin (1948).
9. From J. J. Joseph (1982), p. 10.
10. Ibid. pp. 3–5.
11. Widstrand (1975) p. 60.
12. Data from Joseph (1982), pp. 4–6.
13. Data based mainly on Widstrand, ch. 3.
14. Foreign direct investment is a part of foreign investment.
15. R. Kaplinksy (ed.) (1978), p. 136.
16. For the character of multinational manufacturing in Africa, see Thomas Clive in Widstrand (1975).
17. Members of the other groups are in Widstrand, p. 67.
18. Ibid.
19. Ibid., pp. 82–5.
20. Ibid., p. 85, Table 5.
21. For this local displacement by MNCs, see J. T. Biersteker (1978).
22. E. O. Akeredolu-Ale (1975).
23. Briefly, embodied technical change involves new capital equipment inputs and products whereas the disembodied variety involves skills, management and organisation; neutral technical change does not change the proportion in which inputs are combined in production (ie, constancy of capital–labour ratio) while non-neutral technical change alters input ratios; proprietary technology consists of patents for which fees have to be paid before they can be used, whereas non-proprietary technology is legally non-restricted. See Kaplinksy (1978) ch. 5.
24. For the study of these aspects of technology in Africa, see F. Yachir (1981).
25. R. Kaplinsky (1978) p. 22.
26. F. N. Orgwu (1975) *Bulletin of the Science Association of Nigeria*, vol. 1.
27. Biersterker (1978).
28. UNCTAD Secretariat in *Africa Development*, vol. 2, no. 2, 1977, p. 35.
29. See B. Onimode (1982) p. 187, Table 12.6.
30. Yachir (1981) p. 216.
31. See Organisation for Economic Cooperation and Development (OECD) *The Level and Structure of Research and Development Efforts in OECD Member Countries* (Paris; OECD, 1967).
32. See UNCTAD Secretariat (1977) in *Africa Development*, vol. 2, no. 2, 1977, p. 33.
33. D. S. Thomas (1976).
34. Kaplinsky (1978) p. 237.
35. UNCTAD Secretariat (1977) p. 35.
36. Yachir (1981) p. 166.
37. UNCTAD Secretariat (1977) p. 33.
38. On cheap labour policies in Africa, see A. T. Nzula et al. (1979).

39. See Yachir (1981) p. 216.

40. On the over-concentration of industries in Lagos and other urban centres, see L. Schatzl (1973).

41. See J. F. Rweyemamu (ed.) (1980).

42. Ibid., pp. 95, 150, 181, Tables 8 & 9.

43. For these perverse features of multinationals see Clive Thomas in Widstrand (1975).

44. On the superiority of the capital-goods-first strategy over the textiles-first strategy, see M. Desai (1979) ch. 17.

45. See Warren (1978) in *New Left Review*, 81, September, pp. 3–4.

46. For details, see Kwame Nkrumah (1974) chs. 7 & 8 and K. Panter-Brick (ed.) (1978).

47. On the politics of the MNCs, see M. Tanzer (1974).

48. For a good study of this imperialist cultural offensive, see R. Constantino (1978).

49. This symbiotic collusion has been well documented. See A. G. Frank (1970, '72 and '80).

4 The Export of Capital from Africa

Global imperialism's decapitalisation of Africa through the MNCs, analysed in Chapter 3, will be documented in this chapter as the imperialists' systematic export of capital from Africa. This is not simply a matter of reciprocal international capital movements, in which the inflow of capital from the rest of the world has to be matched by the outflow of capital or out-payments from Africa to the rest of the world. Indeed, even on the basis of reciprocal in- and out-payments of international trade, because Africa is underdeveloped and receiving so-called foreign aid, the inflow of capital to the continent should exceed the corresponding outflow, and should give a net inflow of capital to Africa.

On the contrary, however, the perverse effects of MNCs' activities, as well as the increasingly unfavourable terms of Africa's international trade with global capitalism, have combined to generate persistent *net export of capital from Africa*. In effect, Africa, officially the poorest continent in the world, has been persistently subsidising global imperialism. This is one central factor that has been exacerbating the escalating crisis in Africa; and this phenomenon has been neither accidental nor fortuitous. On the contrary, the systematic net export of capital from Africa to the industrialised capitalist countries (ICCs) is the heart of the global system of unequal development which imperialism represents and sustains. The deliberate plundering of Africa through the export of capital takes seven main forms:

1. net capital export by the MNCs through the repatriation of super-profits;
2. transfer-pricing by the MNCs;
3. unequal exchange and the poor terms and balance of trade of African countries;
4. mark-up inflation by multinationals;
5. increasing interest charges on external debts, i.e., the rising burden of external debt service;
6. technology rent from patents, trade-marks, copyright, etc.;
7. inflated contracts.

Multinationals are by far the most important agents of this capital export from Africa, usually aided and abetted by corrupt state functionaries among the *petit-bourgeois* class strata in African and other Third World countries. Worsening terms and balance of trade, as well as rising external debt repayment, are also indirectly caused by MNCs, by their major participation in import–export trade and profit repatriation, that fuel balance of payments deficits and force external debt problems on poor countries. In addition to the aggregate data on capital export from Africa in these ways, country profiles will also be examined.

Multinationals' pillage of Africa

> The transnationals continued to siphon out a major share of the investable surpluses produced by the mines, the farms and the factories of the new states. They drained off large amounts directly in the form of profits, interest and dividends. In those years, 1965/75, US corporations alone, sent home $601 million, 25 per cent more than they had invested. They drained out untold millions more through unreported profits of their affiliates based in other core industrial nations. In a growing number of cases, transnational firms disguised their acquisition of investable surpluses as managerial and licensing fees, or compensation paid by African governments for purchases of shares in the business.[1]

The pillage of African countries, like the MNCs' plunder of the rest of the Third World, constitutes world imperialism's systematic decapitalisation of these poor countries. This large-scale transfer of economic surplus from Africa consists of three interrelated parts: commodity; capital and technology transactions; and relationships between the UDCs and the ICCs. Resource transfer from Africa through commodity trade, effected essentially via unequal exchange, is treated separately in Chapter 8. Technological pillage through the high cost of imported technology involving technology rent, royalties on patents, licensing fees and technical commissions are analysed later in this chapter. Decapitalisation by multinational monopoly capital or foreign investment, through the repatriation of foreign investment income in the forms of monopoly super-profits, dividends, interest, transfer-pricing and over-invoicing (the last two being essentially tax-evading devices used in transactions between the multinationals) are explored here. It should be noted, however, that as multinational activities cover capital, technology and commodities, the separate treatment of these three sources of resource transfer from Africa is dictated largely by the need for analytical clarity rather than any other consideration.

Multinational super-profits in Africa: an overview

Although owing to the secrecy that shrouds bourgeois profits detailed empirical evidence of the imperialist decapitalisation of Africa is difficult, and such data as are available, tend to be incomplete and outdated, three strands of evidence are, nevertheless, available. These relate to: (1) some of the overall profits of multinational activities in Africa which are summarised here; (2) case-studies of multinational pillage in individual African countries; and (3) the accumulating data on the net export of capital from the Third World by imperialism.

With respect to the MNCs' overall profits, the quotation above indicates that US multinationals alone repatriated $601 million from Africa during 1965/75 – an annual average of $60.1 million for this one country alone. The data in Table 3.3,

Chapter 3, and its source, indicates that the US accounted for an average of about 50% of all DAC foreign direct investment during 1967/76, so that if about $60.1 million was sent home annually, then as profits are proportional to foreign direct investment, all the multinationals in Africa repatriated an average of about $120.2 million annually, that is, twice the US amount. These data exclude South Africa. Moreover, many of the non-US MNCs from such former colonial powers as Britain and France, may be expected to be more entrenched, better favoured and, therefore, more profitable than the US MNCs. Some of the profit data for individual countries given in Table 4.1 also indicate that the MNCs could repatriate more than $60 million annually from their super-profits in countries such as South Africa, Nigeria, etc. This would make the repatriated annual profit of $120.2 million from the whole of Africa during 1965/75 an underestimate.

The data in Table 4.1 on the annual profits on foreign direct investment by US MNCs also indicate the enormous super-profits of monopoly capital in Africa.

Table 4.1
Annual earnings on direct private investment — US firms
(book value in $ million)

	1960	*1964*	*1967*	*1970*
Total All Areas	*3,566*	*5,061*	*6,017*	*8,733*
Africa, total*	33	380	453	845
% profit	3%	21%	19%	24%
South Africa	50	87	128	141
% profit	17%	20%	20%	17%
Libya	(a)	258	292	557
% profit	—	68%	65%	55%
Liberia	(b)	18	16	28
% profit	—	10%	9%	14%
Other countries	—	-17	17	119
Middle East	734	813	1,004	1,176
% profit	64%	61%	57%	71%

* Excluding South Africa;
(a) included in North Africa (-69);
(b) included in West Africa (37).

Source: S. Smith, p. 56.

The earnings of US multinationals in the whole of Africa in 1970 were, therefore, about $1 billion – and they have increased enormously over the past one and a half decades, especially owing to the oil boom in countries such as Nigeria, Libya, etc. Again, if US MNCs alone earned almost $1 billion in 1970, all the MNCs may be expected to have earned about $2 billion in that year. Over the years, as these super-profits rose, multinationals have been siphoning incredible amounts of investible surpluses from Africa.

Further evidence on multinational super-profits in Africa is derivable from the data for individual countries. Thus Nabudere reported that in 1971, the outflow of investment funds from the former East African Federation (Tanzania, Kenya and Uganda) was 933 million East African (EA) shillings.[2] As shown in Table 3.1, Chapter 3, these three countries received $700 million out of the total DFI of $4,668 million from the DAC countries in 1978; that is, the three countries' share of Africa's foreign direct investment was about 6.7% in that year. If we assume constancy of relative shares in foreign direct investment between 1971 and 1978, then the outflow of 933 million EA shillings from the three countries represented approximately 6.7% of the total outflow of capital from Africa. This gives the estimated total outflow of investment funds from Africa in 1971 as about 14 billion EA shillings. Even if at that time the exchange rate was seven shillings to the dollar, this gives a total annual outflow of $2 billion. This can then be cumulated to the present in order to obtain an indication of the colossal amount of economic surplus MNCs have been extracting from Africa. Yet, these huge figures represent multinational earnings on capital alone – apart from the extensive siphoning of African resources through the unequal exchange of traded commodities and the exploitative monopoly rents on technology.

Country cases of multinational pillage

The MNCs' predatory activities can, perhaps, best be appreciated by examining selected individual African "host" countries. Some prime examples of these havens of multinational activities are South Africa, Kenya, Nigeria, Zaire and Ivory Coast.

South Africa: is in fact a synonym for multilateral imperialism in Africa as the apartheid regime has developed into the continent's sub-imperialist centre. The racist state capitalism of South Africa is an exploitative alliance between the state, the MNCs and private South African capital.[3] Foreign direct investment, which was only R2,757 million[4] in 1956 rose to R4,990 million in 1968 and to R9,163 million in 1973 before accounting for about 25% of total investment in the country by 1976 (see Table 3.3, Chapter 3).

Table 4.2 shows that the sectoral distribution of multinational investment in South Africa is concentrated in manufacturing, finance, mining and trade, in that declining order. While manufacturing alone accounted for over 35% of total foreign investment, finance took about 25%. It is remarkable that social services, agriculture and even construction offer the least attraction to the MNCs.

The crucial significance of these multinational investments are highlighted when they are related to total capital formation in apartheid as shown in Table 4.3.

These very high percentages of total investment from abroad exclude short-term capital and the immense export of technology to South Africa by the multinationals.

The profits extracted by the MNCs from South Africa are among the highest in the world. Even at a conservative rate of return of 10%, these multinational profits amount to about R916.3 million annually. US MNCs reported rates of return of 16% to 18% from their South African operations in 1970/74, and even 25%. In mining, smelting and oil refining, these US firms earn over 40% rate of return on their South African investment.

Table 4.2
Foreign investment in the private sector in South Africa (including Namibia), 31 December 1973 (million rands)

	Agri-culture	*Mining*	*Manu-facturing*	*Utilities*	*Construc-tion*	*Trade*	*Transport*	*Finance, Insurance, & real estate*	*Community social personal service*	*Individuals & organisations not included elsewhere*	*Total*
Direct investment:	42	420	2,458	1	61	798	109	1,489	5	68	5,451
EEC	25	256	1,590	1	48	477	75	1,173	1	39	3,685
Rest of Europe	2	6	213	—	11	68	—	51	1	5	357
North & South America	6	157	608	—	1	234	27	154	3	15	1,205
Non-direct investment:	5	928	1,177	332	6	235	75	789	29	136	3,712
EEC	3	570	745	228	3	136	59	510	16	78	2,348
Rest of Europe	—	191	117	94	—	18	4	79	13	4	520
North & South America	—	112	154	10	1	33	3	90	—	13	416
Total investment:	*47*	*1,348*	*3,635*	*333*	*67*	*1,033*	*184*	*2,278*	*34*	*204*	*9,163*
EEC	28	826	2,335	229	51	613	134	1,683	17	117	6,033
Rest of Europe	2	197	330	94	11	86	4	130	14	9	877
North & South America	6	269	762	10	2	267	30	244	3	28	1,621

Source: A. Seidman & N. S. Makgetla. p. 58.

Table 4.3
Role of foreign capital in financing gross domestic investment in South Africa, 1968/77 (million rands)

Year	*Capital inflow from rest of world*[a]	*Gross Domestic Investment* [b]	*Foreign Capital as % of gross domestic investmen*
1968	340	—	—
1969	176	—	—
1970	427	3,149	13.6
1971	438	3,695	11.9
1972	628	4,243	14.8
1973	214	4,850	5.4
1974	761	5,976	12.7
1975	746	7,868	22.2
1976	989	8,913	11.1
1977	278	8,994	3.1

[a] long-term capital inflow;
[b] total fixed investment (includes reinvestment of profits of MNCs).

Source: S. Smith, p. 59.

Indirect evidence of the multinationals' enormous super-profits in the apartheid regime is the super-exploitation of the majority of black workers in South Africa. As profits equal total revenue minus total costs, and total costs equal mainly capital and labour costs, since labour costs tend to be a large component of total costs, the greater the reduction of these labour costs through the exploitation of labour with very low wages and other inhuman working conditions, the higher the level of profits will be. The shamefully low slave-wages of black workers under apartheid are depicted in Table 4.4.

Table 4.4
Average annual wages of South African workers, 1970/76 (rands)

	1970	*1972*	*1974*	*1976*
Average earnings:				
Whites	3,240	3,797	4,767	5,867
Coloureds	931	1,156	1,497	1,895
Asiatics	1,044	1,335	1,741	2,367
Africans	476	577	861	1,269
Total minimum living level or poverty datum line (PDL)[a]	—	—	—	1,653.12

[a] This poverty datum line was computed for a family of five for November 1976 as R137.76 and it is multiplied here by 12 to convert it to an annual figure comparable to the annual wage data.

Source: A. Seidman & N. S. Makgetla, pp. 70–1.

The huge gaps between the wages of whites and those of Africans, Coloured and Asiatics represent part of the super-profits from apartheid, an indication that racism is an immensely profitable capitalist business in South Africa as elsewhere. Systematically, Africans earned less than 20% of the wages paid to whites for the same jobs. Table 4.4 also shows that in 1976 African wages fell below the poverty datum line (PDL) by about 25%.

The major multinational profit grabbers in South Africa are from Britain, USA and the other imperialist countries. The most important of these MNCs constitute the Oppenheimer empire with 28 MNCs by 1970. The other multinational giants in the apartheid system are the Anglo-American Corporation, Rio Tinto Zinc, Union Carbide, South-West Africa Company, with interests in the Consol Gold Fields, etc. These multinationals are so powerful and so diversified into different sectors and branches of industry such as mining, manufacturing, banking, insurance, transport, and so on, that they constitute a separate social system within the country.[5] Their full list runs into hundreds of affiliates of the major MNCs from virtually all the imperialist countries. It is these giant MNCs and their home governments that sustain and nurture South Africa's vicious, inhuman, racist state capitalism. This is done through such mechanisms as sanctions-breaking, especially by the oil MNCs, like BP that illegally supply apartheid with petroleum products, and other multinationals that provide military equipment, nuclear know-how, capital and other critical materials for strengthening the savage oppression and exploitation perpetrated by apartheid.

Kenya: is also a neocolonial enclave which, unlike South Africa, is still underdeveloped and highly impoverished. Happily, the predatory activities of the MNCs in Kenya have been studied fairly extensively and show that by 1971/72, the total FDI in the country was K£125 million[6] with the following annual inflows (in million shillings): 1966, 125;[7] 1968, 168, 1970, 338; 1971, 276.

The detailed breakdown of the sources of these multinational funds is provided in Table 4.5.

Table 4.5
Estimated book value of direct foreign investment in Kenya, 1971/72 (K£ million)

Source of Investment	*Amount*	*% of Total*
Britain	87	67
USA	26	20
West Germany	6	5
France	5	4
Japan	1	1
Total	*125*	*100.0*

Source: R. Kaplinsky, p. 136.

As in South Africa and most of the former British colonies, British and US MNCs dominate the total foreign direct investment. The total US direct investment in Kenya was $74.47 million in 1972 with $34.79 million in manufacturing and $26.45

Table 4.6
Net private long-term capital inflows to Kenya, 1964/73[a]

	1964	*1965*	*1966*	*1967*	*1968*	*1969*	*1970*	*1971*	*1972*	*1973*[b]
Total Amount (K£ million):	-15.0	1.5	1.0	8.0	9.1	13.0	14.9	17.9	15.3	16.0
As % of total capital formation	—	3	2	9	10	14	13	12	10	9
As % of investment by enterprises and non-profit institutions	—	4	2	12	14	19	18	16	13	12
As % of current account (trade) deficit	—	—	15	37	63	48	85	43	63	61

[a] These figures are clearly not net of capital outflows.
[b] Provisional.

Source: R. Kaplinsky, p. 137.

million in petroleum.[8] The annual inflows of foreign direct investments into Kenya and their shares of total domestic capital formation are shown in Table 4.6.

It is important to note that even though the figures in Table 4.6 tend to indicate that foreign direct investment is a small proportion of total domestic capital formation (only 14% at its peak in 1969), they, in fact, account for 15% to 85% of the deficits on Kenya's current (trade) account. This is how MNCs intensify poor countries' structural dependence on imperialism.

The sectoral distribution of these multinational investments in Kenya shows high concentration in manufacturing, petroleum, agriculture, commerce, mining and transport as shown in Table 4.7.

Table 4.7
Capital employed in 61 MNC-controlled subsidiaries surveyed in Kenya, 1971/72

Sector	*Capital employed (K£)*	*% of Total*	*No. of firms reporting*
Primarily manufacturing firms	38,716,382	45.0	37
Primarily petroleum refining & distributing firms	18,850,000	21.9	4
Primarily agric. firms	13,901,739	16.2	3
Primarily commercial firms	8,762,037	10.2	13
Primarily mineral extractive firms	4,780,000	5.6	2
Passenger transportation firms	1,018,437	1.2	2
Total	*86,028,595*	*100.1*	*61*

Source: Kaplinsky, p. 141, Table 4.4

As in other countries, MNCs increasingly shift from their early havens in extractive and commercial activities into manufacturing, which is the fastest growing sector of most economies. In 1967 and 1968, MNCs accounted for 57–60% of manufacturing, while the 1967/73 and 1974/78 development plans reserved over 50% of expected manufacturing investment to about eight MNCs.[9] In Kenya, unlike most other countries, it is important that the multinational presence in agriculture is highly significant – accounting for 16.2% of total investment in Table 4.7.

In spite of the paucity of profit data, the super-profits from these multinational activities amounted to over K£13 million as far back as 1970 and to more than 562 million East African shillings in 1971[10] as shown in Table 4.8.

It should be noted that the figures in Table 4.8 are for repatriated profits only, and that these are only a part of the total profits of the MNCs. For a small country like Kenya, the annual repatriation of about K£20 million from 1967 to 1970, which would have risen since then, constitutes a vast pillage of that impoverished country. The high rates of return associated with these imperialist profits are indicated in Table 4.9 in the petroleum sector.

Table 4.8
Kenya: Outflows (–) of private capital (K£ million)

	1964	*1965*	*1966*	*1967*	*1968*	*1969*	*1970*
International investment income (profits going abroad)	–9.8	–9.0	–12.5	–14.0	–14.1	–12.6	–6.6
Transfer-pricing or over-invoicing of imported intermediate goods[a]	n.a.	n.a.	n.a.	–5.0	–5.0	–5.0	–5.0
Over-invoicing of imported consumer goods[b]	–2.0	–2.0	–2.0	–2.0	–2.0	–2.0	–2.0
Total exported profits	*–11.8*	*–11.0*	*–14.5*	*–21.0*	*–21.1*	*–19.6*	*–23.6*

[a] This is a correction for concealed capital export from Kenya in the form of 5 to 10% transfer-pricing or over-invoicing reported by an ILO mission;
[b] This is for the 10% over-invoicing by the Asian community in Kenya. On both [a] and [b], see Colin Leys, p. 138.
n.a. = not available.

Source: Colin Leys (1976), pp. 137–8, Table 4.3, row 1.

These very high rates of return were only possible from true super-profits, and these rates of return are much higher than the average rate of return of 10% or less that capital earns in the imperialist countries.

Table 4.9
Estimated rates of return for a Mombasa refinery (%)

	1965[a]	*1966*[a]	*1969*[a]
Under debt-equity ratio of 2:			
Return to equity	56.6	21.0	62.2
Return to total investment	24.9	13.0	26.7
Under debt-equity ratio of 1:			
Return to equity	43.8	17.5	48.3
Return to total investment	26.4	13.3	28.7

[a] Year for which price and output data are taken as typical.

Source: Kaplinsky, p. 281.

The major MNCs responsible for the pillage of the Kenyan economy are Unilever, Chandarias, Union Carbide, Firestone, United Steel, Del Monte, Mitsui, Nomura, Schweppes, Inchcape, Lonrho and the oil majors – ENI, Shell-BP, Exxon, Mobil, Texaco and Chevron. Some of these large MNCs include Mitchell Cotts, Motor Mart and Exchange (a Lonrho affiliate), Mackenzie Dalgety (an Inchcape Group subsidiary), Marshalls E.A., the Twentsche Overseas Trading Group

(Dutch) and Gailey and Roberts Ltd. (a Unilever subsidiary), all in commerce; Shell-BP, Esso and Agip in oil and petrol distribution; Barclays and Standard Banks (both British) control over 50% of banking with the third largest bank being 40% owned by the British MNC, National and Grindlays; ETCO, the largest haulage firm (Lonrho subsidiary), the British Electric Traction Co. controlling bus monopolies in Nairobi and Mombasa, and the United Touring Co. Ltd., a large tourist transport firm, all in transportation. Magadi Soda Co. (an ICI subsidiary) has been producing over 80% of Kenya's mineral output; and the American Continental Ore dominates the fluorspar mining project. In agriculture, in 1972, Brooke Bond (British) produced 23.5% of Kenya's tea and controlled 37.8% of the country's tea exports. Other British MNCs in agriculture are the Finlay Group, Mitchell Cotts, Inchcape, Lonrho and James Warren, owning most of the remaining tea estates. In coffee, the second largest export earner in Kenya (tea and coffee together accounted for 45.5% of the value of all exports in 1972), much of the plantation output came from such MNCs as Socfinaf (a French–Belgian subsidiary), Brooke Bond, Lonrho and James Warren; while Brooke Bond handled 16% of the coffee exports, Lonrho jointly handled the warehousing of the total crop with the government.

Nigeria: depicts a similarly depressing picture of multinational domination and exploitation. From 1485 when the Portuguese, John de A'veiro, landed in the old Benin Kingdom, to the formation of the English African Company in 1588 and the establishment of the United Africa Company (UAC) in 1879 after the Royal Niger Company, Nigeria has remained a major haven of imperialist pillage. In the predominant oil sector of the economy, multinational investment totalled $250 million by 1977. The total volume of FDI in the country is shown in Table 4.10. Britain remains the dominant holder of FDI in the country; but her hegemony has been strongly challenged by the USA, which emerged from World War II as the leader of world imperialism. The sectoral distribution of this multinational investment in Nigeria is equally instructive (Table 4.11).

Consistently, the extractive industries comprising oil and other mining activities have remained the haven of FDI, followed by distribution, banking and finance with the third place held by manufacturing. The share of building and construction has been rising steadily, particularly since the oil boom from 1974. Happily, land alienation and latifundia of the Eastern and Southern African and Latin American types have not occurred in Nigeria so far. But the proposed attraction of FDI to the agricultural sector[11] as part of the petit-bourgeois solution to the agricultural stagnation of the country may unfortunately alter the situation for the worse.

The MNCs that controlled over 90% of crude oil production, exports of which consistently account for about 90% of total export earnings and total government revenue since 1974, have a tight grip on the economy. Their tanker fleet monopolise crude oil export and participate actively in the import and internal distribution of petroleum products. The Nigerian National Petroleum Corporation (NNPC) which handles the marketing of the country's crude oil and its domestic refining has only a nominal share of oil production.[12] In the manufacturing sector, FDI accounted for 26.4% of total investment in 1965, 39.5% in 1970, 25.2% in 1973 and 32.9% in 1975, and 68.80% of total deposits with 247 out of 445 bank branches.

Table 4.10
Cumulative foreign private investment by origin (book value of fixed assets) 1965/75 (₦ million)

Year	*Britain: Amount*	*% of total*	*USA: Amount*	*% of total*	*Western Europe (excl. Britain): Amount*	*% of total*	*Others*	*Grand total*
1965	327.6	78.2	78.2	13.4	132.4	22.6	47.2	*585.4*
1970	234.2	32.1	289.0	40.6	130.6	18.3	68.0	*721.8*
1973	581.8	44.2	383.5	29.2	257.7	19.6	91.9	*1,314.9*
1975	902.2	48.3	572.6	30.6	212.5	11.4	181.9	*1,869.2*

Note: ₦1 was approximately $1.5 during 1965/75.

Source: Central Bank of Nigeria, *Economic and Financial Review*, June 1973 and June 1979.

Table 4.11
Cumulative foreign private investment in Nigeria by type of activity (%)

Year	*Mining & quarrying*	*Manufacturing & processing*	*Agric., forestry & fishing*	*Transport & communications*	*Building & construction*	*Trading & business services*[a]	*Miscella-neous*
1962	36.7	17.3	2.0	1.1	3.8	38.4	0.7
1965	43.7	18.5	1.5	1.5	5.3	24.6	4.9
1970	51.4	22.4	1.1	1.4	1.4	20.6	1.7
1972	54.7	22.7	0.6	0.8	2.2	15.1	3.6
1974	45.3	28.7	1.1	1.2	3.5	17.7	2.5
1976	39.4	23.6	1.0	0.5	5.3	26.8	3.6

[a] Includes banking and financial services.

Source: B. Onimode et al. (1983), p. 7.

The super-profits from these multinational activities are difficult to estimate in Nigeria as elsewhere because of the secrecy that surrounds bourgeois exploitation generally. But the following facts emerge from some of the available evidence: three oil MNCs, Shell-BP, Gulf and Mobil, declared dividends of ₦677.8 million in 1973 alone, while 22 MNCs in different sectors declared total pre-tax profits of ₦229.8 million in 1981 and ₦259.6 million in 1982. Some of the high rates of return associated with these super-profits are shown in Table 4.12.

Table 4.12
Rates of return on multinational investment in Nigeria, 1976/78

MNC	*Rates of return (%)*		
	1976	*1977*	*1978*
Paterson Zochonis	35.4	28.0	14.7
Boots Co	43.0	31.8	—
Leventis Technical	26.5	32.9	8.9
Thomas Wyatt	20.9	28.6	24.0
BEWAC	16.8	4.2	-6.3
Metal Box	—	16.2	9.2
Vono Products	—	26.2	17.9
CFAO	21.2	13.0	11.1
Total	—	10.1	12.9
Tate & Lyle	—	12.2	12.3
West African Portland Cement	—	4.5	4.7
Nigerian Hoechst	—	5.0	2.0

Source: B. Onimode et al. (1983), p. 14.

These high rates of return to the MNCs have been documented separately for the manufacturing sector. They show that in 1977/78 the ratio of net profits before tax to net assets ranged from 60.6 for paints to 42.3 for food products, 34.3 for fabricated metal products and 24.9 for pharmaceuticals and toiletries.[13]

The major MNCs responsible for this massive looting of the Nigerian economy span the main sectors of the economy. In oil, there are the oil majors: Shell (BP was nationalised in 1979 for its apartheid connection), Mobil, Gulf, Agip, Elf and Texaco–Chevron; in manufacturing, there are UAC, Lonrho, Unilever, Leventis, Hoechst, Pfizer, Leyland and Guinness; in services (commerce, banking and finance) are Union Bank (formerly Barclays until its apartheid link was attacked in 1979), First Bank (formerly Standard), United Bank for Africa (UBA), Chase Manhattan, International Bank for West Africa (IBWA), British–American and American International Insurance Companies, United Trading Company (UTC), Kingsway, SCOA and R. T. Briscoe in the vehicle trade; and in the burgeoning construction sector are Julius Berger, Dumez, Strabag, Solel Boneh, Tilbury and others. The other significant MNCs are the International Telegraph and Telephone Company (ITT of Chilean fame), the Amalgamated Tin Mines and Taylor Woodrow.

Zaire: is another hot-bed of multinational activity and imperialist intrigue in Africa. By 1970, it had hosted more than £120 million in FDI. The scarcity of data on Zaire permits of only glimpses of the multinational operations there. The major multinational enclaves are mining[14] (gold, diamonds, copper, uranium, etc.), transport, finance, distribution and manufacturing. Perhaps the most important MNC in Zaire before the nationalisation of the copper industry in 1967 was the Belgian–British owned Union Minière. It alone was hauling in an annual super-profit of $60 million by 1970. The portfolio shares of Union Minière were valued at £120 million in 1965 with 31 interests by 1970. Its interests are supported by Société Générale de Belgique, the Anglo-American Corporation and Tanganyika Concessions.[15] The major American MNCs are CSSO Central Africa (1960), US Plywood Corporation, SOCOBELAM, AFRIDEX, Socobanque, Somilu and BAUXI-CONGO. The main Belgian multinationals are OTRACO, Unitra Investment Company, Cie du Katanga, Forminière (mining), Cicicongo (transport) and Forces du Bas-Congo (distribution). Together, these imperialist multinationals have looted Zaire to the point of total collapse – under the expert and allegedly neutral supervision of the ubiquitous IMF.

Ivory Coast: is another imperialist citadel in Africa, where over 9% of French people in the country were actually born there, with a total French population of 34,838 on 1 January, 1976 – one-quarter of this French population are *coopérants* or French technical assistants.[16] Before the opening of a Stock Exchange in Abidjan in 1976 (after the Lagos and Nairobi Stock Exchanges), 60% of the country's industrial sector had been controlled by foreign firms by 1973. Most of this FDI in the manufacturing sector was concentrated in textiles, sugar, coffee and palm oil industries. Commerce is the traditional haven of foreign capital in the country, with banking and insurance the other major sectors dominated by MNCs.

In the textile industry, the base of the booming industrial sector, the three dominant multinational groups by 1976 were as shown in Table 4.13.

Table 4.13
Major textile multinationals in Ivory Coast

Process	*Group 1*	*Group 2*	*Group 3*
Pattern printing	Gonfreville (1959)	ICODI (1964)	UNIWAX (1970) SOTEXI (1967)
Spinning & weaving	Gonfreville (1921, 1965, 1974)	COTIVO (1976)	UTEXI (1974)
Clothing manufacture	Gonfreville (1967)	Blue Bell Côte d'Ivoire (1975)	

Notes: Gonfreville is Etablissements Gonfreville, the first French textile company;
SOTEXI is an affiliate of UTEXI – Ivorian state owns 20% of UTEXI-SOTEXI capital;
SOTEXI = Societe Industrielle Textile de Cote d'Ivoire;
COTIVO = Cotonniere Ivoirienne and is owned 70% by ICODI;
UNIWAX is a Unilever Subsidiary;
Blue Bell is 51% owned by the US Reigel Textile Corporation, 19% owned by ICODI and 30% by Blue Bell Ivory Coast.

Source: H. S. Marcussen and J. E. Torp, p. 109.

Table 4.14 shows the structure of ownership of the Ivorian textile industry by 1 January 1976.

Table 4.14
Ownership structure of Ivorian textile industry (%)

	Ivorian State	*Private Ivorians*	*French capital*	*French trading*	*Non-French capital*
ICODI	33.0	—	8.3	38.7	15.2
SOTEXI	20.0	—	5.0	30.0	30.0
ERG	32.8	23.1	10.0	10.0	10.0[a]
Total % at 1/10/77	22.9	15.4	32.0	combined	29.6[b]
Total million francs at 1/10/77	3,330	2,238	4,653	combined	4,305

[a] capital supplied by a multinational finance firm;
[b] combines private and public capital;
ERG Etablissements R. Gonfreville.

Source: H. S. Marcussen and J. E. Torp, p. 111.

The Japanese Nichimen company was also planning a silk industry based on the MULBERRY plantation at Ndouci in the south of the country. The sugar industry is controlled by Lonrho, which started operation in 1974, the French ADRA company, the Franco-Belgian company of SOMDIAA, the French engineering company SODETEG, two Belgian companies, ABR and SCOFINCO, and the Dutch company AVA ENCO. In coffee treatment and trade is SERIC, a French company established in 1970 and financed by a consortium under the management of Jean Gal. The old commercial sector is dominated by the French CFAO and SCOA import–export houses.

Net export of capital from Africa by the multinationals

> Official US data showed that over the decade of 1965 to 1975, with the exception of 1968, US firms – despite their relatively recent entry – shipped more capital out in a direct form every year from independent African countries than they invested there.[17]

This excess of capital outflows over capital inflows to Africa is what constitutes the net export of capital from Africa; and this holds not only for US firms but for other MNCs in Africa and the Third World generally.[18] Thus for the predominantly British and American MNCs in Kenya, it has been reported that:

> the forms of capital export already considered, including dividend and interest payments, appear to amount to nearly twice the amount of private foreign investment in the years 1967/70, when private foreign investment ran at a high level, and were equivalent to about a quarter of all capital formation – in other words, enough to make a fairly decisive difference to the chances of an autonomous path of capital growth (development). The net export of private

> capital over the whole period 1964/70 . . . corrected for the effects of transfer pricing and over-invoicing . . . seems likely to have been of the order of £80 million.[19]

The US firms quoted first above were reported to have sent home $601 million, which was "25% more than they had invested", that is, during 1965/75 they made a net export of capital from Africa of the order of $150.25 million, or an average of $15 million annually.

Table 4.15 shows the export of capital in one decade for Nigeria.

Table 4.15
Flow of payments on foreign direct investment in Nigeria, 1970/80 (US$ million)

Year	*Outflow*	*Inflow*	*Net Outflow*
1970	–385.0	+205.0	–180.0
1971	–475.5	+285.8	–189.7
1972	–609.1	+305.1	–304.0
1973	–937.0	+373.1	–563.9
1974	–610.9	+275.4	–335.5
1975	–627.7	+471.7	–156.0
1976	–579.6	+339.4	–240.2
1977	–783.4	+439.0	–344.4
1978	–408.8	+212.8	–196.0
1979	–205.4	+310.1	–104.7
1980	–875.9	+600.0	–275.9
Total	*–6,498.3*	*+3,817.4*	*–2,680.9*

Source: United Nations Centre on Transnational Corporations, *Transactions Corporations in World Development, A Third Survey*, New York, 1983, p. 289. Quoted in Alkasum Abba et al. 1985, p. 59.

It is important to note that the net export of capital of $2.7 billion in Table 4.15 is for foreign direct investment alone. It excludes capital transfer from the country through transfer-pricing, unequal exchange, rising interest charges on external debt, technological rent and inflated contracts. When all these are added, the total net export of capital from Nigeria during one decade of oil boom will be truly staggering. An irony of the situation is that by 1983 the same country that suffered this huge net export of capital was begging for an IMF loan of $2 billion.

In Kenya, Colin Leys reported the data reproduced in Table 4.16.

Table 4.16 shows net export of capital from Kenya for every year during 1964/70, and given the persistence, and even intensification, of neocolonialist policies by the Kenyan *petit-bourgeoisie*, the pattern of net export of capital in this Table may very well have worsened.[20] For most years, the net export of capital exceeded the corresponding inflow of capital.

Nabudere also reported similar net export of capital for the former East African Federation of Tanzania, Kenya and Uganda.

Table 4.16
Recorded inflows (+) and outflows (–) of private capital (K£ million)

Item	*1964*	*1965*	*1966*	*1967*	*1968*	*1969*	*1970*
International investment income (Profits going abroad)	–9.8	–9.0	–12.5	–14.0	–14.1	–12.6	–6.6
Concealed capital export via over-invoicing of imported intermediate goods[a]	—	—	—	–5.0	–5.0	–5.0	–5.0
Concealed capital export via over-invoicing of imported consumer goods[b]	—	–2.0	–2.0	–2.0	–2.0	–2.0	–2.0
Private transfer payments	–3.1	–1.5	+0.1	–0.7	0.0	+1.0	–0.5
Sub-total	*–12.9*	*–12.5*	*–14.4*	*–21.7*	*–21.1*	*–18.6*	*–14.1*
Private foreign investment in Kenya (including reinvestment of local profits)	–5.0	+1.5	+1.0	+8.0	+9.1	+12.6	+11.3
Net Flows (Inflows minus outflows)	–7.9	–11.0	–13.4	–13.7	–12.0	–6.0	–2.8

[a] This is based on Leys' estimate of the ILO mission that revealed transfer-pricing or over-invoicing of 5 to 10% of the value of imported intermediate goods as reported by him on p. 138;
[b] Based on Leys' estimate of over-invoicing of imported consumer goods of about 10% by the Asian community as reported by him on p. 138.

Source: Colin Leys, pp. 137–8.

Table 4.17
Foreign direct investment flows in East Africa, 1966/71 (million shillings)

	Kenya			*Tanzania*			*Uganda*		
Year	*Inflow (+)*	*Outflow (–)*	*Net flow*	*Inflow (+)*	*Outflow (–)*	*Net flow*	*Inflow (+)*	*Outflow (–)*	*Net flow*
1966	+125	–374	–249	+54	–192	–134	+44	–169	–125
1967	+118	–400	–282	+39	–159	–120	+32	–167	–135
1968	+168	–452	–284	+64	– 96	– 32*	+22	–141	–119
1969	+248	–438	–190*	+76	– 96	– 20*	+26	–151	–125
1970	+338	–568	–230*	+76	–101	– 25*	+21	–128	–107
1971	+276	–562	–286	+67	–188	–121	+22	–183	–161

Note: The negative net flows (–) are net export of capital.

Source: Dan Nabudere (1982) Vol. 2, p. 152.

Significantly the net flow is negative, showing net export of capital, for each country in all years. Indeed, the net export of capital exceeds the inflow of capital in all the countries, except on five out of the eighteen occasions in Table 4.17 (see asterisks in the Table). The net export of capital frequently more than doubled the inflow of capital, even for Tanzania, in spite of its "African socialism".

The Ivory Coast also offers supportive data on the net export of capital from Africa by MNCs. For each year during 1968/73, it has been estimated that repatriation of profits and capital was in excess of new private foreign investments and reinvestment by the multinational subsidiaries. For each of those years, while foreign firms repatriated between 9.2 billion and 12.7 billion francs (cfa) – an annual average of over $60 million from the country – they reinvested an annual average of about 4.0 billion francs (cfa) or $24 million.[21] Even with greater government restriction on MNCs' repatriation of profits through the expansion of the public investment programme, the pattern probably changed little after 1973, given the domination of the economy by imperialist capital, as documented earlier.

For Africa as a whole, Arrighi and Saul have indicated the extent of the export of capital in the form of repatriated investment income, and calculated the required growth rate of FDI in order to offset the outflow of capital (see Table 4.18).

Table 4.18
Rates of growth of foreign investment necessary to offset the outflow of investment income (percentages)

	Rate of profit (%)			
Maturation period of foreign investment:	*10*	*15*	*20*	*25*
3 years	8	11	14	16
4 years	7	10	12	14
5 years	7	9	11	13

Source: G. Arrighi & J. S. Saul (1973), p. 133.

The four different rates of profit in Table 4.18 are 10, 15, 20 and 25%. Thus, at a 20% rate of profit, an investment that will mature (become profitable) in four years requires 12% growth rate of foreign investment in order to offset the outflow of capital which such an investment will generate (see 12% circled in the table). These growth rates of foreign investment (for different maturity lags or gestation periods and different profit rates) are required if the outflow of investment income (capital export from Africa) is not to exceed the corresponding gross foreign investment. From the past record of inflow of foreign investment into Africa, these required growth rates of foreign investment are unlikely to be realised, and this implies that the net outflow of capital from Africa is most likely to continue (as it has occurred in the above examples) and even increase in Africa.

For the net export of capital from other regions of the Third World similar to those reported here, A. K. Cairncross and A. G. Frank have reported the relevant data (see Note 18).

Transfer-pricing, mark-up inflation, unequal exchange, balance of payments crises and external debts

MNCs have also been decapitalising Africa and the rest of the Third World through transfer-pricing, mark-up and imported inflation, unequal exchange, which creates balance of payments crises and the external debts incurred in order to resolve the external payments crises. *Transfer-pricing involves both under-invoicing of exports and over-invoicing of imports*. With under-invoicing of exports, the MNCs reduce or understate the recorded prices of their exports to their parent or sister MNCs, while in the over-invoicing of imports, they inflate the prices of their imports from their overseas parents or affiliates. The objective of transfer-pricing through the under-invoicing of exports and the over-invoicing of imports is to conceal the repatriation of surplus from the "host" countries. To achieve this, when MNCs under-invoice their exports to related overseas MNCs, their total sales revenue, total profits and profit tax in the "host" country are reduced, while reducing the total costs of exports (e.g., of intermediate inputs) to their sister MNCs abroad, and thereby increasing the realisable profits of such companies (since profit = total revenue minus total cost). Since the MNCs are maximising accumulation on a *global* scale and can transfer funds from one country to another, it is immaterial whether their profit in one country is reduced (for example in a country with high profit tax and/or stringent exchange control on profit repatriation), while the profit of their subsidiary in another country is increased correspondingly. With the over-invoicing of imported machinery, spare parts, raw materials, intermediate inputs, consumer goods and skilled labour, the total cost of the MNC in the country where the over-invoicing of imports occurs is increased and the profit is thereby reduced for a given level of sales. This reduced profit, or even loss, is recouped in a foreign sister company from which the over-invoiced imports originated, and is seen as increased sales revenue and higher profits, for a given level of costs.

In Kenya as Colin Leys reported the over-invoicing of imported intermediate inputs by the MNCs increased their repatriated profits by 5 to 10% or £5 million annually during 1967/70, according to an ILO report, while the over-invoicing of imported consumer goods by the Asian community in Kenya also concealed capital export by about 10% or £2 million annually during 1965/70.[22]

In Ethiopia, transfer-pricing for concealing imperialists' export of capital has also been documented.[23] It was estimated that if one company's reported losses, which were 14 times its original equity contribution, had been adjusted for the under-invoicing of exports, the accumulated losses would have been transformed into a profit 50 times its share capital in five years. Another foreign company processing primary products under-priced its output by 56% and this increased the company's real profits by 39 times for two years. In 1970, the over-invoicing of imported products by another foreign company raised the repatriated return on capital from 405,063 Ethiopian dollars to 963,771. For the country as a whole, the over-invoicing of imported machinery and intermediate inputs amounted to 64 million Ethiopian dollars.

Mark-up and imported inflation by MNCs are also important mechanisms for exporting surplus from Africa. Mark-up inflation, which is the percentage increase in the sales prices of commodities over production costs, has been enthroned by the monopolistic power of MNCs. The dominant control over sources of raw materials and product supply that MNCs enjoy also gives them dominant or significant market shares in various product lines, industries and sectors. Multinationals exploit this monopolistic power as sole suppliers, sole buyers and price-leaders to determine the percentage profit they desire, and simply impose this profit rate as their mark-up over production cost. This mark-up pricing, both in their home and host countries, is also one of the dominant sources of inflation, which they import into Third World countries through the export of their products to those countries.[24] The other source of inflation all over the capitalist world is the massive but unproductive deficit financing or deficit budgets of the governments of these countries. Much of this deficit financing is demanded by the MNCs, and the state strives to prop up tottering private capital under the growing system of state capitalism and the military–industrial complex. Though MNCs blame inflation on trade unions, these imperialist profit gluttons in fact start the inflationary process by mark-up pricing, and further raise their prices to wipe out the workers' gains from any increases in money wages.[25]

The additional surplus which MNCs export from Africa through this inflationary pricing can be seen in three ways. One is through the excess inflationary prices over what otherwise would have been stable prices. The total surplus extorted from this source is equal to the product of the excess or inflationary prices multiplied by the volume of multinational sales. The financial or credit component of this inflationary surplus extraction is achieved through the increase in the nominal or money rate of interest over the real rate of interest, or the real rate of return to capital.[26] The total loss of surplus from this source equals the rate of inflation times the volume of financial or credit transactions. Bourgeois economics regards this as the inflationary tax, part of which accrues to the multinational financial institutions. The second feature of this surplus squeeze through credit inflation is the rise in the external debt of Third World countries through this inflationary rise in the nominal rate of interest. Thus as the total external debt of the Third World stood at $595.8 billion[27] in 1983, a 1% rise in the nominal rate of interest through inflation increases this debt burden in one year by $5.96 billion – which is transferred abroad as capital export in the form of debt service payment. The third way of measuring this loss of surplus by Africa through inflation is through the loss of the purchasing power of money, or the reduction in the volume of real goods and services available to people due to increases in the cost of living. This reduction in the real value of money($\frac{M}{P}$, where M is the volume of cash holdings or cash balances and P is the price level) corresponds to a fall in real income in Africa. Part of this loss is recouped in the imperialist countries through surplus transfer via the higher cost of monetary transactions. The amount of capital which the MNCs export from Africa through inflation thus runs into several million dollars annually.

Unequal exchange, or the imperialism of Africa's external trade through the MNCs, is another mechanism of surplus drain from the continent. For the Third World as a whole, Gibson has shown that in the trade between the advanced capitalist countries and the periphery of world capitalism, $10 billion of value was transferred through unequal exchange in 1969 alone between the two trading parties.[28] The documented secular deterioration in the terms of the poor countries' trade and the volatile instability of their export earnings are reflections of this export of surplus from these countries by imperialism (see Table 4.19).

Table 4.19
Changes in export prices and in the terms of trade, 1965/83 (average annual %)

Country group	*1965–73*	*1973–80*	*1981*	*1981 export value ($ billion)*	*1982*	*1983*[a]
Changes in Export Prices:						
Developing countries – food	6.6	7.8	–16.1	74.8	–14.1	5.2
Developing countries – metals & minerals	1.6	5.6	–12.0	26.9	–8.0	–2.2
Industrial countries – manufactures	4.7	10.9	–4.2	134.6	–1.8	–3.2
Changes in Terms of Trade:						
Low-Income Africa[b]	–0.1	–1.5	–9.9	6.6	–0.9	4.6

[a] Estimated;
[b] Excludes oil exporters.

Source: World Development Report (1984), p. 24.

The negative changes indicate losses of potential surplus to Africa and corresponding gains to imperialism. The changes in export prices for food, metals and minerals, which affect Africa seriously, are clearly worse than the corresponding changes in the export prices for manufactured products. The changes in the terms of trade for most of Africa were persistently negative for almost two decades from 1965 to 1982. When these falls in export prices are multiplied by the total volume of Africa's exports, the concealed export of surplus from Africa from this unequal exchange runs into billions of dollars each year. Thus in 1981 when food export prices for the Third World fell by 16.1%, the total food export for these countries was $74.8 billion,[29] implying that the export loss from the price fall was $5.3 billion. If Africa's share of this is estimated as even one-fifth, this puts Africa's loss from food export alone at over $1 billion in 1981. The total estimated losses due to unequal exchange can be stated as shown in Table 4.20 ($ billion).

Even if we reduce Africa's share of these losses, they still run into hundreds of million dollars; Africa has also been paying for increases in the prices of selected manufactured goods. From these considerations, the concealed export of capital from Africa through unequal exchange is clearly a source of the decapitalisation of the continent.

The World Bank has also volunteered this additional empirical evidence of the export of capital from Africa through unequal exchange.

These export losses in turn impose huge balance of payments deficits and serious balance of payments crises on these poor countries, and force them into debilitating external debt peonage. Table 4.22 shows the estimated relevant figures for 1983.

Table 4.20
Estimated losses to Third World due to unequal exchange

Item	*1981 export value*	*1981 export price fall*	*Third World loss*	*Africa's loss at 1/5 of Third World loss*
Food	74.8	−16.1	5.3	1.1
Metals & minerals	26.9	−12.0	3.6	0.73
Low-income Africa	6.6[a]	− 9.9	0.6	0.13
Total	*134.6*	—	*9.5*	*2.0*

[a] This value used with the 9.9 fall in the terms of trade is not really double-counting as it represents Africa's other exports.

Table 4.21
Changes in terms of trade and the associated loss of income in Sub-Saharan Africa, 1980/82

Country group	*Percentage change in terms of trade between 1980 and 1982*	*Associated loss of income in 1982 over 1980 as a percentage of GDP*[a]
Low-income	−14.5	+2.4
Low-income semi-arid	−2.6	+0.5
Low-income other	−16.0	+2.6
Middle-income oil importers	−11.1	+3.0
Middle-income oil exporters	−1.8	−0.5
Total	*−4.7*	*1.2*

[a] Calculated by multiplying the percentage fall in the terms of trade by the share of exports in GDP. Plus sign shows income loss and minus sign shows income gain.

Source: World Bank (1984) *Toward Sustained Development in Sub-Saharan Africa* (Washington).

Between 1985 and 1986, it was also reported by the Economic Commission for Africa (ECA) that Africa lost $19 billion through poor export conditions.

Table 4.22
Africa's trade and external debts: 1983

Item	*Low-income Africa (billions of constant 1980 $)*
Net export of goods and non-factor services	–4.3
Current account balance[a]	–4.3
Debt outstanding and disbursed	22.2
Debt service as % of exports	24.8%

[a] Excludes official transfers.

Source: World Development Report 1984, pp. 38–9.

The *displacement of local capital* is an integral component of the decapitalisation of Africa by MNCs. This type of local displacement is interrelated with entrepreneurial displacement, because when local capital is displaced, the local production and the local capacity for enterprise, which organises the local capital for domestic production, are also dislodged. Since some of the displaced local capital, production and entrepreneurship are often not relocated locally in another place, industry or sector, such dislodged local resources are simply atrophied and wasted. Losses associated with such displacement of local resources are among the critical adverse effects of multinational activities, which intensify the contradictions of underdevelopment.

As the displacement of local production and local entrepreneurship (and other skilled manpower) are typically associated with the displacement of local capital, the discussion will focus on local capital displacement. The displacement of other local resources is thus implied by the displacement of local capital as capital, entrepreneurship, skilled labour and production are all combined in the enterprise or firm. The displacement of local capital in Africa by MNCs has been widely documented and it takes two forms. One is displacement due to the earlier entry of foreign capital into an industry: this is really pre-emption of local capital rather than displacement (some have called it pre-emptive displacement). The other is where foreign capital dislodges local capital that was already operating in an industry before the entry of the foreign capital. Both types of displacement started with colonialism, but the balance of evidence seems to suggest that the displacement of local existing capital – however simple and small – by foreign capital has been the more significant.

To appreciate the nature of this displacement of local capital by foreign capital, it is important to understand the nature of the pre-colonial African economy. A major point here is that up to the 17th century, Africa was not generally less developed than other parts of the world. This means that local capital, entrepreneurship and production, albeit on a pre-capitalist basis, existed extensively in pre-colonial Africa, especially in such activities as mining, construction, cloth-making, black-smithing and the processing of soap, alcohol, leather, and so on. Even in the post-colonial era, some indigenous capital predated foreign capital in many enterprises because they enjoyed several advantages, for example, local raw materials, mastery of the required simple technology, existence of local demand for their products, availability of labour force, relative absence of economies of large-scale production, and political protection through tariff, quota, prohibition and related barriers against imports.

Basically, foreign monopoly capital assaulted and displaced this *pre-existing indigenous capital* through the convergence of class interests. This was first between the colonial administration and the owners of imperialist capital and, later in the post-colonial era, between the African bureaucratic bourgeoisie that controlled the post-colonial state and imperialist capital. This was why under colonialism, the entire colonised territory was declared "crown land" (as in Nigeria in 1937), which conferred monopoly rights on mineral and other natural resources on foreign capital. Having thus eliminated or weakened local capital's resource base, indigenous capital, technology and skilled manpower were, under colonialism, often banned or restricted from the manufacture or processing of certain raw materials, and the market for indigenous production was finally eliminated by conferring upon colonialist merchants monopoly rights of imports of previously produced local products. With virtually no opportunities to participate with their capital, entrepreneurship and skills in the highly limited incoming colonial enterprises, local capital and enterprise were inevitably rendered impotent. In the post-colonial state, the granting of "pioneer" status, tariff relief on imported inputs, tax holidays, accelerated depreciation and related over-generous incentives to foreign capital, which pre-existing indigenous enterprises did not enjoy, aided imperialist capital to out-compete and dislodge local capital. In addition, foreign monopoly capital typically exploits market imperfections, such as the use of patents for technological advantage (that is, input market imperfection) and product differentiation or branding with trade marks (output market imperfection) as well as the advantages of large capital (including easier borrowing from the expatriate banks that dominate the financial sector and discriminate against Africans in their lending policies), specialised management and marketing techniques, including high pressure advertisement, and the corruption of African state officials in order to gain illegal concessions.[30] In some cases, price competition (for example, price cutting to eliminate weak local firms before raising product price), direct take-over of pre-existing local firms, and collusive agreement among expatriate firms to secure monopoly advantages, have been used to dislodge pre-existing indigenous capital.

With *pre-emptive displacement*, where foreign capital was the first to establish in an industry, both under colonialism and in the post-colonial era, several mechanisms have also been employed. Under colonialism, the state was employed to confer monopoly and oligopoly advantages on foreign capital, thus preventing the entry of, or effective competition from, local capital. The commonest of these colonial barriers to entry against local capital were the colonial state monopoly of natural resources (the crown land procedure), the prohibition of African enterprise in certain activities (for example, manufacturing and processing of certain raw materials) and direct discriminatory legislation against indigenous capital. Good examples of the latter two in Nigeria were the colonial banning of African fabrication, and colonial banking legislation which raised initial capital requirement against indigenous banks.[31] In the post-colonial era, state lobbying and discriminatory legislation (for example, raising capital requirement) as well as imperfect competition in the input and product markets have been used. Monopoly rights over scarce raw materials (for example, mineral rights) and patented production processes exploit input market imperfections, while price manipulation or price war (for example, lowering prices to ruin new entrants into an industry before raising prices again) are all common. Collusive agreements such as mergers of foreign firms and product differentiation (with trade marks) to cater to the elite tastes of Westernised Africans enjoying the privileges of gross inequality in income distribution, have also been employed. Then, as has been noted, there are monopoly advantages conferred on foreign capital by ownership or access to large capital, advanced technology, and specialised management and marketing techniques, including soporific advertising.[32]

In addition, successful competition from local capital has been frequently eliminated by the direct takeover of indigenous enterprises by imperialist capital. It is partly to combat some of these mechanisms of local capital displacement that socialisation (nationalisation with workers' management), nationalisation and indigenisation (local equity participation in foreign enterprises) of expatriate enterprises have been employed by African and other Third World governments. Unfortunately, while indigenisation yields profit-sharing with the MNCs without any real control over them, nationalisation often leads to mere bureaucratisation, as the nationalised foreign enterprises are handed over as parastatals to capitalist-oriented civil servants and technocrats, who often ruin such enterprises through corruption and inefficiency. This is why the socialisation of the MNCs is the real solution. It offers the opportunity to run such socialised ventures in the interest of the direct producers themselves, rather than in the interest of their exploiters.

Additional sources of capital export from Africa are *technology rent*[33] and inflated contracts. On capital transfer through technology, a general impression can be formed from the fact that US firms in 1972 earned $2.76 billion in overseas receipts of royalties and fees for technology transfer, that 85% to 90% of this sum went to multinationals and that three-quarters of that originated from their foreign subsidiaries.[34] Most of this money is made from the sale of patents, trade-marks, copyright and the over-pricing of technologically "locked-in" inputs. Unfortunately, data on these high technological costs and the capital they export from Africa are very scarce. In Nigeria, some available data show that between 1970 and 1977, 600 technology contracts were recorded for oil exploration and production at a total cost of $1.2 billion.[35] Though some capital goods and technical services were offered in exchange, their usual over-pricing meant that much of the contract costs represented net export of capital. Other African countries have similar experiences on account of their external dependence on multinational technology.[36]

The *inflation of contracts* by multinationals through the collusion of corrupt and unpatriotic local compradors is another major source of capital export from Africa. The wide differential in comparative unit contract costs among African countries as indicated in Table 4.23 is one example of evidence of this.

Table 4.23
Unit cost of irrigation schemes in West Africa, 1977/78

Country	*Cost per hectare (in Naira)*
Liberia	250.00
Ivory Coast	500.00
Ghana	1,068.00
Nigeria (average)	2,470.00
Nigeria (Bakalori dam)	7,540.00

Source: A. Abba et al. (1985) *The Nigerian Economic Crisis – Causes and Solutions* (Zaria; ASUU), p. 31.

These wide differences in unit cost are not accounted for solely by national differences in true cost of production – they reflect profiteering in construction, especially against OPEC countries by imperialist multinationals with a grudge against OPEC oil prices.

Table 4.24
Unit cost of construction project in Africa (in Naira)

Project	*Nigeria*	*Algeria*	*Kenya*
Residential building	350/M^2	313/M^2	132/M^2
Multi-storey office block	450/M^2	—	207/M^2
Single carriage road (2 lanes)	294,000/km	149,252/km	105,353/km
Dual carriageway (4 lanes)	0.8 to 1.2 million/km	587,015/km	278,961/km

Source: A. Abba et al., p. 62.

Table 4.24 similarly reveals over-pricing. Although data on actual export of capital from contracts are not available, these indications point to huge capital transfer by such multinationals as Dumex, Julius Berger, Solel Boneh, Strabag, etc. from highly inflated contracts in Africa.

Notes

1. A. Seidman & N. S. Makgetla (1980) p. 49.
2. Dan Nabudere (1982) vol. 2, p. 152.
3. For a comprehensive and recent study of MNCs in South Africa, see A. Seidman & N. S. Makgetla (1980).
4. In 1950 and 1960, 1 rand was equal to US$2.79, to US$1.40 in 1970, US$1.44 in 1973 and US$1.15 in 1976/79.
5. For some of the intricate network of interests held by these MNCs in South Africa, see Kwame Nkrumah (1974), ch. 7.
6. See R. Kaplinsky (ed.) (1978), p. 136.
7. There used to be 20 shillings in the £ and by 1979, $1 was equal to about 8 shillings.
8. Kaplinsky (1978) p. 141, Table 4.3.
9. Ibid., p. 137.
10. The 1971 figure is from Dan Nabudere (1982) vol. 2 p. 152, Table 13.
11. The revised 1984 budget proposed to expand foreign participation in the agricultural sector to 80%, beyond the 40% allowed by the existing indigenisation programme; this was shelved by mid-1985 and the 40% ceiling maintained.
12. On the sectoral activities of these MNCs, see B. Onimode et al. (1983) and K. Panter-Brick (ed.) (1978).
13. Onimode et al. (1983) p. 61.
14. For multinational operations in Zairean mining, see G. Lanning & M. Mueller (1975). See also Nzongola-Ntalaja (ed.) (1986).
15. See Kwame Nkrumah (1974).
16. This discussion of FDI in Ivory Coast is based on F. Yachir (ed.) (1981) ch. 7, and H. S. Marcussen and J. E. Torp (1982), especially ch. 4.
17. A. Seidman & N. S. Makgetla (1980) p. 49.
18. A. G. Frank reported that while the capital inflow into Latin America during 1950/65 was $3.8 billion, the associated capital outflow was $11.3 billion and A. K. Caincross reported that while British capital export during 1870–1913 was £2.4 billion, the corresponding profit repatriated was £4.1 billion. See A. G. Frank (1972), and A. K. Cairncross (1953) p. 180.
19. Colin Leys (1976) p. 138; parentheses mine.
20. On the possible exacerbation of neocolonialism in Kenya, see *Independent Kenya* (1982) by a group of undisclosed Kenyan patriots.
21. F. Yachir (ed.) (1981) p. 121.
22. Colin Leys, (1976) p. 138.
23. See F. Yachir (1981) pp. 194–6.
24. On the inflationary spiral through mark-up pricing by MNCs, see Gamble and Watson (1976), and J. O'Connor (1973).
25. On this conflict between labour and capital in the inflationary process, see Bob Rowthorn (1980).
26. Symbolically, the nominal rate of interest $i = r + \Delta P/P$, r = real rate of interest and $\Delta P/P$ = the rate of inflation, i.e., the difference between the money rate of interest i and the real rate of interest r equals the rate of inflation.
27. See World Bank (1984) p. 31.
28. B. Gibson (1980) in *Review of Radical Political Economics*, vol. 12, no. 3; and Fall and A. Emmanuel (1972).
29. World Bank (1984) pp. 24 & 26.

30. For these mechanisms of displacement of local capital, see R. Kaplinsky (ed.) (1978) ch. 4 & pp. 121–31.

31. See B. Onimode (1982), chs. 6 & 7.

32. For other studies of the displacement of local capital by MNCs, see E. O. Akeredolu-Ale (1975); Nabudere (1982) vol. 2; C. Widstand (1975); T. J. Biersteker (1978).

33. See C. Vaitsos (1970).

34. United States Department of Commerce, *Survey of Current Business*, December 1973, p. 14 and *Africa Development*, vol. 2, no. 2, 1977, p. 35.

35. B. Onimode et al. (1983), p. 33.

36. See F. Yachir (ed.) (1981).

5 Class Formations, Inequality and the Post-colonial State in Africa

> Those who affirm – in our case correctly – that the motive force of history is the class struggle would certainly agree to a revision of this affirmation to make it more precise and give it an even wider field of application if they had a better knowledge of the essential characteristics of certain colonized peoples, that is to say, peoples dominated by imperialism. In fact in the general evolution of humanity and each of the peoples of which it is composed, classes appear neither as a generalized and simultaneous phenomenon throughout the totality of these groups, nor as a finished, perfect, uniform and spontaneous whole. The definition of classes within one or several human groups is a fundamental consequence of the progressive development of the productive forces and of the characteristics of the wealth produced by the group or usurped from others. That is to say that *the socio-economic phenomenon "class" is created and develops as a function of at least two essential and interdependent variables – the level of productive forces and the pattern of ownership of the means of production.*[1]

The correct conceptualisation of social class is important because of the central role of the category in understanding and analysing the dynamics of African societies. In particular, class formations underlie the structures of inequality and the functioning of the post-colonial state. Just as social classes are defined fundamentally with respect to the ownership and control of the means of production in social reproduction, structural inequalities also derive basically from differences in the places which individuals, social groups and regions occupy in the organisation of social production. Similarly, the structure and function of the state – of any state – cannot be understood correctly without an adequate appreciation of the configuration of class forces in society. Indeed, the levels of class consciousness, class organisation and class action are crucial for any serious and socially relevant analysis and insight, not only into these closely interwoven phenomena, but also for the dialectical understanding of the other major phenomena in the dynamics of African societies, such as imperialist domination, food crisis, industrialisation and so on. This is because class straddles the most fundamental aspects of human life as it determines the distribution of resources in society and the power relations implied by this distribution.

Class formations in Africa

Despite the cultural–ideological mystifications of bourgeois social science, the reality of class formations in Africa has been so firmly established, and the obscurantism of "classless Africa" so thoroughly debunked, as not to delay us here on the polemics of African social classes.[2] Though bourgeois sociology conceives of class as a descriptive category of social stratification subject to empirical elaboration in specific societies, so that it has different class concepts, class determination is, scientifically, not a matter of empirical observation alone, but of theoretical and empirical investigation of the relations of production that constitute the foundation of society.

Hence the existence of social classes is predicated on the analysis of the mode of production, which offers the basis of resolving the contradiction between the general law of class formation and the concrete forms this law takes in specific societies. Thus, Africa's social classes may be embryonic but they exist, and differ among African countries according to the uneven development on the continent. From this perspective, while the authors of "classless Africa" and "African socialism" attempt a wholesale social amnesia, the apostles of cultural pluralism[3] absolutise natural differences among people (such as language, race, religion, and so on) into eternal laws of nature.[4] The studied objective of both forms of unscientific and crude empiricism is to combat Marxian class analysis and the imminent social change that it generates. The conceptual framework for the scientific analysis of social classes through the modality of the development of productive forces and their relations of production, which together constitute the mode of production for the periodisation of history, demonstrate these facts abundantly.

Africa's transitional social formations

> In the period of transition, while African societies retained many features that were undisputably communal, it also accepted the principle that some families or clans or lineages were destined to rule and others were not. This was true not only of cultivators but of pastoralists as well. In fact, livestock became unevenly distributed much more than land; and those families with the largest herds became socially and politically dominant.
>
> • • • •
>
> To be specific, it must be noted that colonialism crushed by force the surviving feudal states of North Africa; that the French wiped out the large Muslim states of the Western Sudan, as well as Dahomey and Kingdoms in Madagascar; the British eliminated Egypt, the Mahdist Sudan, Asante, Benin, the Yoruba kingdoms, Swaziland, Matabeleland, the Lozi and the East African Lake kingdoms as great states. It should further be noted that a multiplicity of smaller and growing states were removed from the face of Africa by the Belgians, Portuguese, British, French, Germans, Spaniards and Italians. Finally, those that appeared to survive were nothing but puppet creations. For instance, the Sultan of Morocco retained nominal existence under colonial rule which started in 1912; and the same applied to the Bey of Tunis; but Morocco and Tunisia were

just as much under the power of French colonial administrators as neighbouring Algeria, where the feudal rulers were removed altogether.[5]

This graphic account of the distant origins of Africa's contemporary social formations from pre-colonial and colonial times, underlines the need to adopt the global perspective of the development of capitalism as a single organic world system of domination and subordination. The historical incorporation of different societies into this global capitalism has involved varying forms of subjugation and exploitation. In Africa, it involved enslavement, colonial plunder and imperialist cultural penetration. The four broad phases of incorporation into world economy correspond to three loose phases of social formation and of class formation. In the pre-colonial era, Africa was first incorporated into a pre-capitalist world economy before the first Industrial Revolution (c. 1750). Thus, up to the 17th century, Africa was not generally inferior to the rest of the world. This early incorporation was through so-called "legitimate trade" and, from 1441, when the first slaves were on sale in Lisbon, brutal enslavement. Then, between c. 1750 and the scramble for Africa, Africa was incorporated into a second phase of an increasingly unified world capitalist system through what Rosa Luxemburg defined as exploitation of pre-capitalist (African and other Third World) societies by industrial capitalism. But both phases of pre-colonial incorporation of Africa coincided with basically transitional social formations as structured articulations of modes of production dominated in different parts of the continent by feudal or tributary modes of production, as in Nigeria, Uganda and similar countries. Depending on their levels of articulation, these pre-colonial social formations, based largely on feudal land relations, exhibited such combinations of antagonistic social classes as landlords/chiefs and tenants/free-holders; freemen/slave-owners and slaves, and even big merchant traders and nascent petty commodity producers. It was these social formations in varying transition to petty commodity production[6] and feudalism that, as Walter Rodney states in the quotation above, were terminated.

This culminated in Africa's third and colonial incorporation into global capitalism. Corporate imperialism's new demands for markets and cheap sources of raw materials dictated the need for the colonised societies to be restructured and dominated in order to meet the reproductive requirements of global capitalist expansion through agrarian capitalism, colonial exploitation and the dissemination of capitalist values. The articulation of modes of production in colonial Africa corresponded to two basic patterns – the outright imposition of the capitalist mode by the colonialists and the more general mutilation of pre-capitalist modes to meet the requirements of export commodity production for Europe. This second variant has been identified with three colonial zones:[7] (1) Africa of the colonial trade economy, mainly in West Africa; (2) Africa of the concession-owning companies in the central Congo River basin, Congo–Brazzaville, Congo–Kinshasa, Gabon and the Central African Republic; and (3) Africa of the labour reserves for colonial mines in the eastern and southern parts. As the severe distortions and plunder of the colonies blocked their full transformation into capitalist systems, the new African social formations were again transitional (to capitalist formations) but dominated by capitalist forms with varying remnants of pre-capitalist modes of production. Correspondingly, the major social classes under colonialism were the imperialist bourgeoisie, whose imported representatives controlled the colonial state apparatus and economy; the local *petit-bourgeoisie* comprising the traditional aristocracy of traditional rulers and landlords, usurers, a comprador bourgeoisie of merchant intermediaries, a nascent salariat, professionals and politicians; and the class of working people – wage employees, peasants, students, and so on.

After nominal independence, imperialism again changed the form, but not the substance, of Africa's subordination to world capitalism by substituting economic domination under neocolonialism in place of direct political control. In this post-colonial era of multilateral imperialism, the persistence of serious economic distortions, intensive exploitation by multinational corporations and the utter chaos of ideas and values mean that Africa's transition to capitalism has remained atrophied. The social formations of the African societies have thus been transitional – in most of Africa, they are *transitional neocolonial capitalist formations* dominated by the capitalist mode of production, while a few but increasing numbers of these countries have *transitional socialist formations*. The social classes that correspond to these transitional social formations in the neocolonial capitalist countries consist of the imperialist or imported bourgeoisie in the multinationals and the state apparatuses (bureaucracy, military, and so on), especially in the Francophone countries; the petit or bureaucratic[8] bourgeoisie, comprising a small ruling group of top politicians or military brass and top bureaucrats – the "political class" or elite – the traditional aristocracy, comprador bourgeoisie, professionals and lower salariat; and the class of working people. Thus, Africa's transitional social formations are predominantly mutations of the capitalist social formations in the metropolitan countries, and the different modes of production with their social relations that have been articulated in these African social formations provide the determination of the different social classes in the continent.

The bourgeoisie in Africa

The bourgeoisie in Africa is numerically greater than the African *petit-bourgeoisie*, as the former comprises two class fractions – the imperialist or imported bourgeoisie and the African *petit-bourgeoisie* proper, whose full identity is the African *petit-bourgeoisie* or bureaucratic bourgeoisie. By structural lineage, the imported bourgeoisie is technically a fraction of the imperialist bourgeoisie in the metropolitan countries, the Middle East and India, whose membership of the bourgeoisie in Africa again emphasises the global organic unity of world capitalism. Historically, this imperialist bourgeoisie has varied origins, with some dating back to the slave era, but the majority of them migrated to Africa as part of the colonial intrusion, as colonial state personnel and multinational agents, with more of them joining the post-colonial incursion into the continent with the collapse of the colonial monopolies under multilateral imperialism. Thus, many of them, like the apartheid predators of South Africa, the French in the Francophone countries, the Lebanese and the Indians of East and West Africa, have lived in the continent for several generations – like the ubiquitous owners of the Chandaria multinational in Kenya.[9] Though racial minorities, this imperialist bourgeoisie exercises on-the-spot supervision of the domination of the African economies through, in the majority of cases, ownership and control of foreign monopoly capital (and even imposes minority racial domination as in South Africa and Namibia) and through direct control of state apparatuses (bureaucracy, military, parastatals and so on) in the former French colonies.

The principal roles of this imperialist bourgeoisie have to be understood within the logic of international capitalism and the objective need of imperialism to subordinate Africa to it. This foreign bourgeoisie performs its general function of the internationalisation of capital by using Africa and other peripheral countries to meet the global reproductive requirements of capital in three ways. 1) is by serving as purveyors of foreign monopoly capital to sustain and use monopoly power over capital, technology and marketing to dominate and exploit such key sectors of African economies as manufacturing, oil, finance, mining, etc. The multinational corporations of this imperialist bourgeoisie are the main catalysts for fashioning economic domination or African dependence and exploitation; 2) these expatriates also export enormous surplus from Africa to the imperialist countries through their exploitative relationships, as discussed in Chapter 4; and 3) this imperialist bourgeoisie sustains a symbiotic and exploitative alliance with Africa's *petit-bourgeoisie* for three main purposes. These are: 1) to ensure the intergenerational reproduction of both the imperialist and African *petit-bourgeoisie*; 2) to secure the survival of the fragile post-colonial state, which protects and supervises the neocolonial relationships that subordinate most of Africa to world capitalism, through economic and military aid; and 3) to be able to disseminate imperialist and capitalist values, especially through the free operation of the MNCs and the willing collaboration of the comprador state. But, needless to say, in Africa's transitional socialist formations, this imperialist bourgeoisie and its African *petit-bourgeois* collaborators have either been liquidated or seriously marginalised to an essentially conspiratorial status.

The African *petit-bourgeoisie*

> [We have declared in favour of] a Central African bourgeoisie. That's what we have decided, because we think that that's what the future of our country will be. And I say to this Central African elite, which is daily growing before our eyes: don't be ashamed to be bourgeois, don't be ashamed to become wealthy. (David Dacko, former president, Central African Republic, 16 October 1961.)

Though Dacko's early commitment to the African *petit-bourgeoisie* was too successful and led to his overthrow, he testified to some of the structural peculiarities of that class. Its unusual evolution as a manufactured elite (rather than one that grew naturally through capital ownership and accumulation in social production), tied to the nature of the post-colonial state it inherited and, therefore, condemned from birth as corrupt and enfeebled class agents and allies of the imperialist bourgeoisie, with a tenuous independent existence because of imperialist capital's hijacking of its economy is well known. Historically, the evolution of this *petit-bourgeoisie* can be traced to the ruling classes of precolonial social formations.[10] The uneven development and hierarchy of capitalist interests in Africa have meant that this traditional bourgeoisie was expanded and effectively transformed under colonialism. This was by such measures as the imposition of agrarian capitalism and the rural differentiation it generated, the local personnel recruitment into the colonial state apparatus, and the general economic and political change, especially as it affected the professions and the nationalist movement. After flag independence, this *petit-bourgeoisie* was again transformed into a bureaucratic bourgeoisie through access to political power by its small ruling group and the initiation or expansion of state bureaucratic capitalism with its technocratic MNC-dominated staff.

Correspondingly, the membership of Africa's *petit-bourgeoisie* consists of some five broad class fractions:[11] 1) a ruling group – also styled "political class" or elite of major politicians, top bureaucrats in ministries and parastatals, the military brass, the higher clergy and top academics; 2) traditional aristocrats of chiefs, landlords and emergent capitalist farmers, deriving economic power over production through land allocation, and ideological power as fathers of their people; they have lost political power and are a decomposing reactionary class fraction; 3) comprador bourgeoisie, mainly of local business intermediaries for imperialism, such as import–export merchants and shopkeepers, with a small indigenous group of businessmen owing their capital more to local extractive and industrial enterprises often in partnership with foreigners and the manipulation of the state (especially in the more expanded neocolonial capitalist countries like Nigeria, Kenya, Ivory Coast, etc.); 4) "middle class" of professionals in the bureaucracy, other professions and petty artisans; and 5) lower salariat in the state apparatuses (ministries, parastatals, uniformed forces, educational institutions, and so on).

The dominant features of this *petit-bourgeoisie* are its heterogeneous production relations depicted above, its dependent character, state basis and political role. On its dependence on the imperialist bourgeoisie, Fanon has noted:

> The so-called "national bourgeoisies" in Africa, in this sense, are *neither national nor bourgeois*. They lack both the historical maturity of their metropolitan counterpart and the latter's objective economic base. The natural process of the development of the authentic national bourgeoisies and the national capitalisms in Africa was irreversibly arrested by these countries coming into contact with advanced capitalism.[12]

The domination of this bureaucratic bourgeoisie has been identified with several institutional mechanisms: economically, through MNCs, international banks like those of the Euro-dollar market, multilateral aid agencies such as the IMF and World Bank and international commodity markets; politically and militarily, through national imperialist governments like those of the USA, Britain, West Germany, France, and so on; and culturally through the international media (TV, radio like the BBC, and newspapers), educational and cultural organisations such as Zonta International, the Rotary Club and so on. Collectively, these force the African *petit-bourgeoisie* into an etiolated state similar to that of its precolonial predecessors who were liquidated by colonialism and the neocolonial forces subordinated to imperialism.

The state basis of this *petit-bourgeoisie* lies in the fact that its development was based not on the classic private ownership of capital, but on the manipulation of the state. The growth of state bureaucratic capitalism, which makes little distinction between public and private property, has been the main instrument for the development of the *petit-bourgeoisie* through political buccaneers and kleptocratic bureaucrats and their ilk, who manipulate state power for corrupt private property accumulation. This process has been documented extensively in many African countries such as Nigeria,[13] where some political fugitives each own more than a billion dollars in external assets; and in Zaire as stated in Chapter 5. Meantime, both countries pile up external debts in billions of dollars. For these reasons, the African *petit-bourgeoisie*'s domestic political role is ambivalent in that this bourgeoisie faces two ways: national and imperialist. It poses a rhetorical opposition to the imperialist bourgeoisie, especially in its Pan-African and economic nationalism, and *simultaneously* accepts symbiotic subordinate collaboration with these same imperialists. This vacillating stance thus forces this *petit-bourgeoisie* into intermittent conflict, both with its imperialist class allies and its domestic working people, as will be discussed at the end of this chapter. In some cases, the intransigence of the imperialist bourgeoisie forces the bureaucratic bourgeoisie on to the revolutionary path, as for example in Algeria, the former Portuguese colonies, Southern Africa and Ghana.

The ideology of Africa's *petit-bourgeoisie* flows essentially from its historical development and structural peculiarities. It should be noted that *petit-bourgeoisie* here is used in a broader sense than Poulantzas' "traditional and new petit-bourgeoisie", which are more applicable to metropolitan social formations. This is particularly with respect to the statement that "the petit-bourgeoisie has nowhere ever been the politically dominant class".[14] Poulantzas' *petit-bourgeoisie* corresponds to the middle class and lower salariat of the African *petit-bourgeoisie*. A central feature of *petit-bourgeois* ideology is that it is a terrain of struggle between bourgeois ideology proper and working-class ideology, which is mediated by *petit-bourgeois* preoccupations so that this ideology is more applicable to the lower strata of the African bureaucratic bourgeoisie. But *petit-bourgeois* ideology remains a mutant caricature of bourgeois ideology to suit *petit-bourgeois* aspirations.

As the contemporary *petit-bourgeoisie* in Africa is associated with the post-colonial state, its ideology reflects the preoccupations of that state. These ideological positions include, first, the proclamation of the end of ideological debate at nominal independence, through the imposition of false consensus politics in a "we-all-know-the-problem" posture that reduces politics to mere administration. This arises due to fear of working people's radicalism and the fragile legitimacy of the *petit-bourgeoisie* in power. Then the "power fetishism" of the new *petit-bourgeois* inheritors of the colonial state induces them to postulate a neutral and benevolent state à la Keynes – yet every state is an instrument of class domination. This leads to the advocacy of such state variants as "welfare state", "corporate state", "African socialism" and "social ceasarism", which are debased forms of state socialism. State bureaucratic capitalism is then imposed as the path of development – both to serve corrupt primitive accumulation of capital through the manipulation of state power, and to mislead the working people that there is public control that promises socialism. Forms of "defensive radicalism" or "pre-emptive radicalism", such as "African socialism", "African humanism", etc. are then adopted to contain the revolutionary pressures arising from the mass consciousness of abject poverty and the injustice of growing inequality. As part of this revolutionary containment, reformist illusions then lead the *petit-bourgeoisie* to such policies as redistributive taxation, wages review, incomes policy, etc. all designed to veil and sustain capitalist exploitation because of a morbid fear of revolutionary change. To consolidate the tenuous sense of national integration and the fragile legitimacy of authority, we may hear quoted Samuel Johnson's declaration that "patriotism is the last refuge of a scoundrel", in appeals for unity, law and order, and conformism in the post-colonial state.

Among the lower strata of the *petit-bourgeoisie*, the major ideological foundations are a mixture of bourgeois and proletarian ideologies that exhibit left-wing technocracy, demanding greater participation, decentralisation and true value for mental labour, without questioning the dichotomy between manual and mental labour. There is also the myth of social promotion generated from the social mobility of bourgeois stratification sociology, seeking the democratisation of meritocracy via education, which is supposed to enable anyone to get to the top, regardless of class origin. But unfortunately, the strong individualism and relative isolation of members of the lower strata of the *petit-bourgeoisie* make it difficult for them to organise themselves into an autonomous political party in the long-run. Hence the cumulative frustrations of this "middle class", arising from domination and exploitation, find expression in revolts that reflect a cult of violence or *petit-bourgeois* ultra-leftism – because of contempt for the organisational question needed to deal with social problems.

As a result of these contradictory tendencies that reflect the false consciousness of the *petit-bourgeoisie*, its ideological positions are unstable, being constantly contested by bourgeois and proletarian demands. In addition to its basic insecurity, especially at the lower levels, this explains why, when they are threatened with proletarianisation, large sections of the *petit-bourgeoisie* usually provide ready support for fascist leaders. This is noticeable from the delight this class exhibits towards military rule. It also explains why such large lower strata of the *petit-bourgeoisie* may adopt working-class positions – but such support is usually fickle and subject to a dilution or compromising of the original proletarian positions. But the *ideological polarisation* and opportunistic character of the *petit-bourgeoisie* offers an opportunity for subjective class recruitment from their ranks by both reactionary elites and the proletariat.

The African working people

> These ties determine some aspects of its ideology, organizational level, and, in the long-run now, the trend of the workers' movement. The proletariat's semi-peasant psychology hampers the development of its class-consciousness, the emergence and growth of its organizations and the dissemination of its ideology.[15]

The protagonists of the class analysis of African working people insist that the

African worker is a "man of two worlds" – not a permanent, urbanised and proletarianised class that is fully separated from the means of production and having nothing but his exploitative chains to lose, but amorphous, migrant target worker with lingering rural land rights.

There is also the continuing "labour aristocracy" debate,[16] according to which many African workers are regarded as highly paid, not really exploited as rural people, and, therefore, prone to political conservatism. For these reasons, the revolutionary proletarian consciousness of these workers is very low, or even considered to be non-existent, due to their commitment to an ethnic consciousness that is fed by their rural roots. The peasantry are also regarded as engaged in subsistence production under communal or kinship bonds, rather than exercising individual control over land, or being landless or land-hungry, so that the cultural isolation of rural areas impedes the development of their class consciousness. Hence, it is alleged that the class of working people is yet to emerge in Africa.

Against these sporadically correct observations and facile conclusion, is the empirical fact of the existence of generations of African workers since colonial times, with only few of them exercising any residual formal rights to land. The labour aristocracy thesis also confronts the problems that only few workers (for example, unprogressive officials of some trade unions) can really be regarded as labour aristocrats, since some of those so labelled are really members of the lower strata of the *petit-bourgeoisie*. Moreover, the super-exploitation of workers in Africa, and the rest of the Third World, is so intensive that their real living standards are often lower than those of many rural dwellers – and in any case, rural–urban income differentials are useless for class differentiation. As for the level of class consciousness: the long history of labour activism and participation in political movements dating back to the early days of protracted resistance to colonisation, not to mention the decisive role of the broad masses in the nationalist movement, involving interminable demonstrations, strikes, imprisonment and pitched battles against armed policemen and soldiers, and the post-colonial formations of labour parties such as the Socialist Workers' and Farmers' Party (SWAPF) of Nigeria, the Mau-Mau freedom movement in Kenya, the Cameroon Peoples' Union (UPC), and so on, all testify to the long stirring of revolutionary consciousness among African workers. There may thus be two branches of the African working class – the labour aristocrats in MNCs, who are skilled, white-collar, highly-paid workers; and the majority of super-exploited rural–urban workers whose ideological consciousness, organisational development, size and history are functions of the specific countries and social formations in which they are located. The overall extent of the African working class (factory-type wage workers) is still small, but it has been growing rapidly and the savage exploitation to which it is subjected offsets its relative ideological backwardness.

On the peasant front, the myth of the amorphous peasantry is largely an anthropological illusion from the dual economy syndrome; most rural dwellers are now roped into global capitalism as petty commodity producers, migrant workers and their dependants. This means that the primary relations of production binding these peasants are basically capitalist, but the peasantry are neither fully proletarianised nor are they mere subsistence producers. Their ideological consciousness has been predominantly a function of the high level of illiteracy, the rural isolation that submerges them in Paulo Freire's "culture of silence"[17] and the level of development of different African countries. But after the peasant role in the Mau Mau resistance in Kenya, the *Agbekoya* (peasants against oppression) rebellion in Western Nigeria in 1969 and other similar episodes, particularly the successful mobilisation of the peasantry in Algeria, Zimbabwe, Namibia, South Africa and the former Portuguese colonies, the level of awareness of the peasantry may be low, but their revolutionary potential is indisputable. Moreover, it is important to note the continuum of differentiation among the peasantry since the imposition of colonial agrarian capitalism. There are now urban-based capitalist farmers owning large tracts of land, often approximating to Latin America's rural *latifundia* (for example, the "telephone farmers" among Kenya's city dwellers), hiring farm labour, with modern machinery and producing for the market; kulaks or wealthiest rural-based peasants, both of which groups are part of the agricultural or traditional *petit-bourgeoisie*; rich, middle and poor peasants, who in that decreasing order are capitalist relative to the feudal tenant producer (for example, under share-cropping) and the migrant worker.

The roles of the African working people in their domestic and continental affairs are related to their size and organisation.[18] While working people, comprising mainly the working class and peasantry constitute about 80% of the population of each African country, the numerical strength of the working class is less than 20% of the population, or just about 25% of the class of working people. In Nigeria, for example, the 44 industrial unions that constitute the central Nigerian Labour Congress (NLC) numbered about 2.5 million workers in 1983 out of a total population of about 95 million. In 1983, sub-Saharan Africa's total labour force (population aged 15–64 years) was estimated at 196.5 million or 50% of the total population of 393 million, with, in 1981, about 69% or 135.6 million in agriculture, about 13% in industry and approximately 18.5% in services.[19]

One of the highest expressions of the organisational development of African workers is the formation of the Organisation of African Trade Union Unity (OATUU) whose 1984 congress was held in Lagos in February 1985. In addition, there has also been a gradual departure from the conservative "company-house" basis of labour organisation by enterprise to the more robust and larger industrial union based on all the enterprises in an industry. But the levels of worker education and trade union leadership are still very low.

On the specific question of working-people's socio-political role there are four major perspectives. While Marx saw the working class alone as the revolutionary class under capitalism, Lenin viewed it as the pre-eminent force in a revolutionary alliance with the poorest strata of the peasantry, and Mao considered it as providing the leadership cadres for mobilising the marginalised peasantry into revolutionary offensive. But Fanon dismissed the workers' progressive potential relative to the poor peasants in Africa. The empirical evidence in post-colonial Africa indicates the possible progressive role of the working class subject to the constraint of the prevailing social formation, as attempted socialist transformations in Guinea, Tanzania, Benin Republic, Ghana, Ethiopia and Burkina-Faso (formerly Upper Volta) have shown.

Even in the countries where working people have not displayed a radical potential, this may be due to the phenomenon of "dual consciousness", which generates a surface manifestation of acquiescence with the cumulative growth of latent awareness of exploitation typically triggered off into explosion by even minor incidents. Sporadic, spasmodic and unstructured mass violence in Africa such as the *Agbekoya* rebellion in Western Nigeria, rice riots in Liberia in 1979, Sierra Leone, Morocco and related incidents, may be examples that reflect this dual consciousness among Africa's broad masses. But against this view is the argument that working class counter-ideology to the predominant *petit-bourgeois* ideology is a loose populist sentiment,[20] that workers' demands are not relevant to the non-urban masses and that the working people generally fail to sustain a radical political alternative once the dust has settled on their immediate grievances. In spite of the partial veracity of these claims, it remains true that since nominal independence, there has been progessive atrophy of mass support for the *petit-bourgeois* parties (unlike in colonial times) since political power crystallised in their hands; that the corporate interests of the working people emerged from colonialism intact and with clearer articulation; and that the inability to accommodate these mass aspirations fully in the post-colonial patronage system has constituted the central ingredient of the growth of revolutionary pressures and the dynamics of class struggles in contemporary Africa.

As most of the foregoing discussions of class formations of the *petit-bourgeoisie* and the working people apply more directly to Africa's transitional capitalist formations, it is important to emphasise the different developments in the socialist-oriented African social formations. The main differences are such that the first two of them relate to the bourgeoisie and the other four to the working people, and they are as follows:

(1) the people's revolution has eliminated or externalised the imperialist bourgeoisie in these transitional socialist countries; MNCs operate there mainly on contract, joint venture and with restricted freedom;

(2) the petit or bureaucratic bourgeoisie with its ideology has either been routed or marginalised;

(3) the alliance between the working class and the peasantry has been formalised in varying degrees;

(4) the new ideology of the working people is the dominant ideology in these countries;

(5) the problems of developing the consciousness and organisation of the working people are very high on the political agenda, as demonstrated by the formation of working people's parties as in Ethiopia in 1984;

(6) international proletarianism is being developed in the context of concrete cooperation with other socialist countries of the world. The problems of socialist transition in these countries are discussed fully in Chapter 13.

Patterns of class struggles in Africa

Since class struggle is fundamentally political combat aimed at capturing state power, the state forms in Africa broadly define the main patterns of class struggles – just as the character of social classes objectively defines both the emergence and nature of the state itself. In this regard, the three basic forms of the state in contemporary Africa are associated with three major scenarios of class struggles, corresponding to struggles within transitional or neocolonial capitalist social formations, transitional socialist formations and colonial formations, in that order of numerical importance.

In the neocolonial capitalist formations such as in Nigeria, Kenya, Ivory Coast, Zaire, for example, the decisive class struggles are both inter-class and intra-elite. The inter-class conflicts are sharpest between the working people (especially workers, students and radical intellectuals) and the combined bureaucratic and imported bourgeoisie, who usually close ranks in clashes with the broad masses. The major issues are the grinding mass poverty unleashed by policies of underdevelopment and the super-exploitation of the people, with specific reference points being wage demands to cope with growing inequality and pauperising inflation, shortages of food and other essential commodities; the demand for greater political participation, and adequate educational, health, housing and related facilities. These result in anti-capitalist, anti-feudal and anti-imperialist agitations involving mass demonstrations, strikes, riots and occasionally culminating in revolutionary *coups d'etat* as, for example, in Ethiopia, Burkina-Faso, Ghana, Liberia (though the struggle there has aborted).

In these inter-class struggles, the bureaucratic bourgeoisie and their imperialist allies generally resort to strategies of ideological, political and economic *containment*, which are part of their class ideology. Thus their ideological containment proclaims a false end of ideology by positing common cause and common commitment, and the political containment strategy attempts to depoliticise the population by neo-fascist impositions of one-party rule in class polarised societies, and by *petit-bourgeois* military rule, to prevent the legitimate questioning of the national policy choices made by the *petit-bourgeois* leadership. Economic containment finds expression in the eclecticism of mixed economy, ambivalence towards self-reliance, with regression towards increased external dependence and state bureaucratic capitalism. Both latent and overt coercion in the forms of growing repression and violence in the guise of fascist "law, order and discipline", with the ruthless incarceration of political opponents are also employed, in a vain attempt to stifle the growing revolutionary pressures fuelled by deepening mass misery and worsening structural inequalities.

The intra-class conflicts in these neocolonial capitalist formations pitch the bureaucratic bourgeoisie against the imported oligarchy, and the civilian against the military fractions of the *petit-bourgeoisie*, with minor scuffles between the traditional oligarchy, the ruling group and the comprador bourgeoisie. The nationalist and anti-colonial posturing of the bureaucratic bourgeoisie in its bid for elevation in the international capitalist hierarchy, through the expansion of its fragile domestic economic base, leads it into conflict with its intransigent imperialist mentors. Africanisation or indigenisation, greater local control over MNCs and pro-liberationist posturing thus lead to sharp conflicts with the imperialist oligarchy, which often mastermind a stooge *coup d'etat* against the "wayward" local *petit-bourgeoisie*, as occurred in 1966 with the overthrow of Nkrumah in Ghana, in 1970 with Idi Amin's coup against Obote, in 1975 with the toppling of Gowon in Nigeria, and the abortive coup of February 1976 in Nigeria in which the military head of state, General Murtala Muhammed, was assassinated.

Within the bureaucratic bourgeoisie, the inability of its civilian ruling group to successfully contain the crisis of the legitimacy of power and the revolutionary pressures from the working people, satisfy the corporate ambition of the military fraction of the *petit-bourgeoisie* and allow imperialism to engage in the unbridled exploitation of the neocolony, typically lead to a spate of coups and counter-coups. Except where such coups establish revolutionary regimes, as in Ethiopia, Burkina and so on, they do not eliminate the bureaucratic bourgeoisie, but merely replace its dominant or hegemonic fraction. This is because such so-called corrective military regimes leave the state apparatus (especially the bureaucracy) intact, recruit widely from the civilian elite and typically end up in basically the same contradictions of corrupt private accumulation, growing inequality, mass poverty, and so on in which they took over the state. The basic point is, that both civilian and military fractions of the bureaucratic bourgeoisie share essentially the same *petit-bourgeois* class ideology and aspirations and differ marginally only in their tactics. These issues are elaborated below in the analysis of the post-colonial state in Africa.

The class struggles in the transitional socialist countries are basically anti-imperialist and anti-capitalist and for the consolidation of the gains of the working people. This is the task of transitional socialist construction which requires the dictatorship of the working people over the remnants of the imported and local bourgeoisie. One virulent aspect of these struggles is the internal and imperialist-inspired armed subversion of these countries by separatist rebel groups led by fleeing *petit-bourgeois* renegades like Jonas Savimbi who leads the UNITA in alliance with South Africa against Angola, the South African backed MNR against Mozambique and the Eritrean and Somali offensives against the Ethiopian revolution. These issues are discussed more fully in Chapter 12.

In the colonial social formations, class struggles are increasingly less muted as the liberation struggles have scored historic victories in Algeria, the former Portuguese colonies and in Zimbabwe, before being concentrated now in South Africa and Namibia. The twin issues there are colonial and racial domination and exploitation. The working people's struggles are, therefore, simultaneously anti-racial, anti-colonial and anti-capitalist. Predictably, just as Africa, the socialist countries and the proletarian forces in the imperialist countries have pitched tent with the liberation movements, the ANC and SWAPO, the world imperialist bourgeoisie has been scandalously strengthening South Africa as its sub-imperialist outpost in Africa. The issues involved, of course, are not merely political freedom, but racial democracy and the socialist restructuring of those countries. In all cases, these class struggles are also mediated by the structures of inequality in Africa.

The structure of inequality in Africa

The foregoing class analysis of Africa also highlights the structure of inequality in the region, because social classes or relations of production are also relations of inequality. The situation of Africa's class formations within the context of the global capitalist system thus requires the discussion of structural inequalities in their international capitalist setting. This demands a three dimensional perspective of inequality in Africa – inequality within individual countries, among countries, and between Africa and the rest of the world, especially the imperialist countries. The most serious problem of inequality on the continent is intra-country, as the resolution of this is also fundamental to the elimination of the other levels of inequality.

In order to focus the analysis on the critical intra-country level, we may quickly indicate the magnitude of the inequality at the other two levels, using such ready indicators as per capita income, consumption and so on. Thus, while the average per capita income in the industrialised capitalist countries (ICCs) of Western Europe, North America and Japan was $11,070 in 1983 (with $14,110.00 in USA), it hovered precariously between barely $250 and $840 in Africa – being less than $500 or less than 5% of that of the ICCs in 25 African countries.[21] In 1982 the ratio of population per physician was 554:1 in the ICCs and about 5,500:1 in Africa. Similarly, while in 1980 the average adult literacy rate in Africa was 29.8%, the European average was 99%. Income inequality is also greater in Africa than in the ICCs: while Africa's poorest 10% gets about 5% of total income and the top 10% gets about 35%, the corresponding percentages in the ICCs are 7% for the poorest and 23% for the richest.

There is also considerable inequality among the African countries on account of their different levels of development. Most of these differences are reflected in Table 5.1 that provides figures for the sub-regional disparity of income for 1982.[22]

Table 5.1
Africa's sub-regional income inequality, 1982

Sub-region	*No. of countries*	*Approx. pop. (m.)*	*Approx. GNP ($ bn.)*
East & South-East	17	147.0	42.0
Central, South & South-West	12	71.0	65.3
Western	18	153.0	85.0
Northern	5	88.0	92.0

Source: Computed from World Bank, *World Development Report* (1985), pp. 218–9.

By country, the per capita income in 1982 was less than $200 in four African countries, below $500 in 25, between $501 and $1,000 in eight, and above $1,000 in only six countries (including South Africa); with the lowest of $80 in Chad, the highest of $8,510 in Libya while Zaire had only $190. The adult literacy rate in a sample of 21 countries in 1976, was: below 10% in three countries, 11% to 20% in eight, 21% to 50% in six and above 50% in only four, with the lowest literacy rate being 8% in Niger, 10% in Mali and Senegal, highest at 66% in Tanzania, 62% in Tunisia, 60% in Somalia and about 30% in Nigeria. The share of manufacturing in

GNP was below 10% in 20 African countries in 1982, 11% to 20% in 12 others, and 21% to 30% in only three countries; the lowest were 2% in Guinea, and 3% in Zaire; the highest were 27% in Egypt and 25% in Zimbabwe (the South African figure is not available), with the overall manufacturing share in GNP averaging about 17% for Africa and 35% for the ICCs.

Capitalism, class structure and inequality

Contrary to the mystifications of bourgeois economics, the basic generating cause of structural inequalities at all levels – within and between countries and regions of the world – is the private ownership of the means of production and the unequal classes it generates. The basic form of this private ownership and its class system in contemporary Africa is determined by international capitalism. Indeed, in spite of the pedantic posturing of bourgeois economics to explain structural inequalities in terms of its marginal productivity theory of distribution, according to which differences in income and wealth reflect interpersonal differences in contribution to the social product, it is now clear that bourgeois social science has no consistent theory of distribution that explains inequalities. As Professor Lipsey confesses: "We must, at the moment, admit defeat; we must admit that we cannot at all deal with this important class of problems (of income distribution)".[23]

By contrast, Marxist theory demonstrates that every system of capitalism, whether metropolitan or necolonial (peripheral), generates inegalitarian social structures, both intergenerationally and spatially. This is due fundamentally to the private ownership of the means of production, unequal power over the distribution of resources and the antagonistic social classes or relations of production that these produce. Hence, far from being the results of the aberrational defects of the system (such as imperfect competition), structural inequalities are in-built, organic and functional concomitants of the contradictions and irrationality of the capitalist system. This explains why class differences are also associated with inequality in the ownership of private property, in income, power over the distribution of resources, political power over decision-making and access to such social facilities as education, health, housing, and so on. Even different social classes are segregated spatially, not only between rural and urban areas, but between the planned and salubrious estates of the rich and the decrepit sprawling slums of "the wretched of the earth". The capitalist system is thus a "winner-takes-all" game, as the dominant class also corners most of the wealth, income, power and privileges of society. Therefore, no reformist social engineering, such as redistributive taxation, incomes policy, the welfare state and so on, can eliminate capitalist inequalities without the fundamental restructuring of juridical property relations and the elimination of exploitation, as the persistence of inequality under the welfare state demonstrates – even in the Scandinavian countries with the most populist and reformist welfare programmes.

Moreover, inequality is not merely integral to capitalism as a mere irrationality – inequality is basically functional for capitalism in several ways.

First, the existence of inequality and the appearance of income promotion and social mobility serve to extract greater labour input for capitalism. This ensures the possibility of extracting more relative surplus value through the exploitation of the labour force for capital accumulation. The bourgeois rat-race of "keeping up with the Joneses" secures this, and explains why even the super-exploited masses of Africa derive vicarious satisfaction from the abusively ostentatious consumption habits of their *petit-bourgeois* oppressors.

Secondly, income inequality serves to sustain the occupational hierarchy of the capitalist system. Clearly, if the system of domination through the hierarchical organisational structures of capitalism is to be maintained, there must be a parallel income profile to rationalise it and to sustain the bourgeois myth of social mobility in order to contain the frustrations and revolutionary pressures of the system.

Thirdly, among the ranks of the bureaucratic bourgeoisie, inequality performs a social control function of constantly reminding its dissenting and iconoclastic members that "it could be worse". Just as they could rise higher in the bourgeois hierarchy, they might also fall lower – hence the fear of proletarianisation among the *petit-bourgeois*.

Finally, capitalist inequality performs the oppressive function of ensuring that even the dirtiest, most dangerous and degrading jobs will be done. The division of labour is such that those at the bottom of the distributional ladder have no choice; if they want to survive physically they are obliged to accept the meanest jobs that capitalism requires to be performed. This is because the broad masses have been dispossessed of the ownership of the means of production and, therefore, must sell their only possession – labour power – in performance of the dirtiest jobs, just as they must accept exploitation by capital – at least in the short-run.

But inequality is also a major source of systemic weakness for the capitalist system. The relative social deprivation and injustice that it constitutes, and the poverty it generates, are major incendiaries for the potential revolutionary fire under capitalism. As the victims of structural inequalities feel cheated and frustrated, this generates cumulative impulses of apathy, cynicism and even hatred, which not only undermine popular morale and productivity, but can lead to hatred of the system and provide subversive impulses towards it. The remote causes of popular revolts, unstructured violence and even coups and social revolutions can be traced to inequality, as for example, in the bloody overthrow of Tolbert's perverse patronage regime in Liberia in 1980.

Structural inequalities in Africa

The analysis of structural inequalities within African countries unfortunately confronts the major lacuna of data scarcity. Nevertheless, it is possible and necessary to outline the main issues involved and to summarise the available empirical evidence. It is important to first identify the major indices of inequality within the individual countries before attempting to quantify them. In this regard, it is possible to focus on the following seven critical indicators of structural inequalities: (1) income, whether nominal or real; (2) wealth in the form of ownership, of the means of production such as capital and land as well as such goods as cars, residential houses, refrigerators, etc.; (3) education, especially formal literacy that gives access to white-collar jobs; (4) political power as exercised in decision-making at different levels in parties, ministries, parastatals, corporations, etc.; (5) control over resource allocation, which is more bureaucratic than political and is exercised mainly in ministries and parastatals; (6) access to, and adequacy of environmental facilities such as health-care, housing, water, electricity, sealed roads, etc; (7) spatial location, especially the rural/urban and estate/slum dichotomy, which also includes regional inequality within a country. Even though the most visible indices of inequality are income level, spatial, educational and degree of wealth, it is clear from the class basis of inequality that the most critical variables are the inseparable twins – power and property. They are also among the least visible aspects of inequality, not only because of the secrecy that shrouds bourgeois wealth and power, but more fundamentally because of the deceptive problem of *appearance* under capitalism, which veils its most fundamental structures, such as those of exploitation and surplus value, on the basis of the predominant market or exchange appearances of capitalism. Similarly, the structures of ownership of private wealth and the exercise of power are not easily identifiable or quantifiable for individual capitalist countries.

Accordingly, the best available data on inequality in Africa are for income, which is also one of the most visible criteria of inequality, because differences in personal incomes give rise to differences in life style, consumption, housing and so on. The country data on income inequality that will be summarised here are for Africa, then the West African sub-region as a whole, Nigeria and Kenya. One indication of income inequality in *Africa as a whole* is the ratio between graduate and lowest salaries in the Civil Services of some African countries (see Table 5.2).

Table 5.2
Ratios of Civil Service salaries in Africa, 1963/72

Country	*Graduate entry point (1)* 1963/64	*Graduate entry point (1)* 1971/72	*Bottom of civil service scale (2)* 1963/64	*Bottom of civil service scale (2)* 1971/72	*Ratio of (1) to (2)* 1963/64	*Ratio of (1) to (2)* 1971/72
Ghana (cedis)	1,360	1,608	214	252	6	6
Kenya (K£)	798	1,128	120	135	7	8
Malawi (M£)	700	749	132	141	11	11
Nigeria (N£)	762	762	105	129	7	6
Sierra Leone (leones)	1,368	1,368	216	228	6	6
Tanzania (T£)	702	739	108	162	7	5
Uganda (U£)	798	798	90	111	9	7
Zambia (Z£)	875	1,386	78	102	11	14

Source: J. F. Rweyemamu (ed.) (1980) *Industrialisation and Income Distribution in Africa* (Dakar; CODESRIA), p. 159.

These figures understate the actual salary disparities as they do not include the highest salaries of Permanent Secretaries, which are often double the entry scale for graduates; if this adjustment is made, the actual disparity ratios will hover around

1:20. In the private sector of these countries, where minimum salaries are about equivalent to ₦1,500 per annum and maximum salaries are above ₦50,000, the income disparities are even higher; and comparing rural/urban incomes, reveals an even greater income inequality.

Table 5.3 summarises the available evidence on inequality for the *West African* region.

Table 5.3
Income distribution in West Africa

	% of poor in total	*% of poor's share in total income*	*% of rich in total*	*% of rich's share in total income*
Nigeria	62.8	39.8	1.1	15.3
Ghana	52.0	35.4	6.1	12.9
Sierra Leone	51.6	13.6	1.8	16.2
Liberia	73.7	24.6	3.9	60.4

Note: No date was given for this table in the source, but it refers to 1967/72.
Source: Computed from World Bank, *World Development Report* (1985), p. 180.

Table 5.3 shows that while for the poor, income share is about a half to one-third of their population share, for the rich, income share is about 15 times their population share, except in Ghana where it is about twice. In Nigeria, the picture of income inequality is indicated in Tables 5.3a and 5.3b.

Table 5.3a
Percentage share of Gross Income for Different Income Levels in Nigeria, 1969/72

Year	*Poorest 20%*	*Poorest 60%*	*Middle 40–60%*	*Highest 20%*	*Highest 5%*
1969/70	8.50	27.00	10.00	56.00	40.00
1970/71	8.00	27.50	11.00	57.00	41.00
1971/72	7.50	28.00	13.50	58.00	41.00
Average: all years	8.00	27.50	11.50	57.00	40.67

Source: Computed from World Bank, *World Development Report* (1985), p. 186.

Table 5.3a shows that the highest 20% of income earners received about seven times the share of the poorest 20%, and twice the income share of the poorest 60%, while the highest 5% received about one and a half times the income share of the poorest 60%. These figures are reflected in the income concentration ratios for the country. The last column of Table 5.3b is remarkable in two respects. One: it shows that income inequality has been increasing over the years as the income factor required to achieve equality (the equalisation coefficient) has been rising – the oil boom from 1974 may be expected to have worsened this trend of growing inequality. Two: a

Table 5.3b
Gini Index of Concentration in Nigeria

Year	*Gross Income*	*Net Income*	*Equalisation coefficient*
1969/70	0.6183	0.5975	3.4
1970/71	0.6034	0.5794	4.0
1971/72	0.5518	0.5245	5.0

Source: Computed from World Bank, *World Development Report* (1985), p. 186.

significant aspect of the table is the high value of the equalisation coefficient in each year. This is best appreciated by noting that the coefficient of perfect equality of income distribution is unity or 1.0, so the greater the equalisation coefficient is above 1.0, the greater the extent of inequality.

Table 5.4 provides the corresponding evidence of income inequality for Liberia.

Table 5.4
Income Distribution in Liberia, 1970

	Population		*Income per capita*	*Income*	
	('000)	*%*	*($)*	*Total ($)*	*%*
Rural	1,123	73.7	70	78,610	24.6
Urban:					
Unemployed	52	3.4	75	3,900	1.2
Concessions	109	7.2	100	10,900	3.4
Unskilled Job	52	3.4	150	7,800	2.4
Skilled	128	8.4	200	25,600	8.0
Managerial, professional & others	59	3.9	3,272	193,020	60.4
Total	*1,523*	*100.0*	*210*	*319,830*	*100.0*

Source: Computed from World Bank, *World Development Report* (1985), p. 165.

As Table 5.4 indicates, in Liberia 3.9% of top income earners received 60.4% of total income, leaving 73.7% of the lowest income earners with barely 24.6% of total income.

In Kenya, the data on income inequality are summarised in Table 5.5 and Figure 5.1.

The Lorenz Curve or graph of income inequality associated with Table 5.5 is in Figure 5.1.

In Figure 5.1 the main diagonal line, 00, is the line of equal distribution of income. Along it is shown, for example, 20% of the population will get 20% of total income; the more skewed to the right of this main diagonal 00 the actual curve is, the greater the inequality of income distribution. Thus while the poorest 63% of households

Table 5.5
Kenya: Estimated Income Distribution, 1972/74

Yearly income (K£)	*No. of households*	*Total income (K£ m.)*	*Cumulative % of households*	*Cumulative % income*
20	330,000	6.6	14	2
40	1,140,000	45.6	63	18
90	330,000	29.7	77	28
160	240,000	38.4	87	41
400	220,000	88.0	96	71
800	50,000	40.0	98	85
1,500	30,000	45.0	99	100
Total	*2,340,000*	*293.3*	*100*	*100*

Source; Computed from World Bank, *World Development Report* (1985), p. 95.

Figure 5.1
Lorenz Curve of Income Distribution in Kenya

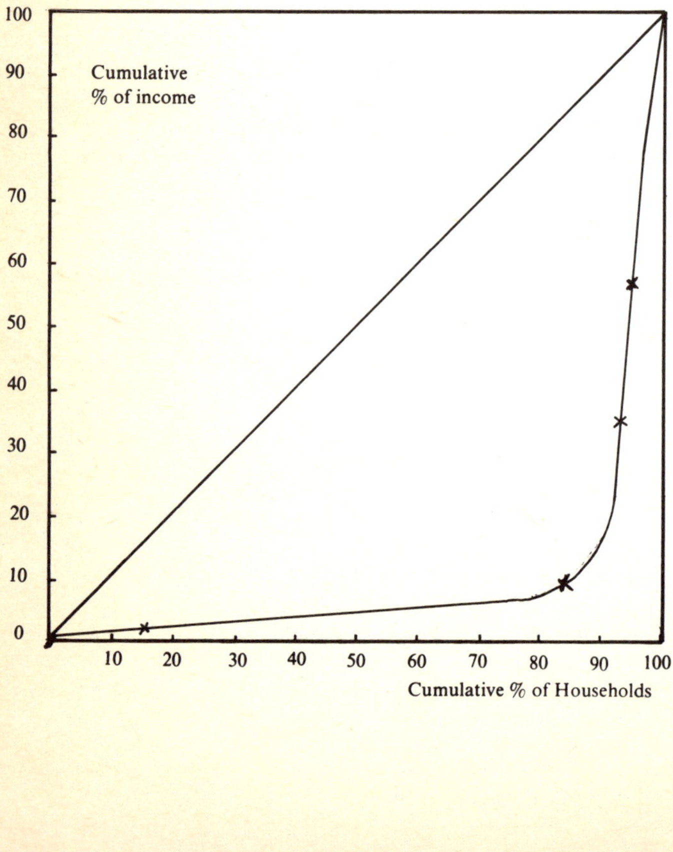

earn 18% of total income, the richest 12% (99% minus 87% of households) earn 59% of total income (100% minus 41% of income). The associated concentration ratio or Lorenz index of inequality is much higher than the 0.44 concentration ratio which Simon Kuznets obtained for developing countries generally.[24]

Data on the distribution of wealth in Africa are even more scanty, essentially owing to the secrecy that shrouds private property in bourgeois societies. But there is direct evidence of wealth inequality for Kenya, and partial data for Nigeria (see Tables 5.6 and 5.7).

Table 5.6
Kenya: approximate distribution of non-farm assets (but including plantations) 1971

Type of Wealth	*Value in K£ m.*	
	Asian	*Non-Asian*
Industry or plantations	70	120
Shares in public companies	20	30
Real estate	200	15
Trade	100	25
Cash	35	35
Total	*425*	*225*

Source: Colin Leys (1976), p. 120.

Unfortunately, the data show only inequality in the distribution of wealth between Asians and non-Asians, and not the inequality of wealth ownership among the African majority of the Kenyan population.

In Nigeria, the partial evidence on wealth distribution is with respect to shareholding which has been a significant aspect of private property since the indigenisation programmes of 1972/77 (Table 5.7).

Table 5.7
Distribution of shareholding by type of shareholder and value of shares held, 1970 (%)

Value of share held (Naira)	*Type of Shareholder*	
	Nigerian individuals (%)	*Expatriate individuals (%)*
1– 99	54.1	41.3
100– 1,000	36.4	49.8
1,001– 5,000	42.1	33.6
5,001– 10,000	31.2	43.0
10,001– 20,000	28.1	29.7
20,001– 50,000	13.0	38.3
50,001–100,000	8.3	28.7
above 100,000	3.7	23.3
Total	*32.6*	*39.82*

Source: W.O, Uzoaga & J. U. Alozienwa (1974) in *Nigerian Journal of Economics and Social Studies*, vol. 16, no. 3, November, p. 466.

While only 3.7% of Nigerians could hold shares of over ₦100,000, 54.1% of them cluster round shares of only ₦1 – and the larger the share values, the smaller the population percentage holding them. Of course, expatriate owners of foreign monopoly capital dominate all classes of shareholding, except those of ₦1 and ₦1,001 to ₦5,000.

These patterns of inequality of income and wealth also reflect underlying inequalities in the distribution of education and power, particularly as incomes flow from paid employment, which is a direct function of education, and from ownership of wealth (farm and non-farm assets, including land). With Africa's overall literacy rate hovering around 29.8% in 1980, and below 20% in over 20 African countries (including Niger with 8%, and Senegal and Mali, 10%), educational inequality is even more pronounced than income and wealth inequality, since even the poorest person has some income or asset. Ownership of wealth, especially among African nationals is, in turn, largely a function of access to political power, as the state apparatus is used widely for both legitimate and corrupt property accumulation under state bureaucratic capitalism.

Rural–urban inequality is even more graphic in Africa than many other forms of distributional inequity, but data on it are equally scanty. In 1980, for all Africa, the average percentage of urban population in the total population was 25.4. The available evidence on rural–urban inequality in West Africa and Kenya are presented in Tables 5.8 and 5.9.

Table 5.8
West Africa: Rural/Urban Income Differentials

Country	*Average urban income*	*Average rural income*	*Rural/urban differential*
Nigeria (N£s)	96	53	0.55
Ghana (cedis)	38	33	0.87
Sierra Leone (leones)	42	18	0.43
Liberia (dollars)	600	70	0.12
Average differential	—	—	0.49

These low urban and rural incomes seem to be those of the working people only, as the incomes of the urban *petit-bourgeoisie* are much higher. Thus the average rural/urban income differential is 0.49, thus, rural dwellers, on average, earn slightly less than half of the income of urban dwellers. This degree of rural–urban inequality was highest in Liberia, lowest in Ghana and about 50% in Nigeria and Sierra Leone. It is important to note, however, that the rural–urban dichotomy is more than income differential; it centres critically on the distribution of power, education, wealth, social amenities and so on.

Unfortunately, the available rural–urban income data for Kenya are for 1969 and outdated, but they do give an idea of the distributional picture at that time (Table 5.9).

Table 5.9
Kenya: average annual rural–urban incomes, 1969

Urban		*Rural*	
Income earners	*K£*	*Income earners*	*K£*
Private sector workers	300+	Workers in 'Services'	201
Unionised public and private sector workers	100-200 (150)	Workers on estates & large farms	69
Part time and occasional workers	60-100 (80)	Non-agricultural employees	56
Occasionally employed & unemployed	Below 60	Seasonal workers on small-holdings, and squatters	Below 25 (13)

Source: Colin Leys (1976), pp. 178, 182.

These rural incomes are also roughly half the urban incomes for different categories of urban and rural income earners. Unfortunately, the rural workers exclude the self-employed peasants and their dependants, who are typically the majority of rural dwellers. If these peasant incomes are included, the extent of rural–urban income inequality will even be higher than in Tables 5.8 and 5.9.

As indicated earlier, the distribution of such social facilities as health, housing, water, electricity, roads, etc. also accentuates both rural–urban and intra-urban inequality. Here the relevant concept is the *density of environmental facilities*, both across regions and neighbourhoods. Thus, the city in Africa is a social form predicated on a division of labour and serving as a point of class command in a global system of inequality. The urban centre thus corresponds to a spatial definition of inequality with its sprawling slums and shanty suburbs, and its rich and exclusive estates, like Ikoyi and Victoria Island in Lagos. A remarkable Dakar slum even captures the essence of this environmental inequality in its metaphorical name of *Hariala*, meaning "waiting for God" (for redemption) – on account of the hopelessness of its earthly plight. The rural–urban inequality in the distribution of social facilities in every African country is insufferable, as the majority of the population is trapped and submerged in a sub-human culture of silence, misery and isolation. In these rural areas we encounter unreliable access feeder roads, no water, no light and not even the most rudimentary health facility. The hapless plight of this hyper-oppressed rural majority is a most eloquent testimony to the utter bankruptcy and inhuman lack of conscience of the African *petit-bourgeoisie* and its colonial predecessors.

The disturbing pattern of structural inequalities that emerges for Africa thus shows that while the level of development of social classes (in terms of size, consciousness and organisation) is lower than in the industrialised countries, the extent of inequality in Africa is much greater – perhaps greater than in any other Third World country – and in underdeveloped countries generally also greater than in the advanced capitalist countries. Since we trace structural inequalities to social classes (that is, to relations of production or ownership) and their distribution of political power (control of the state), these inferences necessitate an investigation into the nature of the state in Africa, both as a source of class formations and an object of class struggle, as well as a source of structural inequalities.

The post-colonial state in Africa

"More or less consciously, the British and the French (and other colonialists) were eager to hand their power to elites who would keep the African world safe for capitalism, above all for their own capitalism."[25]

The nature of colonial disengagement from most of Africa, and the Third World generally, ensured that the post-colonial state would become a neocolonial state in order to preserve the same, basic colonial relationships of domination and exploitation. Theorising about the post-colonial state in Africa is, therefore, anchored to the elucidation of the state in the contexts of neocolonialism, the basic underdevelopment of the post-colonial economies (hence the investigation of the role of the state in the economy and its transformation), the processes of class formations and the issue of the relative autonomy of the state in performing its theoretical functions.

Models of the post-colonial state

In the analysis of these different aspects of the state in post-colonial social formations, some alternative interpretations have been advanced. One, a variation of modernisation theory, postulates a non-capitalist state whose class character is neither bourgeois nor proletarian. The benign elite (civilian and military) that control this state are regarded as modernisers. Green and Seidman's[26] left variant of this benign interpretation sees the post-colonial state as socialist-oriented, but the task of socialist transformation is for the state as a whole (i.e., the elite) and not for a class – the elite is seen to be building socialism, but not as a class. Besides contradicting the Marxist theory of the state as a class institution, the voluntary class suicide implied by this model of an elite-building socialism is really a facade, as the illusion of "African socialism" clearly demonstrates.

A closely related model of the post-colonial state considers it as the inheritance of unformed classes.[27] A "political class" of petit-bourgeois salariat controls the state with relative autonomy and volatility in the political area. This means that the class character of the state is undetermined and that class fractions can even build socialism. Unfortunately, this analysis is static and undialectical with teleological categories like "class in formation".

Then there are two models of the post-colonial state as an oligarchy. The one by Meillassoux, Fitch and Oppenheimer[28] conceives of the consolidation of a wholly formed *oligarchy or class of bureaucrats* around the post-colonial state apparatus (with such bureaucrats as experts in education, government and business employment) with its antagonistic class not fully defined. The bureaucratic class does not own the means of production but controls them constitutionally and its state is subordinate to imperialism. This corresponds to the one-party state where the public sector is created by nationalisation under "African socialism" as in Mali and Ghana in the 1960s. But even in these countries, members of the class of working people are co-opted into the class of bureaucrats, and their opposing class consists mainly of the remnants of the *petit-bourgeoisie*. Hence the classless society in this "socialism" is fake and the socialist construction typically atrophied. The model is also silent on the post-colonial states pursuing the neocolonial capitalist path under multi-party rule, as in Nigeria, Kenya and so on. The other oligarchy model[29] considers power in the post-colonial state as held by a *global and imperialist financial oligarchy* that controls capital and the state, so that independence has brought no major change to the colonial state. A more conciliatory variant of this by Tandon concedes that independence changed the government but not the state in post-colonial society. A local bourgeoisie without capital does exist, and it employs foreign capital and operates as the "servicing agents" of imperialism. In a similar vein, Freyhold regards the "governing class" that holds power in post-colonial societies not as a ruling class; the imperialist bourgeoisie is seen as the ruling class, and it performs the core functions of the state as well as controlling the economy.

All versions of this imperialist oligarchy model stretch neocolonialism too far. Even in the reactionary Francophone countries like Ivory Coast, Gabon and Cameroon, which have defence agreements with France, a local *petit-bourgeoisie* owning agricultural, commercial and even modest industrial capital is emerging, and it exercises some measure of sovereignty over the post-colonial state, etc., through nominal control over mineral rights; control over the coercive apparatus of the state such as police, prisons and even military matters; control of what Poulantzas calls "training and subjection" for the state bureaucracy, and so on. Such developments and functions may be nominal and ineffective, but they exist.

More generally, this imperialist oligarchy thesis sounds like Bill Warren's crude instrumentalist construction of the internationalisation of capital which is supposed to neutralise the nation-state. As Shivji argues, the oligarchy theorists also echo the theses of Kautsky and Kievsky, with the former postulating a united world finance capital under a peaceful imperialism, and the latter claiming falsely, like Bill Warren, that in the era of finance capital, national self-determination is impossible. Fortunately, imperialism is never as monolithic, and the power of its bourgeoisie is nowhere as pervasive as these interpretations suggest.

A more general analysis of the post-colonial state has to start with the main distinguishing features of the centrality of the state in post-colonial social formations.[30] One is the prominence of the post-colonial state, which is due not only to colonial legacy, but to the reality of contemporary production processes in Africa. As Alavi put it,

> The apparatus of the state furthermore assumes a new and relatively autonomous *economic* role, which is not paralleled in the classical bourgeois state. The state in the post-colonial society directly appropriates a very large part of the economic surplus and deploys it in bureaucratically directed economic activity in the name of promoting economic development.[31]

This view is, however, exaggerated because the economic role of the state in *petit-bourgeois* post-colonial society is essentially that of promoting state capitalism, as in the classical bourgeois state; the difference being that, in the former, this role corresponds to state bureaucratic capitalism, while in the latter it corresponds to state monopoly capitalism. In the post-colonial transitional socialist formations, this economic role of the state is that of socialist construction, which under "African socialism" degenerates into greater state bureaucratic capitalism, or at best state socialism.

The second main feature of the post-colonial state is its over-developed superstructure relative to the overall structure (for example, of production). This is because the inherited colonial state was a mere extension of the imperialist state superstructure under colonialism, when the military, police, prisons, bureaucracy, and so on, were overseas branches of the same imperialist superstructure. At nominal independence, the powerful bureaucratic–military apparatus and government mechanisms of the erstwhile colonial state were severed from their imperialist structure. This post-colonial state superstructure is so powerful and relatively over-developed because under colonialism, government was mainly by coercion and a strong enough coercive apparatus was required for subduing *all* indigenous social classes – as against the need for subduing only the working people. But even here, the post-colonial state bureaucracy is relatively weaker than its coercive apparatus because of the less relevant role of the bureaucracy under colonialism, the withdrawal of most imperialist bureaucrats and their slow replacement after nominal independence.

The third characteristic of the post-colonial state is that its hegemonic position must be created. There are three main contending capitals: imperialist monopoly capital, state capital and private indigenous capital. The chaos of ideas and social relations following the termination of colonial rule meant that everything of basic social meaning must be re-created. "In politics, there were no durable political institutions, no democratic cultural traditions, no widely diffused social ideals, and no full sense of national identity . . . neither liberty, nor equality, nor fraternity was possible."[32] As the independence arrangement did not resolve the class contradictions, the state is regarded not as a class construct, but rather the state of a society divided into classes, a state symbolising the unity of the social formation and providing ideological cement for the capitalist system. As the inheritors of the post-colonial state entrenched colonial privileges, class struggle, which was muted under colonialism, develops apace. The precise character of the post-colonial state depends on the underlying transitional social formation. Where this is neocolonial capitalist, as in most of contemporary Africa, various fractions of the bureaucratic bourgeoisie, or even different social classes, forge local alliances to control the state; in extreme cases, this culminates in the one-party state, embracing a coalition of the bureaucratic bourgeoisie, both civilian and military, and the working people, to suppress class opposition. These local power alliances then form external alliances with different rival imperialist powers as in Kenya and Nigeria, for example. These shifting alliances correspond to a "crisis of hegemony", popularly called political instability. But these different neocolonial alliances have different degrees of independence from the imperialist countries, depending primarily on the relative strength of their economies, the maturity of their leadership and the capability of their bureaucracy. In the transitional socialist formations, the *petit-bourgeoisie* commits class suicide (with varying degrees of conviction), constitutes itself into a vanguard and links up with the working people to share state power and build socialism. Under "African socialism", this power-sharing and transformation is more rhetorical than real.

In the transitional capitalist formations, the neocolonial middlemen, mediators or intermediaries, mainly politicians and civil servants (with local support in the military and the other professions such as academic) promote neocolonial policies to entrench themselves. Thus, the innermost vocation (of the *petit-bourgeoisie*) seems to be to keep in the (imperialist) running and to be part of the "racket". Called the *wabenzi* (the owners of Mercedes Benz cars) in East and Central Africa and the *oboku* owners (local Nigerian slang for Mercedes Benz car owners) these neocolonialists have two main roles in global capitalism: (1) to guarantee the continuation of a subordinate role for the post-colonial state in international capitalism; (2) to guarantee the acceptance of neocolonial policies of under-development by the broad masses in their countries. It is primarily this pliant class of *petit-bourgeois* mediators that nurtures the structures of class formations, inequality and underdevelopment in Africa within the post-colonial state.

The relative autonomy of the post-colonial state and social justice

The specific question of the *relative autonomy of the post-colonial state* in Africa is predicated on four basic considerations. 1) The embryonic nature of the classes-in-formation in these countries. This means that there is no strong, homogeneous and dominant bourgeoisie, just as there is no opposing strong, politically conscious and well-organised class of working people. 2) The hegemonic crisis this scenario represents, which corresponds to a typical era of post-war defeat in the classical bourgeois state when there is a relative equilibrium of social classes, or what is called a stalemate in the "people's republic" where social classes are about equally balanced. The state then holds the balance of power to maintain social cohesion, and this scenario is especially conducive to the emergence of fascism with gullible and opportunistic "middle-class" support. The spate of military and dictatorial regimes in Africa and throughout the Third World demonstrates this condition. 3) The character of the social formation and the economic role of the state. Under transitional capitalist social formation, state bureaucratic capitalism ensures a large interventionist role for the state in the economy; and a corresponding leverage for subduing, or at least, regulating, the social classes. Where this state bureaucratic capitalism is associated with a one-party state, as for example, in Kenya, Ivory Coast and Senegal, this enhances the power of the bureaucracy and the relative autonomy of the state. In transitional socialist formations, whether African or scientific, state ownership of the means of production extends the relative autonomy of the state even beyond that of the one-party state bureaucratic capitalism. 4) The claim of the imperial state; the greater this is, other things being equal, the smaller the post-colonial state's relative autonomy.

Generally, this relative autonomy of the post-colonial state tends to be greater than that of the classical bourgeois state, even under state monopoly capitalism; at least, in dealing with the domestic classes in the state (that is, excluding the imperialist bourgeoisie under neocolonialism). This large, relative autonomy of the post-colonial state is exercised primarily by members of the *petit-bourgeoisie* under neocolonialism, and its two adverse consequences are the severe repression of the population, verging on fascism in many cases, and the yawning structural inequalities of these countries. This is particularly significant in view of the economic, political and other containment policies of the African *petit-bourgeoisie* in the face of its growing inability to resolve the escalating crises of the various countries. With a relatively over-developed state apparatus, large relative domestic autonomy and growing social pressures, the tendency towards authoritarianism as represented by one-party rule, military regimes, and so on, is very strong and grave.

All these have critical implications for strategies aimed at eliminating structural inequalities. Three possible scenarios can be envisaged. One is a simple extrapolation of the contemporary situation in which the combination of tight neocolonial grip (with imperialist assistance) attempts to perpetuate the *status quo* with growing inequality and doses of diversionary reformism, such as incomes policy, redistributive taxation and even workers' participation in management. This is likely to be associated with shifting alliances among the bureaucratic bourgeoisie, with coups and other crises. The other possibility is the fascist outcome, where deepening structural inequalities, the escalation of other crises, such as unemployment, inflation, balance of payments problems, and so on, and the consolidation of the *petit-bourgeoisie*, lead to a fascist crack-down, as the survival of the economy and the state are threatened. This has happened in Zaire, Sudan, Idi Amin's Uganda and the Central African Republic. But this is likely to be a transitional phase however long it lasts. The termination of fascist rule may lead either to the crisis syndrome or to the third scenario. Here, the growing super-exploitation of the working people raises their consciousness and organisation which, together with their growing size, may lead them to become more revolutionary. The growing crises of neocolonialism may also lead a revolutionary wing of the *petit-bourgeoisie* (civilian and military) to join forces with the workers, peasants, students and others to initiate revolutionary transformation according to Cabral's model of the post-colonial state. Here, the appreciation of the class roots of inequality and mass poverty in private ownership and power monopoly may lead to a direct assault on the state, which is at the heart of bureaucratic capitalism. This revolutionary transformation has occurred in Ghana, Congo (Brazzaville), Ethiopia and elsewhere in Africa. Its prospects are critically dependent on the pace of class formations, the future course of the African crisis and the peculiar dialectics of class struggle in individual African countries.

Notes

1. A. Cabral (1969) p. 77, emphasis mine.
2. See Kwame Nkrumah (1973); S. Amin & R. Cohen (1977).
3. L. Kuper & M. G. Smith (1969).
4. Van der Berghe (1965).
5. Walter Rodney (1972), pp. 53, 246.
6. See V. I. Lenin (1964).

7. Samir Amin (1977), ch. 2, pp. 67–72.
8. On post-colonial class structure, see Issa Shivji (1976).
9. See R. Kaplinsky (ed.) (1978), ch. 7.
10. On the evolution of the African *petit-bourgeoisie*, see Walter Rodney (1972).
11. See, for example, Nicos Poulantzas (1975).
12. Franz Fanon, quoted in D. L. Cohen & J. Daniel (eds.) (1981) p. 95.
13. S. P. Schatz (1977).
14. N. Poulantzas (1975), p. 297.
15. D. Zakine (1968) in *International Affairs*, no. 4, p. 49.
16. See J. S. Saul, in D. L. Cohen & J. Daniel (eds.) (1981).
17. Paulo Freire (1975).
18. R. Sandbrook & R. Cohen (eds.) (1975) chs. 3, 7, 13, 14.
19. World Bank, *World Development Report 1985* (Washington), pp. 210, 214.
20. Sandbrook & Cohen (eds.) (1975) pp. 281–302.
21. World Development Report 1985, pp. 174–5.
22. Ibid.
23. R. G. Lipsey (1971), p. 481.
24. Simon S. Kuznets (1946).
25. B. Davidson, quoted in P. C. W. Gutkind & I. Wallerstein (eds.) (1976) p. 186.
26. See R. H. Green & A. Seidman (1968).
27. D. L. Cohen & J. Daniel (eds.) (1981) pp. 185–95.
28. Y. Tandon (ed.) (1982).
29. Ibid., pp. 175–9.
30. Consider H. Alavi (1972) in *New Left Review*, no. 74, July–August, pp. 59–82.
31. Ibid., p. 73.
32. B. Magubane (1976) in Gutkind & Wallerstein, (1976), p. 186.

6 Industrialisation Strategy in Africa

Industrialisation is a central theme in the development and social research programmes of Africa and the Third World generally. Indeed, many policy-makers and others regard it as synonymous with national development, certainly as the focal index of "modernisation". This predominant focus derives largely from the sanguine perception of industrialisation as the best index of economic progress, with regard to such attributes as the measure of national productive capacity, manufacturing output, technological development, modern employment opportunities and overall standard of living. Hence, industrialisation is seen not only as desirable, but crucial to social transformation.

Motives for industrialisation

The strategy of ndustrialisation is determined basically by the motives for undertaking industrial development. Whether the strategy is traditional import substitution, or more recent export promotion, the motivating factors in Africa and throughout the Third World are complex. Historically, industrialisation in the periphery started around 1930, in Latin America, after the decline of the primary exports from the specialisation in primary production by the Third World during 1850–1930. In Africa, this industrial process started some 20 years later than in Latin America. The decline of primary exports to the metropolitan countries, which was associated with their development of synthetic substitutes for peripheral exports, thus historically posed the need for the diversification of the production structure in the Third World. In Africa, the prolonged export depression of 1929/45, and the token stimulation of colonial economies in the post war period, as part of world capitalist reconstruction, gave the initial stimulus for this initiation of import-substitution industrialisation (ISI).

This generalised adoption of import substitution, which started in Latin America, and was given intellectual respectability by Albert Hirschman's crude propagation of the strategy,[1] was also informed by motives of foreign exchange savings. The dollar (and other hard currency) shortage of the war and post-war years stimulated this desire. A closely related objective was the change of import structure warranted by the demand for foreign inputs for import-substitute industries. Thus, there was need to reduce the imports of manufactured consumer goods in order to meet the requirements for imported raw materials, intermediate products and capital goods.

The "modernisation" orientation of bourgeois development theorising, especially in the post-war era, also encouraged colonial governments to pursue industrialisation as an index of modernisation. Manufacturing, industry, construction, infrastructure and services were therefore seen as modern sectors that had to be encouraged, as opposed to traditional agriculture. This was particularly necessary since the objective of colonial and post-colonial modernisation has been to make the Third World like Western Europe and North America. Hence the need to transplant the early industrial activities of these metropolitan countries to Africa, using the "textile first" approach, which emphasises the primacy of consumer-good manufacturing in industrialisation and development.

As modernisation proceeds with expanded education, jobs have to be found for school leavers, so the creation of employment opportunities has become a major objective of industrialisation. This is particularly with respect to the economies of scale, or of mass production, associated with industrial enterprises that offer large numbers of job opportunities. The national objective of controlling unemployment thus blends with an emphasis on industrial, especially manufacturing, production.

More recently, especially after nominal independence, many African countries realised their technological backwardness. Industrialisation has, therefore, been seen as a quick method of importing the modern technology embodied in the capital-goods imported for industrial enterprises, as the solution for backward technology. But unfortunately, this has been implemented as naive "technology transfer", which has failed to generate technological development. The generation of sectoral linkages in the economy is related to this technological objective. Here, industrial technologies are considered to be sources of diffusing backward and forward linkages among sectors of the economy, as with agro-allied industries. The generation of quick and large profits or economic surplus from industrial ventures is also seen as a means of realising these structural linkages. This is particularly related to the higher productivity of labour, the income elasticity of demand and the short gestation period of manufacturing enterprises.

More sophisticated versions of these arguments link industrialisation with the "disintegration theory".[2] This is that the imported technology for industrialisation, which typically bears or embodies capitalist relations of production, is critical for breaking-up the pre-capitalist relations of production in the periphery. This disintegration of pre-capitalist relations is essential for the emergence of capitalism, which is the goal of modernisation.

Finally, current social debates and experiments in national self-reliance in Africa and elsewhere correctly perceive industrialisation as a major requirement. Here, the domestic manufacture of consumer and capital goods is required to neutralise the prostrate dependence on the importation of these industrial manufactures from the imperialist countries. This is particularly so if such local industries can be based effectively on local raw materials, indigenous technology and basic national needs (as opposed to narrow elitist desires) as much as possible.

Patterns of import-substitution industrialisation in Africa

Import substitution (IS) was the first strategy of industrialisation to be adopted in the Third World and, as we have seen, spread from Latin America to Africa. It has also remained by far the most popular industrialisation strategy, despite recent gravitations towards export-promotion industrialisation strategy. One major appeal of IS is that it seems the natural way to start industrialisation–producing commodities that are already familiar to consumers and, therefore, with an assured market. By displacing imports, import substitution is also intended to save foreign exchange – but because of the high foreign exchange cost of imported inputs this may not take place. This displacement of foreign imports also satisfies the economic nationalism of, especially, newly independent states. Foreign monopoly capital and technology from the erstwhile multinational exporters are also readily available for import substitutes, because of the high tariffs and other restrictions which threaten to exclude foreign producers of imported manufactures from the peripheral markets. This is the sense in which these import-substitute ventures are really "tariff factories", built behind the protective walls of high tariffs and other protectionist measures. The high tariffs for shutting out or restricting imports that compete with the products of import-substituting enterprises also constitute a lucrative and major source of fiscal revenue. Thus, import duties account for as much as 60% or more of non-oil exporting countries' annual revenue. These factors reinforce the motives for industrialisation in Africa.

On account of the basic similarity of motives for import-substitution industrialisation (ISI), therefore, this strategy typically yields certain patterns of industrialisation in Africa and elsewhere. One of these is the familiar heavy concentration on the manufacture of consumer-goods to the virtual neglect of capital goods. As the imports displaced by import substitution are such basically simple consumer-goods as textiles, beverages, tobacco, soft drinks, beer, and so on, the manufacturing of capital-goods such as machinery, transport equipment and the products of other heavy industries is neglected. This concentration on consumer-goods also fits the prescription of the "textile first" approach to industrialisation.

As the former exporters of the import substitutes are usually multinational corporations (MNCs) (especially early commercial ones like the UAC) they usually dominate the processes of IS, and some of them branched out into manufacturing. Of course, as suggested earlier, these MNCs have strong protectionist motives for engaging in ISI. The foreign ownership of import-substitute industries also gives rise to three further features of import substitution industrialisation: 1) their import dependence; 2) high capital-intensity; and 3) low value-added.[3]

As the use of African inputs constitutes a drain on the foreign exchange of the MNCs' home countries, they prefer, as much as possible, to import their raw materials, intermediate products, capital goods and technology in order to boost their home exports. The MNCs' import of these inputs also offers them opportunities for engaging in transfer-pricing through over-invoicing imported inputs, especially from their foreign subsidiaries, as discussed in Chapter 4. In many cases, more than 75% of African countries' total outlay on IS is consumed by imported inputs.

The import of technology for ISI leads to the high capital-intensity of import-substitute industries. As the MNCs' home countries are relatively more capital abundant than their peripheral "host" countries, the foreign technology imported by the MNCs tends to be more capital-intensive than is warranted by the relative abundance of labour in the poor countries. This is one major reason why ISI employs so few workers, and co-exists with even growing unemployment in the African countries.

For the above two reasons, ISI generates relatively low value-added in the Third World. The manufacturing value-added (mva) in African countries is shown in Table 6.1 for 1970 and 1980. Both the per capita mva and the share of mva in GDP are very low, with the former ranging, in 1980 (constant prices), from a maximum of \$144.04 in Libya to a minimum of \$1.25 in Guinea-Bissau; and the latter ranging from a maximum share of 23.31% in Zimbabwe to a minimum of 1.12% in Guinea-Bissau.

The share of manufacturing in GDP is also typically very low for African countries. In addition to the low share of mva depicted above, the slight sectoral share of manufacturing in 1982[4] was: 14% to 9% for low-income Africa; 20% for middle-income Africa; with a maximum of 27% in Egypt; 13% in Kenya; 12% in Ivory Coast; dropping to 6% in Nigeria; 5% in Ghana, Congo, Mali and Sierra Leone; 4% in Uganda and Chad; 3% in Zaire; and 2% in Guinea. In 1975, in the Economic Community of West African States (ECOWAS), the share of manufacturing and electricity in GDP ranged from a maximum of 20% for Senegal to a minimum of 1.5% for Gambia, and an average of 8.6% for the sub-region.[5]

The growth of manufacturing is another important feature of industrialisation in Africa. In spite of the overall sluggish performance of African economies, the industrial sector has been usually one of the fastest growing sectors of the economy. But this growth performance shows wide variability among countries, as depicted in Table 6.2 for 1970/80. This table shows that the real growth rate of mva during 1975/80 (Column 2) was a maximum of 22.64% in Libya, with an average of about 4%, down to a minimum of –18.76% in Equatorial Guinea. The excess of the real growth rate of mva over that of GDP for 1975/80 (Column 5) was positive in 26 countries and negative in another 26. According to the *World Bank Report* for 1984, the overall average growth rate of manufacturing in Africa during 1970/82 was 3.4%, with 3.2% for low-income, and 5.5% for middle-income countries. The highest growth rate was 12% for Nigeria; the lowest –10% for Togo. The growth rate for other African countries was: Algeria 10.9%; Egypt 9.3%; Kenya 9.0%; Ivory Coast 5.4%; Uganda –8.9%; Central African Republic –4.3%; Zimbabwe –4.1%; Chad –3.2%; Zaire –2.3%; and Ghana –1.5%.

The small size of manufacturing establishments is equally typical of African industrialisation. Just as the total volume of industrial production is small relative to GDP, as shown above, the relative size of each industrial enterprise also tends to be small. Typically this is the consequence of the small size of the internal market for industrial products, the narrow elite tastes for which manufacturing caters, the overall low per capita income in these countries and the low export orientation of industrialisation. Thus, in Nigeria in 1973, small-scale industries employing ten or

Table 6.1
Manufacturing value added (MVA) per capita and share of MVA in GDP, developing Africa by country, and country share in MVA of developing Africa, 1970 and 1980[a]

Country/ territory	*MVA per capita (US$)*			*Share, MVA in GDP at factor cost (in per cent)*			*Country share in MVA of developing Africa (in per cent)*		
	1970	*1980 (constant)*	*1980 (current)*	*1970*	*1980 (constant)*	*1980 (current)*	*1970*	*1980 (constant)*	*1980 (current)*
Main oil-exporters (4):	13.78	25.57	91.71	5.20	6.39	5.01	18.460	28.339	35.089
Algeria	30.29	43.42	134.65	11.16	11.11	8.12	7.478	8.570	9.532
Gabon	23.37	120.58	456.32	4.12	10.16	7.66	0.213	0.715	0.971
Libya A. J.	32.37	144.04	270.54	1.79	5.59	2.20	1.191	4.598	3.097
Nigeria	9.16	17.39	72.05	4.43	5.21	5.01	9.578	14.456	21.489
Least developed (21):	7.79	7.47	25.48	8.69	8.10	7.27	15.155	11.235	13.735
Benin	6.87	6.33	13.73	8.35	6.32	5.21	0.346	0.186	0.188
Botswana	9.52	25.82	67.87	7.84	10.31	6.92	0.106	0.219	0.206
Burundi	4.34	5.53	19.23	6.77	7.81	11.62	0.284	0.256	0.319
Cape Verde	4.91	4.73	17.14	5.23	5.88	5.58	0.024	0.017	0.022
Central African Rep.	13.45	12.59	41.28	13.09	13.95	13.99	0.439	0.303	0.357
Chad	4.49	3.66	19.44	5.49	5.20	9.14	0.303	0.178	0.339
Comoros	6.41	2.42	9.98	6.69	4.70	5.26	0.033	0.015	0.022
Ethiopia	6.82	7.07	13.19	9.55	9.74	10.64	3.107	2.428	1.625
Gambia	6.09	2.93	9.33	5.10	2.64	2.58	0.052	0.019	0.022
Guinea	4.51	4.62	10.27	2.89	3.01	3.10	0.327	0.250	0.199
Guinea-Bissau	1.29	1.25	4.30	1.07	1.12	1.75	0.012	0.008	0.009
Lesotho	1.51	4.56	11.00	2.71	5.02	4.93	0.030	0.066	0.057
Malawi	10.22	15.95	36.22	15.36	16.11	15.66	0.850	1.042	0.849
Mali	5.11	5.22	22.27	10.54	10.83	13.17	0.496	0.373	0.571
Niger	5.73	5.75	21.34	6.04	5.73	5.31	0.426	0.331	0.441
Rwanda	2.00	10.16	28.08	3.47	12.21	12.84	0.131	0.527	0.522
Somalia	5.02	6.82	29.04	6.49	8.25	8.61	0.259	0.269	0.411
Sudan	13.58	10.19	32.33	10.18	7.09	7.01	3.558	2.016	2.294
Tanzania U.R.	8.80	8.23	24.57	10.08	7.75	7.87	2.143	1.591	1.703
Uganda	9.08	4.26	57.28	7.50	4.80	4.76	1.646	0.628	3.027
Upper Volta	5.77	6.97	20.92	10.88	14.57	13.88	0.583	0.513	0.552

Other (27):	23.25	27.76	65.56	12.69	13.70	12.13	66.386	60.422	51.176
Angola	14.28	6.57	11.81	5.18	4.91	2.58	1.472	0.476	0.306
Cameroon	15.26	18.00	68.08	10.02	9.06	9.64	1.904	1.659	2.250
Congo	13.25	12.01	39.68	6.63	5.24	4.62	0.290	0.200	0.237
Djibouti	23.98	19.91	71.71	6.09	8.53	8.60	0.074	0.071	0.091
Egypt	35.54	47.46	67.00	19.60	17.67	14.02	21.902	21.340	10.804
Equatorial Guinea	9.62	2.33	9.20	3.77	4.21	5.22	0.052	0.009	0.013
Ghana	29.30	20.92	105.25	12.15	12.51	9.66	4.675	2.773	5.005
Ivory Coast	23.66	36.08	117.98	11.40	13.48	10.38	2.513	3.126	3.666
Kenya	15.00	22.57	47.68	12.13	16.02	12.49	3.218	3.997	3.028
Liberia	11.33	14.59	32.55	4.00	5.55	4.98	0.281	0.289	0.232
Madagascar	13.33	12.49	41.65	11.51	11.97	11.49	1.666	1.153	1.379
Mauritania	8.15	8.95	27.31	4.93	6.24	6.31	0.174	0.143	0.157
Mauritius	31.66	65.90	154.77	16.01	21.26	17.99	0.486	0.680	0.573
Morocco	35.58	42.49	122.70	15.86	15.51	17.50	9.836	9.178	9.507
Mozambique	12.84	9.57	22.70	5.89	6.12	8.65	1.920	1.051	0.894
Namibia	54.55	57.08	84.84	9.35	8.28	4.85	0.777	0.605	0.322
Reunion	39.15	38.78	152.65	4.94	3.26	3.67	0.323	0.230	0.324
Sao Tome and Principe	8.49	7.50	21.31	4.81	5.43	4.74	0.011	0.007	0.007
Senegal	27.66	26.06	66.74	15.93	18.24	16.89	2.257	1.588	1.459
Seychelles	6.15	20.43	98.29	1.59	4.21	6.20	0.006	0.015	0.027
Sierra Leone	8.90	9.64	26.92	6.45	7.32	7.20	0.453	0.359	0.360
Swaziland	30.33	68.19	177.04	12.35	18.29	23.52	0.236	0.398	0.370
Togo	12.53	7.54	22.61	10.24	6.18	5.70	0.454	0.207	0.223
Tunisia	23.16	48.66	111.06	9.22	11.23	10.03	2.131	3.286	2.690
Zaire	5.12	3.65	8.16	7.55	6.50	8.36	2.053	1.134	0.910
Zambia	23.44	31.07	87.44	6.53	10.00	14.93	1.812	1.957	1.957
Zimbabwe	55.10	55.51	150.46	21.30	23.31	23.80	5.410	4.491	4.367
Developing Africa:									
Total (52)	*16.29*	*21.07*	*58.75*	*9.50*	*9.77*	*7.63*	*5.408*[b]	*9.258*[b]	*25.811*[b]

[a] 1970 data in 1970 prices and 1980 data shown in current and constant 1970 prices.
[b] Value in US$ millions.

Source: Computer printouts supplied by ECA Statistics Division. with calculations by the UNIDO Secretariat.

Table 6.2

Real growth rates in manufacturing value added (MVA) and difference between MVA and GDP growth, averages for 1970–75, 1975–80 and 1970–80, with 1980 price deflator for manufacturing and ratio of manufacturing and GDP price deflators, developing Africa, by country

Country/ territory	*MVA real growth rate (per cent)*[a]			*MVA real growth rate minus GDP real growth rate (per cent)*[a]			*MVA price deflator, 1980 (1970–100)*[b]	*Deflator corrected for change in US$ value of local currency*[b]	*MVA price deflator 1980/ GDP price deflator 1980 (1970–100) in %*[b]
	1970–75 (1)	*1975–80 (2)*	*1970–80 (3)*	*1970–75 (4)*	*1975–80 (5)*	*1970–80 (6)*	*(7)*	*(8)*	*(9)*
Main oil-exporters (4):	11.60	9.11	10.36	4.14	0.74	2.44	250.20	320.64	70.96
Algeria	7.05	8.28	7.66	-1.48	2.64	0.57	240.10	310.13	73.09
Gabon	28.80	11.57	20.19	9.38	8.93	9.16	284.50	378.44	75.41
Libya A.J.	20.16	22.64	21.40	13.40	13.60	13.50	153.52	187.30	39.31
Nigeria	15.29	7.03	11.16	8.17	-2.30	2.93	322.69	414.41	96.03
Least developed (21):	3.04	2.07	2.56	0.21	-1.39	-0.59	348.94	393.51	107.66
Benin	5.77	-5.74	0.02	2.51	-6.75	-2.12	211.60	281.47	82.52
Botswana	15.86	14.71	15.28	7.28	1.68	4.48	224.46	262.93	67.18
Burundi	4.43	4.63	4.53	3.26	-0.24	1.51	358.00	347.98	148.85
Cape Verde	1.65	1.96	1.81	3.50	-1.12	1.19	481.90	361.63	94.63
Central African Rep.	-0.27	3.94	1.84	-0.68	2.17	0.75	246.60	328.02	100.32
Chad	6.18	-5.32	0.43	3.40	-4.15	-0.38	402.40	455.59	175.58
Comoros	3.70	-6.37	-1.34	1.46	-6.88	-2.72	314.55	411.42	112.02
Ethiopia	1.07	5.05	3.06	-1.19	1.76	0.28	154.45	186.53	109.27
Gambia	21.81	-13.49	4.16	16.46	-14.06	1.20	267.21	319.55	97.93
Guinea	2.58	3.23	2.91	-0.32	1.45	0.57	157.70	222.28	102.85
Guinea-Bissau	0.14	2.61	1.37	-2.10	3.36	0.57	403.90	343.28	155.46
Lesotho	45.74	5.98	25.86	38.44	-2.50	17.97	262.05	241.40	98.16
Malawi	11.20	4.62	7.91	1.81	-0.51	0.65	220.27	227.14	97.22
Mali	3.06	2.82	2.94	0.28	0.85	0.56	320.00	426.67	121.69
Niger	2.52	4.42	3.47	3.11	-3.75	-0.32	279.20	371.39	92.73
Rwanda	68.31	6.28	37.30	58.93	1.45	30.19	256.50	276.25	105.15
Somalia	9.66	2.56	6.11	5.17	0.17	2.67	375.44	291.06	104.36
Sudan	3.99	1.87	2.93	1.07	-2.01	-0.47	455.80	317.42	99.00
Tanzania U.R.	4.81	0.44	2.62	0.31	-5.38	-2.54	342.89	298.41	101.57
Uganda	-2.69	-5.37	-4.03	-2.88	-5.45	-4.16	1,213.25	1,344.55	99.11
Upper Volta	7.89	1.54	4.71	6.77	0.15	3.46	225.10	300.05	95.20

Other (27):	5.25	3.88	4.57	1.59	0.07	0.83	359.35	351.78	99.87
Angola	-2.07	-1.57	-1.82	4.31	0.09	2.20	308.80	179.62	52.46
Cameroon	2.15	6.26	4.21	-2.64	0.73	-0.95	283.70	378.16	106.38
Congo	-0.99	4.98	1.99	-8.24	3.84	-2.20	248.50	330.55	88.19
Djibouti	10.81	0.49	5.65	4.78	2.83	3.80	299.90	360.05	100.81
Egypt	4.06	6.50	5.28	-0.36	-1.81	-1.10	227.22	141.14	79.35
Equatorial Guinea	-2.29	-18.76	-10.53	6.86	-4.77	1.04	371.40	392.45	123.07
Ghana	2.60	-1.52	0.54	1.16	-0.22	0.47	1,356.26	503.21	77.22
Ivory Coast	6.72	9.20	7.96	0.69	3.04	1.86	247.90	327.00	76.99
Kenya	8.25	7.70	7.98	3.50	2.66	3.08	219.49	211.21	77.95
Liberia	12.18	0.60	6.39	8.80	0.97	3.92	223.04	223.04	89.74
Madagascar	2.34	1.23	1.79	1.26	0.36	0.46	251.30	333.58	95.99
Mauritania	0.41	6.90	3.66	-1.82	6.75	2.47	252.10	305.10	101.05
Mauritius	11.44	7.33	9.38	3.86	2.35	3.10	327.71	234.86	84.61
Morocco	6.55	3.11	4.83	1.33	-1.81	-0.24	220.70	288.80	112.83
Mozambique	6.22	-3.37	1.42	7.86	-3.36	0.60	407.42	237.09	141.30
Namibia	2.58	3.45	3.02	-0.76	-1.58	-1.16	175.00	148.64	58.54
Reunion	-1.23	6.09	2.43	-8.04	0.14	-3.95	297.30	394.66	112.78
Sao Tome and Principe	0.50	0.39	0.44	5.06	-2.60	1.22	346.40	284.85	87.54
Senegal	4.37	0.15	2.26	1.88	1.17	1.52	192.50	256.06	92.57
Seychelles	25.93	12.99	19.46	21.75	6.21	13.98	647.06	481.59	147.55
Sierra Leone	7.26	-0.12	3.57	5.86	-2.12	1.75	352.35	279.40	98.37
Swaziland	17.07	5.98	11.53	9.96	-0.73	4.62	305.81	259.74	128.62
Togo	-3.64	-0.35	-1.99	-5.70	-3.64	4.67	225.30	299.59	92.22
Tunisia	13.50	7.60	10.55	3.47	1.32	2.40	175.40	228.23	89.35
Zaire	3.78	-4.43	-0.32	-0.14	-2.75	-1.44	1,175.30	223.59	129.67
Zambia	19.99	-1.11	9.44	14.84	-0.15	7.35	310.64	281.44	149.34
Zimbabwe	6.53	1.04	3.78	0.06	1.83	0.94	253.87	271.06	102.09

[a] 1970 US $ basis.

[b] Deflators for the three country groupings calculated on an unweighted arithmetic basis.

Source: Computer printouts supplied by ECA Statistics Division, with calculations by the UNIDO Secretariat.

fewer people accounted for 55.3% of all textile and clothing industries, 25.8% of metals, metal products and machinery, and 11.7% of wood and wood product (furniture) factories.[6] A 1945 survey of Kenyan manufacturing firms found the average issued capital of the MNCs to be £665,726; those of local public firms was £396,083; and those of local private firms only £97,068.[7] These essential features of African industrialisation bear directly on the shortcomings of ISI.

The distortions of ISI in Africa

The major distortions of ISI in Africa centre on its perverse priorities and resource misallocation. An important aspect of these defects relates to industrial composition with respect to the manufacturing of semi-luxury and luxury consumer goods, the chronic shortage of essential manufactured goods, and the virtual absence of the capital-good manufacturing sub-sector of heavy industries. On account of the "textile-first" approach to industrialisation, the product lines or product mix of African industries consist mainly of simple commodities such as textiles, food and beverages, footwear, cigarettes and car assembly. In 1978, for example, these consumer goods accounted for 64% of total manufacturing employment, 62% of establishments, 57% of wages and salaries, and 53% of manufacturing value-added. By contrast, the corresponding shares of capital goods in manufacturing employment establishments, wages and salaries, and value-added were 16%, 17%, 19% and 20%, respectively.[8] As a result of this poor industrial priority, manufactured imports loom large in Africa's total import bill. Thus, in Nigeria in 1978 and 1981, capital goods still accounted for 70% and 60%, respectively, of total imports, while the corresponding import shares of consumer goods for the two years were 26% and 30%, respectively. A related aspect of this product mix is that it panders to perverse imported consumption habits rather than to the basic needs of the broad masses. This is exacerbated by the gross inequality of income distribution, which exaggerates the conspicuous effective demand of the elite minority for car assembly, brewery, lace, carpet and related products, while neglecting the essential commodities required by the majority of the dispossessed population.

A closely related distortion in African industrialisation is the massive import of raw materials and spare parts. Thus, in Nigeria, the import of raw materials and fuel accounted for 24% and 25% of total imports for 1978 and 1981, respectively. The two deleterious consequences of this import dependence are the huge drain of meagre foreign exchange earnings, which contributes to the balance of payments crisis of African countries, and the low value-added of manufacturing. Yet, Africa is one of the most richly endowed regions of the world in raw materials. The paradox of enormous resource endowment and input import has arisen from the domination of African industrialisation by MNCs, which prefer to import raw materials and technology from their foreign subsidiaries and home countries.

The inappropriateness of imported industrial technology to African resource endowment is another serious distortion of ISI. The basic issue here is that because the imported technology is based on foreign factor proportions, which are more capital-abundant, Africa is saddled with capital-intensive enterprises relative to her abundant labour supply. This is illustrated in Table 6.3.

Table 6.3
Capital–labour ratios in Nigerian and Japanese manufacturing industries, 1967

Industry	*Capital–Labour Ratio* *Nigeria*	*Japan*
Food products	2:455	0:130
Beverages	3:410	—
Tobacco products	1:880	—
Textiles	1:154	0:120
Footwear & clothing	0:769	—
Wood & furniture	0:834	0:110
Paper & printing	1:042	0:121
Leather products	0:571	0:060
Rubber products	0:561	0:111
Chemicals, petrol, coal	1:415	0:400
Non-metal mineral product	3:144	0:140
Metals	1:068	0:510
Machinery	0:537	0:160
Transport equipment	0:925	0:131
Miscellaneous products	0:991	—

Sources: Federal Office of Statistics (1967) *Industrial Survey* (Lagos) and UN (1967) *Yearbook of National Accounts Statistics* (New York).

Whereas Japan has relatively more capital than Nigeria, the capital-intensity in Nigeria was higher than in Japan; and it is still likely to be higher, given the basically unchanged manufacturing technology in Nigeria. The implications of this inappropriate industrial technology include the exaggerated demand for capital, especially imperialist capital with its associated high costs, the undue dependence on imported technology and the relative underutilisation of African resources, especially labour and raw materials.

These issues are directly connected with the foreign domination of African industrialisation and its orientation towards imperialist standards.[9] ISI particularly encourages multinational domination as the establishment of "tariff factories" to prevent the shutting out of imperialist products clearly demonstrates in Chapter 4. This has been a central source of many distortions in African industrialisation, like its distorted priorities, import dependence, inappropriate technology and related problems. This large role of foreign capital in African industries accounts for the enormous repatriation of industrial profits, the slow expansion of industrialisation and the prostrate technological dependence of Africa, like the rest of the Third World.

Then, on account of the relatively capital-intensive technology of ISI and its high import content, African industrialisation is associated with growing unemployment. This is particularly acute among young school leavers in urban areas. As industrial profits are repatriated rather than reinvested, the industrial sector, which is the fastest growing sector and should absorb young school leavers, is unable to expand and offer adequate employment opportunities. This is exacerbated by the increasing proletarianisation of the peasantry. The concentration of industries in urban areas and the rapid urbanisation this encourages also accentuates this growing unemployment. The stagnation, or even collapse, of the rural economy in African countries is a partial consequence of these developments. The deterioration of the rural economy forces more people to migrate to urban centres in search of what are simply inadequate jobs.

For these reasons, ISI has been regarded as crypto-industrialisation, as its implied backward linkage to intermediate and heavy industries is technically feasible, but confronts major barriers such as the small size of many African countries. This allows MNCs to exploit the raw materials, labour and markets of less developed countries (LDCs) with *minimum technological transfer and maximum dependence on imported inputs*. Import substitution industrialisation thus reverses the historical industrialisation experiences of small ICCs such as Britain, Belgium, Italy and so on.[10] It produces an industrial structure with extremely feeble internal links, low value-added, limited employment and income potential, relative to the enormous problems of underdevelopment, and little or no rational continuity with the future phases of industrialisation.

Equally serious is the effect of ISI on the increasing structural inequalities in Africa, as discussed in Chapter 5. This is manifested in differentials between urban and rural development, as most industries concentrate in urban areas, in wage differentials, the emergence of the "labour aristocracy" and in class differentiation. Industrialisation has been driving a wedge between urban and rural wages and incomes, and between industrial and other sectoral remunerations. Thus, while agriculture stagnates or declines and manufacturing grows, the inter-sectoral income differentials between the two sectors have widened. Similarly, a relatively better-paid stratum of workers, especially in the MNCs and urban centres, have emerged to constitute the labour aristocracy within the African working class. In the same direction, industrialisation with the indigenisation of African economies has operated to reinforce the emergence of the African *petit-bourgeoisie* with an increasing industrial fraction, especially in Nigeria, Kenya and elsewhere.

Differences between industrialisation in Africa and the advanced countries

There are important differences between the industrialisation of the advanced countries, both capitalist and socialist, and the industrialisation of Africa.[11] In the industrialised capitalist countries (ICCs), the agrarian revolution preceded the industrial revolution so that agriculture was able to produce raw materials for agro-allied industries such as textiles, footwear and so on; cheap food for the industrial proletariat; and foreign exchange for the cheap import of additional raw materials and food, especially through the exploitation of the colonies. But in Africa, industrial take-off has been preceding any major breakthrough in agriculture and, as Africa has no colonies to exploit, this has been contributing to industrial bottlenecks with respect to agricultural raw materials, the development of agro-allied industries and food supply. Similarly, while the ICCs relied essentially on the textile-first strategy and local raw materials for their initial industrialisation before the colonial scramble of the 19th century (except the earlier colonisation, plunder and the decolonisation of Latin America up to the early 19th century) Africa started industrialisation with textiles first, but through the MNCs and with heavy dependence on imported inputs. Even when the ICCs started importing raw materials and food, this was mostly from the colonies and ex-colonies, by expropriation and at exploitatively low prices; methods no longer open to Africa for her industrialisation. Furthermore, a large part of the products of industrialisation in ICCs have always been for export, especially for dumping in the lucrative monopolised markets of the colonies and neocolonies. This export thrust was why Britain became "the workshop of the world" during her early Industrial Revolution, and why there have been two imperialist world wars over the division and redivision of access to foreign resources and markets. Unfortunately, African industries have been facing the viciously protectionist markets of the ICCs and the competitive markets of other Third World countries dominated by multinational products.

In addition, there are also differences and minor similarities between the industrialisation of the socialist countries and Africa. Both are similar with respect to their initial status as liberated territories from outright colonial rule or from imperialist domination, so that both were relatively backward compared to the ICCs at the start of their industrialisation. The differences centre on the deliberate capital-good dominance of manufacturing, symbolised by Stalin's "technological phase-skipping" (meaning skipping the lower phase of simple consumer-good manufacturing technology and starting with heavy industries in order to catch up quickly with the imperialist countries) in the USSR during the industrialisation debate between Stalin and Trotsky.[12] But in Africa, the ICCs' "textile-first" strategy prevails, despite the manifest urgency of industrialisation and development. Similarly, the socialist countries started industrialisation with militant national self-reliance, using local raw materials, indigenous technology and producing for the basic needs of the majority of their population. This robust self-reliance was what earned them the metaphor of "iron curtain" countries from the imperialists, whose exploitative monopoly capital, raw materials, technology and manufactured products were firmly shut out. By contrast, African industrialisation is rife with grovelling external dependence; Japan imported technology for early industrialisation, but soon adapted and quickly internalised it, while Africa seems doomed to continuous import.

Whereas in both advanced capitalist and socialist countries, industrial production and indigenous technological development were organically linked, though separated during the second industrial revolution when science and applied research became predominant, the reverse applies in Africa.[13] The inventions of the Industrial Revolution such as Kay's spinning shuttle improved by Hargreaves, Arkwright and Crompton, Tenny's mule and Watt's steam engine perfected by Newcomen, for example, were the creations of direct industrial and indigenous producers, rather than the moribund imports of some ubiquitous MNCs as in

Africa. This "learning by doing" which, through lack of control over direct production processes, foreign domination of industrialisation has denied Africa, is one major reason why African countries not only import the wrong technology, but are unable to modify, adapt and internalise foreign technology.

As a result, Africa is neither implementing the capitalist, the socialist nor a systematic African model of industrialisation. The resulting hotch-potch strategy has succeeded only too well in imposing avoidable structural distortions and retarding the pace of industrialisation and technological development.

Industry and agriculture in Africa

The interrelationship between industrialisation and agriculture typically involves three major dimensions.[14] These are the intersectoral flows of resources from agriculture to industry, from industry to agriculture, and the rate of exchange between agricultural and industrial products. The four major resource-flows from agriculture to industry are raw materials, food, export earnings and labour force. For these reasons, in the industrialised countries, the agrarian revolution preceded or coincided with the industrial revolution. In this way, agriculture was able to provide adequate raw materials for industry, especially for the development of agro-allied industries. This is part of the logic of the textile-first approach to industrialisation[15] in which agriculture provides the raw cotton and wool for textile manufacturing, and produces other inputs for such related manufacturing activities as leather works, fruit-canning, rubber products, brewery, beverages, tobacco, and so on. But in Africa, the distortion of the industrialisation process imposes the burden of importing basic raw materials for industry, and this has led to the closure of several factories owing to the shortage of foreign exchange to import inputs. The agrarian crisis in many African countries has also forced many agro-allied industries to fold-up due to inadequate supplies of their agricultural raw materials, for example, cotton, vegetable oil, rubber, etc.

The supply of food for the industrial labour force is also a basic agro-industrial linkage, as the availability of cheap food helps to keep down the cost of living, keep wages low, ensure moderate industrial labour costs and thus adequate profit to induce a high level of investment in industry. This was the basic issue behind the protracted struggle over the Corn Laws in England (whose repeal was sponsored by British industrialists in order to ensure cheap food import and low labour costs, even though the food import hurt the agricultural bourgeoisie). Unfortunately, Africa's agrarian crisis has resulted in a serious food scarcity that requires increasing and debilitating food import, thus raising labour costs and reducing investible resources for industry.

Similarly, agricultural exports, especially in primary producing countries, earn the essential foreign exchange for importing the capital goods, technology, and other inputs for industrialisation. Hence Third World countries' severe export fluctuations due to falling export demand and poor terms of trade which greatly constrain their industrialisation. This is particularly severe because of the perverse monocultural dependence of many of these countries on one or two export crops, for example, cocoa in Nigeria before 1967, coffee in Ethiopia, tea in Kenya. In addition, the development of agriculture, especially through its mechanisation and rising productivity, should release labour for industrial production. This proletarianisation of the peasantry was achieved through the enslavement of African peoples, and the expropriation of the European peasantry via the enclosure movement,[16] under which large tracts of land were expropriated from the peasantry for capitalist agriculture, forcing the dispossessed peasants into wage slavery. In Africa, this proletarianisation of the peasantry was started by the colonial regimes, through forcible land expropriation, taxation to be paid in money in largely rural barter economies and forced labour.[17] Under contemporary neocolonialism, this transfer of rural agricultural labour to industrial employment involves the collapse of the rural economy, through neglect and peasant repression, and the expropriation of rural land by urban land speculators. These are the "telephone farmers" in Kenya, retired public functionaries such as generals and permanent secretaries turned capitalist farmers in Nigeria who are developing incipient latifundia through a bogus Land Use Act (first passed as the Land Use Decree in 1978).

The failure of African industrialisation so far has ensured the meagre transfer of resources from industry to agriculture in the forms of agricultural machinery and equipment, insecticides and manufactured consumer goods. Thus, in the dialectics of the deepening crisis in Africa, both industrial and agrarian failures have been mutually reinforcing. Yet, in the industrialised countries, the organic link between industry and agriculture has always been emphasised by the massive injection of industrial capital as well as intermediate and consumer goods into the generation or consolidation of their agrarian transformation. In Africa, the structural distortions of industrialisation impose the additional burden of importing these capital goods, insecticides and manufactured consumer goods for the agricultural sector.

Finally, the structural link between industry and agriculture involves the terms of trade or rate of exchange between the products of the two sectors. In the industrialised countries, just as agricultural products were made relatively cheap to stimulate industrialisation, industrial commodities were also mass-produced, and agricultural prices were even supported (the US still maintains a massive agricultural support programme) to encourage agriculture. But most African countries have been unable to streamline or rationalise the terms of trade between their industrial and agrarian sectors. Evidence of this is apparent in the very low agricultural prices, especially those paid by the Marketing Boards,[18] and the lack of protection of domestic agricultural prices against the vagaries of the international market. The consequence has been the unfavourable terms of trade facing the agricultural sector, due partly to the soaring prices of industrial products induced largely by the inflationary mark-up pricing of the MNCs. This is one important source of the agricultural sector's inability to offer more credible support for African industrialisation, partly through the depression of agricultural incomes, which inhibits the demand for industrial products and restricts the growth of industries as "the division of labour is limited by the extent of the market".

Import substitution and the myth of technology transfer

One major aspect of the official and popular appeal of industrialisation is the development of technology and its associated skilled labour. As industrialisation was initiated by foreign capital which embodies advanced technology, the reliance on the MNCs for ISI has also involved a parallel reliance on the "transfer of technology" to Third World countries. The assumed desirability of this strategy of technological development has led to the exertion of energies to reduce the high cost of technology transfer and to accelerate its pace.

But the idea of technology transfer from the ICCs to the Third World is a myth.[19] Conceptually, technology may be imported, adapted and *reproduced locally*, but it cannot be "transferred" in isolation because it is bound up with concrete production processes and bears definite relations of production. Thus, no technology is transferred when oil MNCs employ local labour to pump oil, even with the use of the most sophisticated drilling rigs. Similarly car assembly plants involve no transfer of technology when the highest task assigned to local labour is riveting, and ITT transfers no technology when it employs African workers to dig holes and fill them in. Moreover, much of the technology being transferred to Africa and throughout the Third World from the ICCs is inappropriate, capital-intensive, wasteful in resource utilisation, bears capitalist relations of production and is supportive of foreign consumption patterns. These are clearly undesirable technological attributes for Africa.

Moreover, the tight monopoly domination and restriction of technology by MNCs under the industrial property system of patents, trade-marks, licensing, and so on, impose definite limits on technology transfer. This is why these MNCs conduct their research and development (R & D) activities in their home countries and insist on an expatriate quota for monopolising even the limited technology they import into the Third World. These are the major sources of the imperialist exploitation of "technology rent" through the over-pricing of restricted technology, and the transfer of much of the surplus value that the Third World generates through whatever productivity gains are realised.

Technology transfer also serves to consolidate imperialism's domination of poor countries through the underlying capitalist relations of production built into its technology, thus closely integrating Africa and other poor regions into its exploitative world orbit. This is achieved both through external dependence for technology transfer and the hierarchical organisation of work (for example, between installation and execution) built into capitalist technology.

For these reasons, technology transfer also denies self-reliance and autonomous development to the Third World. The issue here is that while in the 19th century, Japan, France, Germany, for example, imported technology from Britain and quickly reproduced it for their national production, currently the transfer of technology is mainly by MNCs and not internalised by the importing countries. This is due both to the qualitative change in imperialism, which has turned technology itself into a commodity and an object of monopoly, and to the naive illusion that technology can be mechanically transferred between countries. In reality, however, technology transfer involves only a geographical shift in that the technology is installed for production, without altering the international distribution of technological capabilities between the ICCs and the Third World.

Finally, in the "age of ideology", cold-war, inter-imperialist rivalry and the growing intensity of national liberation struggles, the ideological role of technology renders any faith in its mechanical international transfer a costly myth. Technology is now a powerful instrument of ideological domination both by imperialism and local ruling classes in the periphery. As Marx stated, those who control the means of material production also control the means of mental production. This is particularly true vis-à-vis the separation of technology from production, and the forging of a new link between science education and technology, which makes technology an object of labour specialisation. Technology is also used increasingly as a means of spreading capitalist relations of production and, hence, for exploitation. For these reasons, the imperialists have also been mystifying technology as something beyond the capability of people in poor countries, in a clearly racist manner. This is why some have dubbed technology as "a new white magic for the Third World".[20]

The real alternative technological strategy for Africa and the Third World in general is the development of indigenous technology. The canvassing of so-called *intermediate technology* is another technological illusion. It is unrealistic to suggest that poor countries should revert to the industrialised countries' 19th-century technology. That technology was specific to the resource endowment, production structure and related social configurations of those countries at that time, and today in Africa and elsewhere these factors differ. Why, at the close of the 20th century, should an oil-producing African country impose upon itself the excess baggage of a coal-intensive steam engine in pursuit of a bogus intermediate technology? Similarly, the present production structure in Africa and other poor regions is radically different from that of 19th century Europe. The linear conception of history implied by this return to intermediate technology is equally false – history proceeds in a zig-zag manner with leaps and setbacks.

The development of indigenous technology must, however, explicitly recognise the *political* determinant of technological change, through the effective control of national resources and production. Thus, 19th century technology was developed by direct producers such as Arkwright, Watt, Bessemer, for example, partly because they controlled their own production processes. African countries must, therefore, regain effective control over the use of their national resources and their production processes in different sectors in order to develop their own technology. In the process, international standards and restrictive practices involving patents, trade-marks, and so on, should be discarded, while *traditional artisan technology* should systematically supplement modern technology, and foreign technology should be carefully screened before being imported, modified, adapted and reproduced locally.

False start in industrial export promotion

Another false strategy of industrialisation in Africa is the emphasis on export-led industrialisation, especially by the World Bank.[21] The basic arguments for this are the limited internal markets of most African countries, the need to encourage intra-African trade and cooperation, and the desirability of collective ISI and collective self-reliance, which requires the establishment of regional and sub-regional industries exporting their products to neighbouring countries. It is also considered that the relatively low quality of African manufactured products can be improved by subjecting their producers to the high standards of international competition through exporting such products.

Against these arguments is the fact of World Bank pressure for export-led industrialisation in the Third World. This is allegedly the major way of enlarging the small internal markets for industrial products and sustaining more industries. Export-led industrialisation is also supposed to generate additional foreign exchange to supplement the meagre foreign earnings of these countries and improve their balance of payments. But this argument ignores the fact that current industrialisation has not tapped much of the potential internal market for industrial products, due to the elitist orientation of these industries producing luxury and semi-luxury goods. Evidence of this is, for example, the chronic acute shortage of essential products such as milk, sugar, cement, and so on which are still imported massively into these countries. A more equitable redistribution of income and the revival of these countries' rural economies will also expand their internal markets for industrial products.

The need for increased foreign exchange earnings from industrial exports is also incorrectly premissed on sustaining (and even increasing) the current excessively large foreign sector of these countries, and maintaining their huge import bills. Yet, these are the major sources of their chronic externally induced economic fluctuations, exploitation through unequal exchange, balance of payments crises and dependence. Additionally, if this outward-looking or dependent strategy of development has resulted in the current deepening crisis engulfing Africa, it is irrational and untenable to insist on the intensification of this futile approach as a solution to the decadence of these countries.

Moreover, this emphasis on export promotion perpetuates one of the basic distortions of African economies in terms of the asymmetrical relationship between production and consumption patterns. Africa already produces too much of what she does not consume, and consumes too much of what she does not produce. Export-oriented industrialisation will only exacerbate this perversion to the neglect of the basic needs of the majority of African peoples. The increased external dependence implied by export-led industries will only compound the external problems of these countries.

Export promoters in the World Bank and elsewhere tend to ignore the point that given the ICCs' increasing protectionist posture, the low international competitiveness of African industries, partly due to their relative infancy, and low intra-African trade due to the similarity of production patterns, export-led industrialisation's upper reaches are very limited and it erects strict barriers. For example, neither various rounds of UNCTAD, North–South dialogue, demands for a new international economic order (NIEO), the Lomé Convention for granting EEC trade preferences to African countries, and so on, have made any significant progress in expanding the export market for the less-developed countries' (LDCs) manufactured and other products. The implication is that the World Bank and other export promoters, like the "import substituters" before them, are leading

Africa along another blind alley to another dead end. This is not to deny that some Latin American and South-East Asian countries, for example, Brazil, Argentina and Hong Kong, now export sizeable industrial products, but these are mainly to the poorer Third World countries, especially in Africa. When these poorer countries industrialise and are expected primarily to export to each other, or to the so-called newly industrialised countries (NICs), or the ICCs, this will be wishful thinking. Poland was said to have been induced to borrow heavily from imperialist sources for export industrialisation but when its manufactures rolled from the factories, the imperialist countries shut their doors to them and this has been one major source of the Polish crisis of the 1980s.

Quantitatively, the manufactured exports of all African countries during 1965/73 was merely 4.5% of world total, with 0.5% for 1973/80 and 0.9% for 1980/85.[22] The structure of industrial exports within ECOWAS in recent years is depicted in Table 6.4.

Table 6.4
Percentage structure of manufactured exports in ECOWAS; 1975

Country	*Beverages & tobacco*	*Chemicals*	*Manufactured goods*	*Machinery & equipment*	*Mixed manufactures*
Benin	1.4%	0.3%	3.2%	2.1%	0.7%
Cape Verde	7.6	—	6.0	1.4	0.5
Gambia	—	—	—	—	—
Ghana	0.0	0.1	8.7	2.1	0.1
Guinea	—	—	—	—	—
Guinea Bissau	—	—	—	—	—
Ivory Coast	0.0	0.6	2.6	0.6	0.3
Liberia	0.0	0.5	0.5	0.4	0.2
Mali	0.6	1.0	5.6	0.7	1.0
Mauritania	0.0	0.0	0.5	4.0	0.1
Niger	0.6	0.0	0.5	0.7	0.3
Nigeria	0.0	0.0	0.6	0.1	0.0
Senegal	1.5	2.0	5.0	2.5	3.0
Sierra Leone	—	—	61.1	—	—
Togo	0.0	0.1	2.0	1.5	1.1
Upper Volta	0.5	0.3	5.0	1.0	2.0

Source: V. P. Diejomaoh and M. H. Eyoha (eds.) (1980), pp. 42–3.

Table 6.5 indicates the manufactured exports of Ghana, Morocco and Egypt to the ICCs during 1962/70.

The very low levels of these manufactured exports within ECOWAS and elsewhere, and their slow growth rate do not offer a firm basis for an export-led industrialisation strategy for Africa.

The World Bank's pressure for export-oriented industrialisation in Africa and throughout the Third World is thus misplaced. The primary orientation of the

Table 6.5
Some manufactured exports of Africa

	Export Value ($ million) 1962	1971	*Annual average % increase* 1962/70
Ghana	32.2	102.1	16.8
Morocco	65.6	100.6	4.2
Egypt	26.3	34.0	3.0

Source: UN (1974) *Trade in Manufactures of Developing Countries and Territories, 1972 Review* (New York).

industrialisation of these countries should be the satisfaction of the basic needs of the majority of their population. This is especially necessary on account of the acute shortage of most manufactured products in these countries. Besides satisfying their domestic requirements, their industrialisation strategy should aim at export markets in two thrusts – one through collective ISI and collective self-reliance on a regional and sub-regional basis; the other through the export of residual manufactures.

Alternative strategies of industrialisation in Africa

The central focus of alternative strategies of industrialisation in Africa should be the *resource-demand model* based on available resources and the demand for basic needs, and the Soviet industrialisation model based on the manufacture of capital goods.[23] In the Soviet model, the limitation of feasible capital-good output in small African countries can be removed through collective self-reliance based on regional and sub-regional cooperation, as envisaged in the *Lagos Plan of Action*. The dominant features of the combination of these two models of industrialisation (resource-demand and Soviet) are the critical roles of basic needs, national resource endowment, domestic technological development, the linkages and growth elasticities of different industries, capital goods, the elimination of imperialist domination of industrialisation and the full exploitation of agricultural linkages.

Needs, resources, technology and growth elasticities

First, the industrialisation process should start with the investigation of the structure of the basic needs or mass demand of the majority of the population with respect to food, clothing, housing, health care and so on. The major resource contents or implications of these mass basic needs should be ascertained. Then the scope for adjusting the mass needs and the existing consumption profile to the resource endowment of the individual countries should be determined. These explorations are warranted by the "iron laws of transformation": (a) the necessity of planning the convergence of consumption patterns with broad basic needs; (b) the requirement for the planned convergence of consumption patterns with the domestic output of goods and services; (c) the necessity of planning domestic production to converge on domestic resources.

These requirements derive from the fact that historically, there is a long-term tendency for the global and national income elasticities of demand for imports to exceed those of domestic products. This implies that income changes and their distribution produce demand changes which reinforce the divergence between domestic resource use and the domestic demand profile – and ISI has worsened this. Hence it is necessary to *identify the industrial products that constitute the backbone of modern industrial consumption*. Such industries constitute the empirical range of strategic linkages and the core of an effective and consistent industrialisation programme. They include iron/steel and textiles as the core – others are paper, plastics, rubber, glass, leather, cement, wood, fuel, drugs, aluminium and industrial chemicals (alkalis, chlorine and sulphuric acid) with energy, construction and housing. The input–output matrices of the industrialised countries reveal that the bulk of industrial value-added are derived from these industries which embody most of the raw material contents of industrial products. They also tend to have relatively higher growth elasticities and linkages (forward and backward) than most other industries. Hence, if these industrial products are not manufactured locally, their organic linkages and accelerator effects will lie abroad in the countries from which they are imported. Thus the growth of domestic demand will transfer the bulk of industrial value-added abroad and retard domestic industrialisation, as it has so far done in Africa.

Schematically, the above needs-resource linkages are indicated in Figure 6.1.[24]

Figure 6.1
Needs-resource linkages

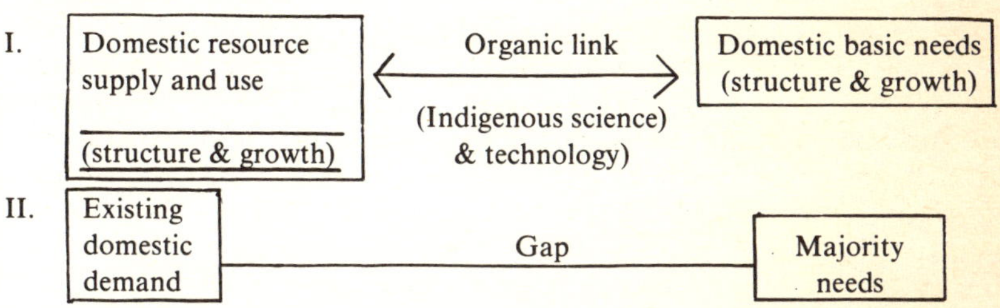

Panel II of Figure 6.1 shows the gap between the existing perverse demand and the majority needs which should be closed through consumption restructuring. Panel I depicts the organic link between broad needs and resource use. The structural link is the indigenous technological matrix which requires science and research to build. Panel I highlights the inherent identification of technology with a specific configuration of resource availability and use, on the one hand, and the demands on them arising from the basic needs of the majority of the population on the other. By implication, an effective programme of indigenous technological development cannot be based on transfer from abroad, but on local *control* of resources, production processes and consumption profile – hence the political issue in technological development.

Priority to capital goods and collective self-reliance

Given the virtual absence of capital-good manufacturing in African and other poor countries, as well as its pivotal role as a development catalyst, as the Soviet industrialisation model demonstrates, African industrialisation must accord high priority to heavy industries. The limited internal capacity and market for capital-good output, due to the meagre capital and technological resources and market, of many small African countries, demand a collective strategy anchored to the collective self-reliance at regional and sub-regional levels canvassed in the *Lagos Plan.*[25] Groups of contiguous African countries should pool their investment, technical, mineral and other resources, to establish joint heavy industries such as machine tool, rollers and boilers, petro-chemical, transport and construction equipment, and so on. This should solve the resource bottle-neck that constrains capital-good industrialisation.

Figure 6.2
Comparative growth rates of capital and consumer goods

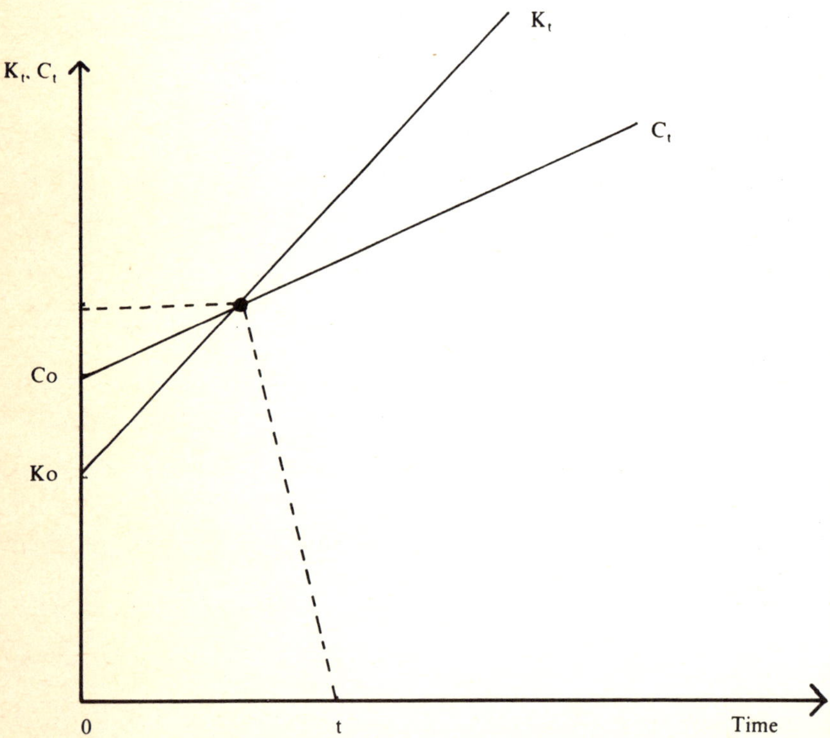

Note: K_t, C_t are the time paths of capital and consumer goods, repectively; Ko and Co are their initial levels at the initial period, t=o.

It remains to demonstrate the theoretical and empirical superiority of this capital-good strategy over consumer-good manufacturing;[26] see Figure 6.2.

Figure 6.2 illustrates that although consumer goods have an initial headstart at Co over capital goods at Ko, and consumer goods have a higher growth rate initially (up to time t), capital goods eventually generate a higher rate of growth after both sub-sectors of industry equalise their growth rates at time t. This is because capital goods build a compound growth-factor into the development process, and empirically have a higher growth elasticity than do consumer goods.[27]

These alternative strategies of industrialisation also emphasise the reduction of the role of foreign capital through the MNCs. If individual African countries cannot challenge them effectively, groups of countries in regional and sub-regional cooperation can. There are two interrelated issues here. One is to reduce the proportionate share of MNCs in the industrial stake of each country by increasing

Table 6.6
Inter-sectoral linkages in the Nigerian economy, 1973 (%)

Production Sector/Industry	*Backward linkage*	*Forward linkage*
Agriculture	7.0	17.1
Livestock	1.1	85.2
Forestry	1.0	54.2
Fishing	5.4	0.3
Oil mining	3.9	4.9
Other mining and quarrying	33.3	99.8
Food, drinks, beverages & tobacco	49.0	13.0
Textiles, wearing apparel and leather products	67.0	14.5
Wood and wood products	53.0	95.5
Paper and paper products, printing and publishing	53.5	75.2
Drugs and chemicals	30.9	32.7
Rubber and plastic products	41.1	61.7
Basic metal products	57.5	55.1
Fabricated metal products, machinery & equipment	19.8	3.7
Other manufactured products	34.1	15.0
Electricity and water	34.1	77.6
Building and construction	38.1	5.1
Transport	28.6	79.2
Communication	33.4	77.8
Distribution trade	13.9	15.8
Finance and insurance	15.9	35.8
Producer of government services	—	—
Hotel and catering	37.2	4.7
Professional, business and others	32.0	90.7
Housing	12.5	9.3

Source: Calculated from National Accounts of Nigeria, 1973–75 Lagos, p. 133.

the national share, either private indigenous or state, or both. The other is to terminate the distorted and exploitative activities of these imperialist multinationals through their outright socialisation: nationalisation with workers' control.

In these different ways, it should be easy to take full advantage of the intersectoral linkages between industry and agriculture. The almost empty cells of the input–output coefficients between these sectors can be filled by utilising more local agricultural raw materials, food and labour in the industrial process. The elimination of prostrate dependence on imported raw materials imposed by the MNCs is a major requirement here. Another is the vigorous revival of the agricultural sector in order to generate enough surplus, beyond its own sectoral requirements, to advance industrialisation. Restructuring the industrial sector should also enable it to produce capital, intermediate and consumer goods to accelerate Africa's agrarian revolution. In these ways, both industry and agriculture will be progressively linked organically and their transformation become mutually reinforcing.

Notes

1. Albert Hirschman (1958).
2. See D. L. Cohen and J. Daniel (eds.) (1981), ch. 1.
3. The main features of African industrialisation are analysed in J. F. Rweyemamu (ed.) (1980); and F. Yachir (ed.) (1981).
4. World Bank, *World Development Report, 1984* (Washington).
5. V. P. Diejomaoh and M. A. Iyoha (eds.) (1980), p. 39.
6. F. Yachir (ed.) (1981), p. 146.
7. R. Kaplinsky (ed.) (1978), p. 52.
8. UNIDO Secretariat.
9. The foreign domination of manufacturing in Africa is an integral element of the internationalisation of capital and production. See H. S. Marcussen and J. E. Torp (1982), chs.1, 6 & 7.
10. See S . Clarkson (1979).
11. On differences between African and earlier industrialisation patterns, see S. Amin (1974), 2 vols., chs. 1 & 4.
12. S. Clarkson (1979), ch. 2.
13. On this technological issue, see S. Amin (1977), chs. 9 & 10.
14. The relationship between industry and agriculture centres on the crucial question of proportionality in development planning. See S. Clarkson (1979), ch. 5.
15. This textile-first approach is the priority concern in the bogus strategy of development by import substitution favoured by A. Hirschman (1958).
16. The enclosure movement was the massive acquisition and fencing of arable land in England for the agrarian revolution around 1700/50. See T. K. Derry and T. L. Jarman (1956).
17. A. T. Nzula et al. (1979).
18. G. K. Helleiner (1964), in *Economic Journal*, vol. 74, no. 295, September.
19. See S. Amin (1977), ch. 10 and in *Africa Development*, vol. 2, no. 22, 1977.
20. N. Girvan (1977) in *Africa Development*, vol. 2, no. 2, pp. 5–7.

21. World Bank (1984) chs. 4 & 5.
22. World Bank, *World Development Report, 1986* (Washington).
23. See S. Clarkson (1979), chs. 3, 5 & 7.
24. See Clive Thomas, in C. Widstrand (ed.) (1975).
25. OAU (1981) *The Lagos Plan of Action for the Economic Development of Africa, 1980–2000* (Addis Ababa).
26. E. Domar, in A. Nove and D. M. Nuti (1972).
27. K. N. Raj, in C. H. Feinstein (ed.) (1967).

7 The Agrarian Crisis in Africa

The agrarian crisis is, perhaps, the most visible aspect of the African crisis; it is certainly the deepest and the most widely discussed. This is particularly so with respect to the deteriorating food crisis, shortage of raw materials, dwindling agricultural export earnings and the virtual collapse of the rural economy. The desperate agricultural paralysis is, however, not just a material problem of growing inadequacy of agrarian supplies, but also a profound tragedy compounded by such natural disasters as drought and desertification. The tragic human core of the crisis centres round the intensification of problems such as starvation, malnutrition, infant mortality, increasing refugees, and landlessness.

The duality of this *material and human crisis* that defines the tenor of Africa's agrarian decay imposes a basic responsibility to analyse and comprehend the situation in its bipolarity. Indeed, it will be argued later that one basic source of the persistent agricultural failure in Africa has been misplaced obsession with the physical/technical aspects of the crisis, to the virtual neglect of its basic human dimension. This agrarian materialism is personified by the envisaged agricultural development in terms of green revolution – an essentially vegetative preoccupation. Yet, even the material crisis in African agriculture is impossible to comprehend adequately without situating it in its fundamental human context. From this perspective, even the food crisis becomes more than a mere quantitative trauma.

The food crisis in Africa

Africa's food crisis is the most dramatic element of the agrarian crisis plaguing the continent. It relates both to absolute and relative shortages of food supplies at prices affordable to the majority of the African population and their governments. The crisis affects the staple foods, mainly involving cereals such as maize, millet and sorghum, as well as rice, (soya) beans, wheat and barley, which are grown in concentrated areas, and root crops: cassava, yam, sweet potatoes and coco-yam. It is possible to identify three aspects of the crisis, namely, persistent food deficits, increasing food import and declining food production. The deficiency is reflected in the fact that in 1981 total food import required was 18 million tons but only eight million tons could be paid for at concessionary prices. Thus, the per capita food consumption in Africa in 1980 was reported to be 15% below that at the beginning of the 1970s, and 20% below per capita consumption at the start of the 1960s. In most of sub-Saharan Africa, calorie intake per capita is below minimum nutritional standards, being 90% below minimum in some 18 countries. Despite food aid and food import, about 20% of Africa's population still consume less than the minimum required for healthy growth. The number of severely hungry and malnourished Africans has also been estimated to increase from nearly 80 million or about 20% in 1972/74, to 100 million or 26% in 1984. Correspondingly, child mortality in sub-Saharan Africa, which was 50% higher than the average for developing countries in the 1950s, is currently 200% of the average.[2]

Rising food imports

These growing food deficits have been forcing increasing numbers of African countries to resort to food aid and food imports. The initial food import started in the 1960s, when food prices were low, as food aid from the huge accumulation of surplus grain in North America. This food aid encouraged reliance on external food supply and the relative neglect of agriculture, until food import became a regular feature of Africa's food economy by the 1970s. Then there was a change in world food trade, with rising commercial demand for grain imports. Thus in the 1960s, the volume of grain imports doubled while the total cost rose by only 50%. But during 1970/78, the cost of grain imports to sub-Saharan Africa increased by 100%, and many countries could not pay for their required imports. These rising food imports are depicted in Table 7.1.

Table 7.1
The growth of sub-Saharan Africa's food imports, 1961/82

Commodity	*Average annual change in volume (%)*		*Average annual value (US$ m.)*		
	1961/63 to 1969/71	*1969/71 to 1980/82*	*1961/63*	*1969/71*	*1980/82*
Rice	4.9	12.4	63	91	961
Wheat	12.9	10.9	30	81	648
Maize	8.7	14.4	12	32	381
Other cereals	8.7	0.2	9	21	58
Cereals total	*9.0*	*12.7*	*114*	*225*	*2,321*
Dairy products	7.2	—	44	109	670
Sugar	2.5	6.5	84	109	836
Meat	1.3	10.7	20	24	267
Animal & vegetable oils	10.3	14.9	20	48	465
Total for sub-Saharan Africa:	*4.3*	—	*749*	*1,137*	*6,833*
Total for oil exporters:	*1.5*	—	*151*	*207*	*2,738*
Total for others:	*5.1*	—	*598*	*930*	*4,095*

Source: World Bank (1984) *Toward Sustained Development in Sub-Saharan Africa*, p. 79.

The figures in Table 7.1 exclude food aid imports, which rose from 1.2 million metric tons in 1978 to 2.2 million metric tons in 1982.[3] The picture of increasing external dependence for food is clear, particularly since the 1970s when the average annual growth rate of volume imports has been about 10%, while the import value jumped from $1.1 bn. to $6.8 bn., with cereals accounting for one-third of the total food imports. Yet, apart from wheat, all of these imported foodstuffs are producible in Africa.

The disaggregated picture on a country basis, and the share of food imports in total imports are even more disturbing, as shown in Table 7.2. For most of the 24 countries, the value of food import increased by more than 200% between 1972 and 1979. Moreover, while the maximum share of food import in any country was 26% (Senegal) in 1972, it stood at the same 26% (Somalia) in 1979. But the minimum value of food import for all the countries – $3.2 m. in Gambia in 1972 – rose to a minimum of $12.6 m. (Chad) by 1979, while the maximum food import bill for any country, which was $179.6 m. for Nigeria in 1972 rose to a maximum of $1.3 bn. by 1979. The total cereal imports in 1982 have been estimated at 9.3 m. tons, which implies that one in five people in sub-Saharan Africa were fed on imports – and this was the equivalent of the urban population in the region.[4]

Declining food production

Africa's rising food deficits and food imports reflect not only increasing demand for food, but relatively declining food production (not just slow increase or stagnant supply). It has been reported that sub-Saharan Africa is the only region in the world where per capita food production has fallen during the past 20 years (see Table 7.1). The associated decline in total and per capita food production is shown in Table 7.2.

From Table 7.2, the growth rate of food production, which greatly outstripped the population growth rate during 1960/70, fell below population growth after 1970. This produced the negative per capita growth rates of food production (which are the differences between the growth rate of total food production and the growth rate of population) for 30 countries out of the 39 in this table. These negative per capita growth rates range from –0.2 for Nigeria during 1970/82 to –6.0 for Botswana.

The associated sluggish rise, or even decline, in the production of major crops is equally suggestive of the food crisis, see Table 7.3.

The growth rates of the output of these major crops exceed the average annual population growth rate of 2.8% for only five of the 13 crops: sorghum, wheat, palm kernels, pulses and sugar. It is even negative for three crops: coconuts, groundnuts and seed cotton.

The effects of drought have exacerbated these food production problems. In the 24 countries most severely affected by drought,[5] annual per capita cereal production was reportedly declining at an average of 2% annually since 1970. This worst drought since 1970 started in southern Africa in 1982, spread to the Sahel zone in 1983 and persisted till 1984. Food production in the worst affected countries fell by 15% between 1981 and 1983. For 1981/82, it was estimated that these countries needed 5.5 m. tons of food import annually, nearly double the normal level. The crops most severely affected are groundnuts in Senegal, coffee in Ivory

Table 7.2
Decline in total and per capita food production, 1960/82

Country	*Average annual growth rate of production volume (%)*		*Average annual growth rate of per capita production (%)*	
	1960/70	*1970/82*	*1960/70*	*1970/82*
Chad	-0.3	2.4	-2.2	0.4
Mali	1.3	2.5	-1.2	-0.2
Burkina Faso	3.2	2.1	1.2	0.4
Somalia	2.8	1.0	0.0	-1.8
Niger	2.7	4.1	-0.7	0.8
Gambia, The	4.3	-1.0	2.1	-4.1
Ethiopia	2.9	1.7	0.5	0.3
Guinea-Bissau	—	0.7	—	—
Zaire	4.3	1.3	2.3	-1.7
Malawi	4.9	2.9	2.0	-0.1
Uganda	3.4	1.7	0.4	-1.0
Rwanda	4.5	3.5	1.9	0.1
Burundi	4.6	1.6	3.2	-0.6
Tanzania	5.5	2.1	2.7	-1.3
C.A.R.	0.8	1.9	-0.8	-0.2
Benin	3.2	2.6	0.6	-0.1
Guinea	2.7	1.5	1.2	-0.5
Madagascar	2.7	1.7	0.5	-0.9
Togo	5.5	2.3	2.4	-0.3
Ghana	2.6	-0.2	0.3	-3.1
Kenya	3.6	2.0	0.4	-1.9
Sierra Leone	3.7	1.1	2.0	-0.8
Mozambique	2.3	-1.0	0.2	-5.1
Sudan	5.4	2.9	3.1	-0.3
Mauritania	2.1	1.4	-0.2	-0.9
Liberia	0.4	3.0	-2.7	-0.5
Senegal	-0.4	1.5	-2.6	-1.2
Lesotho	0.1	0.2	-1.9	-2.1
Zambia	3.5	1.8	0.9	-1.3
Zimbabwe	1.5	1.6	-2.0	-1.6
Botswana	0.9	-2.0	-1.7	-6.0
Ivory Coast	5.2	6.0	1.4	1.0
Swaziland	0.8	3.9	5.9	0.7
Mauritius	1.5	0.8	-0.7	-0.6
Nigeria	0.5	2.5	-2.0	-0.1
Cameroon	4.6	2.1	2.5	-0.9
Congo Peoples' Republic	-2.8	0.9	-5.1	-2.0
Gabon	3.3	0.7	2.9	-0.7
Angola	2.8	0.4	0.7	-0.2
Sub-Saharan Africa	2.5	1.7	0.2	-0.9

Source: World Bank (1984) *Toward Sustained Development in Sub-Saharan Africa*, p. 77.

Coast and cocoa in Ghana, where output fell by 40%, 50% and 17% respectively.

Thus in 1980, cereal production in 25 African countries totalled only about 17.7 million tons which was three million tons below the 1978 level. In addition, several countries need additional food supply of about 0.5 million tons for the increasing number of over four million refugees and displaced people.

Table 7.3
Sub-Saharan Africa's production of major crops, 1969/82

Crop	*Average annual change in volume (%)* 1969/71 to 1977/79	1977/79 to 1980/82
Cereals:		
Maize	1.3	0.8
Millet	0.4	1.6
Rice (paddy)	2.9	1.7
Sorghum	1.6	3.5
Wheat	-0.2	3.9
Total cereals	*1.3*	*1.9*
Oil & oil seeds:		
Coconuts	0.9	-0.8
Groundnuts in shell	-0.9	-3.6
Palm kernels	-0.9	3.8
Palm oil	2.2	1.3
Other crops:		
Pulses	1.1	3.8
Roots & tubers	1.8	1.7
Seed cotton	-2.5	-3.0
Sugar	2.5	4.5

Source: World Bank (1984) *Toward Sustained Development* . . ., p. 78.

Other agricultural deficiencies

The agrarian crisis in Africa is also reflected in declining export earnings, very low incomes and low internal demand, inadequate raw materials and food supply for industrialisation and the collapse of the rural economy. Most African countries rely on exports of *cash crops* such as coffee, tea, cocoa, cotton, palm products (oil and kernels), groundnuts, rubber, tobacco, sisal, sugar and timber, for most of their foreign exchange earnings and internal government revenue. The share of these agricultural exports in total exports was at least 50% in 25 countries, at least 90% in nine countries and 99% in Equatorial Guinea by 1977. Similarly 12 countries depended on only one major export crop for over 70% of their income, while over 90% of Gambia's export earnings are from groundnuts.

The agrarian crisis has been severely reducing these *agricultural exports.*

These are very depressing export trends. Whereas the average annual change in these export volumes was negative for only eight of the 20 commodities listed in Table 7.4 during 1961/71, it was positive for only three (that is, negative for 17) in 1972/82. These average annual decreases were over 5% for ten of the 17 cases and over 2% for 13 of them. The world shares of sub-Saharan Africa's exports also declined for 17 of the 20 commodities during 1971/82. The agricultural export data for seven cash crops in Table 7.5 reveal the same trend (in metric tons).

Table 7.4
Sub-Saharan Africa's export of major crops: growth and shares

Commodity	*Average annual change in volume (%)* 1961/63 to 1969/71	1969/72 to 1980/82	*Sub-Saharan Africa's share of world exports (%)* 1961/63	1969/71	1980/82
Beverages:					
Cocoa	0.2	-0.3	79.9	75.9	69.3
Coffee	3.4	-0.2	25.6	29.3	25.9
Tea	9.0	4.1	8.7	14.4	9.3
Cereals:					
Maize	-1.9	-5.1	2.5	1.4	0.4
Wheat	1.2	-16.2	0.1	0.1	0.0
Rice	0.7	-12.5	0.9	0.8	0.1
Other cereals	-6.0	13.3	4.1	1.4	2.5
Oil & oil seeds:					
G/nut oil	2.2	-6.0	53.8	57.6	27.8
G/nuts (shelled)	-6.1	-13.9	85.5	69.1	18.0
Oil seed cake & meal	5.3	-3.8	9.5	8.3	2.2
Palm kernel oil	8.9	-1.3	55.2	54.8	21.6
Palm kernels	-6.2	-9.6	90.4	82.2	75.8
Palm oil	-8.6	-5.1	55.0	16.4	3.0
Sesame seed	3.8	-6.2	68.6	75.3	40.7
Bananas	-1.7	-5.4	10.9	6.5	3.0
Cotton	5.6	-3.5	10.8	15.5	9.2
Rubber	3.0	-2.9	6.8	6.8	4.4
Sisal	-2.1	-8.7	60.7	59.7	60.4
Sugar	3.2	1.4	4.7	5.6	4.8
Tobacco	-3.1	6.6	12.1	8.2	11.8

Source: World Bank (1984) *Toward Sustained Development* . . ., pp. 80–1.

Table 7.5
Agricultural export data for seven cash crops, 1969/79

Three-year average	*Estate Production*[a]	*Peasant production*[b]	*Total crop export*
1969/72	240,003	391,771	631,774
1976/79	161,856	335,805	497,661
% change	-32.6	-14.3	-21.2

[a] Estate tea and total sisal;
[b] Cashew, cotton, tobacco, all coffee, smallholder tea, pyrethrum.

Source: Dinham & Hines (1983), p. 129.

The *terms of trade* (ratio of export prices to import prices) for these agricultural exports have also been declining along with the decline in the overall terms of trade for the continent. Thus, during 1980/82, the overall terms of trade for sub-Saharan Africa fell by –4.7%, leading to a loss of 1.2% of the GDP for the entire region. For the region's low-income countries, the decline in the terms of trade was –14.5% and the associated percentage loss in GDP was 2.4%, while the corresponding figures for the middle-income oil importers were –11.1% and 3% respectively.

Very *low and declining per capita income* and small national markets are the logical consequences of these declining agricultural outputs and prices. Thus, while in 1982 the per capita income for sub-Saharan Africa stood at barely $491, its average annual growth rate for 1960/82 was a mere 1.5%, compared with a per capita income of about $12,000 in the industrialised capitalist countries in 1982. Actual peasant incomes in Africa have been persistently much lower than these per capita figures; in fact, these per capita incomes have been declining in many African countries.

Table 7.6
Annual percentage change of per capita income in Africa, 1960/83

Country group	*1960/70*	*1970/80*	*1981*	*1982*	*1983*
Low-income countries	1.5	–0.9	–1.9	–2.5	–0.3
Middle-income oil importers	1.5	1.2	0.6	–0.7	–3.4
Middle-income oil exporters	1.1	1.6	–6.7	–4.7	–7.3
Total:	*1.3*	*0.7*	*–4.0*	*–3.3*	*–3.8*

Source: World Bank (1984), *Toward Sustained Development* . . ., p. 10.

It has been suggested that these per capita incomes will continue to fall during 1985/95. Thus, by 1995, real incomes in Africa will be so low that 65% to 80% of the population will be living below the poverty line, compared with about 60% in 1984. These low and declining incomes for the African majority also imply limited demand for industrial products and the inhibition of the domestic expansion of industrialisation. These factors combine to produce about 75% of the world's poorest countries in Africa.

Inadequate raw materials for agro-allied industries, and cheap food for the rapidly expanding labour force are additional adverse consequences of the agrarian crisis in Africa. It is true that the import-orientation of multinational-dominated industrialisation means that there is an in-built preference for imported raw materials. But even state and indigenous private agro-allied industries, such as textile, tyre, soap, sugar, paper, brewery, fruit canning and other food processing ventures, have had to resort to importing their raw materials or shut-down because of inadequate domestic supplies. This increasing import of raw materials has also been adding to the foreign exchange shortages (with dwindling export earnings) and to the balance of payments crises of many African countries. In Nigeria, for example, import of raw materials has been a major fiscal and political issue in the management of the economic crisis of the 1980s, and a cause of plant shut-downs and massive retrenchment of workers.

In addition to famine, there have been food riots and demonstrations, such as the rice riots of April 1979 in Liberia which eventually led to a coup in 1980, and the Sudanese urban food demonstrations in mid-1979 and January 1982, which contributed to the coup against fascist Nimeiry in 1985. In urban areas especially, the increasing restlessness over food has been due to prices rising above the previous artificially low levels imposed by governments in consideration of city dwellers' political power and influence. The demand for food, particularly by the urban population, which has been increasing at about 5% annually and is expected to double by the turn of the century, has led to a greater food scarcity in the face of declining production. Thus, the cost of living has risen, provoking demands for wage increases and thereby raising labour costs to industry in what is often regarded wrongly as cost–push inflation. Yet, behind this growing scarcity of food for the proletariat are two basic problems. One is the poor storage and distribution or marketing of foodstuffs, based on a long chain of exploitative, parasitic and unproductive *middlemen*, who either allow food to rot on the farms while millions starve in cities, or impose profiteering food prices on urban dwellers. The second is that while in other regions the agrarian revolution preceded the industrial revolution, thereby ensuring cheap food and raw materials, as well as low wages for industrial production, in Africa, the order has been reversed, with agriculture lagging behind and crippling industry.

In Africa, the collective consequences of these agricultural problems is the virtual collapse of the rural economy and theatened social disintegration. This parlous state of Africa's rural areas is reflected in the degrading misery that condemns millions to live below the poverty line with decimating disease and pervasive illiteracy; in constant and widespread famine, starvation and malnutrition: with very low and declining incomes, and neither water, electric light nor motorable access roads; in increasing landlessness and consequent emigration from the rural areas.

Rural genocide and the proletarianisation of the peasantry

The human tragedy[6] that constitutes the core of the agrarian crisis in Africa is most visible with respect to the decimation of rural areas and the proletarianisation of the peasantry. Several mechanisms and factors define the essence of the decimation perpetrated against Africa's rural communities. One is their physical liquidation by armed officials that frequently occurs when peasants legitimately protest against the unjust acquisition of their land by the urbanised elite. Thus, the 60,000 peasants affected by the Talata-Mafara irrigation project in Nigeria "were unable to farm, were given no compensation and finally, when they protested, the State used guns against them".[7] In 1981, there was the Bakalori episode in Nigeria when several peasants, protesting against the unjust acquisition of their land, were murdered by the police. The famines, starvation and malnutrition suffered by the rural peasantry is eloquently documented in *Seeds of Famine*,[8] based on an evaluation of the Sahel Development Programe in Senegal, Mali and Niger. One in every 200 Africans is now a refugee, and Africa, "with less than a tenth of the world's population, has more than a quarter of the world's 10 million refugees".

Rural children also bear a disproportionately high share of the cost of agrarian failure in Africa. In 1982 the infant mortality rate for 0–1-year-olds was around 89 per 1,000 and 23 per 1,000 for 1–4-year-olds in sub-Saharan Africa as a whole, and much higher for rural areas. While in 1982, in sub-Saharan Africa, infant mortality was 50% higher than elsewhere in the developing countries, it was almost double the average in 1984, and, "In Zambia's poorer northern regions, height-for-age ratios have fallen in all age categories under 15 years." Rural Africa is also rife with preventible but decimating diseases and epidemics, such as cholera, diarrhoea and other water-borne diseases, which by 1982 had reduced the life expectancy to below the African average of about 57 years. Increasing irrigation for large-scale rural agricultural projects has also stepped up the risks of contracting these diseases, while the very poor health facilities in the rural areas make them the more deadly.

With less than the average literacy rate of about 10% for sub-Saharan Africa, the rural areas are submerged in a "culture of silence" and, without electricity, of darkness. This systematic denial of social amenities is predicated on the powerlessness of the rural dwellers. Even as food producers, they receive only a fraction of the prices paid by food consumers, because rural people do not control food marketing to urban centres; while as "cash"-croppers, they exercise no power within the marketing board system that determines prices. Nor do they participate in the distribution of agricultural inputs and credit facilities. At national and regional state levels, they vote but are rarely voted for, so that they do not participate in policy making, even with respect to agriculture and other aspects of rural life that affect them directly.

In these different ways, peasants are the mute victims of hapless social oppression by the urbanised elites. They are subjected to crippling multiple taxation involving income, poll, cattle, export, development, and even water tax whether or not they have access to a treated water supply. In the grossly unequal distribution of income, wealth, power and social amenities the peasantry is last in line. Rural incomes are barely 10% of urban incomes in Africa, yet rural dwellers constitute the majority of their countries' population. It is this blatant victimisation that in 1969 provoked the *Agbekoya* revolt[10] in the former Western State of Nigeria, and similar incidents elsewhere in Africa.

A major consequence of this increasing rural victimisation is the growing proletarianisation of the African peasantry which takes two principal forms: 1) the conversion of peasants into farm labourers, often on land alienated from them by urban land speculators; and 2) seasonal or permanent rural migration to urban areas. This is reminiscent of the capitalist expropriation of the European peasantry, for example in Britain, under the enclosure movement for the agrarian revolution.

In Africa, this expropriation of the peasantry is typically involuntary and – by indirect manipulation – voluntary. Involuntary proletarianisation is usually the consequence of the drive of modern agrarian capitalism in Africa, which generally involves the establishment of a large mechanised farm and/or the construction of a large irrigation project with a dam to serve 20,000 hectares of land or more. For example, the Sahel Development Programme was designed for 26 million people over several countries; Zambia's 1981 scheme of $500 million required 18 mechanised farms, each of 20,000 hectares; Senegal's eastern Caramance scheme was designed for 30,000 hectares; while Nigeria's Green Revolution programme was to cover 76,000 hectares.[11] The plan is usually to turn the peasant owners of such large farms into hired farm labourers. Similarly for the peasant victims of large irrigation projects, whose plight is often worse as they often have to mortgage their land to small bankers, businessmen and bureaucrats, as in Talata-Mafara, Kadawa and elsewhere in Nigeria. Some of the displaced peasants who cannot get jobs as Marx's wage slaves, simply have to abandon their rural homes and head for the uncertainty of the cities,[12] where, as unskilled workers, they often become night guards, construction hands or simply unemployed – and later join the growing band of Africa's armed robbers.

In less blatant cases, rising population density, soil erosion, desertification, drought and similar ecological disasters force peasants off their land. Land hunger and soil erosion are common in south-eastern Nigeria. In these cases of natural disaster, many of the peasants migrate to other agricultural areas, where they may become share-croppers or pay some land tributes, usually in kind, to their hosts. But these circumstances frequently force some peasants off the land seasonally or permanently.

Peasants often abandon agriculture "voluntarily" due to the harsh effects of competing imports, such as imported rice and maize, for their local produce. Thus, in Ondo State and elsewhere in Nigeria and in other countries, many peasants have been ruined and forced off the land by such unimaginative food import policies. In other cases, very low agricultural prices, either enforced by government for cash crops through the produce marketing boards; imposed officially, to ensure cheap food for urban dwellers and maintain low wages, or by exploitative middlemen, make agriculture unviable and drive peasants into wage employment or into unemployment. There are also informed peasants who find the tedium of rural agriculture with back-breaking hoe and cutlass so tough – particularly as they grow older – and the level of unskilled wages relative to their low agricultural incomes so attractive, that they opt for wage employment. Such peasants may retain their small holdings, but cultivate them only part-time or seasonally, in order to meet their family food requirements.

In these different ways, agriculture has been losing much of its labour supply to wage employment through the proletarianisation of the peasantry. In addition to expanding formal education, which does not encourage a return to the land, the rural economy has been facing an increasing drain of its population and slipping inexorably into decay. The causes of these agricultural problems are bound up with the history of the development of agriculture in Africa.

The development of agriculture in Africa

Broadly speaking, four agricultural groups in Africa can be identified: peasants (the majority); small farmers or middle peasants; kulaks, or indigenous plantation-owning rural capitalists; and planters or foreign agrarian capitalists operating mainly cash crop plantations as settlers in southern and Francophone Africa.[13] The capitalist *latifundia* of Latin America and South-East Asia is rare or at most incipient in Africa; the classical feudalist is also uncommon, except in the form of tribute-paying cultivators among migrant growers and the religious-based practices in Islamic areas from the northern parts of West Africa upwards.

These different cultivators correspond essentially to different levels of development of pre-capitalist social formations (PCSFs) and to varying degrees of these PCSFs' resistance to their transformation into agrarian capitalist formations. Where the traditional or indigenous resistance was successfully overcome, we have the agrarian capitalism of the imperialist planter, the indigenous plantations of local kulaks and the Arab North African type tribute-payers. These are all fully integrated into the international capitalist system through the cultivation of export crops. But where the transformation of the indigenous social formation is incomplete, there is, nevertheless, a trend towards agrarian capitalism through integration into the world market (for cash crop growers) and into the capitalist exchange system of petty commodity production (for food growers). Both may take on the appearance of feudal forms based on religion, especially in Islamic areas, or on local custom, as in the southern parts of West and East-Central Africa. In areas with poorly developed PCSFs with indigenous tenacity, there may emerge predominantly large units of small peasant holdings with "sporadic agrarian micro-capitalism" or petty commodity production within village communities, producing mainly for family subsistence with limited surplus for exchange, as amongst most indigenous food growers. In all cases, these agrarian forms in Africa face a growing agrarian crisis arising from population pressure on the land, exploitative prices, etc.

Historically, the development of agriculture in Africa can be analysed in four phases: up to the 16th century; 1600 to 1807; 1807 to 1960; and post-independence.[14] The first era pre-dates the vigorous slave epoch, and coincided with the period of food agriculture under the indigenous communal (village) social formation. Agricultural organisation was communal with an egalitarian orientation based mainly on age and sex. The major objectives of production were food security in which self-sufficiency was pursued to the point of three-year grain storage against drought in such countries as Burkina Faso. Between 1600 and the formal moves to abolish slavery in 1807, the Euro-American slave trade involving depopulation to the extent of 30 to 100 million, disrupted the communal system and destroyed its internal cohesion and self-reliance. This era established the slave social formation which dominated the remnants of the communal mode of production. Food production remained predominant, but slave labour was used to generate more surplus for the rudiments of petty commodity foodstuffs production such as pepper, palm oil and kernels, and cash produce such as ivory, and so on, all of which was subordinated to the hunting and trading in human cargoes. This was the beginning of rural differentiation and agrarian production for exchange.

From the initial abolition of slavery in 1807 to the end of formal colonialism, cash crop farming and colonial agrarian capitalism were entrenched. First, there was a switch from slavery to other exports, such as palm oil, rubber and other raw materials, and some Africans diverted slave profits to plantation agriculture. Subsequently, the increasing demand for these raw materials from the mass-production factories of the industrial revolution in Europe, motivated European traders to challenge the African monopoly of the palm oil trade, especially in the Niger Delta[15] and elsewhere. This led to increasing demands by European traders for their home governments' intervention in Africa, through the establishment of consuls, missions and fraudulent treaties – the bridgeheads of colonisation.

The articulation of the colonial capitalist modes of production has been identified with three broad patterns: 1) the colonial economy as in West Africa; 2) the concession-owning companies in Congo and Equatorial Africa; and 3) the labour reserves in Central and Southern Africa.[16] Three types of rural localities corresponding to the labour reserves have been indicated:[17] 1) places of installed (plantation) capitalism with pre-capitalist elements as in East, Central and Southern Africa; 2) areas of kulak evolution, where indigenous African farmers use hired/migrant labour, resulting in gradations of capitalist farmers, middle farmers and farm labourers (with class contradictions between peasant strata and industrial, commercial and financial capitalists), especially in western, central and eastern Africa; 3) areas of blocked capitalist development, supplying labour-power and maintained or trapped in that status through the prevention of cash crop production as in colonial Kenya and Tanzania, the manipulation of export prices against the country and the bogus defence of African "tradition" as in apartheid bantustans. Other agrarian forms correspond to prototype agrarian feudalism, that is gradually converting landlords into capitalist farmers; and pastoral feudalism, in the emirates of West and North Africa, and the frontier zones of new agricultural cultivation similar to installed agrarian capitalism, as with Polly Hill's migrant cocoa farmers of Ghana.

These correspond broadly to three major colonial agrarian structures: 1) full capitalist development and production, especially in South Africa, Zimbabwe and other imperialist settler enclaves; 2) primitive capitalist accumulation from pre-capitalist modes for the initiation of capitalism (agrarian and commercial) by the interventionist colonial state as in eastern, western and central Africa; and 3) the persistence of village, largely subsistence, production in areas supplying labour power for capitalist industrial production, as in the remote hinterlands of most African countries.

The sub-regional patterns of these colonial agrarian modes reveal four types.[18] In West Africa, the indigenes initiated or controlled the move to commercial cash crop production, thus relatively few colonial trading and mining companies existed. The other three broad categories span East, Central and Southern Africa where there were settler plantations, concession companies and forced labour. One of the best known settler plantations was the palm oil plantation, established in the Congo in 1911 by William Hesketh Lever, the initiator of Lever Brothers, now Unilever, one of the world's biggest food businesses. Under this scheme, imperialist settlers annexed large areas for export crops, without the initial encouragement of colonial power. In Kenya, for example, Africans were even forbidden to grow cash crops in competition with the settlers. In 1926, Firestone Rubber Company signed a concession with the Liberian government for one million acres at *4 cents per acre*. In the early 1920s Brooke Bond also established its first tea plantation in Kenya. In the late 19th century, colonial powers granted concession companies sole rights over land, labour and fruits of the forest and soil over extensive areas. Equatorial territories thus suffered most, being burdened with the worst examples of concession plantations. One example was King Leopold of Belgium's concession company in the Congo Basin, yielding huge profits from rubber and ivory exports after 1895. Between the 1880s and 1908 the population of the area was halved due to the brutality of forced labour. Other concession companies controlled French and German Equatorial Africa around 1900. Chad, Gabon, Central African Republic and Congo-Brazzaville were divided among 40 such French companies with a 30-year charter. In 1898, the South Cameroons Company, with mainly Belgian capital, was conceded about 20 million acres in perpetuity, for rubber collection, without payment. The fourth category was based on coercion, involving forced labour and compulsorily cultivated crops, where Africans were forced – at times under guns – to grow agricultural supplies for Europe; this barbarous system was practised in the Portuguese colonies, German Tanganyika, French Equatorial Africa and French Sudan.

In the post-colonial era, while a few African countries have engaged in socialist restructuring of their agricultural sectors, most of them have been implementing programmes of agrarian capitalism in four main directions. One is dealing with the imperialist agricultural plantations through nationalisation, joint ventures and collaboration with modest controls. An example was Mozambique's Sena Sugar Estates, with owners in Britain and Portugal. After independence in 1974, the company began to reduce production until 1977 when 70% of its crop was unharvested because of alleged low sugar prices. This reveals the difficulty of controlling such plantation companies that have greater economic strength than their "host" governments. Under joint venture, for example, Mobutu has reportedly shown favour to the imperialist plantation companies rather than to Zairean workers and peasants, as revealed by his collaborative dealings with Unilever and the palm oil plantations. As Unilever reduced production from Zaire's independence in the 1960s, Zaire had to seek a World Bank aid package of $47.4 million for the Oil Palm Development Project, with one Unilever subsidiary and two other multinationals under generous concessions to the companies. Another joint agricultural venture is Bud Senegal between the Senegalese government and Bud Antle Inc., a large US food conglomerate, an affiliate of the House of Bud in Brussels, which grew vegetables until it failed and had to be acquired by the government in 1976 and closed down in 1979. Other countries such as Nigeria, Kenya, Ivory Coast, Liberia, Mauritius, Malawi, Swaziland, and others, simply collaborate with foreign agricultural plantations with nominal legal and financial controls.

Other post-colonial agricultural policies favour: 1) large-scale mechanised farms run by private (local and foreign) capitalists and the state; 2) traditional peasant farming; and 3) agricultural marketing cooperatives. In all three cases, typical government policies centre around technical injections, restructuring production relations and hoping to raise output under traditional peasant production. Among the technical policies are new inputs, mechanisation, use of fertilisers and a general orientation towards large farms and Green Revolution. A further policy is the deliberate change of agrarian relations, especially land tenure, aimed at replacing traditional farming with capitalist property relations in order to create a "capitalist gentry" or "yeoman class". But this counter-revolutionary strategy will diffuse the middle peasants and hasten the emergence of landlessness as does the creation of large farms. Another policy is to exhort peasants to use new inputs, credit facilities, with the agricultural bureaucracy and the foreign oil companies hawking chemicals to transform agricultural production without directly confronting feudal or traditional land tenure or property rights. All these policies are applying pressure to modify the indigenous pre-capitalist mode of production to fit new technical and institutional forms under the domination of imperialist monopoly capital that controls large capital, new inputs and machines.

The major defects of these essentially neocolonial policies are: pandering to greater external dependence; superficial populist character; excessive authoritarian control; and exploitative capitalist orientation. Dependence on imported inputs means that the drive towards agrarian capitalism will be distorted and fitful, as its import bill contributes to balance of payments crises, retrenchment, proletarianisation, increasing urban poor, and crime, which threaten the stability of the state and lead to exhortations to "go back to the land". The cooperatives involved in these post-colonial policies often produce capitalist relations (for example, hiring labour) and are instruments for controlling peasants and production as well as being veritable electoral bases. In addition, the authoritarian control is a bridge between foreign capital, technology and the peasantry. This leads to high production costs, surplus extraction by the state, especially through marketing boards and cooperatives, which inspire resentment and encourage low productivity. The farm settlement scheme is one good example of such authoritarianism. In these different ways, such agrarian policies intensify capitalist exploitation, contradictions and crisis.

Basic generating causes of the agrarian crisis

On account of the growing significance of the World Bank and the International Monetary Fund (IMF) in African crises, and especially as the World Bank is involved in many agricultural projects addressed to the agrarian crisis and has prepared three Reports on the situation,[19] it is relevant to examine the causes of the agrarian crisis as perceived by the World Bank.

Defects of the World Bank view

Basically, the Bank attributes the basic causes of the agrarian crisis in sub-Saharan Africa to inadequate incentives with respect to output prices, input costs, and so on, and inefficient systems of marketing, transport, extension and other support services. These are sub-divided into both short- and long-run constraints which ultimately are attributed to such causes as: poor climate and soils; management problems or inappropriate policies, for example, poor pricing, marketing and transportation, over-valued exchange rates, white elephant state farms reflecting too large a role for the public sector and too small for the private sector; human problems, such as over-population, inadequate education, health and institutional facilities; technical inadequacies involving poor inputs and insufficient research and development, as well as an anti-agricultural bias among foreign aid donors. Hence most of the responsibility for the agrarian catastrophe rests primarily on the national governments, and secondarily on aid donors and development theorists. The World Bank, which over the past 30 years helped to elaborate and support the development principles and projects that have generated the African disaster, in its own opinion bears no responsibility.

The World Bank's remedies for the crisis revolve around internal policy reforms to be backed by external aid.

> The internal structural problems and external constraints impeding African economic growth have been exacerbated by domestic policy inadequacies . . . trade and exchange-rate policies [which] have overprotected agriculture, held back agriculture . . . the public sector has become overextended.[20]

Hence African governments are invited to devalue their exchange rates in order to raise agricultural producer prices; import and supply new seeds, insecticides, fertilisers and tractors for agriculture, allow more aggressive capitalism; and throw their countries open to iniquitous aid donors and their multinational handmaidens. We say no!

This is a patently imperialist and neocolonial policy package of increased external dependence couched in the supposedly neutral garb of a purely technical and multilateral aid institution.

Many of these policies, such as devaluation, importation of new inputs, capitalist farms and multinational initiative, as well as aid projects, including the World Bank's own agricultural projects, have been implemented for years in various parts of Africa with disastrous consequences. The economies of Ghana and Zaire collapsed, despite massive devaluations in 1972 and 1976 (in Ghana and Zaire, respectively) and the cheap sale of state enterprises under Busia in Ghana. Capitalist farms and multimillion dollar World Bank and other aid projects have not prevented the agrarian crisis in such model neocolonial capitalist countries as Nigeria, Kenya, Ivory Coast, Senegal, and so on. Agrarian capitalism and external dependence are the heart of the African agricultural crisis, so they cannot be the solution.

More precisely, the World Bank's diagnosis and prescription are defective in that they are limited to the symptoms and superficial manifestations of the crisis instead of investigating their deeper generating causes. There are half-truths in the observed inadequacies of African agriculture, such as low prices, low technology, poor transport and marketing, illiteracy, and so forth. But what caused these deficiencies? The World Bank Reports fail to: a) offer an in-depth analysis and critique of the socio-economic systems in African countries; b) explain why capitalism revolutionised agriculture in Europe and North America but not in Africa; c) evaluate the international division of labour that imposes primary production on Africa; and d) undertake an appraisal of the Bank's own agricultural programmes in Africa.[21]

Fundamentally, underdeveloped agriculture has been preserved in Africa because, as has often been observed, it is profitable for certain powerful classes and class fractions.[22] In this regard, it is significant to note that capitalist accumulation proceeds both by: a) prior primitive accumulation of commercial or merchant and finance capital in pre-capitalist social formations (PCSFs) at the expense of petty commodity production (or of first-stage capitalism); and b) expanded reproduction through the reinvestment of capitalist surplus value. Thus imperialism, colonialism and contemporary neocolonialism have been preserving pre-capitalist and underdeveloped agriculture in Africa as a strategy of primitive accumulation by political and economic means or instances. Politically, this primitive accumulation from the PCSFs has been involving taxes, seizure of land and livestock without compensation, compulsory crop-growing, forced labour, enslavement, state loans under colonialism, and now exploitative foreign aid as well as control of trade channels. The economic means through market processes centre around unequal exchange. The exploitation of peasants and craftsmen by merchant capital, and by low organic composition of capital and cheap labour is also significant here. These are the sources of low prices, poor technology, rural powerlessness and decay in agriculture.

There have also been contradictions between colonial capitalism and PCSFs under this primitive accumulation whose long-term effects have contributed to the agrarian crisis. One conflict centred on the restriction of commodity production for sale, as with the prohibition of cash crops in colonial Kenya and Tanzania to prevent competition with settler planters and to prevent the creation of a productive alternative to involuntary labour migration into capitalist employment. The other contradiction was the colonial truncation of indigenous modes of production to the point where they were capable of only reproducing their labour-power. Colonialism thus limited the destruction of the PCSFs, because a cheap labour reserve was essential and because it promoted the exodus of semi-proletarianised labour. Thus, the change in rural production relations with respect to land ownership and the division of labour was prevented from the differentiation that would yield rapid internal proletarianisation. The same mechanism is observable in post-colonial reluctance to confront unprogressive rural production practices directly.

The distorted character of neocolonial capitalism, particularly its domination by imperialist and unproductive commercial activities, and the post-colonial state's undemocratic class structure, also contribute to agrarian crisis. The domination of the neocolonial state by the same *petit-bourgeois* class fractions (for example, compradors, capitalist bureaucrats, soldiers, capitalist farmers) that own, control or protect commercial, agrarian, and foreign monopoly capital in the economy, militates against agricultural transformation. In sub-Saharan Africa so far, the kulak and other agrarian capitalist forces are in a minority in the state structure. Hence their competitors among the other fractions of the bureaucratic bourgeoisie within the state collude with imperialists to divert national resources from agriculture into commercial, industrial and other activities. Even where the agricultural *petit-bourgeois* class fraction gains temporary control of the state and diverts large resources of inputs, credit, and so on, to the agricultural sector (as in

Nigeria since 1974), most of these resources are cornered by the new agrarian capitalist gentry of retired civilian officials and soldiers. They often dissipate these resources in corrupt and wasteful contracts for import of fertilisers, chemicals, machinery, and so on, much of which is inappropriate and ineffective. The combination of resource denial and resource misuse arising from this perverse capitalist model, and the class structure of the state, thus deny appropriate priority to the requirements of the majority of peasant producers, and perpetuate agricultural stagnation.

Furthermore, with rapid urbanisation at about 5% annually, which exceeds the overall rate of population growth and food production, the political power and influence of the urban centres have been growing rapidly. Governments (especially post-colonial) have thus had to maintain the price of food and other agricultural products artificially low. This is one source of the observed poor terms of trade facing agriculture in relation to industry, which has discouraged agricultural production. As increased food demand has been forcing up such artificially low food prices, labour restlessness over the cost of living, and even food riots, have occurred.

Post-colonial governments have been driven more desperately towards the "political need for quick results and the deceptive simplicity of a single solution". Large farms constitute one such approach. Unfortunately, these ill-conceived large mechanised projects rely on larger imports and inappropriate technology as well as creating rural landlessness. Not surprisingly, many of these large agricultural schemes and their multinational involvement, including those sponsored by the World Bank, have been grand failures.

Currency devaluation has also been a faulty response (together with technical inputs) to Africa's agrarian crisis. First, from repeated experience, devaluation does not necessarily increase producer prices in local currency because under a Third World devaluation, prices in foreign currencies are not usually maintained. Moreover, as local prices tend to adjust to import prices because of Third World countries' external dependence, the effects of an African currency devaluation, both on comparative price structures and the balance of payments, tend to cancel out. Worse still, the observed low supply elasticity of primary exports and the low elasticity of the foreign demand for them combine to transfer the possible gains from devaluation to the foreign consumers of African exports. For African oil exporters that are OPEC members, where crude oil accounts for over 80% of their exports, OPEC's fixed output quota and prices mean that currency devaluation offers no solution to the agrarian crisis in those countries.

Critique of the Green Revolution

Partly on account of World Bank prescription and the political need for quick results from a single but simple solution, bureaucrats urge governments to adopt the Green Revolution (GR)[23] of large-scale agricultural schemes. Such bureaucrats prefer to see the agrarian crisis in terms of the inadequacies of peasant production rather than in more general problems. The adoption of this strategy is also motivated by the apparent success of modern agriculture in the imperialist countries and of GR in South-East Asia. This is in addition to the strong external pressures and arguments (by the World Bank, FAO, and so on) for governments to adopt the latest technology. Foreign aid agencies such as the World Bank and USAID (US Agency for International Development) are also more willing to support large projects than less spectacular programmes that aid peasants. Moreover, agrarian multinationals or agribusiness are anxious to advise on new large schemes and supply the new inputs. Thus, before it was wound up, the FAO's Industrial Cooperative Programme (ICP) created in 1966, was being advised by more than 100 agribusiness companies; the UN Development Programme (UNDP) established the Industrial Council for Development (ICD) which assisted agribusiness with respect to supplying new seeds; and ICD's $2 billion FAO tsetse fly eradication project in parts of West, Central and Eastern Africa was similarly operated.

Basically the GR comprises two elements: 1) private large-scale farms managed by multinationals or parastatals with reduced role for government; and 2) raising the productivity of small farmers and peasants through integrated Agricultural Development Projects (ADPs) for improving rural infrastructure. Both imply an attempt at increased agricultural production *without* changing production structures and organisation. In Nigeria, for example, the GR is an omnibus strategy that succeeded the 1976/78 Operation Feed the Nation (OFN, which was cynically dubbed Operation Fool the Nation on account of its colossal cost and failure). The GR thus embraces integrated rural development; integrated ADPs; large-scale river basin development authorities (about eight); a national accelerated food production programme (NAFPP); an agricultural credit guarantee scheme; Nigeria Agricultural Cooperative Bank; joint-venture agricultural enterprises; food-for-all programme; a back-to-the-land campaign; a tree planting campaign; and national agricultural shows and supportive transport, marketing and processing facilities with National Grain and National Root Crop Production Companies. In spite of these the agrarian crisis in Nigeria has escalated.

ADPs are financed jointly by the World Bank, and Federal and State governments by offering farm inputs (seeds, chemicals, fertilisers and machinery), credit, irrigation, extension service, training, and so forth. By 1970, in this integrated rural development programme, ₦150 million was spent on three state pioneer projects, and by 1984, there were pioneer projects in seven states. The estimated total cost for the whole national programme (net of fertiliser) by 1990 is ₦3 billion (about $3.69 billion at mid-1985 exchange rate).

But the Green Revolution strategy is caught in several contradictions. It seeks national self-reliance and agrarian self-sufficiency, yet it bypasses national human and physical capital and relies on imports. It also neglects the basic requirements of the majority peasants and small farmers. As a result, even though it serves to divert enormous resources to the agricultural sector, these do not benefit the rural majority. Its agricultural credit scheme also displays a profound lack of understanding of the peasantry, many of whom regard borrowing or indebtedness as an affront to their dignity. The demands for collateral security, feasibility study certificate of occupancy for land to be cultivated and so on are also counter-productive. The GR also betrays a myopic technical infrastructural conception of agrarian problems, and ignores such social relations as land tenure, mode of rural labour organisation and the structure of foreign exchange relations; agriculture in Nigeria and many other countries is a net loser of foreign exchange. This compounds the problem of large imports of agricultural inputs, food and raw materials.

Where it has been adopted in, for example, Brazil, India, Pakistan, and the Philippines, the GR has exacerbated structural inequalities. Rather than raising and stabilising rural incomes and living standards, the GR has differentiated them. As its focus is partisan on selected farmers, the effect of GR has tended to raise the level of absolute poverty in rural areas. The technology implied by the GR is relatively capital intensive and inappropriate for African conditions. Its intensive cultivation rather than traditional shifting cultivation makes excessive demands on the scanty nutrients of Africa's fragile soils. Its large irrigation schemes have also accelerated landlessness and proletarianisation, increased salinity, reduced aquatic life and increased the prevalence of water-borne diseases. The flow of many rivers (for example, the huge River Niger in West Africa) has also been seriously jeopardised to the detriment of inland navigation.

Green Revolution and agribusiness multinationals

A particularly disturbing aspect of Green Revolution and its model of large-scale agriculture is the increasing dependence of African countries on major agricultural multinationals, especially those engaged in producing agricultural chemicals and machinery, as well as those engaged in grain processing and importing.[24] The Big Five among these MNCs are Continental, Cargill, Louis Dreyfus, Bunge and Andre. There is a strong link between large-scale agricultural programmes, aid agencies and these MNCs. The aid agencies guarantee contract payments on large projects and eliminate the financial risk; the MNCs thus gain enormously from aid. It has been estimated that about 75% of USAID assistance funds are spent in the US in this way: "every dollar that American taxpayers pay into the World Bank generates about $10 in procurement contracts for US companies" for the supply of irrigation equipment, food processing technologies, seeds, fertilisers, chemicals, farm implements, and management contracts for technical skills and training.

In Zaire, Continental Grain, one of the Big Five agribusiness MNCs that control world grain trade became Zaire's sole importer of wheat and manufacturer of flour. Zambia's $500 million ten-year national food production programme, which started in 1981 for self-sufficiency in food by 1991, was financed largely by bilateral aid and international organisations. All the consultants are foreign personnel. Tate and Lyle did a technical study and won a contract to develop Mswebe State farm in the Central Province as a joint venture with government. French, Japanese, EEC and other foreign experts are involved in other farms. There is similar high involvement of agricultural multinationals and aid agencies in the Sahel Development Programme discussed earlier. In Nigeria, the government planned to raise foreign equity participation in agriculture from 40% to 80%, (this 1984 plan was shelved in August 1985 due to popular opposition) and various multinationals, such as Texagri, Lever Brothers, for example, are already developing large farms supposedly to meet the acute shortage of raw materials.

But agricultural multinationals, aid agencies and their large capitalist farms are quite unlikely to solve Africa's agrarian problem. These schemes are not only too expensive for African countries, but their inappropriate technologies accelerate the deterioration of social relations and of the ecology. Such projects also divert attention from the underlying problems of rural poverty, which they aggravate by creating landlessness.

The East German consultants who helped establish the Zambian state farms believe they cannot be successfully operated. René Dumont's report on: "Towards Another Development in Rural Africa", argues that the direction of post-independence agricultural policies on the continent has "accentuated rural underdevelopment, has widened the gap between urban rich and all poor people . . . it has aggravated malnutrition." An evaluation report on the giant Sahel Development Programme in *Seeds of Famine* (Frank and Chasin, 1980) stated that the Programme is not working, is over-ambitious and producing effects opposite to those intended, by increasing external dependency, worsening vulnerability to drought and famine, as well as widening social inequalities. It is "a captive to the overall negative relationships between the Western capitalist nations and the people of the Sahel."

Agricultural organisation, land relations and peasant power

Any serious and realistic strategy that will provide a lasting solution to Africa's agrarian crisis must be based on an understanding of the problem both in its human and material setting. Because the peasantry must form the bedrock of such a strategy it is necessary to appreciate both the nature of the peasantry in their diverse varieties and the forces that cripple their agricultural performance.[25] Besides agricultural multinationals, capitalist (settler) planters and "native" kulaks, there are "cash-cropping peasantry, marginal-subsistence peasantry and labour-exporting peasantry" in Africa's agrarian scene; but the peasantry constitute the vast majority of about 70% of all agricultural producers. Agrarian transformation programmes must, therefore, revolve round them.

The transformation of African agriculture against this background must address five basic issues:[26] 1) peasant power; 2) state structure; 3) agricultural reorganisation; 4) land relations; and 5) technical change. It is inconceivable that African agriculture can be permanently transformed without the peasant majority's effective exercise of political and economic power. They must have a say in the disposition of the products of their labour-power, in resource allocation to agriculture and, therefore, in broad decision-making, especially as it affects their lives at all levels. They must participate in land allocation, input distribution, produce buying, marketing boards, and so on. This also involves the transformation of the *petit-bourgeois* class structure of the neocolonial state apparatus that subordinates and exploits the peasantry. The agrarian class fractions must be promoted in terms of their competition with the compradors, bureaucrats and other *petit-bourgeois* class fractions that currently dominate

African governments. Within the agrarian strata, the power and interests of the peasant majority must also be elevated vis-à-vis those of the agricultural multinationals, settler planters and "native" kulaks. Ideally, this requires a revolutionary transformation of the state, but even before that materialises, the reformist programmes of the post-colonial state must deliberately elevate the legitimate interests of the rural majority – even as a concession to the liberal democratic ideal.

Then African governments must squarely face or review the basic question of the organisational basis of agriculture. The five broad organisational forms corresponding to differing roles of MNCs and aid agencies, capitalist settler planters and "native" kulaks, the state and the peasantry are: 1) multinational agribusiness with foreign aid; 2) private (indigenous and settler) capitalist farms; 3) state farms (with or without MNCs and aid); 4) peasant producer cooperatives (with or without cooperative marketing); 5) small peasant holdings.

The dominant trend so far centres round individual peasant holdings with a big push towards large-scale farms of varying mixtures of types 1) to 3) above. The current direction seems to favour large-scale capitalist farms ultimately (model 2)) with the current experiments with agricultural MNCs, state farms and peasant holdings being regarded as a transitional stage warranted by the current weakness of local private capital. The privatisation and indigenisation of state and foreign enterprises, respectively, point in this direction. Yet, from the foregoing, the emphasis on large-scale farms of models 1) to 3) above is misplaced because it neglects the peasant majority and exacerbates external dependence by relying unduly and uncritically on imported inputs. A more viable self-reliant and mass-based agricultural organisation should instead rest on: a) cooperative peasant producers; b) mechanised state farms of moderate size; c) individual peasant holdings, in that order. The core of the programme should be peasant producer cooperatives. They rest squarely on the majority of the peasantry, depend on internal resources and directly liberate and elevate the peasants. These peasant cooperatives are the heart of Chinese agrarian success against the fumbling of Green Revolution and hunger in India and elsewhere.

Rural land relations must also be transformed from their current complex and confused juridical forms that include communal, feudal, freehold and other holdings. If the state is too conservative to undertake the comprehensive nationalisation of land, peasant cooperatives should be given titles to pool land and other agricultural resources. Whatever strategy is adopted, growing landlessness, arbitrary dispossession of the peasantry by urban land speculators and persistent rural land disputes must be stopped. Once land rights are settled, appropriate measures can be designed to deal with such problems as erosion, desertification and drought. The settlement of these rural relations will also eliminate, or at least ameliorate, growing social inequalities, both between urban and rural areas and within the rural economy. Here, the egalitarian principle that informs the cooperative movement will be a major advantage.

Finally, the purely technical problems that constrain African agriculture, which have been fairly well documented, also require urgent attention. Among others, these include tedious labour, poor seeds, inadequate water supply, scanty physical and social infrastructure. But they do not have to be solved by greater imports and dependence on aid; pooling peasant resources and other internal measures can cope with many of them. Thus rural feeder roads, clinics and schools, cooperative marketing, judicious mechanisation, local training and the like are better substituted in place of the current external dependence for solutions to these problems. These technical constraints have been treated last here, not because they should be attended to last, but because they are essentially dependent on the resolution of the other constraints. In practice, the suggested measures can be implemented simultaneously, or as particular circumstances warrant in each country and local area.

Political framework for agricultural reorganisation

It is crucial to emphasise that the resolution of the agrarian crisis in Africa is fundamentally *political*.[27] A certain kind of political framework must be created from the national government down to the rural grassroot level before the necessary economic, technical and social measures proposed above can be implemented successfully. Even the formulation of these policies requires a progressive political orientation towards the peasant majority, social justice and national reconstruction. This progressive disposition to change may have to be forced on the national leadership through political pressures from below – from the peasants and other working people.

This political environment is crucial because there will be several difficulties and practical obstacles to programmes of peasant liberation and rural transformation. Some of the familiar obstacles include the following:

1. the resistance of traditional rulers, customary landholders and local authorities who will fear loss of power, wealth and prestige from successful rural transformation;
2. the subversive activities of local elites, especially urban-based land speculators who profiteer on the dispossession of the peasantry, particularly in peri-urban areas;
3. the relative inertia of the peasantry due to its massive illiteracy, isolationism and parochialism, which may even make them ready allies of their elite exploiters;
4. the relative weakness of the post-colonial state with respect to its capacity to provide needed funds, extension workers and other support for programmes of rural development;
5. scarcity of imported inputs needed for rural transformation such as agricultural equipment, infrastructural materials for roads, water, health-care, and so on.

But these difficulties are surmountable. To overcome these problems requires serious political education of the rural population, their effective mass mobilisation and the creation of appropriate institutions, preferably manned partly by the peasants themselves – even at the initial stages. The political education of the peasantry must teach the following:

(a) basic literacy through literacy campaign or adult education so that it becomes easier to communicate written instruction and methods (for example, of cultivation with new inputs) to the peasantry;

(b) rudimentary political skills such as organising meetings, representation, voting, canvassing, and so on;

(c) democratic rights and duties towards the local community and the state in order to inculcate the communal spirit;

(d) how peasants can organise themselves to fight local reaction and any other attack on their rights, and to defend their property and privileges;

(e) other skills, such as simple book-keeping, first aid, home economics, and so forth.

In addition, there is need for the mass mobilisation of the peasantry around the basic issues of land rights, production and political power. An imaginative development campaign based on peasant organisations linked from the grassroots through local government to state/provincial government and then to national government and state power is essential here. The emphasis should be on the effective political participation of peasants in decision-making at all levels. This will ensure that rural development emerges as self-development with peasants exercising effective control over their environment and lives.

New supportive institutional structures, such as a land redistribution law, agricultural or cooperative credit banks, rural infrastructural bureaux, equipment service centres, democratic commodity boards and subsidised new agricultural input bodies, will all be needed. In all cases, peasants should be directly represented on these bodies to emphasise their democratic content and grassroot preoccupation. All these require the decisive political reorientation of state power.

Notes

1. B. Dinham & C. Hines (1983) ch. 6.
2. World Bank (1984) *Toward Sustained Development in Sub-Saharan Africa; A Joint Programme of Action* (Washington), p. 9.
3. Ibid., p. 78.
4. Ibid., p. 10.
5. These poorest countries are Angola, Benin, Botswana, Burkina Faso, Cape Verde, Central African Republic, Chad, Ethiopia, Gambia, Ghana, Guinea, Guinea-Bissau, Lesotho, Mali, Mauritania, Mozambique, São Tomé and Principe, Senegal, Somalia, Swaziland, Tanzania, Togo, Zambia and Zimbabwe.
6. See M. Herskovits (1962).
7. Dinham & Hines (1983) pp. 152–3.
8. R. W. Franke & B. H. Chasin (1980); Susan George (1976).
9. World Bank (1984) p. 9.
10. Tunde Adeniran (1974) in *Journal of Black Studies*, vol. 4, no. 4, June.
11. Dinham & Hines (1983) ch. 6.
12. See M. J. Esman (1978).
13. For a related analysis of agrarian forms, see S. Amin (1974), vol. 2, pp. 380–2.
14. Dinham & Hines (1983) ch. 1, have similar phases up to the post-colonial capitalist era.

15. See K. O. Dike (1960).
16. Samir Amin, ch. 2 in D. L. Cohen & J. Daniel (eds.) (1981).
17. See L. Cliffe, ch. 4 in P. C. W. Gutkind & Wallerstein (eds.) (1976); see also Polly Hill (1970).
18. Dinham & Hines (1983) pp. 18–23.
19. These are: (1) World Bank *Accelerated Development in Sub-Saharan Africa* (1981); (2) *Sub-Saharan Africa – Progress Report on Development Prospects and Programmes* (1983); (3) *Toward Sustained Development in Sub-Saharan Africa: A Joint Programme of Action* (1984).
20. Ibid.
21. See Cheryl Payer (1982).
22. L. Cliffe, in Gutkind & Wallerstein (eds.) (1976).
23. See I. Ahmed (1976) in *International Labour Review*, July–August; K. Griffin (1979).
24. F. R. Frankel (1971).
25. See A. V. Chayanov (1966) and (1971).
26. See J. S. Saul (1974) in *Review of African Political Economy*, August–November, pp. 41–68; M. Stahl (1974); and K. Sutton (1974) in *Afrika Spectrum*, 74 (1), pp. 50–68.
27. Consider M. Stahl (1974).

8 Africa's Foreign Trade and Debts

Africa's unfavourable foreign trade and rising external debts are major elements in the escalating crisis of the continent. They warrant especially critical analysis because of the common assertions in bourgeois development theory that "trade is the engine of growth" and that the integration of Third World countries into the international capitalist system, through trade in merchandise, technology and capital, is a precondition for their structural transformation and the liquidation of underdevelopment. Yet, many will agree today that the combination of narrow specialisation in primary production, concentrated trading partners, growing food imports and balance of payments crises together with the burgeoning external debts that these factors generate are the most visible expressions of the African crisis. They also reflect the underlying perverse structure of the African economy, its non-viable mode of integration into the world economy and consequent underdevelopment. This is with respect to such basic indices as the share of external trade in the economy of each African country, the commodity composition of exports, intra-African trade, unequal exchange, trade fluctuations and the degeneration of trade deficits into chronic balance of payments crises. Beyond these, it is also appropriate here to relate the controversy over "internal production relations – external exchange relations" to Africa, that is, the question of whether circulation determines production (and underdevelopment) in the periphery.

Comparative advantage, capitalist international division of labour and trade dependence

To understand Africa's contemporary trade predicament fully, it is necessary to underline its theoretical and historical origins. This will demonstrate clearly that the trade and debt crisis is not just a matter of the operation of purely economic forces, and cannot, therefore, be resolved by allowing for the increased sway of market forces, as the *economism* of bourgeois theory and imperialist policy (especially the IMF and the World Bank) persistently demand. Briefly, the current foreign trade and debt profiles of African and other Third World countries are the consequences of the capitalist international division of labour which is based on the bourgeois classical and neo-classical theory of comparative advantage.[1] While the original classical or Ricardian theory was formulated in labour values and based on the labour theory of value, the neo-classical version is elaborated in relative prices and is derived from their sterile subjective utility theory of value. Thus, the neo-classical version is retrogressive in that it inhibits the direct comparison of relative labour productivities between countries, as in the Ricardian model. Stripped to its essentials the bourgeois theory of comparative advantage (or the theory of comparative cost) maintains that all countries gain from free trade if they specialise in the production of those commodities in which they have comparative cost advantage, and exchange those products for commodities in whose production they have comparative cost disadvantage. So, if African countries produce primary products more cheaply than other countries (that is, the industrialised countries), then Africa should concentrate on producing primary products, and exchange these for the manufactured products that the industrialised countries produce relatively more cheaply. Thus, in Ricardo's famous example of trade in cloth and wine between England and Portugal, even though Portugal had a comparative advantage in the production of both products, it had even greater relative advantage in the production of wine than in cloth production. So Portugal should specialise in producing wine and exchange this with cloth to be produced in England, as this would raise the total output of both countries and benefit both of them. Ricardo's comparative costs were given as shown in Table 8.1.

Table 8.1
Comparative advantage and trade between two countries

In Portugal	*In England*	*Relative advantage of Portugal over England*
1 wine = 80 hrs	1 wine = 120 hrs	In wine = 1.50
1 cloth = 90 hrs	1 cloth =100 hrs	In cloth = 1.11
Internal exchange ratio = 1 wine for 0.89 cloth	Internal exchange ratio = 1 wine for 1.20 cloth	International exchange ratio to lie within the internal exchange ratios, e.g., 1 wine for 1 cloth

Source: David Ricardo (1921).

While this theory appeals to common sense and is optimistic, it is nevertheless, a very unsatisfactory basis for international trade on several grounds.[2] Besides the familiar criticisms that the theory requires exceptional assumptions or conditions, like no transport cost in trade, constant returns to scale in production, two countries – two products – two inputs (2 x 2 x 2), treatment of relative and not absolute optimum in the expression of total gains from trade, the apologetic–ideological nature of "advantage" that does not correspond to comparative labour productivities in the neo-classical version, etc., the theory of comparative advantage is inadequate in four main respects.

First, it uses a static theory to deal with the dynamic problem of international trade. In this regard, Emmanuel has pointed out that even the British who have become major textile exporters since the Industrial Revolution had no initial comparative advantage in textile production (since Britain does not grow cotton, and traditionally wove wool) and used to import cloth from Flanders. The theory thus ignores the whole process of "learning by doing" and the impact of technical progress – though belated efforts have been made to construct dynamic models, of comparative advantage, which are still unsatisfactory.[3] Second, both the Ricardian and neo-classical models of comparative advantage are addressed to trade between countries which are both operating the capitalist mode of production in its pure state. This is clear, even in the Ricardian model, from the treatment of wages and even exchange itself. Yet, international trade is not restricted to trade between capitalist countries alone, and African as well as Third World trade with the industrialised countries is between pre-capitalist modes of production in many cases (for example, in cash crops) and the capitalist mode. Increasingly, however, most Third World exports are now produced in modern capitalist enterprises.

More seriously, the theory of comparative advantage in its economism panders to *unequal exchange*. The configuration of prices and money wages, even under factor–price equalisation, means that most of the benefits of trade accrue to the capitalists in the trading countries through rising profits. This is because the advantage of specialisation is to lower the value of labour-power in the trading countries and thus raise the rate of surplus value. Consequently, unequal exchange can take three forms. One is where wages are unequal even though the organic composition of capital (bourgeois capital–labour ratio) may be similar. Then the low-wage country (Africa and the rest of Third World) gets, for the exchange of units of labour of the same productivity, less than its partner; two, organic compositions can differ between countries even though wages or rates of surplus value are equal. Then an hour of total (direct and indirect) labour of the more developed country with higher organic composition gets more products in the international market than an hour of labour from a less developed country; three corresponds to unequal exchange arising from the undervaluation of the simple labour of the pre-capitalist mode of production (or less capitalistic country) relative to the complex labour of capitalism or the more capitalistic country. The formal undervaluation of pre-capitalist labour here is not simply unequal market wages, because it corresponds to the fact that the pre-industrial worker is quasi-proletarian, supplementing his money wages with subsistence production or extended family support.

Finally, the economistic mould of the models of comparative advantage prevents the theory from answering some basic questions in international trade.[4] These include: (1) why underdeveloped countries are restricted to specialisation in sectors/products with limited increases in productivity in these activities, that is, why does their productivity in these activities not rise, or why do they not develop comparative advantage in other activities over several decades? (2) What are the functions of exchange, beyond raising the total output and incomes of the trading partners, in the international capitalist system? (3) Why do we observe more rapid development of trade between industrialised countries that are similar and have similar distribution of comparative productivities, than between the Third World and the industrialised capitalist countries? (4) Why are there varying and successive forms of specialisation in the Third World, with these countries supplying most raw materials from modern capitalist enterprises?

In order to answer these questions, the theory of comparative advantage must transcend economism and deal with the economic, political and social factors involved in the imperialist domination of Third World countries, and the inherent imperative of global capitalism to expand markets both in its processes of primitive and expanded reproduction. Beyond comparative advantage, the political economy of the policies involved in these processes determines the character and functioning of the international capitalist division of labour.

Imperialist division of labour and trade dependence

The answers to the four questions above, as well as the explanations of the patterns of specialisation and trade vicissitudes in Africa and the rest of the Third World, are bound up with the logic of the global imperialist division of labour. In Africa, this international specialisation between the advanced capitalist countries and the poor countries corresponds to three broad phases. In all the three periods, the changing requirements of capitalist accumulation informed the policies pursued by the imperialist countries to modify and restrict the direction of specialisation and trade in Africa. In the first pre-colonial phase, from about 1450, African countries were naturally primary producers like the rest of the world before the Industrial Revolution. The European and American demand for slaves distorted this early pattern of African specialisation in the direction of export of slaves for the primitive accumulation of capital in Europe, North America and the Middle East. In addition to the slave trade, this early foreign trade also featured primary exports of pepper, ivory, leather, palm oil and kernels etc. from Africa. After the Industrial Revolution, from about 1750, slavery became increasingly unprofitable and restrictive of the "free" wage labour required by capitalism. Hence, between 1750 and the partition of Africa in 1884/85, Africa specialised more in the production of raw materials such as cash crops and minerals required by European factories, and less on slaves and food production. Europe's increasing search for overseas markets in this era also meant the beginning of restrictions on Africa's internal specialisation, for example, through deliberate colonial policy banning the fabrication of raw materials and also the competition of European fabricated exports which displaced the African market for their local production.

During the second phase of colonial specialisation, the imperialist division of labour was formalised between capitalist Europe and the pre-capitalist periphery. Capitalist accumulation then depended on expanded reproduction in the metropoles and on essentially primitive accumulation in the colonies. Both forms of capital accumulation converged on the deliberate colonial policy of imposing specialisation in primary production on Africa and banning not only industrial production, but even cash crop agriculture, as occurred in colonial Kenya and Tanzania. Even the internal markets for African production were increasingly monopolised by imperialist manufactured products, thus further restricting the scope of African specialisation. This was the era of compulsory crops, forced labour, prohibited fabrication and restricted cash crops. Colonial capital thus organised the proletarianisation of Africa and the rest of the Third World partly for primitive accumulation in the colonies and partly in aid of expanded reproduction in Europe, by creating labour reserves for permanent and increasing surplus labour-power relative to the demand for it. This is the opposite of the false labour surplus theory of W. A. Lewis and other dualists who suggest that surplus labour diminished through its increasing absorption by the expanding industrial or modern sector. Thus, it is not economism and its "laws of the market" that explain the persistent specialisation of Africa in backward primary production, and the evolution of the system of wage labour under colonialism, but rather, the deliberate policies of primitive accumulation tailored to the requirements of the imperialist division of labour and its system of expanded reproduction.

In the post-colonial era, as expanded reproduction in the metropoles faced increasing crises (from falling rate of profit, under-consumption, disproportionality, inter-imperialist rivalry, rising prices of raw materials, and so on), both primitive and expanded accumulation coexist in Africa as elsewhere in the periphery. This meant that in addition to sustaining the colonial policies of primitive accumulation, such as increasing labour surplus and proletarianisation (maybe with less overt coercion), imperialism designed other policies to sustain African specialisation in primary production including: multinationals' domination of the post-colonial economies; increasing imperialist monopoly of technology, both under the second international capitalist division of labour (between MNCs and "host" country firms); trade protectionism against exports of manufactures from underdeveloped countries; and the active collaboration of the post-colonial states in sustaining neo-colonial dependency.

These are the collective forces that combine to impose specialisation in primary production on African countries, tailor global imperialist trade primarily to the requirements of expanded reproduction in the metropoles and to primitive accumulation in the periphery. They also create varying degrees of specialisation through the MNCs in the poor countries and ensure that inter-imperialist trade expands faster than both intra-peripheral and centre-periphery trade. Such distortions also involve the external dependence of the poor countries, especially with respect to foreign trade. Thus, the debate about the relationship between "internal production relations and external exchange relations", or whether circulation determines production in the periphery, depends upon the period under consideration. Before the slave trade era, the internal mode of production largely determined Africa's external exchange relations, but since then, the domination of imperialist capital under the capitalist international division of labour has meant that the centre countries of that system and their exchange requirements have been exerting decisive influence on Africa's internal production patterns. Even with such mineral exporters as the OPEC countries, the largely external demand for their oil conditions the extent, and even the mode, of their internal production by MNCs.

The structure of Africa's foreign trade

The composition of Africa's import–export trade in goods and services (the trade in capital was analysed partly in chapter 3 with respect to the MNCs and will be examined below with respect to external debts) is striking in four main respects.

These are the relative size of foreign trade in the economy of each country, the dominance of a few commodities in the export bundles, the primary nature of the exports and the concentrated destinations and origins of exports and imports, respectively. These are what generate the low level of intra-African trade, very poor, deteriorating terms of trade, trade deficits, wide fluctuations in export earnings, balance of payments crises and the rising external debts of African countries.

The extent of sub-Saharan Africa's dependence on foreign trade is indicated by the share of exports plus imports in GDP, or the ratio of merchandise trade to national product as shown in Table 8.2. From the table, these import–export shares in national product were highest at 111.2% in Benin, lowest at 8.2% in Uganda and hovered around 40% to 50% for most of the other countries. The corresponding merchandise share in national product is between 10% and 20% for most of the industrialised countries (both socialist and capitalist). The average share of merchandise trade in GDP is thus about twice as high in Africa as in the

Table 8.2
Selected sub-Saharan African countries' trade dependence, 1982 (%)

Country	*GDP (in $ million)*	*Exports (in $ million)*	*Imports (in $ million)*	$\frac{\text{Export + Import}}{\text{GDP}} \times 100\ (\%)$
Chad	400	101	132	58.3
Burkina Faso	1,000	56	346	40.2
Niger	1,560	333	442	49.7
Ethiopia	4,010	404	787	29.7
Zaire	5,380	569	480	19.5
Malawi	1,320	262	314	43.6
Uganda	8,630	371	339	8.2 (minimum)
Tanzania	4,530	480	1,046	33.7
Benin	830	34	889	111.2 (maximum)
Guinea	1,750	411	296	40.4
Ghana	31,220	873	705	5.1
Kenya	5,340	979	1,683	49.9
Sudan	9,290	499	1,285	19.2
Senegal	2,510	477	974	57.8
Zambia	3,830	1,059	831	49.4
Zimbabwe	5,900	663	704	23.2
Ivory Coast	7,560	2,235	2,090	57.2
Nigeria	71.720	19,484	20,821	56.2
Cameroon	7,370	998	1,205	29.9
Congo	2,170	923	970	87.2
Gabon	3,254	2,161	724	88.7

Source: Computed from World Bank (1984), *Toward Sustained Development in Sub-Saharan Africa*, pp. 59, 63.

metropoles. This makes the African countries not only more externally dependent, but more vulnerable to the mercurial vagaries of imperialist international trade.

Even more seriously, this relatively high trade dependence is anchored to monocultural economies in which one or two commodities account for over 50% of all exports, and support over 50% of all imports as indicated in Table 8.3.

Table 8.3
African dependence on major export crops, 1977/79

Country	*Crop/Commodity*	*Percentage of export earnings*	
		1977	*1979*
Burundi	Coffee	94	93
Mauritius	Sugar	94	68
Gambia	Groundnuts	90	n.a.
Uganda	Coffee	82	27
Chad	Cotton	80	n.a.
Ethiopia	Coffee	75	69
Rwanda	Coffee	73	71
Eq. Guinea	Cocoa	66	n.a.
Somalia	Live animals	61	71
G. Bissau	Groundnuts	60	n.a.
Sudan	Cotton	60	65
Ghana	Cocoa	61	n.a.
Kenya	Coffee	54	27
Swaziland	Sugar	54	n.a.
Lesotho	Wool & mohair	50	n.a.
Mali	Cotton	50	47
Senegal	Groundnuts	50	37
Nigeria[a]	Crude oil	About 80	About 80

[a] Africa's other oil exporters, such as Algeria, Libya, Congo, Cameroon and Gabon also rely on crude oil exports for over 50% of their export earnings;
n.a. = not available.

Source: B. Dinham & C. Hines (1983), p. 187.

Table 8.3 reveals that even though this monocultural dependence declined between 1977 and 1979, seven out of the eleven countries for which data were available in the latter year still depended on one major commodity for over 50% of their export earnings. Even up to the present, one to three commodities account for over 75% of the export earnings of over 75% of African countries, as the World Bank's *World Development Report* shows for various years.

Moreover, most of the export commodities of these African countries are persistently primary products like cash crops and minerals. Thus for 1981, fuels (for example, crude oil), minerals and metals (for example, iron ore) accounted for at least 10% of the exports of eight sub-Saharan African countries out of 13 for which data were reported, while other primary products such as cash crops accounted for over 50% of the exports of eleven out of 16 for which data were reported; for over 70% of the exports of nine of them; and for over 90% of the exports of Sudan, Malawi, Ethiopia and Somalia.[5] By contrast, manufactured products of all types accounted for 5% to a maximum of 26% of the exports of only nine of these sub-Saharan African countries in 1981, with 11% each for Senegal and Kenya; 13% for Togo; and 26% for the Central African Republic. Needless to say, before 1981, the export composition was much worse.

On the import side, even though there is a wider range of such imported commodities as food, fuels, other primary products, capital goods and light manufactures, the sub-group of manufactured products has persistently dominated all imports. Thus in 1981, these manufactured products accounted for over 50% of the imports of 14 out of the 16 countries for which data were reported, with 77% for Cameroon; 75% for Malawi; 74% for the CAR; and 72% for Madagascar. The shares of capital goods such as machinery and transport equipment in these imports were about equal to those of light or other manufactures which, together with the heavy imports of food, highlight the consumerist orientation of African imports featuring luxury and semi-luxury items such as expensive cars, rugs, lace, liquor, and so on.

The destinations of Africa's exports and the origins of its imports are also highly concentrated. As the destination of the exports corresponds to the origins of imports, Table 8.4 gives only the export destinations. It is these concentrated export destinations that pose serious problems of export fluctuations, through low foreign demand elasticities for these exports, synthetic substitution for them, the manipulation of their prices to exploitatively low levels and the imposition of trade barriers against them.

The pattern of neocolonial trade dependence in Table 8.4 is very clear, as most of the countries depend on the imperialist countries for their export markets; even more disturbing is that at least 30% of the external trade of these countries is with their former colonisers. Thus Britain, France and Portugal still control the dominant shares of the external trade of their former colonies as is indicated by the trade concentration ratios in Table 8.5.

This is further evidence of how political and other policies have been shaping the direction of Africa's specialisation and trade. Another important feature of these export destinations is the low level of intra-peripheral trade (see column 3, Table 8.5) which implies an even lower level of intra-African trade since Africa is only a part of the developing countries. Also, only 13 of the reported countries had any trade with the third group of export destinations, the socialist countries, and of these, six countries had only 1%; four others had 2% to 4%; Madagascar had 6%; Sudan 7%; and Ghana 10%; shares for some socialist countries, for example, Angola, Congo, Guinea, were not reported. Sub-Saharan Africa's fourth category of trading partners are the rich oil exporters. From Table 8.5, nine countries had export shares ranging from a minimum of 1% for Tanzania and Zimbabwe to a maximum of 68% for Somalia, with 22% for Sudan. The associated indices of export commodity concentration and export market concentration computed for selected African countries are shown in Table 8.5.

Table 8.4
The main destination of sub-Saharan African exports, 1982

Country	*% Exports to ICCs*	*% Exports to Developing Countries*
Chad	44	49
Mali	62	37
Burkina Faso	64	36
Somalia	16	16
Niger	76	24
Ethiopia	66	24
Zaire	92	8
Uganda	88	10
Burundi	76	24
Benin	82	18
Tanzania	57	38
C. African Rep.	83	17
Guinea	87	13
Madagascar	57	37
Togo	63	36
Ghana	77	13
Kenya	53	42
Sierra Leone	80	20
Mozambique	54	43
Sudan	38	33
Liberia	64	35
Mauritania	95	5
Senegal	65	35
Zambia	74	25
Ivory Coast	71	26
Mauritius	—	—
Nigeria	89	9
Cameroon	89	11
Congo	81	19
Angola	67	33
Sub-Saharan Africa	80	17

Source: World Bank, *Toward Sustained Development*, p. 66.

Intra-African trade

The foregoing analysis not only underlines the perverse extraversion of African economies with respect to foreign trade, but it also indicates the possible scope for regional self-reliance and self-sufficiency. The extent of intra-African commodity trade is a good measure of this collective regional cooperation. It will be examined

Table 8.5

Computed indices of export commodity and export market concentration for selected African countries, 1964/65

Country	*Index of export commodity concentration (%)*	*Index of export market concentration (%)*
Algeria	n.a.	n.a.
Angola	n.a.	37.23
Cameroon	63.35	69.74
C. African Rep.	84.42	55.83
Chad	83.36	58.23
Dahomey	71.79	72.70
Ethiopia	74.36	41.00
Gabon	72.44	54.05
Gambia	78.54	74.14
Ghana	77.54	33.51
Guinea	n.a.	30.43
Ivory Coast	76.20	50.75
Kenya	64.54	29.83
Liberia	89.85	47.84
Malagasy	71.47	55.64
Mali	68.99	41.34
Mozambique	n.a.	41.00
Niger	73.72	99.87
Nigeria	68.09	45.03
Sierra Leone	71.32	82.04
Tanzania	65.15	36.80
Congo	n.a.	n.a.
Togo	66.06	54.02
Burkina Faso	68.88	50.93
Uganda	68.45	36.29
Zambia	95.78	39.84
Zimbabwe	44.36	38.81

Source: F. S. Idachaba (1974) 'Instability and Diversification of Foreign Exchange Earnings – The African Experience', in *Nigerian Journal of Economic and Social Studies (NJESS)*, vol. 16, no. 1, p. 22. Predictably, the table reveals that the export commodity concentration indices are higher than the export market concentration indices, because of the greater possibility of diversifying markets rather than commodities. Thus, the more even the distribution of exports, the smaller the market concentration index. When compared with the more recent patterns of commodity and export market concentration, the older data in the table show the high stability of these concentrations[6] – an indication of the low levels of structural and policy changes in these countries over two decades.

with empirical data for the colonial and post-colonial eras and on a comparative basis. Table 8.6 indicates the intra-African trade of selected African countries during the colonial era, for 1950/57.

Table 8.6
Colonial intra-African trade: 1950/57

	Imports (%)	*Exports (%)*	*Total trade (%)*
Angola	2.0	7.0	4.7
Cameroon	6.7	7.1	6.9
French Eq. Africa	8.7	11.3	9.7
French West Africa	8.7	12.6	10.4
Ghana	6.1	2.5	4.2
Nigeria	0.8	1.3	1.0
Sierra Leone	3.0	1.1	2.2

Source: N. A. Cox-George (1963) *NJESS*, vol. 5, no. 1, March, p. 22.

The data show that the former French colonies had greater intra-African trade (6.9% to 10.4%) than did the former British colonies (1% to 4.2%) - even Portuguese Angola had higher intra-African trade than any of the three former British colonies. But overall, the figures confirm the expected extraversion of these former colonies.

Table 8.7 indicates the intra-regional trade as a proportion of total external trade in West Africa.

Table 8.7
West Africa's intra-regional trade, 1966/74

	1966	*1967*	*1968*	*1969*	*1970*	*1971*	*1972*	*1973*	*1974*
Total trade %	3.3	3.5	3.1	2.5	2.2	—	—	—	—
ECOWAS[a] Export %	—	—	—	—	4.0	4.0	2.0	1.0	2.0
ECOWAS Import %	—	—	—	—	4.0	4.0	2.0	2.0	1.0

[a] The ECOWAS data cover 0–9 SITC Commodity groups, that is, crude materials (codes 0–4) and manufactures 5–8.

Sources: NJESS, vol. 18, no. 2, July 1976, p. 295; and V. P. Diejomaoh & M. A. Iyoha (eds.) (1980), pp. 279, 281.

The disturbing factor is not only the low level but the declining and unstable trend of these trade shares, falling from 3.3% in 1966 to 2.2% in1970, and from 4% during 1970/71 to 1% to 2% by 1973/74.

The corresponding intra-regional trade flow for East Africa (Tanzania, Uganda, Kenya) in 1972 by commodity groups is indicated in Table 8.7a.
Though this average level of 11.2% is higher than the West African figure, it is still relatively low, especially for an economic community of several years' standing.

The overall shares of intra-African trade in the region's total exports and imports for 1961, 1965 and 1970 were as shown in Table 8.8.

The figures in Table 8.8 underline the same very low level of intra-African trade, ranging from 5% to a maximum of 8.5% during the 1961/70 period. Worse still was

Table 8.7a
East Africa's intra-regional trade, 1972

Commodity group	*% of total inter-state trade flows*
Food and live animals	25
Beverages and tobacco	4
Inedible crude materials	4
Mineral fuels, lubricants, etc.	18
Animal & vegetable oils & fats	2
Chemicals	13
Manufactured goods	25
Machinery & transport equipment	4
Miscellaneous manufactures	6
Average for the nine groups	11.2

Source: Dan Nabudere (1982) vol. 2, p. 100.

Table 8.8
Intra-African trade shares in total African trade

	Exports ($ million)			*Imports ($ million)*		
Year	*Africa's Total*	*Intra-African*	*%*	*Africa's Total*	*Intra-African*	*%*
1961	4,882	314	6.4	6,200	443	7.1
1965	7.109	602	8.5	6,865	551	8.0
1970	12,310	620	5.0	11,940	612	5.0

Source: NJESS, vol. 17, no. 2, July 1975, p. 63.

the decline to 5% by 1970, even though there was a slight increase between 1961 and 1965.

For 1975, the intra-African shares of the region's total exports and imports are indicated in Table 8.8a.

Table 8.8a
Africa's intra-regional trade, 1975 ($ m.)

	Africa's Total	*Total Intra-African*	*% Intra-African*	*North Africa*	*West Africa*	*Central Africa*	*East Africa*
Exports	35,330.0	1,735.6	4.91	436.98	571.41	156.76	570.01
Imports	38,280.0	1,523.95		344.41	586.29	238.78	354.47

Source: ECA (1980) *Foreign Trade Statistics for Africa*, pp. 27–8, 110–17.

Again, the pattern is basically similar, but since the formation of ECOWAS in 1975 and of the Preferential Free Trade Area of East and Southern Africa later (even with the collapse of the East African Economic Community), the volume of intra-African trade has increased, but it is still around 10% of the continent's total trade.

Comparatively by regions of the world, the shares of intra-regional trade during 1965/66 were as shown in Table 8.9.

Table 8.9
Comparative global intra–regional trade shares

Region	*Share of intra-trade in the total trade of the region (%)*
Africa[a]	7.7
West African sub-region[b]	2.7
Latin America	9.8
Asia & Far East[c]	24.5
Eastern Europe	63.2
Western Europe	64.0

[a] Excludes South Africa;
[b] Excludes Guinea and Liberia;
[c] Excludes the Socialist countries.

Source: UN Conference on Trade and Development, *Handbook of International Trade and Development Statistics*, 1965.

Thus, Africa's intra-regional trade was, and still is, the lowest of all the regions of the world: less than that of Latin America; one-third of that of Asia and the Far East; and barely one-ninth of that of Europe. These low levels of intra-African trade also indicate the high level of external dependence for trade outside Africa.

There are several reasons for these persistently low levels of intra-African trade, of which one is the great similarity of African countries' traded commodities. As primary producers, they export and import similar products. The low level of industrialisation in the region also means that they cannot fabricate each other's primary exports nor supply each other's requirements of manufactures. There are also currency, and even language, barriers – it is often easier for an exporter from an African country to sell directly to, say, Europe and be paid in hard currency than to sell to an African country, get paid in its local currency and then try to convert that into hard currency or go to collect payment in Europe – as most African countries keep their foreign reserves of hard currencies overseas. There are also transport problems in moving commodities by road, rail, water or air between many African countries. Either the transport facility is simply not there, or poor inter-governmental relations, even between neighbouring African countries, due to political differences, make it difficult to move products between such countries; frequent closure of borders is a case in point. Some borders may be closed for months or certain commodities may be banned.

Additionally, neo-colonial ties between African and imperialist countries inhibit intra-African trade. Thus the operations of currency areas like the sterling area and the franc zone lock some African countries into imperialist trade relations, thus inhibiting intra-African trade. In other cases, African trade agreements with imperialist countries, such as the Lomé Convention operated by the EEC and its preferential trade with some African countries, operate to limit intra-African trade. But the growing significance of regional and sub-regional cooperation within the *Lagos Plan of Action* for African cooperation is breaking down some of these barriers – but too slowly.

Unequal exchange, terms of trade and balance of trade

Besides its obtuse extraversion, one of the major problems that restrict Africa's benefits from her integration into the imperialist world economy is the extensive *unequal exchange* that characterises Africa's external trade – and that of the Third World generally. Unequal exchange is reflected partly in the adverse terms of trade as well as in the deficit balance of trade and payments of African and other poor countries. As indicated earlier, unequal exchange arises from differences in wage rates, organic composition of capital and modes of production between countries. Thus, unequal exchange between an industrialised and an underdeveloped country (UDC) may be illustrated as Emmanuel did; see Table 8.10.

In Table 8.10, with trade reckoned in labour values, the income of the advanced country (A) rises from 182–50 (132) to 188–50 (138), but the income of the UDC (B) falls from 146–50 (96) to 134–50 (84). The gains to the advanced country (A) in real terms are even greater – being equal to the differential in the barter terms of trade, that is, they are of the ratio where the gross barter terms of trade are equal to the volume of imports divided by the volume of exports.

Empirically, chapter 4 explained that a 67-sector model of world trade has been used to show that in the trade between the advanced capitalist countries, (A) in Table 8.10, and the periphery (B) in 1969, the transfer of resources from the poor countries to the rich countries by unequal exchange was equal to $10 billion. This was approximately equal to the total transfer of public foreign resources to the Third World countries in 1969. Similarly, it was also shown that in 1969, 38% of the value of Peruvian exports was transferred to the US through unequal exchange.[7] Thus the objections to unequal exchange, such as the claim that it is based on the assumption of complete specialisation or specific commodities traded, that unemployment is self-cancelling because wage disparities disappear in long-run equilibrium through labour mobility, and that the effect of unequal exchange is empirically insignificant, are dubious and untenable.

Africa's terms of trade

Another reflection of the unequal exchange between Africa and the capitalist world relates to Africa's *terms of trade* (the prices of exports divided by the prices of imports) with these imperialist countries. The relevant data for 1970/82 are shown in Table 8.11.

Table 8.10
Illustration of unequal exchange

Region	*Total capital invested* K	*Total capital consumed* C	*Total wages* V	*Surplus value* S	*C+V+S* W	*Cost of production* R	*Rate of profit* $\Sigma s/\Sigma k$ Ψ	*Total profit* P	*Price of production* (R + P) L	
Advanced (A)	240	50	90	30	170	140	20%	48	188	(182)
UDC (B)	120	50	60	60	170	110	20%	24	134	(146)
Total	*360*	*100*	*150*	*90*	*340*	*250*		*72*	*322*	*(328)*

Source: A. Emmanuel (1972), p. 193.

Table 8.11
Africa's terms of trade, 1970/82 (1980 = 100)

Country	*1982*	*Average annual growth rate of terms of trade (%) 1970/82*	*Country*	*1982*	*Average annual growth rate of terms of trade (%) 1970/82*
Chad	99	1.5	Ghana	61	0.2
Mali	102	-1.5	Kenya	87	-0.4
Burkina Faso	97	-2.5	Sierra Leone	84	-3.3
Somalia	111	-3.4	Mozambique	84	-2.0
Niger	89	-5.1	Sudan	85	-0.6
Gambia, the	108	-2.4	Mauritania	97	-5.1
Ethiopia	74	-4.9	Liberia	92	6.0
Zaire	81	-5.9	Senegal	89	-0.3
Malawi	106	-2.7	Zambia	72	-9.0
Uganda	74	-0.5	Zimbabwe	105	n.a.
Rwanda	63	-0.8	Ivory Coast	91	0.6
Burundi	—	—	Mauritius	91	-21
Tanzania	86	1.3	Nigeria	103	15.7
Benin	75	-6.3	Cameroon	71	0.3
C.African Rep.	90	-0.6	Congo	110	17.4
Madagascar	80	-2.3	Gabon	111	17.6
Togo	112	3.7	Angola	104	14.2
			Sub-Saharan Africa		-4.7 (1980 to 1982)

Source: World Bank (1984), *Toward Sustained Development* . . ., pp. 12, 67.

From Table 8.11 it can be seen that these terms of trade were unfavourable (less than 100, implying that the prices of a country's exports were less than the corresponding prices of its imports) for 23 countries out of the 34 listed in 1982. Moreover, the terms of trade during 1970/82 for 21 out of the 32 countries had negative annual growth rates. The deteriorating financial terms of trade were indicated in chapter 4 on resource transfer from Africa.

Table 8.11 conceals the differential pattern of trade between Africa and the imperialist countries on the one hand, and between African countries and the socialist bloc on the other. The more general structure of Africa's trade with imperialist, socialist and Third World countries is depicted in Table 8.12.

Africa's balance of trade and balance of payments

The balance of trade is part of the balance of payments, and is also called the current account balance of international transactions. This balance of trade is the difference between exports and imports of goods (merchandise balance); plus the difference between exports and imports of services (the invisible balance). Thus, the

Table 8.12
Geographical distribution of Africa's external trade, 1979

Area	*Exports (f.o.b.)* $ *millions*	*Percentage*	*Imports (f.o.b.)* $ *millions*	*Percentage*
Industrialised capitalist countries	53,540	84.7	49,988	79.6
Socialist countries of Eastern Europe	1,494	2.4	2,944	4.7
Developing countries:	7,931			
Africa	2,365	3.7	1,593	2.5
Asia/Middle East	814	1.3	4,700	7.5
Other developing countries	539	0.9	—	—
Others	213	0.3	1,203	5.7
World	63,178	100.0	62,793	100.0

Source: UN (1980) *Monthly Bulletin of Statistics*, July.

Table 8.13
Sub-Saharan Africa's annual growth rates of commodity trade-volume and prices (%)

Commodity	*1970/82 Volume: Average annual growth rate (%)*	*1970/82 Prices: Average annual growth rate (%)*	*Commodity*	*1970/82 Volume: Average annual growth rate (%)*	*1970/82 Prices: Average annual growth rate (%)*
Minerals & metals:					
Copper	–0.3	–7.2	G/nuts (meal)	–4.6	–4.1
Iron ore	–5.1	–4.6	G/nuts (oil)	–7.1	–4.0
Bauxite	20.5	1.8	Beef	–7.0	–4.1
Phosphate rock	2.2	1.7	Palm oil	–6.7	–3.2
Manganese ore	3.4	–0.6	Bananas	–6.6	–1.1
Zinc	–2.9	–3.9	Maize	–6.9	–4.2
Tin	–8.5	4.1			
Lead	1.5	–0.9	*Non-food:*		
			Timber	–2.3	3.6
Food & beverages:			Cotton	–4.0	–1.9
Coffee	–1.0	1.8	Tobacco	–4.7	–1.2
Cocoa	–1.2	3.0	Rubber	–3.8	0.0
Sugar	1.2	–2.7	Hides & skins	–1.5	—
Tea	4.0	–2.8	Sisal	–9.7	0.1

Source: World Bank (1984) *Towards Sustained Development . . .*, p. 68.

balance of trade consists of two sub-accounts: 1) *merchandise* balance or account which is the difference between exports and imports of physical commodities or merchandise; 2) *invisible* balance or account consists of the difference between exports and imports of such services as profit on foreign direct investment (called "investment income" in the balance of payments accounts), travel, shipping, insurance and other international services. This balance of trade or current account balance is the most important part of the balance of payments; its second major component is the *capital account*.

The unfavourable effects of Africa's external trade on her trade balances will be examined with respect to the growth rate of the volume of commodity trade during 1970/82; the relative values of exports and imports; the share of the balance of trade in GNP; and the shifts in exports and imports during 1980/90 (see Table 8.13).

Fourteen out of the 24 commodities listed had negative average annual growth rates of trade volume and fifteen had negative average annual growth rates of prices.

The current account balances of the different African countries during 1970 and 1982 are shown in Table 8.14.

In Table 8.14, negative values mean that the value of imports exceeds the value of exports, or that the balance of trade is in deficit or unfavourable; positive values

Table 8.14
Sub-Saharan Africa's trade balance, 1970/82 ($ m.)

	Current account balance			*Current account balance*	
Country	*1970*	*1982*	*Country*	*1970*	*1982*
Chad	2	19	Kenya	–49	–509
Mali	–2	–113	Sierra Leone	–16	–158
Burkina Faso	9	—	Sudan	–42	–248
Somalia	–6	–117	Mauritania	–5	–252
Niger	—	—	Liberia	—	–79
Gambia, The	1	–47	Senegal	–16	—
Ethiopia	–32	–196	Lesotho	—	–50
Zaire	–64	–375	Zambia	108	–252
Malawi	–35	–78	Zimbabwe	—	–706
Uganda	20	–256	Botswana	—	–61
Rwanda	7	90	Swaziland	—	–69
Tanzania	–36	–268	Ivory Coast	–38	15
Benin	–1	—	Mauritius	8	–43
Central African Rep.	–12	–268	Nigeria	–368	–7,324
Guinea	—	—	Cameroon	–30	–525
Madagascar	10	–369	Congo, Peoples Rep.	—	–320
Togo	3	–152	Gabon	–3	680
Ghana	–68	83			

Source: World Bank (1984) *Toward Sustained Development . . .*, p. 69.

depict the reverse. While 18 out of the 34 countries had deficit current account balances totalling about $0.8 billion in 1970, 26 countries had these trade deficits totalling about $12.0 billion by 1982.

For low-income Africa, these current account deficits for 1970/84 were as given in Table 8.15.

Table 8.15
Low-income Africa's current account deficits ($ m.)

Trade item	*1970*	*1973*	*1980*	*1981*	*1982*	*1983*[b]	*1984*[c]
1) Net export of goods and nonfactor services[a]	-381	-607	-5,385	-5,901	-4,590	-4,359	-3,780
2) Net factor income	-161	-274	-901	-1,098	-1,004	-1,029	-1,291
3) Interest payments on medium and long-term loans	80	143	698	643	567	662	1,000
4) Current account balance	-679	-998	-5,837	-6,419	-5,432	-4,900	-4,594

[a] These are the invisible services like travel, shipping, etc;
[b] Estimated;
[c] Projected net exports = export minus import so its minus sign means: import exceeds export. Item 4 is positive because it is regarded as export.

Source: World Development Report 1985, p. 18.

The overall current account deficit (which usually excludes item 3 which is usually in the capital account) deteriorated progressively from 1970 to 1982, before declining to $4.6 billion in 1984. The most important items in these cumulative deficits have been excessive imports of goods and services in item 1), which account for about 50% to 90% of the trade balance. For percentage shares of these current account deficits in Africa's GNP for 1960/84 see Table 8.16.

Over time, the deficits have been increasing as a proportion of GNP, with shares of about -3.5% in the 1960s, -7.0% in the 1970s and about -10% in the 1980s.

These adverse changes in Africa's trade yield the following average annual percentage changes for different trade items for 1980/85 (%).

Thus, the most important item in Africa's balance of payments – the current account balance or the balance of trade – has been in worsening deficit since the 1960s. The other items of the balance of payments: international reserves, long-term foreign investment and external debts have, along with the balance of trade, also been in very bad shape. While foreign investment represents the grip of foreign monopoly capital on Africa, as analysed in chapter 3, the external debts and their debt service burden are analysed below.

The persistently low level of Africa's international reserves is another alarming indicator of the trade crisis plaguing the continent. These reserves of gold and hard currencies (US dollar, pound sterling, Deutschmark, franc, yen, rouble, etc.) are usually held as contingency for financing import necessities in case of shortfalls in

Table 8.16
Africa's current account deficits as percentage of GNP, 1960/84

1960	*1965*	*1970*	*1971*	*1972*	*1973*	*1974*	*1975*	*1976*	*1977*	*1978*	*1979*	*1980*	*1981*	*1982*	*1983*	*1984*
–3.3	–4.1	–3.4	–7.3	–5.6	–4.4	–7.8	–10.2	–7.3	–7.6	–8.3	–7.7	–9.8	–10.5	–12.0	–10.0	–9.4

Source: World Development Report, 1985, p. 17.

Table 8.17
Changes in Africa's exports and imports

Exports of goods and non-factor services	*Exports of manufactures*	*Exports of primary goods*	*Imports of goods and non-factor services*
−1.6	−12.6	−1.2	−2.1

Source: World Development Report, 1985, p. 141.

export earnings, and their normal level is about three months' imports or three months' import coverage – and thus is less of an indicator of a balance of payments crisis.

In 1982, the highest level of these external reserves for sub-Saharan Africa[8] was: $1.9 billion in Nigeria, with a minimum of $8 million in Liberia, Sierra Leone and Gambia, and an average of about $200 million for all African countries. Out of the 30 countries for which data were available in 1982: five had external reserves covering at least three months' imports; 13 countries had less than one month's import coverage; Uganda and Ivory Coast 0.1 month's import coverage; Liberia, Sudan and Tanzania had 0.2 month's coverage; and sub-Saharan Africa as a whole had an average of 1.1 month's import coverage.

For these reasons, especially high external trade dependence, the *multiplier* and *accelerator effects* of expenditures on aggregate consumption and government services in Africa are typically transferred abroad.

The multiplier measures the induced effect of an increase in autonomous expenditure (for consumption, investment or government) on national income, and the accelerator measures the induced impact of an increase in consumption on the level of the investment required to produce the consumer goods. As African countries rely heavily on external trade for imports of consumer, intermediate and capital goods, the effects of these multiplier and accelerator mechanisms are typically transferred abroad.

Foreign trade fluctuations, deficits and external debts

Apart from these chronic and growing trade deficits, wide fluctuation in Africa's foreign trade is also a serious problem. These huge trade deficits and fluctuations have combined to generate balance of payments crises, with the alarming effect of the accumulation of a large and rapidly growing external debt with a debt service burden that has become a major issue of international debate and diplomacy among the OAU, IMF, World Bank and the United Nations.[9]

Some of the data on the trade fluctuations have been computed for the medium and long-term (Table 8.18).

Table 8.18
Computed indices of instability of export earnings for 27 selected African countries, 1946/68

Country	Export instability index (%) I	II	Country	Export instability index (%) I	II
Algeria	25.8	25.3	Gambia	26.4	25.9
Angola	17.5	16.1	Ghana	15.8	16.6
Cameroon	14.3	14.5	Guinea	24.5	24.3
C.A.R.	23.7	23.1	Ivory Coast	22.6	21.1
Chad	17.4	17.3	Kenya	10.0	9.1
Dahomey	32.1	32.5	Liberia	32.2	29.6
Ethiopia	11.7	11.6	Malagasy	18.5	19.0
Gabon	19.1	17.0	Mali	20.3	20.5

Thus, the July 1985 summit of the OAU addressed itself to the economic crisis in Africa with a central focus on the debt problem, and a subsequent August proposal to the UN for a five-year moratorium on Africa's debt service.[10] This was against the backdrop of President Castro's demand for the cancellation of Third World debt (Table 8.19).[11] Between 1985 and 1986, Africa lost $19 billion in export earnings from these trade fluctuations.

Table 8.19
Africa's export instability indices

Country	Export instability index (%) I	II	Country	Export instability index (%) I	II
Mozambique	16.8	15.0			
Niger	25.6	24.9	Togo	30.5	30.1
Nigeria	16.1	15.8	Burkina Faso	41.1	39.2
Sierra Leone	23.7	24.0	Uganda	15.0	14.6
Tanzania	14.3	13.7	Zambia	56.9	54.6
Congo P.R.	27.5	26.1	Zimbabwe	30.4	30.1

Note: I is based on semi-log trend equation and II is based on linear trend equation. F. S. Idachaba (1974) "Instability and Diversification of Foreign Exchange Earnings – The African Experience".

Source: Nigerian Journal of Economic and Social Studies, July 1975, p. 20.

The average rate of export instability for all the countries is 23.3% with 15 countries experiencing rates of export fluctuation of 20% to 56.9%. Zambia had the highest coefficient of variation: 56.9%; and Kenya had the lowest: 9.1%. For more recent years, Table 8.13 showing changes in Africa's trade volume and prices gives an indication of these trade fluctuations, since the export earnings are the products

Table 8.20
Sub-Saharan Africa's outstanding and disbursed external debt 1970/82 ($US m.)

Type of Debt	*1970*	*1971*	*1972*	*1973*	*1974*	*1975*	*1976*	*1977*	*1978*	*1979*	*1980*	*1981*	*1982*
(1) *Total concessional bilateral:*	*2,377*	*2,816*	*3,111*	*3,761*	*4,699*	*5,319*	*6,056*	*7,068*	*7,971*	*8,961*	*10,173*	*10,906*	*11,566*
DAC governments	1,654	1,923	2,019	2,362	2,819	3,162	3,491	3,930	4,269	4,477	5,099	5,170	5,964
OPEC governments	70	78	107	146	261	378	584	819	1,049	1,607	2,022	2,599	3,006
Socialist governments	585	736	896	1,157	1,493	1,630	1,828	2,131	2,406	2,597	2,758	2,888	2,812
Other bilateral	68	73	90	96	126	148	153	188	247	280	293	270	285
(2) *Total official export credits:*	*324*	*345*	*374*	*479*	*674*	*927*	*1,439*	*1,791*	*2,300*	*4,159*	*5,506*	*5,606*	*6,187*
DAC governments	285	304	330	415	520	606	898	1,149	1,533	2,859	3,854	3,851	4,205
OPEC governments	0	0	0	14	96	187	400	488	559	696	856	887	924
Socialist governments	21	27	33	34	42	54	64	72	93	323	404	463	448
Other bilateral	18	15	12	16	16	81	80	84	116	279	393	404	610
(3) *Total multilateral loans:*	*842*	*1,018*	*1,321*	*1,620*	*1,997*	*2,529*	*3,157*	*4,048*	*5,446*	*6,735*	*8,443*	*9,752*	*1,144*
IBRD	590	681	831	924	1,041	1,261	1,493	1,723	2,017	2,262	2,549	2,854	3,327
IDA	226	288	396	547	679	880	1,157	1,147	1,801	2,156	2,573	3,090	3,728
Regional banks	26	48	93	143	193	225	271	424	688	869	1,154	1,342	1,571
Others	0	0	0	5	83	164	237	413	940	1,449	2,168	2,467	2,789
(4) *Total privately guaranteed loans:*	*1,876*	*2,048*	*2,321*	*3,426*	*4,261*	*5,330*	*6,096*	*7,933*	*11,802*	*14,640*	*16,521*	*18,185*	*18,895*
Supplied credits	764	907	1,023	1,286	1,605	217	2,470	3,076	3,535	3,722	3,544	3,459	3,397
Financial institutions	307	453	701	1,361	1,889	2,607	3,371	4,606	7,794	10,370	12,310	14,204	15,120
Bonds	387	398	333	321	310	260	204	212	435	532	654	520	369
Others	436	289	265	458	457	292	51	39	38	15	14	3	10

(5) *Total publicly guarantee loans*	*5,419*	*6,227*	*7,127*	*9,285*	*11,631*	*14,104*	*16,747*	*20,840*	*27,518*	*34,495*	*40,643*	*44,450*	*48,063*
(6) *Total private non-guaranteed debt*	*331*	*360*	*430*	*636*	*832*	*990*	*1,139*	*1,278*	*1,839*	*2,296*	*2,722*	*3,031*	*3,251*
(7) *Total public & private debt*	*5,749*	*6,587*	*6,587*	*7,558*	*9,921*	*12,463*	*15,093*	*17,886*	*22,118*	*29,357*	*36,790*	*43,480*	*51,315*
Total bliateral	*2,701*	*3,161*	*3,485*	*4,240*	*5,373*	*6,245*	*7,494*	*8,859*	*10,270*	*13,120*	*15,678*	*16,512*	*17,754*
Total official	*3,543*	*4,179*	*4,806*	*5,859*	*7,374*	*8,774*	*10,651*	*12,907*	*15,716*	*19,855*	*24,122*	*26,264*	*29,168*
Total private source	*2,206*	*2,406*	*2,751*	*4,061*	*5,093*	*6,319*	*7,235*	*9,210*	*13,641*	*16,936*	*19,243*	*21,216*	*22,147*
Total concessional	*2,618*	*3,127*	*3,549*	*4,379*	*5,544*	*6,456*	*7,567*	*9,143*	*10,961*	*12,833*	*15,192*	*16,759*	*18,368*
Total non-concessional	*3,132*	*3,460*	*4,009*	*5,542*	*6,919*	*8,637*	*10,039*	*12,975*	*18,396*	*23,957*	*28,173*	*30,721*	*32,947*

Notes: (5)=1+(2)+(3)+(4); (7)=(5)+(6); The Parts of (7) do not add up to the total due to overlapping; DAC= Development Assistance Committee of OECD; IBRD = International Bank for Reconstruction and Development (World Bank); IDA = International Development Association.

Source: World Bank *Toward Sustained Development in Sub-Saharan Africa* (Washington), p. 17.

of export volume and price for each year. The net export data in Table 8.14 also offer another indication of fluctuations in the trade receipts.

The rising external debts which Africa has been accumulating in order to accommodate these large and persistent fluctuations in export earnings as well as the associated trade deficit are depicted in Table 8.20.

From Table 8.20, sub-Saharan Africa's total outstanding external debt (unpaid) jumped from barely $5.7 billion in 1970 to $51.3 billion within just over one decade. This implies an average annual increase of about 350%. Item (2) of Table 8.20, total official export credits, most directly reflects the effect of cumulative and rising trade deficits on these external debts. These export credits that are drawn to finance the excess of imports over exports, rose from $0.3 billion in 1970 to $6.2 billion by 1982.

The different measures of the burden of these external debts on "low-income Africa" alone are shown in Table 8.21. By mid-1987, Africa's external debts stood at $200 billion.

Table 8.21
Low-income Africa's debt indicators, 1970/84

Debt indicator	*1970*	*1974*	*1976*	*1978*	*1980*	*1981*	*1982*	*1983*	*1984*
Ratio of debt to GNP (%)	17.5	23.8	27.7	26.9	39.8	43.4	47.7	52.0	54.5
Ratio of debt to exports (%)	75.2	99.5	135.3	162.3	175.8	216.5	260.6	279.5	278.1
Debt service ratio (%)	6.1	8.6	8.5	9.6	12.5	13.8	15.7	16.5	19.9
Ratio of interest service to GNP (%)	0.5	0.7	0.6	0.7	1.3	1.2	1.1	1.4	2.1
Total debt outstanding & disbursed ($ b.)	3	7	10	15	21	23	25	25	27
Private debt as % of total	33.5	39.3	36.6	38.6	29.8	29.3	26.9	22.4	18.4

Source: World Development Report (1985), p. 24.

These ratios clearly show the rapidly rising trend of these external debts, particularly with respect to the debt service ratio (the ratio of the sum of debt repayment plus interest charges to annual export earnings) which is the most critical indicator of external debt burden. Normally, this debt service ratio should not exceed 10% to 15%, which was the ratio in 1981. From 1982, therefore, low-income African countries as a whole exceeded this normal debt burden, that is, they have been collectively over-borrowing since 1983. Indeed, for many individual African countries, the debt service ratio is much higher, and many of them were over-borrowing even before 1982. For 1983, these above-average debt service ratios were as indicated in Table 8.22.

The low figure of 18.6% for Nigeria in 1983 was a benchmark for the figure of 25% announced in the 1985 budget speech; the 1985 debt service ratio for the country has been estimated at 44%, which is much higher than the low-income African average of 19.9% in Table 8.12.

Table 8.22
Africa's debt service ratios, 1983 (%)

Low-income Africa	*Malawi*	*Kenya*	*Egypt*	*Ivory Coast*	*Zimbabwe*	*Morocco*	*Congo*	*Nigeria*	*Tunisia*	*Algeria*
16.5	20.3	20.6	27.5	31.0	31.6	38.2	20.5	18.6	22.3	33.1

Source: World Development Report (1985), pp. 204–5.

The *growth* of these external debts for selected periods has also been very high as shown in Table 8.23.

Table 8.23
Growth of Africa's external debts, 1970/84

Debt item	*1970/73*	*1973/80*	*1981*	*1982*	*1983*	*1984*
Debt outstanding & disbursed	19.7	22.6	10.2	6.9	3.7	4.7
Official	17.3	24.2	10.9	10.6	10.1	10.2
Private	24.4	19.7	8.5	–2.0	–13.5	–14.6

Source: World Development Report (1985), p. 153.

The average annual growth rate for total and official borrowing which shot up during 1973/80 has remained fairly constant at around 10% for official borrowing, though it declined overall between 1981 and 1983 before rising again in 1984.

Africa's external debt policy

The crushing burden of debt service and the rapidly escalating danger of debt peonage in the Third World generally, and in Africa especially, demand the elaboration of a systematic external debt policy for Africa and the Third World both regionally and collectively.[12] The major planks in this overdue external debt policy include the following options:

Collective political action: The external debt problem is even more political than economic. This is both with respect to its adverse political effects on individual debtor countries and with regard to the political stance of the imperialist creditor countries (for example, their formation of a creditors' consortium for collective bargaining, their political use of the IMF and the World Bank to exert leverage and political pressure on the national policies of debtor countries, the foreign policy uses of external lending, and so on). So Third World and African countries should form their own debtors' consortia or debtors' cartels for collective bargaining with the creditor countries, and thus approximate the bilateral monopoly situation initiated by them. Unity is strength in this matter, especially given the relative individual weakness of most Third World countries. The July 1985 OAU summit in Addis Ababa initiated this political thrust just as the September 1983 Caracas Conference and subsequent meetings of Latin American debtor countries have done.

Tough external borrowing restraints: and even embargo by the poor countries, especially with respect to short-term borrowing from the IMF and the pernicious conditions it imposes on behalf of imperialism. "Neither a borrower nor a lender be" should be a good guide. Any essential recourse to external borrowing should avoid short-term funding of imports for consumption.

Scrutiny of existing foreign debts: Many African and Third World debts are fraudulent and should not be honoured. All external debts inherited from previous governments should first be carefully scrutinised and bogus debts, that is those that have not been utilised in the debtor country for national purposes, should be repudiated. There is often nothing (not even a site or drawing) to show for many, fully drawn external debts, which have been embezzled by the so-called leaders of many poor countries in collusion with their imperialist mentors.

Cancellation of Debt servicing options: (a) repudiation of all external debts, as advocated by President Fidel Castro of Cuba on the grounds that the imperialists have plundered the poor countries in excess of the values of these foreign debts (for example, by the super-exploitation of cheap labour and raw materials to provide super-profits for MNCs, by fraudulent transfer-pricing, unequal exchange, inflationary and interest rate manipulation on these debts); (b) Repudiations of only fraudulent debts if (a) is too radical for neocolonial leaders; (c) Debt moratoria, for example, five years' grace on debt repayments; (d) maximum ceiling of about 10% on the annual debt service ratio. A combination of these policy options is required urgently in order to deal effectively with the debilitating effects of these exploitative foreign debts on African and other Third World countries.

Regional and sub-regional cooperation in trade

The intensification of the contradiction of undevelopment that generally plagues all African countries, and the more specific exploitative external trade prospects with very low intra-African trade, have forced African countries into regional and sub-regional groupings since 1960. The Organisation of African Unity (OAU) and the Economic Commission for Africa (ECA) have played significant roles in these efforts towards the economic integration of Africa. The *Lagos Plan of Action for the Economic Development of Africa during 1980 to 2000* that came out of the Monrovia Conference and its report was adopted by the OAU, in Lagos in 1980; this plan embraces the overall strategies in different sectors for regional and sub-regional economic integration. With respect to trade, these integrative efforts can be examined in relation to cooperation in external trade, in monetary and financial integration and the problems associated with these efforts. The major advantages of these integrative efforts centre on the usual *trade creation* or expansion, *trade diversion*[13] from outside to the cooperating countries (from high cost to lower cost sources of trade), the facilitation of monetary and financial arrangements for external payments, the reduction of external dependence on imperialism, and the elimination of exploitative unequal exchange. Although in the following sections merchandise and financial integration are treated separately to emphasise their different strategies, a grouping for merchandise trade typically leads to financial cooperation in order to be more successful.

Cooperation for merchandise trade

Of the eight main attempts in the 1960s and 1980s, towards securing regional and sub-regional cooperation in Africa, four have remained most active. These are:

1) *The Lagos Plan of Action*. This is the blueprint for the continental regional grouping which is still more a statement of hope than one of concrete action, as its major programmes are yet to be implemented. Its major achievements so far are the broad unity of common purpose, the vision, the programmes and the sub-regional strategies that it offers. One major defect of the Plan is its contradictory external dependence.

2) *The ECOWAS*. With 16 members embracing a population of 163.1 million[14] in 1983, it is the largest functioning sub-regional group in Africa. It began, in 1967, with the signing of an agreement for a West African Economic Community of 12 members, but was broadened to its present 16 members by the 1975 treaty. The intention is that it shall become a full common market by 1990 and already it has achieved free movement of persons for stay of up to 90 days, linked its capitals by telecommunication and is making rapid progress towards financial integration. It plans to harmonise foreign tariffs during 1981/89 and to establish a Federation of West African chambers of commerce to produce and consume African commodities. But the development of the community has been generally disappointing: many of its projects not implemented, some members defaulting in their financial contributions, and other decisions not implemented promptly.

3) *The Economic Community of Central Africa (ECCA)* was established in December 1981 to supersede the former, smaller Central African Customs and Economic Union (UDEAC) of the 1960s and 1970s; it also supersedes the earlier movement for the Economic Community of Great Lakes Countries, embracing Zaire, Rwanda and Burundi. Member countries of the ECCA are: Cameroon, Chad, CAR, Congo, Zaire, Guinea and São Tomé and Principe.

4) *The Preferential Trade Area of Eastern and Southern African States (PTA)*, comprises 21 States and was established by treaty in 1982, signed by 10 members by July 1983. Though the PTA was to start on a preferential trade basis, its treaty provides for its eventual evolution into a full economic community.[15]

The other attempts at economic integration in Africa since the 1970s include the SADCC, CEAO, MRU and the EAEC.

5) *The Southern African Development Coordination Conference (SADCC)*, comprising the frontline states of Mozambique, Angola, Zimbabwe, Zambia, Tanzania, Swaziland, Botswana, Lesotho and Malawi was established in April

1980; its members are also members of the PTA. The SADCC was formed to reduce the economic dependence of these countries on South Africa. Though it is not intended to become a customs union or common market, it provides for cooperative development in certain sectors such as agriculture, industry, energy and manpower. It has a small secretariat but uses the services of its members for specialised studies, which have identified projects for which $650 million external aid has so far been pledged. It is hoped that the SADCC will eventually merge into the PTA, especially when the latter becomes an economic community.

6) *Communauté Economique de l'Afrique de l'Ouest* (CEAO) *(West African Economic Community)*, developed from the former West African Customs Union (UDEAO) of former French West African colonies in 1959, and was reorganised in 1966. In 1972, it was again modified into the CEAO with Senegal, Mali, Niger, Burkina Faso, Mauritania and Ivory Coast as members. It was envisaged that it would gradually evolve into a customs union over a 12-year period, starting from 1974. Its three major institutions are the Regional Cooperation Tax, Community Development Fund and the Solidarity Intervention Fund. Both funds have been used to implement some community projects and there is a common currency, except in Mali where the Malian franc is linked to the CFA franc. Unfortunately, the community has remained poor and its intra-community trade has actually declined from 11% of total (CEAO) trade in 1972 to 8.5% in 1977.

7) *The Mano River Union (MRU)* was formed in 1973 by Liberia and Sierra Leone and joined by Guinea in 1980. In common with CEAO it is within ECOWAS, and it is hoped that both will eventually merge into ECOWAS.

8) *North African Cooperation*. Three attempts to form an economic community have been made in North Africa. The first involved Algeria, Libya, Morocco and Tunisia; the second Libya and Egypt, while the third grouped Libya, Sudan and Egypt. But so far little has been achieved because of the instability of these cooperative efforts that tend to be dominated by political, rather than economic, considerations.

9) The former East African Economic Community (EAEC) embracing Tanzania, Uganda and Kenya started under colonialism until 1967 when the Treaty of East African Cooperation was evolved. In the 1960s, as East Africa held the brightest hopes of integration in Africa, the ECA tried, without much success, to expand the EAEC to include Zambia, Rwanda and Burundi. The community had a Development Bank and a transfer tax system, both of which were to ensure the equitable flow of development projects and funds from Kenya, which was most favoured by the community, to the other members. Unfortunately, these did not function adequately and the addition of political and ideological differences among the members (especially under the weight of Idi Amin from 1971) led to the sad collapse of this laudable experiment in July 1977.

Others in the 1960s. In the early independence era, there was also the Ghana–Guinea–Mali Union based on ideological affinity but afflicted by geographical separation, and the fall of Nkrumah in 1966. The Ghana–Upper Volta and the Ghana–Guinea Customs Unions suffered a similar fate, and the West African Free

Trade Area embracing Guinea, Liberia, Sierra Leone and Ivory Coast collapsed mainly on ideological differences. In 1958, the former French colonies of the Congo, Gabon, the Central African Republic and Chad agreed to retain their colonial common services and formed a customs union in 1959. By 1964, they were joined by Cameroon to form the Central African Economic and Customs Union (UDEAC). In 1968, Chad and the CAR pulled out because of growing disparity between them and the rest of the union, although the CAR returned to the union in the following year. It has since survived to the present, and it is hoped will merge with the PTA when it becomes a full economic community.

Monetary and financial cooperation

Attempts at monetary and financial integration in Africa are closely interlinked with the experiments in regional and sub-regional integration generally. There are six broad types of financial cooperation to date.[16]

1) *Clearing House*. This is to facilitate financial payments and receipts involving different national currencies, liberalising exchange and thus promoting faster and wider trade among African countries. There are now three of these clearing houses:
(a) *Central African Clearing House* was established in January 1979 and started operating in September 1981. Zaire, Burundi and Rwanda have started to limit fund movements and control exchange between them as well as their commercial banks. Zaire also has a special financial cooperation agreement with Angola and there have been negotiations to admit Equatorial Guinea and São Tomé and Principe to the Central African Clearing House;
(b) *West African Clearing House* started in June 1975 and embraces all the Central Banks of the ECOWAS countries;
(c) *East and Southern African Clearing House* for the PTA countries under Treaty of cooperation. The operational rules of the clearing house were finalised and submitted to the respective governments for approval in 1982.

2) *Monetary Union*. There is a West African Monetary Union (WAMU) with a Central Bank of West African States (BCEAO), both of which embrace only six countries of the sub-region.

3) *Joint Development Banking*. In August 1985, there were five Development Banks on regional and sub-regional basis; a sixth has folded. These are the African Development Bank (ADB); the West African Development Bank (WADB); the Development Bank of the Central African States (BDEAC); the Development Bank of the Great Lakes Countries (BDEGL); the Development Bank of East and Southern Africa (DBESA), which was included in its Treaty; and the former Development Bank of the former East African Economic Community. The objective of these banks is to pool financial resources to finance large, joint development projects in different sectors.

4) *Bilateral agreements among Central Banks*. This exists for the Central African and the West African Clearing Houses. Such agreement covers exchange regulations, movements of funds, and related payments issues among sub-regional groupings. Such a bilateral monetary agreement has been formed between Morocco and Tunisia and in 1981 others were proposed for North Africa.

5) *African Monetary Fund.* In addition to the African Development Bank, the Lagos Plan of Action proposes an African Mutual Guarantee and Solidarity Fund to operate as a Trade and Investment Bank for the African, Caribbean and Pacific (ACP) Group of States.

6) *African Centre for Monetary Studies, Dakar.* Not a financial institution, but a financial "think tank" for African countries which offers an excellent opportunity for the *Association of African Central Banks* and allied agencies to jointly examine Africa's financial problems, evolve a common monetary tradition and train their staff jointly so that they can easily man regional and sub-regional financial institutions.

Problems and prospects of African integration

As economic integration is an international issue, its most important problem has typically been political in two respects. One is the over-emphasised question of differences in ideological, political, economic and social systems of which ideological orientation (capitalist or socialist) and language are most visible. These differences are compounded by many African leaders' weak political will and lack of commitment to effective integration, which is due to an effective obsession with the national sovereignty of their impoverished and often oppressed populations. Some leaders even create deliberate obstacles to economic integration in order to facilitate them "sitting on their exploited countries". Foreign ideological powers and former colonial exploiters also interfere in an attempt to sabotage Africa's integration. The reality of the enormous human tragedy of the African crisis demands urgent action to reverse these negative attitudes, raise political commitment, and to eliminate such barriers in the legitimate interest of the majority of Africa's populace.

On the purely economic front, four other obstacles have been identified: 1) is the similarity of the production patterns of African countries which has rendered intra-African trade so low; 2) relates to infrastructural problems with different monetary systems, and poor transport and communications links between African countries. Some of the existing mini-economic groupings also tend to inhibit the establishment of larger sub-regional units; 3) the uneven size and development of African countries, especially the different levels of industrialisation, often raise fears of inequitable potential and of actual distribution of the benefits of integration. This distributional problem largely led to the collapse of the East African Economic Community whose advantages were alleged to have accrued mainly to Kenya; there are similar fears about Nigeria's status in ECOWAS and that of Zaire in Central and Southern Africa. Adequate and imaginative compensation schemes to poorer members that will locate development projects in their countries and offer other compensatory resource transfers to members to offset their losses are critical here. Both the richer and poorer members require good judgment in this respect. Finally, it is felt by some countries that the objectives of integrative efforts in Africa are too wide and over-ambitious; this can give rise to despair. The disbursement of meagre resources over regional and sub-regional groupings' carefully selected priorities that initially emphasise such urgent problems as food and trade, and industrial items such as capital and intermediate manufacturing, as well as monetary cooperation, might be easier to tackle in the short run.

The prospects for African economic integration are immense, in spite of these obstacles. It is a historical challenge to African ingenuity and statesmanship to overcome the barriers and reap the huge potential benefits of integration. In this regard, three fundamental considerations should be emphasised. One, that African economic integration is now basically a matter of survival, given the rapid growth and complexity of the African crisis. The combination of this internal crisis with the growing adventurism and desperation of imperialism dictated by its escalating crisis, demand an urgent survivalist response that transcends narrow politico-economic calculations from Africa.

Another is the fact that in the context of contemporary realities, virtually no country is individually viable today. Europe realised this when it imposed the EEC. Africa's plight is worse, and the urgency and necessity for collective self-reliance more compelling. Even import-substitution industrialisation has become collective import substitution. The age of independent national capitalist (and even socialist) development has gone. The growing assault of the multinationals, each of which has much larger resources than most African countries, the large optimum size of most essential industries (in terms of capital), overall interdependence of the world, leave Africa no choice but urgent and greater economic cooperation.

The iconoclasts who may still be suspicious of economic integration because of narrow ideological or socio-political (even economic) considerations bordering on national sovereignty must be prepared to give a convincing answer to the legitimate question: *sovereignty for whom?* If the correct answer is for the mass-majority of our people, and *not* for the minority of largely parasitic, exploitative and oppressive leaders and elites which currently dominate the African scene, then in the name of that mass-oriented sovereignty, African integration must be encouraged and consolidated because of its proven capacity to improve the lot of our desperately poor masses. Hence, *African integration must also become a proper agenda for class struggle* – the broad masses, which stand to gain most from it and from collective self-reliance, must press hard for closer integration by their leaders whose material and political interests may be better served by isolating their countries.[17]

Notes

1. While the classical theory of comparative advantage was elaborated by David Ricardo, the neoclassical version is based on the Heckscher–Ohlin model. For the detailed description and critique of these bourgeois models of comparative advantage, see Arrighi Emmanuel (1972).
2. A. Emmanuel (1972).
3. For example, R. W. Klein (1975) in *American Economic Review*, vol. LXIII, No. 1.
4. Samir Amin (1974), pp. 44–64.
5. World Bank, *World Development Report, 1984*, pp. 236–7.

6. The formulas used for computing these concentration ratio are (a) export commodity concentration index: $X_l = (100)\sqrt{\sum_i \left(\frac{Xij}{X.j}\right)^2}$,

the modified Gini-Hirschman coefficient, where Xij = j^{th} country's exports from the SITC's i^{th} good and X.j is its total exports; (b) export market concentration index: $X_l = (100)\sqrt{\sum_i \left(\frac{Xij}{X.j}\right)^2}$,

where Xij = exports of the jth country to the ith country and X.j is the total commodity export of the jth country in a given year.

7. B. Gibson (1980) in *Review of Radical Political Economics*, vol. 12, no. 3.

8. World Bank, *Toward Sustained Development in Sub-Saharan Africa*, p. 69, Table 13, last 2 columns.

9. Thus, the July 1985 OAU summit was addressed to economic crisis in Africa with a central focus on the five-year moratorium on Africa's debt service. This was against the backdrop of President Castro's demand for the cancellation of Third World debt; *Daily Excelsior* (Mexico), 21 March 1985.

10. See Cheryl Payer (1974) and (1982).

11. See President Fidel Castro's interview in *Daily Excelsior* (Mexico), 21 March 1985.

12. P. Korner et al. (1986).

13. For these benefits of economic integration, see E. Osagie and E. C. Edozien (1982).

14. This excludes the population of Cape Verde which was not given.

15. See UN (1983) *Twenty-five Years of Service to African Development and Integration* (Addis Ababa, ECA).

16. See African Centre for Monetary Studies (1982) "Implementation of the Lagos Plan of Action – Working Notes on the Aspects of Trade and Finance", paper presented at the Seminar organised by the ECA, CODESRIA and IDEP, Addis Ababa, 1–4 March 1982.

17. For studies of economic integration in Africa, see: V. P. Diejomaoh (1983) "The Economic Integration Process in Africa: Experience, Problems and Prospects", paper presented at the 7th World Congress of the International Economic Association, September 5–9, Madrid, Spain; OAU (1981) *Lagos Plan of Action for the Economic Development of Africa* (Addis Ababa, OAU and IILS Geneva); UN (1983) *Twenty-Five Years of Service to African Development and Integration* (Addis Ababa; ECA); A. Hazlewood (1975); P. Robson (1968).

9 Development Planning and Infrastructure

One major reason for this chapter is the growing incongruity between the prevalence, the high prestige and the motivation for development planning and the escalation of the African crisis. Since colonial times, every African country has systematically and continuously elaborated development plans with varying degrees of comprehensiveness and sophistication in order to promote national development and eliminate structural crisis. Many of these countries have ministries, commissions and institutes of development planning at national and even regional or state levels. Even the Economic Commission for Africa (ECA) has an African Regional Institute of Development and Economic Planning (IDEP) based in Dakar, Senegal. Yet, almost all of these planned African economies have been sinking deeper into crisis and underdevelopment. This adamant and growing conflict between the objectives of planning and the observed reality of its contrary and negative effects raises the urgent questions of what is basically wrong with development planning in Africa, and what corrective measures are required. A related concern of this chapter is the fragile status of Africa's physical and social infrastructure in spite of decades of their planned development.

The heritage of colonial planning

The acceptance of development planning as the basic organisational principle of national development in Africa, as elsewhere in the Third World,[1] dates back to the colonial era. After Joseph Stalin first instituted planned development in the Soviet Union, America's Marshall Plan for the reconstruction of Western Europe after the Second World War also inspired European colonialists to introduce development planning to the colonies. Three reasons seem to have initiated this experiment. One was the historical parallel between war-ravaged Europe and the imperialist-ravaged colonies. The second reason was that just as America's Marshall Plan was a form of material and moral compensation (in material terms the US gained enormously from the Second World War just as Europe lost terribly), colonial planned investment was also a kind of "European Marshall Plan". For war-weary Europe, it was a plan of appeasement for containing mounting nationalist agitation. It was also a moral compensation owed by the imperialist predators, not only for their criminal ravage of the colonies, but also for the heroic support of the colonial peoples to Europe against Hitler's terror. Colonial planning was also an instrument for enhancing the efficiency of surplus extraction. The third reason for the initiation of colonial planning can be traced to the broad intellectual developments associated with the aftermath of the Great Depression of 1929/33 and the birth of Keynesian economics with its central focus on state intervention in the growth process. The elaboration of the Harrod–Domar model[2] of development planning and of the crude dualistic models of economic growth are integral to development theorising, which emerged, first with the socialist transformation of the Soviet Union, and later with the extension of Keynesianism. This explains why both colonial and post-colonial bourgeois planning is anchored to Keynesian economics and the simplistic Harrod–Domar model. Thus, in Nigeria, the first colonial development plan was the Ten Year Plan of Development and Welfare for Nigeria, 1946/56.[3]

The acceptance of the basic tenets of colonial planning by both nationalist leaders and the ruling group of the post-colonial state, reflects the significant congruence between the *petit-bourgeois* ideology of these ruling groups, and the principles of colonial planning. These colonial planning tenets are anchored to two major planks: the ideological role of bourgeois development theory and its praxiological elements.[4] The main ideological roles of the former are the reproduction of the *ideal types* of imperialist societies and the proclamation of the "end of ideology dogma". The use of the ideal–typical index method[5] pitches the psychological traits of people in underdeveloped countries, such as collectivism, particularism, low need–achievement motivation, ascribed status, etc. against the alleged ideal characteristics of people in the imperialist countries, such as individualism, universalism, acquisitive aggression, prescribed status and so on. Development planners and other social scientists in the Third World are thus invited to formulate programmes to promote these ideal capitalist traits. Similarly, the end of ideology dogma seeks to eliminate the need for choice between capitalist and socialist development by negating any alternative path of development except the capitalist model. Hence, the major differences between capitalism and socialism are trivialised and their minor similarities magnified, in a vain search for ideological or system convergence between capitalism and socialism, as celebrated by Kenneth Galbraith's metaphysical *New Industrial State*.

The major effect of this false end of ideology dogma on colonial and post-colonial planning is the erroneous conceptualisation of development as mere growth via the crudely abstract Rostovian stages of economic growth,[6] and bogus theories of dualism[7] that preach modernisation in order to transform so-called subsistence sectors of traditional societies into modern sectors. Thus both the colonial and first two post-colonial plans in Nigeria were allegedly laying down Rostow's preconditions for the stage of take-off into self-sustained economic growth.

The praxiological role in bourgeois development theory is even more intimately related to colonial planning. This is with respect to its commitment to mixed economy, the search for a leading sector, the special need for the state to stimulate the private sector with detailed public sector planning and, at best, indicative private sector guidance. In this obtusely technocratic conception of planning, colonialism is exonerated from having played any essential role in generating underdevelopment, and there are no social conflicts except the conflict between present and future consumption. The major roles of the state in this colonial planning are twofold – to transfer large funds to public development through development banks, subsidies, cheap infrastructure and fiscal concessions, all aimed at strengthening the private sector; and to bear the risk of pioneering investment for the private sector to facilitate the future privatisation of successful public investments. The specific strategies associated with this colonial planning include export promotion for the continued production of primary products for export, imperialist-dominated and perverse import-substitution industrialisation and dependence on elusive foreign aid and imperialist direct investment. Thus while loans of £9 million were added to the British contribution of £23 million towards Nigeria's colonial plan of £55 million, the first post-colonial plan of 1962/68 required over 50% foreign funding. Finally, the methodology employed in colonial planning was predominantly the Harrod–Domar variant of Keynesian economics, with naive reliance on static capital-output ratio (COR) and the incremental capital-output ratio (ICOR).

These basic tenets of bourgeois development ideology and colonial planning have constituted the reactionary harbinger of post-colonial planning in Africa as elsewhere in the Third World, as thc basic philosophy, objectives, method and programmes of these neocolonial plans clearly confirm.

Critique of neocolonial capitalist planning

The basic continuity between the character of colonial and post-colonial planning in Africa makes it appropriate to dub these latter plans as *neocolonial capitalist planning*. This is with respect to their fundamental ideological orientation as well as their policies and programmes. An immanent critique of this mode of planning is, perhaps, best articulated in terms of its basic features.

The basic ideological commitment of most post-colonial planning in Africa is to neocolonial capitalism, except in the new socialist states. The capitalist path of development is the model of these plans, whether this is stated explicitly or not. In most cases, this dependent capitalist orientation is couched in terms of building a mixed economy, as in Nigeria, Kenya and other neocolonial states.[8] But in a few cases, for example, Senegal, Zaire, Uganda and even Tanzania, a bogus "African socialism" is proclaimed as a ruse for neocolonial capitalist construction. It is this ideological commitment to capitalism that makes post-colonial planning an exercise in planning for underdevelopment, because capitalism, or its global form, imperialism, is the tap-root of the underdevelopment of the Third World. Planning with a capitalist model embodying predominant imperialist and other exploitative interests is, therefore, to be strengthening the forces of backwardness and underdevelopment.

The role of the state in neocolonial capitalist planning is to initially make the public sector the leading sector of the economy in order to build the private sector of the mixed economy, which is to become the subsequent leading sector. So detailed planning of the public sector is undertaken, while only vague, general indicative guidelines are directed at the weak and embryonic private sector. Some even insist that *petit-bourgeois* planning is simply public sector planning. The state provides massive investment in physical and social infrastructure in preparation for the so-called preconditions for take-off. It also undertakes pioneering and risky investment in other sectors, especially in new and medium to large-scale enterprises, as well as offering massive transfers of public funds to the private sector through development banks, corruptly operated parastatals, over-generous tax concessions and other fiscal incentives, especially to exploitative foreign investors. In a few cases, the state even aspires to control the "commanding heights"[9] of the economy through the domination of such strategic industries as banking, heavy and defence industries, other essential manufacturing, foreign trade, transport and telecommunications, etc. Yet, the point that *powerful private enterprise is incompatible with effective planned development* is frequently missed; in planning it is impossible to mobilise and allocate resources for development if you do not own and control them. Another salient feature of neocolonial capitalist planning is the predominance of imperialist and capitalist interests which derives from the reactionary class configuration that dominates the state and economy. Given this class bias, not surprisingly, this form of planning is seen as a purely technocratic exercise in which social questions and class conflicts are wafted away in the airy breeze of growthmanship, and the reconciliation of the only perceived conflict is the technical one between present and future consumption, which the appropriate planner's discount rate is supposed to resolve. The *petit-bourgeois* intellectuals (mostly reactionary economists) and capitalist-oriented bureaucrats who dominate this planning process thus impose pro-imperialist and elitist policies and programmes in the partisan pursuit of their minority and often unpatriotic class aspirations. Major highlights of these reactionary policies include the intensification of the external dependency relationship, the preservation of the client status of the economy, and export promotion through the uncritical expansion of primary production. Additional features are an import-substitution policy that panders to multinational domination with import-dependent industries and a distorted commitment to a capitalist private sector, involving massive subsidies and other incentives to imperialist and domestic exploiters. Then an outrageously urban-biased investment programme is imposed that bristles with super-expressways, multi-storey buildings, specialist hospitals, and luxury assembly industries, in countries without basic feeder roads, rudimentary clinics, potable drinking water, simple shelter and essential manufactures for the majority of the national population.

These contradictions in the investment programme of *petit-bourgeois* planning highlight its basic lack of a *mass base*[10] in three critical respects. One, that the legitimate aspirations of the mass-majority for such basic *needs* as food, water, shelter, health-care, and so on, are persistently neglected in the objectives, policies and programmes of this type of planning. The second is the scandalous lack of participation of the majority of the working people in the formulation of these plans, despite bucolic rhetoric about grass-roots planning; and the issue is not the pedantic and obscurantist one of the broad masses not being literate or skilled in the art of planning. This diversionary excuse arises only from the narrow and erroneous conception of planning as a purely technocratic exercise. Yet, development planning is fundamentally a *framework for social debate*[11] about the desirable goals of national development, its ideological direction, the priorities of resource use, the equitable distribution of the gains of development, greater mass control over the organisation of production and, ultimately, self-development for groups and individuals. Third is the inability to mobilise the majority of the population for plan implementation. The point is simply that successful and effective planning requires the mobilisation of broad social forces for the execution of plan programmes. Clearly, if the aspirations of the mass-majority are not adequately reflected in the planning process, the energy of the masses cannot be mobilised successfully to implement the plan. This is one basic reason why most neocolonial plans remain unimplemented as mere "paper tigers".

For obvious reasons of partisan vested interest, the leadership of most African and other Third World countries do not back up development planning with adequate political will, especially during plan implementation.[12] Plan discipline is typically weak or non-existent, as the plan document is violated with impunity. The leaders themselves are culpable in this respect – while sound plan projects are not executed, dubious, "white elephant" projects not even included in the plan are hastily executed for perverse political expedience and corrupt corporate reasons. Those who violate the plan are not punished neither are those who implement it rewarded. The fundamental reason for this lax attitude is that *the critical class interests of the neocolonial leadership are opposed to planned development*. This is because successful planning will mobilise and liberate the masses enabling them to acquire economic and political power, and to challenge the dominant class. The leadership of the neocolonial countries, therefore, merely pay lip service to planning and development generally, while effectively pursuing policies of underdevelopment. It is also why the issue of effective development planning is a major area of class struggle.[13]

Financial planning is another defect in *petit-bourgeois* planning, and an instrument of bourgeois class corruption and consolidation. The projects and programmes in these plan documents are typically stated in monetary terms and the progress reports on them also evaluate their implementation in financial terms. Thus in Nigeria's Second Plan (1970/74), the progress report claimed that some projects were implemented 200%,[14] meaning that twice the sum allocated to them had been spent – even though the projects may not have been physically executed to the extent of even 50%. This exercise in delusion has a built-in commitment to kleptocracy, especially with the standard practice of criminal contract inflation. Yet, what is required is the use of material balances[15] in planning that will stipulate physical targets in addition to financial allocations.

Keynesian growthmanship,[16] especially in the Harrod–Domar model, is a common feature of neocolonial planning. This has two main elements. One is the focus on the growth rate of Gross National Product (GNP) or Gross Domestic Product (GDP) and other Keynesian aggregates such as saving, investment, exports, imports, and so on, as the preoccupation of development planning, which is why this type of planning has been dubbed "GDP planning" or the "growth number game". It ignores such other critical national economic variables as the social relations of production, the development of productive forces, the maintenance of proportions in the national economy through the planning of these basic proportions, sectoral linkages and structural transformation. Thus, *petit-bourgeois* planning typically leads to the pathetic anathema of growth without development. The other aspect of this Keynesian planning methodology is the use of the static Harrod–Domar model and the imperialist inspired two-gap approach. While the former hinges national development mainly on the capital-output and the incremental capital-output ratios (COR and ICOR, respectively), the latter insists on seeking external funds to fill the bigger of the alleged two gaps in planning[17] – the savings gap (the difference between planned savings and planned investment) and the trade gap (export minus import). Predictably, the Harrod–Domar model is a recipe for growth without development, and the two-gap model is a formula for external dependence and the intensification of neocolonialism. The timid use of input–output tables in neocolonial planning, with their relative small size, poor data and static input coefficients, is hamstrung by external dependence, which transfers critical structural linkages abroad.[18]

For these reasons, the collective consequences of decades of neocolonial capitalist planning in Africa and the Third World in general have been an unmitigated disaster, and the human tragedy they have precipitated is most eloquently summarised in the deepening crisis throughout the Third World.[19] Many African countries, such as Zaire, Ghana, Sudan, Uganda and even Tanzania, have suffered total collapse, in spite of years of planning "African socialism", and collapse threatens the show-pieces of neocolonialism, like Nigeria, Kenya, Liberia, Senegal, and so on. Elsewhere in the Third World, such as Latin America and South-East Asia, the effect of neocolonial capitalist planning has also been very disappointing.

Planning and the colonial status of African physical and social infrastructure

Besides the escalating crisis of the continent, another major index of the failure of neocolonial capitalist planning in Africa is the essentially colonial status of her physical and social infrastructure. While the physical infrastructure consists of transport and communications such as roads, railways, ports and harbours, river transport, posts, telegraphs and telecommunications, and energy, the social infrastructure comprises mainly housing, water, educational and health facilities. The rapid development of these infrastructural services has been one of the persistent and central objectives of development planning in Africa. Yet, after more than three decades of this so-called planned development, (effectively, planned underdevelopment) infrastructural facilities are still grossly inadequate, basically uncoordinated and so poorly maintained that many are in advanced stages of deterioration and virtual collapse. The situation is such that most African countries can more easily contact Europe, either physically or by post and phone, than any other African country. Indeed, in many of these countries, one has to first connect to a European capital before phoning another African country. Not only has this crippling situation retarded intra-African trade and cooperation, as discussed in chapter 8, but has inhibited trade and development within individual African countries, where foodstuffs rot on the farms and millions starve in cities.

The state of physical infrastructure

One index of the parlous state of African infrastructure is the paucity of data available on it – even at the level of the Economic Commission for Africa (ECA) as it admitted: "for road traffic . . . knowledge remains poor".[20] For what they are worth, the available data are summarised below for Africa's total area of 30.3 million square kilometers.[21]

Roads: In 1970, the total mileage of roads and seasonal tracks in Africa was estimated at 1.1 million km., of which 150,600 km. were of stones or covered with bituminous binder. By 1973, the road network stood at 1.3 million km., or one km. of road per 30 square kms. In 1965, there was a total of 645,000 commercial vehicles and 1.2 million by 1973. Four trans-African highways were under construction in 1985: 1) The Trans-Saharan road through Algiers, Gao in Mali to Arlit in Niger; 2) The Trans-African highway from Lagos to Mombasa in Kenya; 3) the Trans-Sahelian highway from Dakar to Ndjamena in Chad; 4) the Coastal Route from Nouakchott in Mauritania to Lagos.

Railways: In 1971, 90,976 km. of rail lines were estimated for the whole of Africa (including South Africa), and this was equivalent to one km. of rail for 333 square km., or for 380 people. By 1975, the total extent of railways was an estimated 94,000 km. The volume of rail freight traffic was estimated at 53,564 ton-km. in 1975. Table 9.1 shows ECOWAS railway traffic for 1974/77.

One embarrassing aspect of Africa's railways is that they still run from the hinterland to the coast for the evacuation of export products, as the colonialist built them. Little by way of lines parallel to the coast has since been added. One of the most recent of the major rail lines is the Tan-Zam line of over 1,860 km. from Dar es Salaam to the Zambian Copperbelt at Kapiri-Moshi.

Shipping: African sea transport statistics distinguish between international shipping, involving direct links with the rest of the world, international coastal shipping and domestic coastal shipping. There is also domestic river transport, which is very important in a continent with many navigable rivers and poor modes of alternative transport. The total shipping tonnage of the first three types rose 100% between 1965 and 1974 to a total tonnage of 474 million. If that trend was maintained in the following decade, the total tonnage by 1983 would have been around 948 million tons. Yet most of Africa's shipping is still handled by foreign vessels; in Nigeria, by 1985, the National Shipping Line still handled less than 25% of the country's total shipping. The total numbers of Africa's merchant ships is shown in Table 9.2.

Air transport: The development of both international and domestic air transport in Africa is very recent, partly because of past colonial policy and the post-colonial poverty of the continent. By 1975, 25 African airlines were reported to be offering

Table 9.1
ECOWAS railway traffic, 1947/77

Country/Year	Gauge (mm)	Weight kg/m	Length (km) Total	Single Track	Double Track	Passengers	Wagons Goods No.	Goods – Total Capacity (million tons)
Benin–Niger (1977)	1,000	30/25	579	579	—	11	334	8,407
Burkina Faso/						1,040	—	139
Ivory Coast (1977)	—	—	1,314	—	—	(Pass. x km)	—	(tons x km)
Ghana (1975)	1,067	40/30	952	—	—	182	3,287	—
Guinea	1,000	36	662	—	—	20	500	—
Mali (1977)	1,000	30	641	—	—	32	438	13,539
Nigeria (1974)	1,067	40/30	3,523	—	—	55	6,707	282,016
Senegal (1976)	1,000	20/36	1,034	964	70	93	911	27,330
Togo (1976)	1,000	36/33	442	—	—	63	293	4,680
Abidjan–Niger	1,000	30/25	1,174	1,156	18	125	1,290	49,130

Source: ECOWAS (1977) *Study on the Coordination of Transport and Communications*, Vol. 1, pp. 182, 199.

Table 9.2
Merchant Fleet: selected African countries, 1977

Country	*No. of Ships of 100 GRT and above*	*GRT*	*Non-Specialised Cargo Ships*		*Oil Tankers*	
			No.	*GRT*	*No.*	*GRT*
Benin	—	—	—	—	—	—
Cape Verde	3	2,252	2	1,815	—	—
Ivory Coast	15	103,073	15	103,073	—	—
Gambia	1	641	1	641	—	—
Ghana	22	136,041	22	136,041	—	—
Guinea	3	11,200	2	436	—	—
Guinea Bissau	—	—	—	—	—	—
Liberia[a]	2,577	79,701,658	580	3,880,098	910	50,772,231
Nigeria	44	319,557	38	176,088	6	143,496
Senegal	12	12,456	5	4,867	4	3,876
Sierra Leone	3	5,042	3	5,042	—	—
Togo	—	—	—	—	—	—
Total ECOWAS	*103*	*590,262*	*88*	*431,003*	*10*	*147,345*
Algeria	61	1,005,242	34	123,034	17	623,203
Angola	13	19,463	11	17,588	2	1,875
Cameroon	4	72,605	3	25,078	1	47,527
Gabon	7	96,859	4	22,131	2	74,471
Morocco	44	274,003	30	75,456	5	105,584
Zaire	11	95,951	10	82,470	—	—

[a] Liberian flag excluded; these are US data.

Source: ECOWAS (1977) *Study on the Coordination of Transport and Communications*, vol. I, p. 75.

regular freight services with over 300 cargo aircraft (see Table 9.3 for ECOWAS airlines).

Energy: The overall energy situation in Africa is good, but there are two disturbing signs. One is the declining growth rate of the annual production of commercial energy, which fell from 10.4% for low-income sub-Saharan Africa during 1965/73, to 8.4% in 1973/83, and from 30.8% for middle-income sub-Saharan Africa in 1965/73 to –2.5% during 1973/83. In particular, while for low-income sub-Saharan Africa the annual average growth rate of commercial energy consumption was only 1.1% (compared to the annual growth of production of 8.4% during 1973/83), during the same decade, the production growth rate for middle-income sub-Saharan Africa was –2.5%, while the consumption growth rate was 7%, implying an annual deficit of 9.5%. Over the same period the corresponding figures for lower-middle income Africa were 2.2% and 5.5%, with 3.3% deficit over the same period. The other disturbing aspect is the growing energy import bill for the oil importers, especially since the 1973 oil crisis. This heavy import of fuel, which was only 5% of merchandise export for sub-Saharan Africa in 1965, became a major source of the

Table 9.3
Traffic of ECOWAS airlines: 1976

Airlines	*Passenger* *International*	*Passenger* *National*	*Freight* *International*	*Freight* *National*	*Total Pass. x km (million)*	*Total Tons x km (million)*	*Passenger load factor (%)*
Air Afrique[1]	444,561	—	44,044	—	1,370	144	55.5
Air Mali	42,119	17,269	422	7	98.3	0.8	57.2
Ghana Airways	121,061	127.707	1,240	199	234	2.8	64.8
Air Liberia	15,822	—	84	—	4	0.03	32.4
Nigeria Airways	125,172	529,212	1,032	816	634	253	60.9
Air Guinea (1977)	21,000	—	240	—	10	0.1	49[1]
Air Volta (1975)	—	2,767	—	—	—	—	—
Air Mauritania (1977)	10,000	—	300	—	6	0.2	48[2]
Air Ivoire (1977)	—	55,395	—	450	—	—	—
TACV	3,000	72,267	26	61	—	—	—

[1] International traffic only.
[2] The entire traffic.

Source: ECOWAS (1977) *Study on the Coordination of Transport and Communications*, Vol. I, p. 211.

balance of payments crisis of many African countries. The situation thus demands the urgent elaboration of appropriate energy policies, for both oil exporters and importers.

Africa's social infrastructure

The deplorable state of Africa's social infrastructure is better appreciated in human terms than by its physical structures. The state of the two most important components of these social services, health and education, will be summarised with respect to their human indicators (see Tables 9.4 and 9.5).

Table 9.4
Sub-Saharan Africa's health-related indicators

Zone	*Pop. per physican: 1980*	*Pop. per nursing person: 1980*	*Daily calories supply per capita, as % of need: 1982*	*Child death rate (age 1–4) (per 1,000): 1983*	*Crude death rate per 1000 pop: 1982*
Sub-Saharan Africa	21,234	2,978	90	23	17
ICCs[a]	554	180	132	less than 6	9
Low-income semi-arid Africa	33,987	3,620	88	34 (1982)	22
Low-income other	26,585	3,370	86	18	17
Middle-income oil importers	11,223	1,522	100	20 (1982)	17
Middle-income oil exporters	13,327	2,878	91	21 (1982)	16
Nigeria	12,550	3,010	91	17	16

[a] ICCs = industrialised capitalist countries of Western Europe, North American and Japan.
Sources: World Bank, *Toward Sustained Development in sub-Saharan Africa*, pp. 83–6; *World Development Report 1985*, pp. 212–3.

The aggregative data in Table 9.6 hide some glaring disparities. Thus Ethiopia had the highest population per physician of 58,490 in 1980; nine other countries had more than sub-Saharan Africa's average, while Mauritius had the lowest figure of 2,000. Similarly, the number of people per nursing person was highest at 9,840 in Rwanda and lowest at 550 in Kenya. The daily calorie intake per capita as a percentage of requirement was highest at 125 in Mauritius, 100 and more in ten other countries, and least in Guinea-Bissau with 70. The child death rate in 1982 was highest at 50 per 1,000 in Sierra Leone and Gambia, and lowest – three per 1,000 – in Mauritius. The crude death rate was highest at 28 per 1,000 in Guinea Bissau and lowest in Mauritius at seven per 1,000. The prevalence of over-crowded hospitals and other health centres with grossly inadequate beds, drugs and other facilities as well as numerous preventable diseases such as malaria, diarrhoea, cholera, typhoid, for example, all testify to the parlous state of health facilities in Africa.

The reason for this lies partly in the low level of educational development and the pervasive ignorance that imposes a culture of silence on the vast majority of the African population.

Table 9.5
Educational indicators for sub-Saharan Africa, 1982

Zone	*No. enrolled in primary school as % of age group*			*No. enrolled in secondary school as % of age group*	*No. enrolled in higher education as % of population: 20–24*
	Total	*Male*	*Female*		
Sub-Saharan Africa	69	79	56	14	1
ICCs	102	102	102	87	37
Low-income semi-arid (1981)	27	36	19	7	n.a.
Low-income other (1981)	76	86	64	14	n.a.
Middle-income oil importers (1981)	74	82	75	17	n.a.
Middle-income oil exporters (1981)	101	98	75	17	n.a.
Nigeria	98	94 (1981)	70 (1981)	16	n.a.

Source: World Bank (1984), *Toward Sustained Development . . .*, p. 87; *World Development Report 1985*, pp. 222–3.

These figures also conceal wide disparaties in educational development among African countries. First, the overall literacy rate for the continent still hovers around 30%. Thus in 1982, the highest percentage total primary enrolment was 130 in Zimbabwe (second in the world after the United Arab Emirates with 132) and lowest in Niger with 23; the male primary enrolment percentage was also highest in Zimbabwe with 134 (the world's highest) and lowest in Burkina Faso with 28; female primary enrolment was highest in Lesotho with 129 (the third in the world) and lowest in Burkina Faso with 16. While percentage secondary school enrolment was highest in the Congo with 69, it was least in Rwanda with two and only three in Tanzania, Burkina Faso, Burundi and Chad; higher educational enrolment percentage was highest at 15 in Egypt with six in the Congo and Morocco, and lowest at one in eleven other African countries. In many of these countries, the standard or quality of education has been falling rapidly, and the educational systems of many of them have been in serious crisis since the 1970s with worsening under-funding, under-staffing and grossly inadequate supplies of books, laboratory equipment and even buildings.

In housing and water services, reliable data are not available for the whole of Africa, but the country data and experiences are appalling. While the majority of the African population still eke a precarious existence in widely isolated mud huts with thatched roofs and in dilapidated hovels, the rapid urbanisation generated from the high migration from the rural areas has converted most African cities into vast sprawling slums with criminally infested shanty towns, where sewage, lighting and pipe-borne water are rare luxuries. Even in such state capital cities as Ibadan, millions still drink from dirty running streams and other infected sources.

Towards alternative development planning and infrastructural construction

The dominant objectives of alternative development planning and infrastructural construction in Africa are the achievement of self-reliance and effective integration at national and regional levels. In order to succeed, the alternative strategies have to be addressed specifically to the shortcomings of current practices, as well as being informed by a creative vision of the types of societies we want to create in Africa. Hence, far from development planning being anchored to ideological dogma, the ideological question of the appropriate model of development must be keenly contested as it informs the planning format and the pattern of infrastructural development. Within this framework, the desired alternative planning orientation must embrace some minimum mechanisms.

People's democratic planning

The essential requirements of the new planning strategy are mass orientation and democratic process, as opposed to the bureaucratic practices of the contemporary approach. A fundamental element of this is the basic restructuring of the economy from its external dependence to a national, sub-regional and regional self-reliance orientation. This demands, not growth and reforms within the neocolonial capitalist economy with its minority and pro-imperialist obsessions, but radical transformation for the achievement of genuine national economic independence. Just as it is irrational to attempt to optimise in an equitable manner within a slave economy without destroying slavery, it is also untenable to attempt to plan a dependent mixed economy without first restructuring it. This demands terminating its stifling foreign domination and loosely integrated structures.

In order to ensure that planning is consonant with the legitimate aspirations of the broad masses both in rural and urban areas there must be an abiding commitment to supplying the basic needs[22] of the majority of the national population and guide the formulation of plan objectives and policies, as well as the selection of programmes and projects. One major advantage of this mass orientation will be to ensure an adequate domestic market, based on the effective demands of the majority of the populace, which will obviate the limited elite demand that persistently inhibits industrialisation in Third World countries. It will also eliminate the absurd perversion of Africa's so-called planned economies that routinely consume what they do not produce, and produce what they do not consume. In this regard, it is important to emphasise that no effective self-reliance is possible if African countries cannot provide the majority of their population with the essential requirements of food, water, health-care, housing, clothing, and so on, from their own national resources; and this is not a naive argument about autarky.

The creation of a mass democratic base for effective planning will also be facilitated by this alternative approach. Since the implementation of development plans must necessarily depend on the mobilisation of broad social forces and energies, plan formulation must be firmly rooted in the broad masses of the population, rather than on the flimsy support of the minority elite and their imperialist mentors. The mobilisation of idle reserves of scattered rural funds, the utilisation of abundant labour force for capital formation in roads, buildings, agriculture, and similar programmes, are feasible only if planning is anchored to the grass-roots of the population. Grass-root planning in this regard is a two-way process: involving the rural and urban masses in the formulation of plan objectives, policies and programmes to meet their democratic aspirations and mobilising the broad masses to participate actively in the execution of plans.

Proportion planning is also critical to these processes.[23] This is what is loosely termed balanced growth, in bourgeois terminology. Here the major proportions in national economy are between industry and agriculture, the economic sectors and the social services, physical infrastructure and direct production, construction and energy, and so forth. One effective way to satisfy these basic proportions is by the use of *input–output tables* and *social accounting matrices*. Decentralised *optimal planning* is also useful here. These exercises require technical skills, but this is no excuse for converting development planning from a democratic social process into an elitist and obtusely technocratic exercise. It is the failure to observe these critical proportions and structural linkages in planning that leads to embarrassing shortages and surpluses, and even to deepening crisis in Africa, as the differing fortunes of agriculture and distribution clearly show.

The method of material balances[24] should also supplement planning in financial terms in order to enhance plan implementation and check potential plan corruption through the embezzlement of funds and contract inflation. Thus for agriculture, in addition to allocating, say, ₦10 million for food production, the types of food, their hẹctareage and target output should be indicated. It is only against these physical targets that real achievement can be measured. Plan progress reports should include information on the proportion of the stipulated physical targets that have been met.

African leaders must also commit greater *political will* to planned development. So far, there has been too much rhetoric and lip service. There are several ways of generating and committing this political will. One is to create a National Planning Commission, *outside* the civil service framework, and directly responsible to the President and National Assembly, or to the highest executive and legislative authorities. Each Development Plan should also be enacted into law and thus be legally binding on everybody concerned. (Ironically in this regard, the state budget, which is an annual plan, is passed into law but a development plan, which is much larger and comprises several annual budgets, is not passed into law.) Additionally, sanctions should be imposed on those who capriciously violate development plans, while those who implement them should be rewarded – so that plan discipline is not simply a negative punitive matter. The leadership itself should not capriciously engage in plan distortion, by arbitrarily adding or dropping plan projects – the established procedure for plan revision should be followed.

It is equally necessary to recognise, practise and integrate the three plan sequences: the annual plan or budget, the medium-term (three to five year) plan, and the *perspective plan* (10–20 years).[25] Most African countries have no perspective plans and their annual budgets are typically unrelated to their medium-term plans, yet all these plans are addressed to the same resources and the same economy. This is why African and other Third World development efforts tend to be haphazard and uncoordinated, with the result that they fumble from one crisis to another.

Sub-regional and regional planning should also supplement local national planning. Each zone of cooperation should have a planning division to articulate and chart the development of the cooperating unit. Enterprises, such as industries and infrastructural projects, that are beyond the scope of individual countries' resources can be planned and executed at this collective level. The *Lagos Plan*[26] is a bold attempt in this direction, but unfortunately, it is still largely a "paper tiger" yet to be implemented.

Infrastructural development and maintenance

It should be emphasised that the development of more democratic methods of planning and plan implementation is not enough, especially in respect to infrastructural development. It is crucial that new infrastructures and other development projects should be maintained on a continuous basis. The persistent failure to maintain installed infrastructures and equipment in Africa is a major weakness of infrastructural development and planning. Clearly, no matter what the quantity and quality of these facilities, and the democratic participation in their development, if they cannot be repaired and kept in good working and usable condition, their contribution to development will be greatly diminished.

Minor repairs to roads, bridges and other facilities are usually delayed until potholes become gullies and thus qualify for the award of inflated contracts. The narrow-gauge colonial railways are frequently subject to flooding, especially during the wet seasons, the rolling stock is dilapidated and coaches overcrowded. Much the same story of poor maintenance holds for educational institutions, health facilities with inadequate drugs and damaged equipment, buildings and other installations. Yet, it is infinitely cheaper to repair than to replace these infrastructures. What is required are units in the relevant ministries, charged with the responsibility for maintaining facilities, with trained and well equipped personnel. Indeed, training of appropriate technical staff to maintain and repair infrastructural facilities and equipment should be a compulsory element of the contracts to construct or purchase them.

The failure to install mass-oriented infrastructural facilities is a related shortcoming. Rather than elite facilities such as expressways, specialist hospitals and the like, the broad masses of the population require less expensive all-season feeder roads, rural health clinics or polyclinics, boreholes, more integrative railways linking various parts of the country, and dredging of the rivers for all-season navigation. Most African countries' overall capacity to spend on infrastructure is severely limited, but a reallocation of the available funds could achieve better results. The integration of regional planning with development planning to coordinate utilisation of space is also necessary in this regard.

On the other hand, the criminal inflation of infrastructural contracts, for roads, buildings, ports, for example, with 10% kick-backs salted away into foreign bank accounts is a major constraint. If, for example, a contract for a 50 km. road that should cost ₦20 million is inflated to ₦48 million, then ₦28 million that would have provided other infrastructural development is lost. Public enquiries in various Third World countries have disclosed the incidence of contracts paid for but not executed, and others paid for two or three times to different contractors at inflated costs. Oil exporters, like Nigeria for example, lose billions of naira annually through this inflation of contracts. Shoddy construction work is a related problem, but because the contractor has paid a kick-back, the project sponsors and staff approve any standard of work, however poor. The people must instil into their leaders that they must *build for posterity*, especially in view of limited resources and of the infrastructural inadequacies yet to be rectified in the face of deepening crisis.

Intra-African cooperation is also essential here. Happily, some beginning has been made with a few trans-African highways under construction. But their progress is too slow and such ventures are too few relative to the need and opportunities for them. A more purposeful commitment is required and this should start with individual heads of state, the OAU and the ECA, with the cultivation of more friendly cooperation to keep borders open and facilitate effective coordination of projects. The ideological differences among African countries are over-dramatised, but after all, EEC members are not all of the same ideological persuasion, but they share a common commitment to the progress of their countries and the welfare of their people. The African masses must compel their leaders to provide this effective leadership and Pan-Africanism.

The use of direct labour in infrastructure

In concluding this chapter, it is pertinent to raise the immense potentialities of employing *direct* labour, as opposed to *contract* labour for three related purposes: (1) the implementation of plan projects; (2) construction of new infrastructural facilities; and (3) repair and maintenance of existing infrastructures.

Under the conditions of acute shortage of capital in Africa, it is clear that many development projects, for example, dams, irrigation works, and rural projects, could be constructed wholly or partly by the use of direct labour. The relevant Ministries of Works or Construction could prepare estimates of the quantities, and buy construction materials required, and hire workers directly to construct these projects. For the construction of new infrastructures, such as schools, hospitals or health clinics/dispensaries, rural feeder roads, waterworks and so on, the local communities could be mobilised to provide the direct labour. The local or state/national government could provide equipment and other capital support for such projects. In Nigeria, some state governments and the newly created Federal and State Directorates for Rural Development are already employing direct labour for these purposes with great success.

Road maintenance and the maintenance of other infrastructural facilities could also be carried out by the use of direct labour; the proximity of such workers to the infrastructural facilities would be a major advantage. Because they would constantly be using these facilities they could quickly detect the need for repair, mobilise local resources and carry out repairs quickly and cheaply.

Employing direct labour in such ways would have some basic advantages. For example, it would reduce the high and rising cost of construction and maintenance of development projects and infrastructures by eliminating or reducing inflated contracts. Furthermore, just as these inflated contracts slow down the pace of development by reducing the number of potential projects, the use of direct labour is a well-known method of rural capital formation. The relatively abundant labour supply in African countries, especially in rural areas, could thus be mobilised to offset the disadvantage of their relative scarcity of capital. In this way, those communities within which development and infrastructural projects are located could be mobilised to provide the labour (and possibly some local, raw materials), for their construction, while capital requirements (equipment, cement, roofing materials, personnel, drugs, etc.) could be provided by higher agencies.

In addition, by utilising direct instead of contract labour, unemployment could be reduced. Multinational corporations in the construction sector tend to use capital-intensive methods, while the direct labour method is labour-intensive. The direct labour method, by engaging more workers, would help reduce the increasingly high level of unemployment in Africa. Projects that could not be wholly executed by direct labour could be sub-divided: with the capital-intensive parts contracted out, and the labour-intensive components executed by direct labour. For example, in road construction, the capital-intensive earth works (levelling and hardening) and drainage could be contracted, while bush-clearing and asphalting could be done by direct labour.

Notes

1. Even though most Latin American countries achieved their nominal independence before the age of planned development emanating from the Bolshevik Revolution of 1917, their planning was inspired under their neocolonial subordination to the USA.

2. This model was developed separately by R. F. Harrod (1939) in *Economic Journal*, 49, pp. 14–33 and E. Domar (1946) in *Econometrica*, 14, pp. 137–147.

3. *A Ten-Year Plan of Development and Welfare in Nigeria*, Sessional Paper No. 24, 1945.

4. See S. Amin et al. (1978) in *Africa Development*, vol. 3, no. 2.

5. See A. G. Frank (1970), ch. 2.

6. W. W. Rostow (1962).

7. J. H. Boeke (1953).

8. See Paul Mattick (1980), chs. 14, 16 & 20.

9. J. G. Zeilinski (1968).

10. See L. Cliffe & J. S. Saul (ed.) (1975) vol. 2.

11. See Stuart Holland (ed.) (1979), chs. 6 & 10.

12. Consider Edwin Dean (1972).

13. On this fundamental question of the necessity for class struggle in development, see Paul Baran (1968).

14. *Progress Reports on the Second Plan, 1971/74* (1974), Lagos.

15. L. Ya Berry (ed.) (1977), vol. I ch. 4.

16. Stuart Holland (1979), chs. 7 & 8.

17. These two gaps are derived from the Keynesian identity Y = C + I + X – M, implying Y – C – I = X – M. So S – I = X – M (where Y – C = S). The left side is the savings gap and right side is the trade gap. See I. Adelman and H. B. Chenery (1966) in *Review of Economics and Statistics*, XLVIII, February, pp. 1–19.

18. On the limited use of these crude input–output tables for planning, see L. Ya Berry (1977) ch. 10.

19. See A. G. Frank (1980).

20. *African Economic Indicators* (1975), p. 43.

21. Ibid., pp. 43–5. Data on other infrastructures are also from this source and the sources indicated in the tables.

22. J. Friedman (1979) in *World Development*, vol. 7.

23. On planning proportions, see Ya Berry (1977); V. N. Kirichenko (1980); and A. Brody (1970).

24. Ibid.

25. J. G. Zeilinski (1968); and V. N. Kirichenko (1980).

26. OAU (1981) *The Lagos Plan of Action for the Economic Development of Africa, 1980–2000* (Addis Ababa).

10 Social and Political Failures in Africa

Africa's rapidly escalating crisis is both economic and non-economic. One non-economic dimension is the intellectual crisis in the social sciences discussed in Chapter 2. In addition, the continent is plagued by major social and political failures. Effectively then, the African crisis is located not only at the economic foundation but also at the socio-political superstructure of the state and society. Since both are organically linked as the two components of the same social formation, critical interactions between an economic crisis and a crisis of the superstructure can be expected. Fundamental structural linkages therefore exist between Africa's economic crises and the associated socio-political failures.

The economic crisis has contributed to the socio-political crisis with respect to the growing number of economic refugees (that is those displaced from their countries by drought, famine, flooding for example, as opposed to political refugees fleeing from political repression) and the rising unemployment and inequalities, which have led to increased crime and prostitution. The state's fiscal crisis associated with the economic crisis has also contributed to political instability and the collapse of the fledgling welfare state, which has meant persistent mass illiteracy, deteriorating health, housing and related social services. Conversely, the socio-political crisis has partly generated or exacerbated the economic crisis in several ways. One is by way of the massive outright looting of the neocolonial capitalist state in Africa to the point of total or near collapse of the economy by corrupt predatory leaders as in Zaire (under Mobutu), Ghana, Sudan (under Nimeiry), Nigeria, Equatorial Guinea, Uganda, among others. Another relates to the pro-imperialist policies of underdevelopment perpetrated in neocolonial Africa by its *petit-bourgeois* dominant classes, as analysed in Chapter 5. In addition, basic incompetence and economic management have suffered from perversion of the bureaucracy in most African states. The best example of this is, perhaps, the prompt imposition of austerity measures and general sacrifice, in the name of an abused patriotism, for dealing with economic crises. These austerity measures are typically repressive and inequitable with respect to the broad masses.

The conceptualisation of Africa's socio-political crisis

It is thus possible to predicate the social and political failures in Africa on four planes: (1) the deepening socio-political crises; (2) the dashed hopes and legitimate expectations of the African majority since nominal independence; (3) the abysmal gap between socio-political performance and what is feasible in terms of the rich material, human and cultural potentialities; (4) Africa's lagging global status, relative not only to the industrialised countries, but to the other post-colonial regions of Latin America and South-East Asia. In the socio-political crisis, we encounter such political problems as persistent tussles over leadership succession, political repression or outright fascism, as in Idi Amin's Uganda[1] and Bokassa's Central African Empire, separatist irredentism and widespread kleptocracy among highly placed state functionaries. There are also social failures, such as increasing numbers of refugees, both political and economic, rising crimes and increasing numbers of beggars. These failures have contributed to mass disillusion with political independence due to the failure to ameliorate mass poverty, growing inequalities through the Africanisation of colonial privileges, and the increasing proletarianisation of the peasantry, all of which have generated growing alienation of the broad masses from African governments, and this is a major source of the rising tide of revolutionary pressures in Africa.

These basic social failures are all the more culpable because they reflect the wide gap between performance and potential in Africa. Some indices of this shortfall in performance are the persistence of over 70% mass illiteracy, despite the continent's huge wealth, pervasive malnutrition, despite the abundant agricultural endowments of the region, and the prevalence of decimating but preventable, common diseases. On a comparative basis, these socio-political failures have contributed to Africa's lowest social indicators among the regions of the world. Thus, as discussed in Chapter 1, the continent harbours 22 out of the 31 least developed countries in the world.[2]

It is important, however, to emphasise two basic perspectives of the social and political failures in Africa. These are in comparative terms between regions of the world and dynamically over time. Thus the major point of these critical failures will be missed if the issue is trivialised to the non-argument that all regions have their failures. That, if tautological, is true enough, but in Africa these failures are deeper, more pervasive and dehumanising and, therefore, less acceptable than they may be elsewhere, particularly relative to the region's potentials. In dynamic terms, it is particularly alarming that many of these social and political problems (frequent coups and counter-coups, refugees, crime, and so on) have worsened. Even where there has been improvement over the years, the pace has been disappointingly slow, relative to the continent's potentialities.

Clearly, therefore, these are essentially welfare, policy, institutional and structural failures of the superstructure. But they impinge critically on the economy, and are often generated or exacerbated by the economic foundation of African countries' social formations. Welfare failures are, perhaps, the most graphic in terms of the broad masses afflicted due to relative social deprivation and deteriorating human conditions. The policy malaise involves both perverse and poor policy formulation and implementation, and this is most vivid in development plans, annual budgets and social legislation generally. Many will, however, insist that institutional failures underlie many of the other socio-economic failures. Thus Africa's political systems and institutions, such as the party system, bureaucracy, judiciary, education, market mechanism, private property, and so on, simply just do not work. There are also those who may even ascribe the institutional failure to basic structural defects identifiable with the more general structural distortions that characterise underdevelopment. Such socio-political structural disabilities include the post-colonial state itself,[3] the deformities of the social structure bequeathed by colonialism and so on.

Pattern and explanation of major political failures

Africa's major political failures are identifiable in: structural, institutional, policy and welfare areas.[4] These are with respect to the structures of the state, social classes and political power; the performance of the main political institutions: party system, bureaucracy, judiciary and so on; specific political policies with respect to national integration, political participation, the internal national question as it affects ethno-religious issues; and the welfare problem of relative political deprivation, which generates mass alienation, separatism and political refugees. These broad superstructural deformities should, however, be reduced to specific dimensions so as to facilitate both their elucidation and solution. The major political failures will, therefore, be analysed vis-à-vis the generic problem of political instability, political repression, pervasive abuse of office, poor political institutionalisation with defective political culture and failures in political innovation; the twin problems of racism and lingering colonialism in Southern Africa as well as the challenge of imperialism and neocolonialism. Needless to say, these political disabilities are both interrelated among themselves as well as linked up with the economic crisis.

Political instability or crisis of legitimacy

The most graphic and frequently discussed political problem in Africa is the instability of governments, regimes or the state: the frequent changes of government or regime, the musical chair of coups and counter-coups[5] and the persistent problem of change of leadership succession in African countries. Political instability has become so characteristic of these states that they have approached the status of the "banana republics" of Latin America, the life span of whose governments is that of banana trees before being cut down – by frequent coups.

Happily, this matter of political instability in post-colonial African politics has been problematised [6] as, basically, a *crisis of legitimacy*. This is anchored to the theorising about the character and function of the post-colonial state, which emphasises three critical issues: firstly, the fact that throughout Africa colonial disengagement was rigged to favour the most faithful pro-imperialist parties or groups (including Jonas Savimbi's reactionary UNITA in socialist Angola as opposed to the more nationalistic and progressive MPLA). Even if this favoured neocolonialist faction was dominant, this laid the basis for its questionable legitimacy. Secondly, is the betrayal of mandate or trust by the *petit-bourgeoisie* in the post-colonial states. Soon after nominal independence, the all-embracing nationalist movement becomes factionalised by the Africanisation of colonial privileges, the entrenchment of inequalities, persistent mass poverty, and marginalisation of the broad masses from the nationalist slogans of "freedom, equality and fraternity". This mass alienation creates a crisis of legitimacy for the *petit-bourgeois* leadership whose resort to repressive measures, by the use of the authoritarian state inherited from the colonialists, leads to revolutionary pressures from the class of working people, which may find expression in popular insurrection and even military intervention. Thirdly, the intra-class conflicts of the heterogeneous *petit-bourgeoisie*, as well as the clashes and shifting alliances between fractions of the bureaucratic bourgeoisie and the imperialist oligarchy, may also cause a crisis of legitimacy. This is why fractions of the *petit-bourgeoisie* collude with military fractions of their class to subvert the state; and the imperialist oligarchy also conspires with civilian and/or military fractions of the *petit-bourgeoisie* to cause leadership crises as for example the imposition of Idi Amin on Uganda.[7]

In all these cases, the moral authority of the governing fraction or coalition of the bureaucratic bourgeoisie is disputed. This general loss of confidence is more fundamental than the narrow "vote of no confidence" which a government may suffer on specific national issues in the state legislature. This crisis of legitimacy or political instability is fundamentally the consequence of both inter- and intra-class conflicts. Its resolution is typically through a violent change of government, or a sustained leadership stalemate, in which no fraction or coalition of fractions of the contending social classes or class can maintain hegemony over the rest of the country. Extreme cases of this latter resolution of the crisis take the form of civil war or secessionist rebellion as in Lumumba's Congo, in Nigeria, Sudan, Chad, Ethiopia and in post-Amin Uganda.[8] Other aspects of this broad concept of political instability are treated below.

Political repression, separatism and political refugees

Political repression and separatism on account of their pervasive and persistent recurrence in Africa should be separated from general political instability. While political repression is epitomised by Africa's growing fascist and neofascist states such as those of Idi Amin of Uganda, Nguema of Equatorial Guinea, Bokassa of the Central African Republic, Nimeiry of Sudan, separatism takes the form of secession and civil war. The dominant manifestation of political repression in Africa is the hostile harassment, and even proscription, of opposition parties, especially under the rubric of the one-party state in a class divided society. Other examples are: the physical liquidation or disappearance of political opponents, their incarceration and torture without trial; retrenchment and denial of socio-economic opportunities; the imposition of leadership by massive electoral rigging that returns an absurd 99.5% majority; denial of effective political participation, especially to the rural masses and other working people; and the alarming rate of violation of basic human rights that has been attracting Amnesty International to many African States.[9]

Besides the inherited authoritarianism of the colonial state, other causes of political repression in Africa include the material greed of the *petit-bourgeoisie* to monopolise capital accumulation by using the state. As the basic poverty of the state severely limits such accumulation, the competitors must be bribed or blocked. The failure of the post-colonial state and its ruling *petit-bourgeoisie* to solve basic national problems and fulfil its elementary functions with respect to employment, social welfare and so on, also breeds a crisis of unfulfilled expectations. Unable to resolve the growing, legitimate protests arising from these disappointed demands, the comprador state first resorts to *containment ideology*. This stresses an end to national ideological conflict, shifts political emphasis from liberty to "law and order" (called, in Nigeria, "war against indiscipline – WAI") in which politics or debate over goals and means is reduced to mere administration, and the state prefers unity and consensus politics to effective political participation. The defensive radicalism of African socialism is also intended to contain the revolutionary pressures of the masses.[10] As this ideological concealment of the leadership's greed and intolerance is contended, coercive containment is unleashed on the populace with three distinct features. First, the bankrupt leadership hangs tenaciously on to power for over 20 years by any means (including the use of a fascist police state). Then a monolithic one-party state is imposed to depoliticise the broad masses, with all non-conformists being ruthlessly persecuted, imprisoned and murdered. All these are aided by the poor institutionalisation of political processes in the post-colonial state.

Separatism is generated in the African countries by a combination of three major factors. First, the cultural irredentism built into these states by the arbitrary colonial boundaries which often split one ethnic group or nationality across two or more national borders, as in West Africa, Sudan, Southern Africa, and the Afars and Issas in the Horn of Africa.[11] Second, ethno-religious cleavages often erupt into secessionist wars, ignited or fuelled by imperialist intrigues that are designed to secure cheaper access to such basic raw materials as may be located in weaker, and thus more easily manipulated, states. This was the case with the Katanga secession in Lumumba's Congo,[12] and in Nigeria, Ethiopia, and so on. Third, decades of political repression may also force deprived groups and classes into separatist movements. Examples of this are the invasions and threatened secession of Shaba Province in Zaire in 1977 and 1978, and in Uganda under Milton Obote and with General Tito Okello opposed by the National Resistance Army (NRA).

"The refugee crisis"[13] is also one of Africa's major social and political failures; a crisis so serious that the UN declared 1982 as a year of conscientisation and global support for refugees.

> Africa now has around 2.5 million refugees; twenty years ago there were 400,000. One in every 200 Africans is a refugee. The African continent, with less than a tenth of the world's population, has more than a quarter of the world's 10 million refugees.[14]

The growth trend in the number of refugees has been summarised elsewhere.

> Today we deplore more than 5,000,000 refugees in Africa, whereas at the end of the 1950s there were no more than 200,000. In 1970, the number had grown to 750,000 and by 1973 there were already 1,000,000. In 1979, 4,000,000 could be counted. According to the MIUFRP, there is a danger that before the end of this century the figure will be between 15 million and 20 million.[15]

The total number of refugees in Africa between 1981 and 1986 is shown in Table 10.1.

Table 10.1
Refugees in Africa by country: 1981 and 1986

Country	*1981*	*1986*
Algeria	151,000	167,000
Angola	73,000	92,000
Botswana	1,000	5,000
Burundi	200,000	250,000
Cameroon	265,000	13,000
Central African Republic	7,000	42,000
Congo	—	1,000
Djibouti	42,000	25,000
Egypt	5,000	5,500
Ethiopia	60,000	11,000
Gabon	30,000	—
Ghana	250	—
Ivory Coast	—	600
Kenya	3,500	8,000
Lesotho	10,000	11,500
Morocco	500	—
Mozambique	100	1,000
Nigeria	105,000	5,000
Rwanda	10,150	50,000
Senegal	5,000	5,200
Somalia	1,300,000	700,000
Sudan	438,000	1,000,000
Swaziland	6,000	8,000
Tanzania	140,000	180,000
Togo	—	1,800
Uganda	112,400	180,000
Zaire	400,000	317,000
Zambia	36,000	96,000
Zimbabwe	—	46,000
Total	*3,400,675*	*3,221,600*

Source: CIMADE et al. (1986), p. 154.

The major causes of this refugee crisis are wars (civil, border, and so on), political repression by fascist dictators, drought or famine as in the Sahel and Central Africa, especially Burundi, and the collapse of the rural economy. Besides the human hardship this problem imposes upon those involved, the refugees' original home countries face severe problems of depopulation, reduced productive capacity, especially in agriculture, and threatened food shortage that may encourage further population migration. Furthermore, the burden on the host countries to provide food, shelter, clothing, health-care and gainful employment is typically beyond individual countries' capability. Concerted African and international efforts to provide rehabilitation aid for the refugees, and to eliminate or ameliorate the major causes of the refugee crisis are, therefore, essential.

Abuse of office, looting and electoral rigging

The political problems associated with the abuse of office in Africa have increased to the extent that people now assert that in Africa, it is not simply that officials are corrupt, but corruption is official, and that many African states operate a "lootocracy" or government-by-looting of the state treasury. Nigeria's political refugees in Western Europe and the USA thus looted their country of billions of dollars and stacked the money abroad. "Pirate capitalism" has also been used to describe this pervasive corruption for the primitive accumulation of capital.

In December 1985, a swindle of over six billion Nigerian nairas (about $6 billion) was reported in the Johnson Matthey Bank (JMB) in London, allegedly perpetrated by some Asians and Nigerians through Britons in that bank.[16] Similar episodes of executive and bureaucratic plunder of the state exist in other African countries, involving massive embezzlement of funds, kick-back on highly inflated contracts, and so forth.

In addition to constituting a moral failure in its own right, kleptocracy has contributed to Africa's socio-political failures, broadly in four ways: 1) by inflating relative values (of contracts, supplies, prices and so on), corruption impairs the efficiency of the state, both directly, in terms of the performance of ministries and parastatals, and indirectly, by undermining supervision and discipline in the implementation of policies and programmes. This lowering of governmental performance undermines the capacity of the state to perform some of its basic functions of law and order, as well as economic management. 2) the scandal associated with official corruption often precipitates a political crisis through loss of confidence in the government, which may be forced to resign, or is toppled by a military coup that routinely uses corruption as a convenient pretext in many African countries; and 3) massive looting of the state may create economic mismanagement on such a scale as to precipitate an economic crisis, which then becomes a source of political instability and military intervention. A good, recent example was the gross mismanagement of the Nigerian economy by the 1979/83 Shagari administration, which brought the economy to the brink of collapse and culminated in two quick coups between December 1983 and August 1985.[17] The persistent armed resistance to Mobutu in Zaire, the coup against Busia in 1972, the eruption in Liberia in 1980, the collapse of the feudal–capitalist dynasty of Haile Selassie in Ethiopia in 1974, and several other political crises in Africa were precipitated by this same problem. By breeding apathy and cynicism among the masses, such official corruption also operates to erode the legitimacy of government, and this has been a persistent element in the crisis of legitimacy in many African countries.[18]

Political and electoral rigging in order to impose unpopular leaders, or otherwise manipulate the political process in favour of certain candidates, groups and social classes also compounds the political failure and abuse of office in Africa. Although this borders on political repression, or serves to achieve one of its objectives, it is treated separately here to emphasise its basic origin in the arbitrary or even illegal exercise of executive authority. It is a corrupt misuse or abuse of popular mandate which leaders have sworn solemnly to exercise with probity and in the general public interest.

Some critical factors usually facilitate the practice of political and electoral rigging. One is the opportunity to do so with impunity, which usually derives from the relatively high concentration of power over different organs or branches of the state in the hands of the executive leadership. Mass illiteracy in Africa, which inhibits people's knowledge of their civic rights and their capacity to demand and defend them, also facilitates political rigging with impunity; hence, the democratic process requires a high level of literacy among the populace. Education has been denied to the majority of citizens in many African countries in order to make them exploitable in these ways. The feeble performance of many African leaders makes them very unpopular among the broad masses and thus encourages election rigging. But this also requires the additional incentive of a perverse political ambition to achieve power at all costs, not for the public good, but to promote the corrupt ambition of using the state for the primitive accumulation of capital.

This is tied up with the development of bureaucratic state capitalism in Africa, and the rest of the Third World, for corrupt primitive accumulation of capital to strengthen the *petit-bourgeoisie*. Even when these bankrupt governments are patently inefficient and rejected by the people, they cling to power, not to serve the people – but to serve themselves; they are, therefore, impervious to the people's negative verdict on their performance. Also, because they impose themselves on the people and sit on society without moving it forward this is precisely what necessitates their violent overthrow. The rigging game is also facilitated by the patronage nature of the political process, the *rule*, or *what* you know, is not important – only *who* you are and *whom* you know; this makes institutionalisation difficult and rigging easy.

Perverse political culture and poor institutionalisation

Besides material poverty, colonialism also bequeathed a desperate poverty and profound confusion of ideas and values. Hence, thanks to faceless neocolonialism, the post-colonial milieu depicts basic cultural rootlessness even decades after the formal termination of the colonial encounter. The two aspects of the superstructure in which this is very critical are political culture and institutionalisation. While political culture deals with the values, attitudes and norms of society, about the ways its political affairs are to be conducted, institutionalisation concerns the acceptance of the free sway of the rules and due processes formulated for the objective and efficient functioning of political (and such other) institutions as party system, police, judiciary, electoral commission, and so on. Some elements in a society's political culture include democracy (republicanism), authoritarianism or monarchy (divine right of kings or leaders), violence or passivity, accountability, centralisation and collectivism as opposed to decentralisation and individualism, conception of leadership (by succession, gerontocracy or old age, charisma or efficiency for example) and the like.

The combination of African indigenous traditions and colonial heritage has bequeathed a differentiated political culture whose major components are democratic commitment (especially freedom of expression) with an opposing authoritarian and anti-intellectual intolerance to politics inherited from the colonial obsession with law and order; a strong charismatic and gerontocratic approach to leadership, from traditional chieftaincy with a low premium on performance (efficiency) and accountability; a tilting edge to violence derived essentially from the violent nature of slavery, the colonial encounter and the military input into post-colonial politics; and an overt tension between post-colonial monolithism (the one-party syndrome) at the top, and the centrifugal decentralised community spirit at the grass-roots. The contradictions among these political values are thus manifested in Africa's political tensions.

For Africa, the poor institutionalisation or low level of internalisation of the norms of post-colonial institutions has often been cited as a major source of political instability,[19] and been seen as the reason for the spate of coups and counter-coups, and political repression and corruption. The fairly familiar reasons for this weak institutionalisation centre first on the conflict of values inherent in these essentially alien political institutions. As imported institutions grafted on to the deformed indigenous (essentially pre-capitalist) superstructure, they are undermined by the basic clash between the underlying foreign capitalist values and the generally pre-capitalist indigenous values of their African operators.[20] To take one familiar cultural example: opposition connotes *Ota* (enemy, in Yoruba) who is fought to the death, so the political opposition can be killed. Another example is the Chief Executive, President, Prime Minister, or Commissioner who is a kind of chief, an *Oba* or *Sariki* who usually rules by divine right and for life. The African Chief Executive, therefore, tends to see himself, and be seen by many, in that light and tends to play down the need for high performance, accountability and succession. There are several other parallels, such as oath-taking, which was a binding sanction in traditional society such that those who violated their oath were visited by the quick and visible wrath of some ancestral god. Thus in some parts of Nigeria, oath-taking involved swearing with iron, and those who violated this oath were visited with violent death by *Ogun*, the god of iron. But in modern politics, people swear on Bibles and Korans only to turn round to violate their oath with impunity.

The relatively short duration of post-colonial experiments with these alien political institutions may also partly account for their poor entrenchment. By contrast, the operation of liberal, democratic institutions on an autonomous basis has been in existence for more than 200 years in the most stable bourgeois democracies such as Britain, USA, and so on, which experienced traumatic revolutions and world wars before stabilising their systems. It should also be noted that whereas South-East Asia has been relatively politically stable, with India achieving political independence in 1947, the Latin American countries which gained nominal independence in the 1830s were, until recently, still "banana" republics. But even if this argument explains part of the fragile institutionalisation in Africa, it does not exonerate African leaders from their patent political failures.

A continent with a literacy rate of barely 30% also inhibits political institutionalisation. Indeed, the democratic order, or game as some cynics call it, presupposes an educated and enlightened citizenry that is informed not only of its civic rights and duties, but also of the major social debates in society. Where this precondition cannot be met, as in Africa, bourgeois liberal democracy and its supportive institutions founder, if they survive at all. The African *petit-bourgeoisie*'s denial of education to the broad masses is, therefore, a basis for failure and an urgent agenda item for political action.

The illegitimate claims and pressures of the imperialist estate in Africa have also been operating to undermine political institutionalisation. Thus, if imperialism must sustain that neocolonial stooge and multinational pimp as an African head of state, elections must be rigged, the judiciary must be corrupted, the military must be politicised to act against the country and other national institutions must be perverted. This highlights the double standard of imperialism in Africa and throughout the Third World. At home, imperialism strengthens or at least sustains effective institutionalisation, but in Africa and the rest of the periphery of global capitalism, it undermines it for the benefit of the super-exploitation of the broad masses for multinational super-profits.

Failure in political innovation

Besides the *abortive political praxis* that perverse political culture and weak institutionalisation generate in terms of fragile political institutions and mass deprivation of effective political participation, there is also *defective political conceptualisation*. This is Africa's persistent inability to articulate a desired political system, which is part of a more general indictment of post-colonial Africa's failure so far to contribute any significant economic or political model besides discredited "African socialism" and one-party dictatorship of the *petit-bourgeoisie*. On the basis of the rich experiments and heritage in statecraft spanning several kingdoms over many generations, there is no reason why Africa should not have articulated some coherent political arrangements. In this regard, the Latin Americans have contributed dependency theory for dealing with the crisis of underdevelopment.

The failure of political innovation is also not helped by the juggling of parliamentary and presidential systems under multi- or one-party rule. Even the proposal of dyarchy (mixed civil–military rule) is no innovation as this will have to be parliamentary or presidential, both of which constitute a continuation of the old system of political patronage, corruption and failure. The frequent hopping across to Europe and North America for the indolent and sheepish copying of their constitutions and other models is an embarrassment in this regard. Even if there are no models of government to be invented or discovered, African countries can at least be creative about adapting the existing models rather than slavishly replicating different socio-political milieux.

Another aspect of this lack of political conceptualisation and innovation is the tendency towards unscientific obscurantism with manifest cultural–ideological mystification. Indeed, in some quarters, this obscurantism is regarded as Africa's unique contribution to political thought. A dominant example of this is the unscientific mythology of a classless Africa, which is the springboard for "African socialism" and one-party dictatorship.[21] Yet, there is nothing distinctively original about one-party dictatorship, socialism or the denial of class analysis. These obfuscations are, indeed, epistemological barriers to the rational and scientific analysis and understanding of the African world.

A closely related phenomenon, which is intended as an African innovation or the precursor of such an innovation, is the castigation of certain political formulations, especially radical ones, as foreign. Thus in Nigeria and elsewhere, socialism, Marxism or communism are denigrated as foreign ideologies. But the same obscurantists that maintain this bogus stand gleefully embrace and implement capitalist ideology – as if the private ownership of the means of production originated from Africa. This is not to deny that Africa must be creative about the application of socialism. Indeed, it is this creativity that is sought as political innovation, whose conspicuous absence is regarded here as a political failure. The irony of soldiers and other *petit-bourgeois* elements that are foreign from their titles and caps to their boots, and in their professional practice, objecting to scientific ideas because they are allegedly foreign is central to this obscurantism.

What, perhaps, highlights this persistent defect in political conceptualisation and innovation is the absence of serious, scientific ideological orientation in Africa. Fanon made the same point in the elaboration of his robust thesis in *Towards the African Revolution*.[22] This relative ideological vacuum is the consequence of four major factors. These are: 1) the commitment of the *petit-bourgeoisie* to the preservation of their class which is threatened by any serious ideological debate; 2) the associated fear of revolutionary pressures on the continent which point in the direction of a radical ideology; 3) the mass illiteracy which imposes a culture of silence and passivity that inhibits popular demand for ideological discourse; and 4) the overtly reactionary character of imperialist pressures that block and obscure any major ideological enquiry.

Imperialism and Southern Africa

The extent of persistent imperialist grip on Africa, the prevalence of racism and the tenacity of colonialism in Southern Africa are the major anti-imperialist failures in the region. Although they do nothing concrete to combat them, even most conservative forces in Africa recognise the stubborn perpetuation of racism and colonialism in Southern Africa as an insult and a major defeat. Yet, both the internal strength of apartheid and Western imperialism's racist support are not impregnable, as the glorious defeat of the most awesome military–industrial complex in the USA by a poor agricultural North Vietnam in 1975 heroically demonstrated. At the heart of the Southern African debâcle are deficient political conceptualisation and the puppet leadership imposed by neocolonialism on Africa. The poor perception of the problem revolves round the failure to recognise that no African country can be truly safe and independent as long as apartheid survives as a sub-imperialist launching-pad from the Cape, and the refusal to recognise that in the nuclear age, Africa's best security interests lie in collective security, as the age of independent national armies has gone. The increasing destabilisation of the frontline states should be adequate warning. The obstacle posed by predominant neocolonial leadership in Africa is mainly that it poses false problems, proffers false solutions, diverts energy to imaginary threats under the rubric of endless ideological differences of rival imperialist estates in the continued domination and exploitation of the region. This is why mass militant action to dislodge Africa's so-called leaders and put more serious national and regional questions on the political agenda are crucial for the liberation of Southern Africa. These national initiatives should also be combined with systematic demands for purging the OAU of its neocolonial proclivities in order to strengthen its politico-military potential in a militantly pan-Africanist framework.

The major neocolonial threat posed by imperialism to Africa revolves round the persistent destabilisation of nationalist and serious governments, especially by manipulated coups and counter-coups, the imposition of bankrupt leaders and the increasing danger of recolonisation through the combined thrusts of the multinational corporations, growing external debts, and the operations of the International Monetary Fund (IMF) and the World Bank. All these dictate the need for a more serious and systematic study of the nature and function of imperialism in Africa and globally, the mechanisms of necolonialism and the political strategy for combating these reactionary predatory forces in Africa.

The profile of social failures in Africa

Africa's major social traumas cohere at the levels of physical welfare, social relations, identity, values and ideas. The basic signposts in this saga of social domination and humiliation are: relative social deprivation of the majority by the minority; exploitative social relations; neocolonial identity; and miseducation; all of which nurture parochialism.[23] As these social disabilities are intimately bound up with socialisation, mental processes and intellectual reproduction, mass consciousness and basic social relations in African countries, they shape their ideological superstructure, which not only rationalises the economic foundation but dictates even the character of the political processes there. In this deeper sense, the social atrophy can be traced to such major factors as acculturation, cultural dependency, perverse social relations, national degeneration and the structures of social deprivation in Africa.[24]

Socialisation patterns and acculturation

The socialisation processes of inculcating ideas, values, attitudes and norms in young Africans from one generation to another lies at the root of much of the social failure in the region. This is compounded by the mechanisms of acculturation, or acquisition and internalisation, of foreign cultural values through colonialism and neocolonialism. While the main socialising agencies are the family, educational institutions, mass media, religion and the general environment, the dominant forces that constrain them are the sway of foreign monopoly capital owned by the multinational corporations and the structure of social classes or the nature of the post-colonial state.

Imperialism or neocolonialism is the single factor that permeates and shapes these forces of socialisation and acculturation. For example, the institution of the nuclear family is an imperialist concept, imposed by imported Christian religion and bourgeois education, while the basic values of most parents into which their children are socialised in the family are shaped increasingly by the imperialist cultural offensive. Additionally, the predominant neocolonial influence on education, the media and religion, as well as the post colonial economy and state, are all too obvious. Thus the importation of imperialist educational systems which started with colonial missionary schools has led to miseducation with the uncritical inculcation of imperialist bourgeois values and attitudes under a mélange of uncoordinated facts and empty homilies about universalism and crude empiricism.

The result has been a profound cultural confusion[25] under the unabating pressure of the Europeanisation and Americanisation of Africans. The associated patterns of socialisation and acculturation have produced neither Africans nor Euro-Americans, but a culturally rootless and confused population, especially in the urban areas. This confusion and conflict of values and ideas is one basic source of the political tensions and crises on the continent. Concretely, some of the more banal consequences of this scenario are greedy materialism, corruption, armed robbery (encouraged by "Wild West" movies), proliferating prostitution, foreign intellectual domination, and so on. This same cultural confusion and conflict is at the root of the *ambiguity of African behaviour* in all spheres, of the East–West ambivalence in African foreign policy and the marginalisation of Africa in the tumultuous march of human civilization. The implications of these for the African's seal of identity are even more alarming.

Cultural dependency, neocolonial identity and consciousness

Just as the imperialist offensive in Africa has produced neocolonial economies and states, it also produced a cultural dependency not only in the narrow terms of values and attitudes, but in the broader sense of neocolonial identity and consciousness.[26] In this context, while identity is basically a sense of *belonging* – to a nation or to some other human grouping – consciousness is a cognition of the fact that social reality or forms change, and an awareness of the need for radical change. And as Marx aptly explained, it is not the consciousness of people that determines their material existence, but their material mode of existence that determines their consciousness.[27] Thus, as the mode of production changes, so does the level of consciousness corresponding to it. But when consciousness is diverted (by false consciousness or the ideas of the dominant class) necessary changes in the material base or economic foundation of society are delayed. Cultural dependency thus gives rise to diffusion and decline of national consciousness. The issue of nationality or African solidarity has, therefore, increasingly become one of mere identity rather than of a basic consciousness or awareness of sharing common aspirations, goals and destiny. This underlies the increasing disparity between neocolonial identity or subordinate status and consciousness in Africa. Fanon addressed the same problem in his chapter on "The Pitfalls of National Consciousness" in *The Wretched of the Earth*.[28] This growing incongruity between distorted identity and consciousness also largely explains the ambivalence and paradoxes of socio-political behaviour in the region, for example, between being non-aligned *and* pro-West conduct, between the affirmation of an African identity and open or secret collusion with apartheid, between the rhetoric of African liberation and the active suppression of a liberating consciousness in the form of growing revolutionary pressures among the broad masses.

The resolution of these cultural contradictions requires the deliberate cultivation of a *counter-consciousness* which must permeate the generality of the population.[29] This counter-awareness will negate and eliminate the prevailing reactionary and pro-imperialist consciousness which enslaves the populace and encapsulates their liberating energies. Obviously, the starting point must be a thorough and critical appraisal of neocolonial identity and consciousness in each country; this exposure will serve as the theoretical and empirical basis for the radical rejection and neutralisation of this servile consciousness. The family, mass media, schools and other agencies of socialisation and acculturation will then be imbued with alternative and more progressive values, aspirations and purposeful liberation. These basic changes will convert the counter-consciousness into a new consciousness for the urgent liberation of Africa from the debilitating shackles of reactionary cultural dependency and erect the foundation of an authentic and modern African civilization.

Social regeneration and bourgeois values

The predominance of bourgeois values analysed above also determines the forms of social regeneration in Africa. Here, social regeneration is used in the broad sense to embrace the demographic reproduction of the population, its standard of living and the processes of reproducing the social structure with particular reference to the class formations. On the first count, one encounters a Malthusian preoccupation with African numbers and their perverse structure. This is summarised with respect to such demographic statistics[30] as the very rapid rate of population growth of about 3%, which is about the highest in the world, and a high rate of rural–urban migration propelled by the collapse of Africa's rural economy. It has to be admitted that Africa does have a population problem which consists mainly of a very high growth rate that outstrips the growth rates of food production, national income and employment. This is the heart of rising unemployment among young people (15–30 years old), and of starvation. There is also uneven distribution of national populations over the available land. These problems call for a national population policy to limit growth rate and encourage more even distribution of the population between rural and urban areas, as well as between areas of high and low population density.

The social consequence of this demographic profile is even more disconcerting. Here, again, we encounter some of the basic features of Africa's severe underdevelopment, such as: poor standard of living indices, for example, malnutrition, starvation, mass illiteracy, shoddy housing, insanitary water facilities and rudimentary health-care, as discussed in Chapters 1 and 9.[31] The physical and psychological health of the African population, their capacity for self-identity and for developing a critical social consciousness and, therefore, the possibility of their self-liberation depend on these living standard indicators. This is why, predictably, while Africa's standard of living is the lowest in the world with respect to the above indices, her social failures and rate of regeneration are also the worst in the world. If most Africans barely survive because of these disabilities, the overall meaning of their existence, their destiny as a people and their general social performance are critically constrained by the low, specific class regeneration.

This is the third, and perhaps, most disturbing aspect of Africa's social regeneration, which is interrelated with the earlier two. First, even the possibility of transcending the demographic problem and appreciably raising the standard of living depends on the possibility of transforming class relations and the associated *petit-bourgeois* policies and values that produced these regenerational problems in the first instance. Moreover, even if the demographic pattern and the level of material existence were to improve, unless the class cleavages are negated, then the other socio-political failures will endure, which is why the regenerational problem of elite recruitment versus class representation in Africa requires urgent attention.

This is an integral part of the generic problem of growing structural inequalities in Africa. Its specific manifestation here deals with the regeneration or reproduction of different classes under the predominant patronage of the *petit-bourgeoisie*. The concrete question is how the bureaucratic bourgeoisie recruits its members into educational institutions, jobs, political positions, and so on, in relation to the numerical representation of the class of working people in these positions.[32] The glaring evidence is that this elite recruitment and mass exclusion is based on such socially manipulated criteria as birth, wealth, education, "social connection" and, in more banal cases, ethno-religious considerations.[33]

The basic issue here is not whether elites should be interested in recruitment in order to consolidate their position, and use special mechanisms for that purpose, but that the methods of elite regeneration in African countries sharpen inter- and intra-class cleavages through the extreme relative deprivation they create from the virtually separate education of elite children (from kindergarten to foreign universities) to their eventual monopoly of the state and the means of production in the economy. These are what generate the visible and growing frustration, bitterness and mass alienation that constitute sources of systemic paralysis in the post-colonial state.

The effect of bourgeois values on these three aspects of regeneration are fairly obvious. To start with the most familiar, the exclusion from elite recruitment is motivated by the *petit-bourgeois* commitment to social privileges and class domination in order to ensure the reproduction of its reactionary false consciousness in society. This is why the control of ideological institutions such as schools, mass media and the bureaucracy, for the inculcation and dissemination of its capitalist values and attitudes is central to the *petit-bourgeois* strategy.[34] Similarly, the demographic explosion and the very low living standard of the masses are functional for the major bourgeois goals and values in Africa in several ways. This relative overpopulation generates "labour surplus", which is used for depressing wages, keeping labour docile and imposing harsh working conditions in the super-exploitation of labour for the generation of super-profits in Africa. The desperate poverty of the broad masses has been a persistent factor in their electoral corruption in many countries where venal politicians *buy* the ballot papers of poor voters and simply dump them into ballot boxes for electoral rigging.[35] This abject poverty also induces passivity vis-à-vis embezzlement, prostitution and other forms of corruption in post-colonial Africa. And, of course, the "culture of silence" imposed by mass illiteracy serves to marginalise the majority of the population from any real political, and even social, participation and facilitates the imposition of predatory, bankrupt and dictatorial leaders on them.

Social relations and cultural cleavages

The essentially social character of these sources of failure in Africa should be emphasized in order to make their political manifestations more identifiable. This is particularly necessary in a continent where imperialist falsification trivialises every conflict as "tribal" or a manifestation of a bland "pluralism" – thanks to the intellectual ravages of racist colonial social anthropology.[36] Thc basic issucs here are the explanations of the chronic social conflicts and irredentism arising from antagonistic feudo-capitalist social relations of production (with their racist overtones in Southern Africa and other citadels of foreign monopoly capital discussed in Chapter 4) and ethno-religious chauvinism. These cleavages in social relations have already produced a profound social revolution due mainly to the contradictions of feudo-capitalist production relations in Ethiopia; transitional socialist transformation by coups in Ghana, Benin, Burkina Faso, Congo, and so on, and civil war in Sudan, Chad, Nigeria, Uganda, for example.

It may be asked why capitalist social relations of production that prevail in many other regions of the world should be identified as a source of basic political failure in Africa. There are several reasons for this, one of which has to do with the deformed and distorted nature of Africa's social relations of production which reflect the distorted neocolonial capitalist social formation in the region. So, while the predominant production relations are neocolonial capitalist, these are intermingled in varying degrees by such precapitalist production relations as feudal and communal relations. Together with the large claims of the imperialist estate that constrain domestic capitalist reproduction by draining economic surplus, these pre-capitalist social relations have produced blocked capitalist transformation. A major consequence of this is the absence of a national bourgeoisie[37] with a robust and autonomous economic base, and patriotic commitment to the historic mission of the development of a self-reliant capitalist economy – as opposed to pervasive pimping for imperialism by Africa's intermediary *petit-bourgeoisie*.

Another significant aspect of Africa's social relations of production is the fact that they are based more on control than on ownership of the means of production, which is why Africa's neocolonial capitalism is bureaucratic capitalism that often degenerates into "pirate capitalism"[38] through the looting of the state for corrupt accumulation. Even the scanty private ownership of the means of production is dominated by the imperialist estate. On account of these distortions, the character of accumulation is still predominantly *primitive accumulation*, involving the expropriation of the peasantry, as in the 18th-century European experience. The particularly rough edges of primitive accumulation include its resort to physical violence, for example, the forcible alienation of peasant land and the physical suppression of workers and mass demonstrations against blatant exploitation. One social consequence of this primitive accumulation is massive social deprivation. Then for these various reasons, the classical capital–labour antagonisms and class conflict of capitalism are distorted into a mixture of class and feudo-communal antagonisms and conflicts. These ethno-religious cleavages are the consequences of blocked capitalist development that generates the coexistence of fairly strong capitalist and pre-capitalist modes of production (feudalism and communalism). But bourgeois sociology prefers to attribute them to a generic and amorphous pluralism. Other causes of these parochial conflicts that often erupt into fratricidal wars are the relative weakness of the post-colonial state and the refusal to expose relevant ideologies for guiding social debates and national policies. Hence reactionary politicians resort to the manipulation of chauvinistic sentiments of ethnicity and religion in order to divide the masses in a nefarious "divide and rule" strategy. This manipulation then yields ethnic and religious electoral bases for class domination by the *petit-bourgeoisie*.

Social relations and social deprivation

As indicated above, Africa's distorted social relations of production and the nature of primitive accumulation associated with them throw up an immense burden of relative social deprivation. This takes different forms, such as increasing unemployed, destitutes, prostitutes, robbers, landless peasants, the hungry and refugees. They all have two basic features in common – they are located at the bottom of the ladder of the social organisation of production and dispossessed of both ownership and control of the means of production. Indeed, the only labour-power which many of them (the unemployed, landless peasants and so on) own is rendered redundant – not by any natural cause or because society could not use it, but because the capitalist could not earn adequate profit by utilising it.

This is a familiar social scandal of capitalism that has become entrenched in Africa: people are able and willing to work, society would benefit from their labour, but by employing them, the capitalist may not earn enough private profit, therefore society must lose their social contribution and the victims must stay idle, hungry and with no income. And this must happen, no matter the absolute wealth of their country! This is the sense in which these social groups are the victims of a particular system of social relations of production, victims who have been marginalised outside their nation's fortunes. No matter the bourgeois human rights enshrined in constitutions, the natural right to life of these groups is denied or jeopardised.

Furthermore, the groups that direct the social relations of production which marginalise these victims then declare them to be anti-social! National budgets are then beefed up (as in Nigeria's 1986 budget of the human rights regime that kept the police vote at ₦0.4 billion) in order to fight crimes, especially armed robbery. This is not to deny that crimes are bad or that society should not be protected against criminals, but it should be realised that *criminals are usually produced by society*[39] by its sanctioned social relations of production, which deprive many lawful citizens of a legitimate means of livelihood; this denial of their social rights *drives* them into criminal behaviour. As Marx correctly stated, society neither can nor should be explained in terms of the individual, but that the conduct of the individual should be explained in terms of the nature of the society that produced him – because the individual is only the bearer (*Träger*) of a definite class relation, a specific social relation of production.[40]

In other words, those currently socially deprived and who, under the prevailing feudo-capitalist social relations of production in Africa are regarded as criminals, could easily be integrated into social production if the system of social relations of production were altered. This is the pertinent sense in which this social deprivation is a basic failure. Similarly, the other social and political failures in Africa are the collective consequences of particular and non-unique ways of ordering the continent's affairs. The rest of this book grapples with the possibilities of reorganising the region in order to eliminate or ameliorate these disabilities and contain the deepening economic and social crisis.

Notes

1. See, for example, M. Mamdani (1983).
2. On these comparative indicators, see World Bank, *World Development Report, 1985* (Washington).
3. See H. Alavi (1972) in *New Left Review*, 74, July–August, pp. 59–82.
4. For an alternative perspective on these political failures, see Basil Davidson (1974).
5. For the spate of coups, see W. F. Gutteridge (1976); A. Bebler (1973); and Jack Woddis (1977).
6. On the problematic of the post-colonial state in Africa, see: H. Alavi (1979); Y. Tandon (ed.) (1982); and P. C. W. Gutkind & I. Wallerstein (eds) (1976).
7. For examples of these insurrections, see M. Mamdani (1983) and H. Gutteridge (1976).
8. For detailed analyses of these crises, see Patrice Lumumba (1962); B. J. Dudley (1973); M. Mamdani (1983).
9. See Osita C. Eze (1984).
10. See A. M. Babu (1981).
11. For a detailed study of the separatist implications of these arbitrary colonial borders, see M. Asiwaju (1984).
12. See J. Gerard-Libois (1966).
13. See CIMADE, INODEP and MINK (1986).
14. World Bank (1985) p. 9.
15. CIMADE (1986), p. 3.
16. See *African Guardian*, vol. 1, no. 1 (Lagos).
17. See T. Falola and J. Ihonvbere (1985), and *Newswatch* magazine, December 1985.
18. For an Asian example, see R. Constantino (1978), ch. 5, pp. 129–48.
19. Luckman thus explained the causes of Nigeria's first coup in 1966 as partly due to poor institutionalisation in the military. See R. Luckman (1971).
20. See A. Temu and B. Swai (1983).
21. See Issa Shivji (1973).
22. Frantz Fanon (1967).
23. For a related study of social failures in the Third World based on the Philippines, see R. Constantino (1978).

24. These themes are treated marginally in P. Gutkind & P. Waterman (1977), especially Parts IV, V & VI.

25. See R. Constantino (1978), chs. 1, 6, 8 & 13.

26. Ibid., ch. 1.

27. See V. G. Afanasyev (1980), ch. 4.

28. Frantz Fanon (1967), ch. 4.

29. The need for this counter-consciousness is the essence of the message in A. Cabral (1973).

30. For a graphic picture of Africa's demography, see World Bank (1985) ch. 3 and pp. 92–6.

31. Ibid. pp. 57, 76, 86 for indices of Africa's standard of living.

32. On class recruitment, see N. Poulantzas (1978), Part I, ch. 2, Part II, ch. 4.

33. Ibid., Part II.

34. These issues are discussed with respect to educational institutions in M. W. Apple (1979).

35. This scandalous rigging was widely reported in the 1983 elections in Nigeria.

36. For the vehement denunciation of this, see O. Onoge, in P. Gutkind & P. Waterman (eds) (1977), ch. 3.

37. F. Fanon (1976) ch. 4.

38. S. P. Schatz (1985) (Mimeograph).

39. On this, see F. Pappenheim (1968), chs. 3 & 4.

40. See Bob Rowthorn (1980), p. 15.

11 Socialist Experiments in Africa: Old and New

Socialist experiments in Africa may not be immediately conceivable as part of the pedigree of the deepening crisis in Africa. But these experiments can be seen at least as elements of the *African revolution*, which is being canvassed as the vehicle for the resolution of the continental crisis. In reality, the old and new socialist regimes are both integral to the correct appreciation of the African crisis and its rapid liquidation. For one thing, these African socialist experiments are also embroiled in the deepening crisis to varying degrees. For another, a good understanding of these attempts at socialist construction should offer both theoretical insights and praxiological lessons about the possibilities and pitfalls of socialism in Africa. This is especially true after Babu's *African Socialism or Socialist Africa?*[1]

The specific motives of this investigation into old and new socialist experiments in Africa should first be emphasised. First, it is to analyse the general social conditions that have facilitated their emergence, which should be useful to radical forces struggling to establish socialist formations in Africa. Secondly, it aims to examine the main distinguishing features of these socialist experiments with respect to such parameters as their ideologies, policies and general direction. A third objective is to analyse the differing prospects and problems of the two sets of socialist regimes. The issue here is to focus on the progress of ideas and praxis in African socialist struggle over time as well as the effects of the changing African and global environments on the functioning of these socialist regimes. How socialist have some of these self-proclaimed socialist regimes been over time? In the process of these inquiries, it is hoped that some fairly clear lessons in the theory and practice of socialism, which are relevant to the struggle for the African Revolution, can be summarised to guide the future.

These considerations also impinge on the criteria for the division between old and new socialist regimes in Africa. The obvious dividing line is time, and here, a rough approximation is made with the mid-1970s as the bridge. The old socialist experiments include all those before 1975 and the new ones span the period thereafter. The choice of 1975 is essentially arbitrary and is only related to the rapid spate of socialist changes in the major former Portuguese colonies which have heralded the final death-knell of colonialism in Africa. Ideological posture is the second basis for separating the old and new socialist experiments. Generally, the younger socialist regimes have offered a clearer statement of their commitment to socialist revolution under Marxism, whereas the older socialist experiments have been much less precise in their statement of basic ideological commitment.

Old and new African socialist experiments

It is possible to identify 16 old socialist experiments in Africa before 1975, with eleven of them socialist-oriented and the remaining five being self-styled or imitative socialist regimes. By mid-1986, there were ten new socialist experiments at various stages of consolidation in Africa.[2] These old and new socialist states are listed in Table 11.1.

Table 11.1
Old and new socialist states

Old socialist experiments		*New socialist experiments*
Socialist-oriented	*Self-styled socialist*	
Ghana (1957)	Zambia (Humanism)	Ethiopia (1974)
Guinea (1958)	—	Angola (1975)
Mali	Senegal (under Senghor-Negritude)	Mozambique (1975)
Congo-Brazzaville (1963)	Zaire (Mobutu-authenticity)	
Algeria (1964)	Sudan (under Nimeiry)	Guinea-Bissau
Tanzania (1964)	Malawi	Cape-Verde
Benin	—	Seychelles
São Tome & Principe	—	Malagasy
Burundi	—	Ghana (1981)
Egypt (under Nasser from 1959)	—	Burkina-Faso
Libya (1969)	—	Zimbabwe (1980)

There are two sub-groups within the old socialist regimes: the socialist-oriented states are those whose leadership was, or appeared to be, genuinely committed to the socialist transformation of their countries, but did not elaborate and implement scientific socialist programmes based unambiguously on Marxist–Leninist ideology. This was partly because they lacked a mass base with sufficient socialist consciousness for such total socialist commitment. So the leaders had to compromise their socialist programmes with powerful internal and external reaction, as in Guinea, Ghana, and so on. The absence of large socialist groups and a conscious working class in these countries meant that their socialist experiments were largely the result of the ideological clarity and political courage of their leaders. Hence the contradictions, inconsistencies and vulnerability of these old socialist regimes.

For these reasons, for fear of unsettling their tenuous national unity, these socialist-oriented states compromised to build socialism without effective class struggle. Their socialist experiments were founded on *African* socialism as, for example, in Tanzania, Ghana, Guinea,[3] or on *Arab* socialism as in Egypt, Libya and Algeria. In other countries there were modest socialist reforms anchored to the *nationalisation* of enterprises and land without effectively changing the relations of production permanently, and thereby democratising economic and political power.

By contrast, the self-styled or defensive socialist experiments were founded largely on defensive radicalism and ideological rhetoric without genuine commitment to socialist transformation. The strategy was to use radical slogans and cosmetic reforms to stem the rising tide of revolutionary pressure from the broad masses below the stratum of privilege. In this way, bogus *petit-bourgeois* ideologies were entrenched, like *African Socialism* in Nimeiry's Sudan and Malawi, *humanism* in Zambia, *negritude* in Senegal and rootless *authenticity* in Mobutu's Zaire. Under these essentially state capitalist and semi-feudal regimes, the leaders launched single or dominant parties to neutralise political opposition to their basically neocolonial regimes.

The new socialist experiments have, however, benefited from the mistakes, illusions and problems of the earlier socialist experiments. They have been erected on a broader base of mass socialist consciousness and support, involving prolonged armed liberation struggles, in the case of the former Portuguese colonies.

They often proclaim themselves as socialist revolutions led by vanguard single parties based on the alliance of workers, peasants, soldiers, and so on, and guided by Marxist–Leninist ideology, like the Workers' Party of Ethiopia launched in 1984. In these ways, these new socialist states emerged from successful struggle against colonial capitalism as in the former Portuguese colonies and Zimbabwe; against neocolonial capitalism as in Ghana and Burkina Faso; or against feudo-capitalist social formations as in Ethiopia. This makes class struggle the central feature that sharply distinguishes these new socialist states from the two brands of old socialist experiments in Africa.

To summarise, it is possible to establish a set of criteria to distinguish between the old and new socialist experiments in Africa. The most important of such differentiating factors are: mode of emergence, mass base, ideology, class struggle, anti-imperialism, economic structure or dominant relations of production and the control of political power in the state.

Old socialist experiments

It is necessary to focus explicitly on the old socialist experiments in Africa in order to identify their specific and historical character. This will be done with respect to the general features of these regimes, the specific policies and programmes of selected case-studies among them which pin-point their basic achievements and the major shortcomings of their social experiments.

The trap of African socialism

Perhaps, the most graphic summary of the old socialist experiments is the trap of African and Arab socialism[4] in which most of them have been caught. It is this generic factor that conditioned the other significant features of the earlier socialist initiatives on the continent. The ideology of African socialism is a non-scientific socialist option which bases itself pragmatically on the false claim of classless Africa and rejects, or precludes, overt class struggle in the attempt to build socialism. It is conceived in relation to African humanism in its communal expression within the context of the African extended family with such norms as "mutual respect, sharing and work" characteristic of the traditional African family. Its best exponents are Nyerere, Nkrumah, Kaunda and Senghor, with Nasser and Qadafy as the corresponding exponents of Arab socialism based on the tenets of Islam.

The basic world-view of African, or Arab, socialism is metaphysical idealism, a bourgeois philosophy based on subjective or mechanistic materialism. Hence this world-view peddles logical positivism whose critical elements are agnosticism and scepticism with a strong religious bias. Its implied subjective theory of knowledge places a central role on the mind which is said to be able to discover absolute truth in religion when the flesh is denied by the self. Hence this theory of knowledge emphasises "introspection, memory and linguistic juggling". On account of its being influenced by Judaeo-Christian values, African socialism accepts the institution of private property and insists on social justice with it. This is the heart of its basic contradiction – the unscientific and untenable attempt to graft the idealist values of a pre-capitalist communal African social formation with egalitarian distribution of wealth, on an eminently neocolonial capitalist social reality in contemporary Africa, with yawning inequalities in the ownership of property.

Since African socialism is retrieved from a dim past based on the communal social formation, which is assumed to have been classless, the old socialist experiments and African socialism also posit the illusion of classless Africa. Hence class struggle is denied in this socialist construction. But besides the ideological reason for this, the historical circumstances in which the old socialist regimes emerged also encouraged the denial of class conflict. This was bound up with the anti-colonial nationalist struggle that led to the birth of these old socialist states. As all indigenous social forces were united in the monolithic nationalist struggle, and as the post-colonial state distributed the gains of flag independence very unevenly and unjustly, social divisions quickly arose with the Africanisation of colonial privileges by the elites. The frenetic efforts to contain these debilitating social cleavages by the dominant bureaucratic bourgeoisies of the new states quickly led many of them to elevate national integration to the status of defensive ideologies.[5] As all dissent came to be viewed as subversion, politics was reduced to administration in the repressive search for national consensus, with political opposition submerged into the bogus one-party system or banned. So if, as these leaders claim, there are no conflicting political goals and strategies there can be no conflicts giving rise to classes. Even the word "class" was denied as having no equivalents in African languages – because if, as alleged, there is no class reality there can be no class notions in Africa!

Partly because of the suppression of political dissent, but largely because of the fairly easy compromise that led to neocolonial independence and the absence of any long tradition of fighting capitalism on a class, rather than a national basis, mass socialist consciousness was very low during the early socialist experiments. So there were no large socialist groups to offer mass support for consistent and robust socialist policies in the old socialist states. Socialism was thus basically imposed, either by such imaginative and courageous political leaders as Nkrumah, Sekou Toure, Nyerere, for example, or by defensive politicians professing a fake radicalism such as Senghor, Mobutu and other self-styled socialist leaders.

For these reasons, the old socialist states maintained massive persistent concessions to domestic reaction and imperialism within varying forms of neocolonial capitalism. These were all styled "socialism", but in reality were different mixtures of bureaucratic state capitalism with large doses of welfare statism. Even with massive nationalisations in such countries as Guinea, Tanzania, Nkrumah's Ghana and so on, joint ventures and management agreements with imperialism in these countries meant persistent, and often increasing, accommodation with the major imperialist countries. This was partly because of the weaknesses of the economy and bureaucracy in these countries. An extreme example was in 1958, when the French left Guinea in anger and removed even typewriters and cut telephone lines. The level of anti-imperialism in these old socialist states has remained very low, while the economy and state remain dominated by powerful bourgeois-oriented bureaucrats and party officials. Hence it has been suggested that socialism in these states is the socialism of consumption and not of production, with considerable private ownership, particularly in the self-styled socialist states such as Zaire, Senegal, Zambia, and so on. Socialist progress in these circumstances has been associated with the pursuit of private interest. Those who complain that this progress is inadequate are simply told that "Rome was not built in a day".

Selected case studies

The case studies of old socialist experiments in Guinea, Tanzania, Congo-Brazzaville, Nkrumah's Ghana, Nasser's Egypt and Zambia will best illustrate the common features and differing experiences of these regimes.[6]

Guinea (Sekou Toure): When, in 1958, Sekou Toure boldly said "no" to de Gaulle's imperialist proposal that francophone Africa should remain within the French empire, Guinea was declared a socialist state under the single Democratic Party of Guinea (PDG). Two state trade monopolies for external and internal trade were established as the *Comptoir Guinéen du Commerce Extérieur* (CGCE) and the *Comptoir Guinéen du Commerce Intérieur* (CGCI), respectively. This was rapidly followed in 1959 with the elaboration of three- and seven-year development plans and the creation of rural cooperatives and other institutions for national development. These measures established firm state control over the economy, but the three bauxite mines remained joint ventures with foreign monopolies, as the relatively weak Guinea government could control only 49% of their equity shares. These socialist-oriented domestic policies were followed in 1961 with an external political expression of Guinean socialism when the country joined the radical Casablanca Group of African countries opposed to the reactionary Monrovia Group.

Among the gains of this socialist experiment are: an impressive growth rate of 2.8% during 1960/74; and an average annual growth rate in 1973/83 of 3.1% for

GDP, 2.4% for agriculture, 6.7% for industry and 1.9% for services, although in 1983 the per capita income was still only $300 for a population (in mid-1983) of 5.8 million.[7] The Guinean growth rate was the third in French Africa after Gabon and Ivory Coast. In addition: student enrolment rose from barely 40,000 in 1958 to 0.25 million in 1967 and 0.4 million in 1979; the number of persons per physician fell from 54,610 in 1965 to 17,110 in 1980. Politically, the level of mass consciousness has been fairly high, particularly since the 1964 *Loi Cadre* led to radical measures and the Eighth Congress of the PDG in 1967 called for a cultural revolution to remove "the reactionary elements of bourgeois bureaucratic capitalism".

Yet, the Guinea socialist experiment had its defects. Perhaps the most important was the minimisation of internal class struggle in order to muster a national front against imperialism. Besides pandering to the illusion of classless Africa, this led to overlooking serious internal contradictions. Thus since 1961, there was less radical politics and greater accommodation with imperialism, which probably facilitated the abortive imperialist invasion of the country in 1971 that required the assistance of Nigerian troops to crush. In 1963, some enterprises were even denationalised. There have also been persistent reports of inefficiency, involving hasty mechanisation of agriculture, inadequately trained personnel and poor economic and technical infrastructure. These have led to little agricultural development with persistently unrealised plan targets, too few cooperatives, and smuggling across easily breached borders. The *Comptoirs* or state trading monopolies have also been inefficient and recorded losses for years because of their bureaucratic control. There has also been over-centralisation of banking and trade with a proliferation of investment projects. These have led collectively to rising external debts, growing from $314 million in 1970 to $1,216 million in 1983 with a total debt service of $100 million in 1976, and a ratio of external debt service to annual export earning of 40% in 1974 (the highest in Francophone Africa). It was in these circusmtances that a coup toppled the socialist regime a few weeks after Sekou Toure's death in 1984.

This was against the backdrop of the immense political repression reported under Sekou Toure. Given the one-party state structure and the absence of genuine class struggle, opposition was stifled and many critics of the regime had to flee into exile. From there, they were reported to have linked up with imperialist forces and tried several times to topple Sekou Toure.

Tanzania: Independent in 1960, the Zanzibar revolution took place on Sunday 12 January 1964[8] followed by an army mutiny in the former Tanganyika in the same year – which Nigerian troops helped to crush. Later in 1964, the union of Tanganyika and Zanzibar as Tanzania gained momentum and socialism was proclaimed in Tanzania. This was followed by the Arusha Declaration of 5 February 1967. The six basic propositions of the Declaration were: profession of faith in man; rejection of exploitation of man by man; control of major means of production and distribution by workers and peasants; popular democratic government of workers and peasants; faith and dedication to socialism, *especially by party leaders*;[9] and policy of self-reliance.[10] The day after the Arusha Declaration, Nyerere announced "a little nationalising exercise" of the commanding heights of the economy – banks, insurance companies, flour mills, import–export trade, and so on.

Thereafter, Tanzanian socialism was defined in Swahili – the new official national language – as *Ujamaa na Kujitegemea*, a new synthesis of man and society, a search for the ideal polity. Nyerere defined socialism as an attitude of mind, like democracy, so that the possession and non-possession of wealth are irrelevant. *Ujamaa* is thus said to be opposed to both capitalism and "doctrinaire" socialism. It maintains that African life was traditionally socialistic, that the basis of African socialism is not class struggle, but the extended family, since Africa is regarded as classless.

> I doubt if the equivalent for the word "class" exists in any indigenous African language; for language describes the ideas of those who speak it, and the idea of class or caste was non-existent in African society.[11]

Yet, in Nigerian languages, for example, we have words like *mekunnu* for poor masses, *amunisin* for exploiters and *Agbekoya* for "peasants against oppression" in Yoruba; *talakawa* for poor masses and *sarakuna* for the rich in Hausa; and *Osu* for caste in Ibo. Tanzanian socialism also involved a leadership resolution: political leaders were required to renounce all business links and have only one occupation or source of income. Hence the leaders must work and live modestly like the masses.

The steps to be taken towards the establishment of *Ujamaa* were contained in the Arusha Declaration, which has been described as being not a revolution; its main significance is said to lie, not in what it stated, but in the steps for attaining its objectives. The three broad programmes were: a) state control of income distribution; b) new institutions to rejuvenate socialist attitudes and the acceptance of socialist principles (which implied *laissez-faire* in economic affairs, for example, the 1964 five-year plan relied on foreign aid and foreign investment); c) self-reliance, implying that the three main theses in Tanzanian socialism are absence of exploitation, workers' and peasants' control of the major means of production, and democracy. Hence the single party, TANU (Tanzania African National Union), which was built after visits to Yugoslavia and Guinea to study party organisation, was defined as "a Party of Peasants and Workers" and maintained "that it is necessary for the government to be elected and led by Peasants and Workers".

The practical Action Programe for the realisation of *Ujamma* consisted of five major components: 1) *nationalisation of the modern sector* with, a) *a state sector* embracing banks, insurance and foreign trade, and b) *socialist sector* comprising nationalised factories and mills, based on workers' self-management; 2) *agricultural production* to be organised through cooperative and state farms with the cooperatives consisting of, a) socialist cooperatives with the total pooling of all means of production, b) semi-socialist cooperatives with partial pooling of members' resources, and c) mutual-aid cooperatives involving no pooling of means of production. Thus in both the nationalised modern sector and agriculture, non-socialist enterprises were allowed with their capitalist relations of production; 3) *problem of socialist democracy*, whose resolution required that democracy should be based on the working population and not on social parasites as in bourgeois democracy; 4) *political education and political cadre* to provide the basis for raising socialist consciousness and linking the leadership with the broad masses;

5) *settlement schemes* organised around villagisation involved several schemes such as the "Supervised" (for example, village settlement pilot or transformation scheme); the Cooperative Farming Settlements (for specific crops); and the *Ujamaa* schemes for pioneering the socialist path of development.

The *Ujamaa* schemes otherwise known, in Swahili, as the *Ujamaa vijijini* were *Ujamaa* villages. Their objective was to initiate the transformation of society and create "rural economic and social communities where people will live and work together for the good of all". This implied building people's homes around common service centres and not creating scattered homestead plots. The scheme thus aimed to revolutionise rural social relations and promote economic and political mobilisation. The choice was, therefore, to create the social preconditions for revolutionary change in the countryside against the alternative of facing the danger of entrenched rural capitalism. Hence the *Ujamaa* villages were designed as a countervailing initiative to the emergence of rural class differentiation.

Both because of its large scale (involving a population of 20.8 million in mid-1983 and a land area of 945,000 square kilometers) and the strong intellectual backing of the University of Dar es Salaam, the Tanzanian socialist experiment animated, perhaps, the greatest interest of all the old socialist regimes. Its capital was the intellectual citadel for African Marxists in the 1970s, just as Accra was the parallel political vortex for African nationalist radicalism under Nkrumah. Perhaps, the greatest gain from Tanzanian socialism was the wealth of ideological ideas and political praxis it offered to the continent through the prolific outpouring of literature emanating from the Arusha Declaration and the radical Publishing House it encouraged. In sheer grandeur and moral commitment, the experiment endeared itself sympathetically to most radicals, in spite of its flaws. It also succeeded fairly well in raising the socialist consciousness of the Tanzanian masses and offering a model of the decent moral tone of government in a continent riddled with pervasive repression and venality. It was, therefore, not accidental that the offensive to crush Idi Amin's fascism in Uganda was launched from Tanzania.

But in material terms, the socialist experiment did not achieve much. By 1983, per capita income hovered precariously around barely $240 and grew at an average annual rate of 0.9% during 1965/83. Yet the other growth indices of the economy were impressive: the average annual growth rate of GDP was 5.0% for 1965/73 but fell to 3.6% during 1973/83; that of agriculture was 3.1% in 1965/73 and 2.6% in 1973/83; industry recorded 6.9% growth rate for 1965/73 but only 0.2 in 1973/83; the services sector had 6.2% growth rate in 1965/73 and 5.4% in 1973/83. While agriculture accounted for 46% of GDP in 1965, its share rose to 52% in 1983, probably due to villagisation, and the manufacturing value-added which was 190 (in millions of 1975 dollars) fell sharply to 151 by 1982. But the number of people per physician dropped from 21,840 in 1965 to 17,740 to 1980. The greatest gains were in education where the total primary school enrolment as a percentage of the age group rose sharply from 32 in 1965 to 98 in 1982, with even 101 for males, though the corresponding percentage in secondary schools rose from 2 to only 3 between the two years.

The disappointment of Tanzania's African socialism has been summarised most eloquently by its architect, leader and intellectual godfather, Julius Nyerere. On voluntarily relinquishing presidential office in 1985[12] the *Mwalimu* (teacher, as he was fondly called, in Swahili) with his usual moral candour, confessed that *Ujamaa* had not realised its basic objectives, and that the villagisation scheme had been too ambitious and had been a failure. He blamed the failure of his experiment on grandiose policies, poor plan implementation and the basic abject poverty of a resource deficient country.

But these were only partial explanations as Issa Shivji's critique of Tanzania's socialist experiment clearly showed (*Silent Class Struggle*). The fundamental error of the experiment was ideological, as those who earlier distrusted Nyerere's staunch Catholicism and aversion to scientific socialism foresaw in the early 1960s. Thus it is basically unscientific to suppose that the communal values of African traditional life can be grafted on to a state capitalist society in transition to socialism. Neither is it possible to build socialism without class struggle, as was shown by the bureaucratic corruption, creeping capitalism and ambivalence between capitalism and socialism that wrecked nationalisation without workers' control.[13] These internal contradictions also led to persistent reliance on imperialism, especially the EEC countries, for foreign aid and investment. The strings attached to these external bourgeois favours forced more and more concessions to imperialism. It is precisely these ideological inconsistencies that forced Shivji and Babu, both Tanzanians, to publish their scathing criticism of the Tanzanian experiment. Its outstanding external public debt rose to $2.6 billion in 1983, and its debt service as percentage of exports rose from 4.9% to over 7% in 1983 with total exports of only $480 million. So in the 1980s, as the economy almost collapsed, Tanzania became an IMF client.

Congo-Brazzaville (People's Republic): The less known Congolese socialist experiment[14] started with the revolution in July 1963 against Abbe Youlou under the National Movement of the Congolese Revolution. This sole party had two left factions, with the moderates backing President Massamba Debat and the radicals behind the Prime Minister, Pascal Lissouba. The implied struggle for power led to the ousting of Massamba Debat in a coup by Major Ngouabi in August 1969. In 1970, the country pulled out of OCAM, the French-inspired African regional grouping which the Congo had joined in 1965. The Congolese Workers' Party was formed in the same year as the vanguard party for the transition to socialism.

So it can be said that during 1963/69, the Congo was socialist-oriented only because of the suppression of internal class struggle in the interest of the united national front that made the revolution. Thereafter the country adopted Marxism–Leninism as its ideology and backed up the earlier nationalisation of means of production with workers' control of enterprises. After the assassination of Ngouabi in 1977, French, American and other foreign capital were invited to exploit the country's rich oil wealth. This tended to tone down political radicalism.

Being a basically rich country, the socialist experiment on a foundation of oil and other resources has thrown up important gains. Thus with a population of 1.8 million in mid-1983 in a large country of 342 thousand square kilometers, the per capita income of $1,230 in 1983 was the highest in sub-Saharan Africa outside the apartheid enclave. The average annual growth rate of GDP was 6.8% in 1965/73 and 7.9% in 1973/83 with that of industry rising from 9.3% to 12.7% during the two periods, while the agricultural growth rate was 4.1% and 0.4% in those years. The number enrolled in primary schools as a percentage of the school age population was 114 in 1965 with 10 for secondary schools in 1965 and 69 in 1982; the population per physician dropped sharply from 14,210 in 1965 to 5,510 in 1980, which was the lowest in sub-Saharan Africa outside South Africa. But the Congo has also been slipping into the external debt trap as its external debt rose from $144 million in 1970 to $1.5 billion in 1983 with a ratio of debt service to export earnings of 20.5% in 1983.

The main failures of the Congolese socialist experiment are, therefore, not so much political as socio-economic. Though the level of socialist consciousness among the masses is fairly high and the per capita income is also impressive for Africa, the level of mass poverty remains very high. But it is much lower than in Zaire from where hundreds troop across the Congo River boundary in daily search of livelihood – as I witnessed in 1979. This poverty and the waxing imperialist presence pose real problems for this socialist experiment. Indeed, there are those who insist that Congo-Brazzaville is socialist only in name, though the radical posture of the regime cannot be denied.

Nkrumah's Ghana: Shortly after Ghana's independence in March 1957 under the Convention People's Party (CPP), Nkrumah launched a socialist programme under the inspiration of his philosophical consciencism.[15] This was a synthesis of Euro-Christian and Islamic cultures as an ideology for African development. It was intended to provide a theoretical basis for the dynamic unity of African societies under the guiding principles of egalitarianism. The idea was to develop an ideology to contain Christianity, Islam and traditional African society and employ them for harmonious development "towards *a socialism unique to Africa*". The basic elements of consciencism were the separation of church and state because of the authoritarianism of religion; total *positive action* to overwhelm the summation of negative action in order to achieve territorial independence and effective decolonisation; a mass party to push for greater positive action involving increased production, efficient distribution and higher incomes to the people; the ideology of philosophical consciencism saw a correlation between egalitarian principles and Africa's humanist past; non-alignment in the cold war between the socialist and capitalist/imperialist blocks. For the dissemination of these ideas among his party leaders and the masses, Nkrumah took the correct step of establishing an ideological institute at Winneba.

There were two major components of the implementation of African socialism under Nkrumah – radical Pan-Africanism and domestic reformism. Being the first African country to achieve independence since the war, Ghana rightly linked the fate of her socialist experiment with the decolonisation of Africa under an impressively radical Pan-Africanist programme, and non-alignment. Ghana was so successful in this endeavour that Accra became a nationalist vortex, and some of Nkrumah's harsher critics even insisted that this robust decolonisation programme diverted such disproportionate administrative energy and resources that it contributed to the domestic failure of socialism. Among the highlights of this

Pan-Africanism was Macmillan's anti-imperialist "wind of change" which swept away formal colonialism from most of Africa by the early 1960s. It also culminated in the formation of the Organisation of African Unity (OAU) in 1963 from the fusion of the former Pan-Africanist factions, the radical Casablanca Group supported by Ghana and the reactionary Monrovia Group.[16] But Nkrumah's correct advocacy of an African High Command as the anti-imperialist vanguard force of the continent has not yet materialised – in spite of the lessons of NATO and the Warsaw Pact countries and the destabilising role of South Africa's sub-imperialism on the continent.

At the national level, Ghana's old socialist experiment was consummated essentially at the level of state bureaucratic capitalism and radical mass mobilisation. Thus there was nationalisation of enterprises in the major sectors of the economy but these were not placed under workers' self-management, so they succumbed to bureaucratic atrophy and creeping capitalism. On the political front, power was centralised solely in the CPP as a mass populist party with a radical Young Pioneers' Movement for mobilising the youths. Among the achievements of Ghana's old socialist experiment must be included the rapid decolonisation of Africa by the early 1960s and laying a solid domestic infrastructural foundation for social transformation. This was through schemes like the Volta hydro-electric power station, which remains one of the largest in Africa, massive harbour and road construction, free education at all levels with three universities for a population of barely eight million by 1966 when Nkrumah was overthrown.

Unfortunately, Ghana's old socialist experiment was terminated within a decade through the vulnerability of its internal contradictions and imperialist hostility. The basic flaw was the failure to pursue radical internal class struggle rather than the pursuit of an elusive programme of national unity, which led to the scandal of a socialist state with a minister importing a gold-plated bed. Many CPP leaders had no commitment to socialism, and Ghana's state apparatus remained dominated by a *petit-bourgeois* elite with a capitalist-oriented bureaucracy and military that persistently complained about the reformist radicalism of Nkrumah. There was no mass *socialist* consciousness, so that Ghana's socialism was imposed on an unwilling or unradicalised CPP by the force of Nkrumah's charismatic personality with its mystic Messianism. Ironically, it was only during his exile in Guinea with Sekou Toure that Nkrumah attained the ideological maturity revealed in such socialist tracts as *Class Struggle in Africa*.[17] The economic programmes of Ghana's old socialist experiment also lacked effective workers' control, as well as bureaucratic nationalisation. But being a potentially rich country, the level of national economic performance was mediated by Ghana's bold and generous material support to Pan-Africanism, especially to the liberation movements and nationalist struggle generally.

Egypt: After toppling the reactionary regime of King Farouk in a coup on 23 July 1952, Nasser and his fellow radical officers set about transforming Egypt under the inspiration of Arab socialism; they jailed trade unionists and communists. This was essentially another unique form of socialism, guided this time by another traditional culture – Islamic religious values – as in Syria and later Libya and Iran.[18]

Under the Arab Socialist Union, Nasser and his colleagues elaborated reformist socialist principles for the transition of Egypt into modern development in close collaboration with the Soviet Union. But not until 1975 was the Communist Party revived from its earlier repression under this socialist regime.

The major planks in this Islamic socialist experiment were radical land reform and the nationalisation of major enterprises in different sectors. So land was liberated from rural kulaks and redistributed to the impoverished peasantry. But though there were nationalisations of foreign and indigenous enterprises, these were placed under bureaucratic elite management. The result was the consolidation of a massive state bureaucratic capitalism with strong military and agrarian components. Rural capitalism flourished to the point of making Egypt the largest agricultural producer in the Arab world.[19] Despite its radical posture, however, Egypt's socialist union failed to mobilise the masses, abolish exploitative feudo-capitalist relations of production and ensure popular participation.

The achievements and failures of Egypt's socialist experiment were deeply compromised by Nasser's leadership of the Arab world in the Middle East crisis. This necessitated maintaining an immense and costly military machine supported by defence industries and domestic food supplies. Egypt lost the 1967 and 1973 wars against Israel, but that it led the offensive against Zionism and its Western mentors demonstrated the basic resilience of the Egyptian socialist experiment. Before Anwar Sadat dismantled the experiment, after Nasser's death in 1971, such monuments as the Aswan Dam had been erected, the steel industry, defence industries, successful agrarian capitalism established and the infrastructural foundation for the transformation of Egypt had been laid. The 3.8% average annual growth rate of GDP during 1965/73 rose to 8.8% in 1973/83; the corresponding growth rate of industry over the two periods was 3.8% and 10.6%, respectively; and the services sector recorded 4.7% and 11.1% growth rates during the two decades, respectively.[20] In education, while the percentage of students in secondary schools was 26 in 1965, it jumped to 54 in 1982, while the corresponding percentages in higher education institutions rose from 7 to 15 over the two periods. The ratio of population per physician dropped sharply from 2,260 in 1965 to barely 970 in 1980, the second lowest in Africa after Libya.

The ease with which Sadat, and later Mubarak, were able to dismantle Egypt's socialist experiment and expel the Soviets highlighted the failures of the socialist attempt. It reneged on internal class struggle, an error that facilitated the accommodation with imperialism and encouraged the entrenchment of capitalist relations of production.

Zambia: Zambia's reformist socialism is based on the official ideology of Humanism, an expression for African socialism.[21] Although the state is capitalist, there is some desire for socialism, as was the case in Nkrumah's Ghana. However, since independence in 1964, most top Zambians have not shared the government's socialist perspectives. Kaunda has allowed scientific socialism to be taught in schools, and defended it against attacks from the church. Reportedly, there is even a Marxist-oriented Research Bureau within the sole United National Independence Party (UNIP). But the dominant African humanist ideology, which appears to have been imported from Nyerere's African socialism, has been persistently reaffirmed, as on 13 December 1972 when it was declared that Zambia was "a one-party participatory democracy under the philosophy of Humanism" for "taking government to the people".

Thus this social democracy is based on one-party consensus politics, as the opposition African National Congress, led by Harry Nkumbula, had been weak in Zambia. After the August 1967 Mulungushi General Conference of UNIP, the ANC grew, while the UNIP became factionalised, with its splinter United Party banned in 1968. The United Progressive Party (UPP), which was later formed from UNIP, merged into the parent party in 1972 with the declaration of UNIP as the ruling single party. But except in the ANC – apart from *petit-bourgeois* struggles for office – radical ideological differences have not been central to these party changes.

The practical implementation of Humanism has been based on a reformist mixed economy with social goals pursued spasmodically, due to periodic failures of political will and ambivalent public policies. Largely public ownership of the means of production is apparent, but powerful private interests persistently block tendencies towards the establishment of a socialist economy. So there is state bureaucratic capitalism with conflicting interests and policies underlain by the activities of politicians in parastatals that frustrate these public enterprises. Thus, since 1973, increasing public ownership has been accompanied by economic stagnation.

The state sector of the economy includes the dominant copper enclave supported by small industries on the Copperbelt, and this is not progressively integrated with the rest of the economy. Since 1965, outright nationalisations have not been possible, so government has been buying shares and acquiring board control in various enterprises, such as the Industrial Development Corporation (Indeco) and the Zambia Mining Corporation (Zimco), through which the government controls the copper industry cautiously and piecemeal. By the 1968 Mulungushi Reforms (shortly after the Arusha Declaration in Tanzania), the state entered into retail trade building supplies, transport and breweries. The 1969 Matero Reforms gave the government 51% control over mines, while 51% state ownership of banks, insurance firms, and such like, was conferred by the 1970 Reforms. Such reforms have facilitated the emergence of a Zambian quasi-bourgeoisie straddling the public and private sectors of the economy.[22] This has also encouraged pressures for the privatisation of parastatals on the allegation of their economic failures (as in Nigeria since 1985). Thus, following the 1978 draft of the Third Development Plan, President Kaunda ordered the relaxation of central political controls and the leading monopoly status of parastatals.

Before the global depression of 1974/78 and the 1980s, Zambia's reformist socialism generated some economic gains, especially from copper. Thus by 1974, the country was reported to have the highest per capita income and tax revenue in independent Africa. But by 1983, the per capita income stood at only $580 with an average annual growth rate of –1.3% for 1965/83.[23] The corresponding growth rate of GDP was 3% for 1965/73 and 0.2% for 1973/83, and 1.4% for agriculture during the second period, with industry recording –0.3% for 1973/83. The major failures have not, of course, been this poor economic performance only, but the failure to accept a revolutionary alternative – even by the political leadership – the lack of mass socialist consciousness, absence of internal class struggle, capitalist resurgence through privatisation, and growing concessions to imperialism. But Zambian socialism must be commended for the immense sacrifices it has been making as a frontline state for the liberation of Southern Africa, through providing sanctuary and material support for liberation movements and suffering frequent invasion by South Africa. This may partly explain the high scale of internal economic decay in Zambia. This leads to the pressing question of why after 15 years of nationalisation, the almost total reliance on copper has continued.

Senegal: The situation here is similar to that in Zambia. In 1960, Sedar Senghor proclaimed the Senegalese Progressive Union as a form of African socialism around the ideology of negritude.[24] Modibo Keita also proclaimed African socialism in Mali, and Senghor formed the short-lived Senegal–Mali Federation during June–August 1960. During 1966/74, Senegal became a one-party state until 1974 when the so-called "democratic opening" allowed for multi-partyism under Senghor's two basic political currents: social democracy and *petit-bourgeois* liberalism. This persisted until what has been termed his "poetical and grammatical retreat" from power in December 1980. By July 1981, his successor, Abdou Diouf (Senghor's Prime Minister for 11 years) announced "total democratic opening" which led to the formation of some 15 political parties. He has also retreated into "democratic closing" since 1981 under the combined weights of national crisis and virulent US neocolonialism. Since then, the IMF and the World Bank have been imposing privatisation, and Senegal has been offering a base to UNITA in Dakar in spite of Diouf's status as OAU Chairman in 1986. These developments have been provoking the unity of the opposition parties.

New socialist experiments

Selected case studies

Examples of the new socialist experiments in Africa that highlight their common features and peculiarities are Ethiopia, Mozambique, Angola, Rawlings' Ghana, and Zimbabwe. All, at various stages, have declared themselves as Marxist–Leninist states (except Ghana) after being established through social revolution. Their distinguishing characteristics flow mainly from these two basic factors as their actual functioning will reveal below.[25]

Ethiopia ("Revolutionary Motherland or Death"): I had the privilege of watching the Ethiopian Revolution as a participant observer between September 1981 and July 1982.[26] After years of struggle against the fascist feudo-capitalist regime of Emperor Haile Selassie, the Ethiopian Revolution was executed by a broad mass front of students, peasants, the Confederation of Ethiopian Labour Unions (CELU), soldiers, teachers and taxi drivers, between February and September 1974. After rank-and-file soldiers and junior officers formed the Dergue as a military committee in April 1974, it soon became the ruling military council and later the Provisional Military Administrative Council (PMAC). After deposing Haile Selassie in September 1974 and legalising peasant land expropriations in March 1975, it degenerated into a *petit-bourgeois* organ defending capitalist interests by banning strikes and protests as well as outlawing the CELU under General Teferi Bante. These tendencies led to two factions within the military and two within the civilian left.[27]

Within the army, General Bante increasingly represented the radical nationalist officers, while the First Vice-Chairman of the Dergue, Major Mengistu Haile Mariam, led the "transcendentalist" Marxist nationalists of other ranks, pushing for the rapid creation of mass revolutionary consciousness from above. Their rivalry led to a shoot-out in the Dergue in which, on 3 February 1972, General Bante and others were killed and Major Mariam became the leader of the Dergue. Among the civilian left (mainly student movement) the MEISON (All-Ethiopian Socialist Movement) saw the February revolution as a *petit-bourgeois* affair, while its rival, the EPRP (Ethiopian People's Revolutionary Party) saw a mass revolution. Their rivalry led to EPRP's "white terror" against the MEISON and others, until 1977 when Mengistu's ascendancy unleashed "red terror" to stabilise the revolution. With slogans like "Revolutionary Motherland or Death" and "Ethiopia Tikdem" (Ethiopia First), this peasant Revolution is widely regarded as the most thorough socialist revolution after the Bolshevik Revolution in 1917. It has been unambiguously grounded on Marxist–Leninist ideology and firmly affiliated with the world socialist bloc.

The three major planks in the socialist programme are: (a) National Democratic Revolution (NDR) launched in April 1976 for establishing the bourgeois democratic revolution of basic rights and liberties, state control of means of production and for creating a mass base for the Revolution. The NDR is crucial for a largely feudal and pre-industrial society with a very small working class; (b) establishment of the Vanguard party through COPWE (Commission of the Party of Workers of Ethiopia) to train cadres, organise political education, and structure the party organisation which emerged as the Workers' Party of Ethiopia in 1984; (c) workers' control of all enterprises, which has involved the extensive formation of peasant cooperatives, peasant associations, enterprise unions and workers' control committees.

Some of the specific programmes involved in all these include: (1) land proclamations including the "land to the tiller" Proclamation No. 31 of 4 March 1975, and the Urban Land Proclamation of July 1975; (2) nationalisation of Crown assets (August 1974), financial institutions (January 1975), industries (February 1975) and private airlines and supermarkets (May 1975); (3) new labour code with the dissolution of CELU and the establishment of the All-Ethiopian Trade Union (December 1975); (4) the organisation of urban dwellers into *kebeles* and "highers" (like wards and streets) under the Provisional Office for Mass Organisation Affairs (POMOA of April 1976) with *kebele* cooperative shops; (5) educational mobilisation through the *Yekkatit* 66 or political school, with provincial branches and offices closed for two hours weekly for political discussions; and there is also *Zemacha* or National Literacy Campaign launched in 1979 to wipe out illiteracy – a national, mass literacy campaign so well organised that people of all ages go to evening classes so that by about 8.30pm it seems that the whole of Addis is returning from school (Addis Ababa University operates day and evening classes and is open all year round); (6) a national Revolutionary Development Campaign is also tied up with both medium and perspective planning, with the first ten-year plan under way by 1982. Between 1979 and 1985, the literacy campaign had made some 12 million Ethiopians permanently literate in about 15 languages, thus raising the literacy rate from around 11% to 51% within a decade.

The gains of the Ethiopian Revolution have been truly immense against the background of the abject poverty imposed on the country by years of US-supported feudal fascism. The liquidation of the crushing feudal oppression that liberated the rudely abused peasantry and gave them the right to land for the first time in their lives is, perhaps, enough to justify the Ethiopian Revolution. In addition, the Revolution has firmly established mass revolutionary consciousness complete with a revolutionary mass party, an ideological school and an ideological journal (*Maskeram*). The economy has been fully reorganised under central planning, with socialist relations of production and an agrarian sector under state and cooperative farms. Unquestionably, the average living standard has risen. Since 1983, however, the gain in the standard of living has been undermined by famine in the country and the problems in Tigray province. The recurrence of drought calls for durable long-term solutions which the Ethiopian government has been evolving with the assistance of the international community. The educational gains have also been impressive, with the literacy rate rising from barely 11% to about 50% (that is, literacy in the national Amharic and/or English language) by 1982.

The Ethiopian Revolution has survived tremendous problems from internal class struggles, secession (and invasion) and persistent poverty aggravated by famine. Happily, the factionalism within the Dergue with an abortive coup on 10 July 1976 aimed against Mengistu, and the civilian Left rivalry have been resolved in favour of the Revolution, and the counter-revolutionary offensive from the Ogaden south (border with Somalia) was also crushed. So it remains the Eritrean secession and famine with poverty which time will resolve.

But two persistent revolutionary questions should be addressed further: the Eritrean secession, and whether the Revolution is "heretical". While it is true that Eritrea was federated with Ethiopia in 1952 before it was forcibly integrated into Ethiopia in 1962, the current refusal of Eritrea to accept federation with Ethiopia raises several questions without denying the intensity of nationalistic aspirations. (1) Under what circumstances should a socialist Eritrean revolution be organised within and against an ongoing Ethiopian revolution, since the Eritrean struggle started initially against Haile Selassie's feudal autocracy that has been liquidated? (2) Why has the Eritrean revolutionary struggle been supported by Arab reactionary regimes in Nimeiry's Sudan and across the Red Sea – certainly not for progressive purposes? (3) Why was the Eritrean offensive synchronised with the counter-revolutionary and imperialist offensive against the Ethiopian Revolution from the south in the Ogaden in 1977? (4) Why is Eritrea not prepared to be part of a socialist federation of Ethiopia and enjoy guaranteed regional autonomy – because comrades cannot trust comrades? (5) What precisely are the major ideological differences between Eritrea and revolutionary Ethiopia? (6) If the essentially primordial or nationalist logic of Eritrean secession is accepted, which African country will be free from secession due to arbitrary colonial boundaries – indeed, will an independent Eritrea not also be split between the Eritrean Liberation Front (ELF) formed in 1961 and the Eritrean People's Liberation Front formed in 1970 (EPLF)? (7) In terms of the welfare of the majority of Eritreans, is Eritrea likely to be more viable alone (and not become a mere imperialist puppet) or with Ethiopia? (8) If Eritrean secession is granted, what is to become of about 60% of Ethiopia's total industrial investment located in Eritrea?

On the question posed by René Lefort on whether the Ethiopian Revolution is "heretical", my own answer is "No". This is without denying mistakes in the Revolution. With the launching of the Workers Party of Ethiopia in 1984, the Revolution can no longer be considered as a military coup. At any point in time, in any revolution, the leadership must consist predominantly of people with a particular background. In Ethiopia between 1974 and 1977, the EPRP's insistence on the immediate establishment of a workers' mass party in a pre-industrial society without a sizeable working class was really a call for the EPRP to take over power with General Bante's military faction. But Mengistu also assumed power with a military faction, the MEISON and other Marxist forces. It is ideologically correct for Mengistu to insist that the vanguard party should be led by genuine revolutionaries who will not betray the revolution – as happened so many times in Africa, as with Ghana's CPP and elsewhere. In any case, if there are truly Marxist soldiers, why can they not participate in the leadership of the vanguard party? An African Marxist state with a population of 40.9 million by mid-1983 is simply too serious a stake to gamble with on grounds of shaky ideological purity. Marxists should rally round to consolidate the Ethiopian Revolution, and thus correct and prevent its mistakes.

Mozambique: Mozambique achieved its revolution for national independence on 25 June 1975 after the assassination of Eduardo Mondlane, President of its liberation movement, FRELIMO, early in 1969 during the long and bitter armed struggle against the Portuguese ultra-colonialists under fascist Salazar.[28] During the armed struggle, FRELIMO, like the FLN (National Liberation Front of Algeria) in Algeria, the national liberation movements in the other former Portuguese colonies of Guinea-Bissau, Cape Verde and Angola as well as the liberation movements in Zimbabwe, Namibia (SWAPO) and South Africa (ANC), made it quite clear that they were fighting to make a *social revolution*. This means the liquidation of the colonial state, racism and colonial capitalism through the transformation of the entire colonial social order or social formation, embracing the state, economy and society. Hence at independence, when Samora Machel became national President and Marcelino Dos Santos became Vice-President, FRELIMO emerged as the central political organ of Mozambique.

At its Third Congress in December 1977, FRELIMO thus adopted Marxism–Leninism as the national ideology and transformed itself from a liberation front into the vanguard party of the "worker–peasant alliance". Its socialist-oriented cadres and anti-capitalist policies were built gradually during the armed struggle.

The political structure of the young revolutionary state is thus based on one-party proletarian democracy as formulated during FRELIMO's First Congress in 1962.

The political organisation of the revolution was also built during the armed struggle around the liberated areas; the political structure of the liberated areas consisted of the FRELIMO party. People's militias, based on the local party organisation and the zonal military leadership, were erected in the villages. In this way, the entire national population was engaged in political action, and economic life was organised around producers' cooperatives under the supervision of the relevant local party branch. There were thus individual and cooperative *shambas* for the liberation army. FRELIMO's Second Congress, in July 1968, endorsed this organisational structure in preparation for national independence.

During the liberation wars FRELIMO's organisational structure consisted of four main organs: Congress, Central Committee, Executive Committee, and the Political and Military Committee.[29] The Congress is the supreme organ of FRELIMO, while the Central Committee which comprised about 20 members during the war, constituted the liberation force and the provisional government. It exercised legislative, executive and judicial powers, and was divided into Departments for Finance, External Affairs, Administration, Information, Publicity and Propaganda, Education and Social Affairs. The Executive Committee exercised daily executive functions and later comprised the President, Vice-President and departmental secretaries. I saw these structures inside Mozambique in 1979.

The current post-colonial problems of the Mozambican revolution are partly inherited from the period of the armed struggle. The main problems then were ethnicism and regionalism, the army and the material needs of the liberated areas. Ethnic and regional cleavages arose from the power of the ethnic chiefs associated with the administrative void after a FRELIMO victory in an area. This problem was so serious that in October 1966 FRELIMO's Central Committee declared prophetically that the battle against it was as crucial as the anti-colonial struggle itself. This primordiality was, in part, the harbinger of the counter-revolutionary activities of the Mozambican National Resistance Movement (MNR). The second problem centred round the army with the notion of two types of FRELIMO members in civil and military life. This duality tended to encourage rivalry, factionalism, recrimination and divided loyalty to the party. Then there was the difficulty of meeting the material requirements of the population in the liberated areas, which had 0.8 million people even before 1966. The virtual plunder and benign neglect of the former colony with virtually no rural infrastructure and an illiteracy rate of over 95% compounded these problems. Then there are allegations of mulatto domination of state organs and the marginalisation of blacks.

These difficulties foreshadowed the emergence of the counter-revolutionary MNR movement which has been waging an armed rebellion, with South African support, against the FRELIMO government.[30] A major motive for the base and assistance given to these rebels to operate from inside South Africa is to stop Mozambique's principled support of the liberation movements (ANC and SWAPO) fighting apartheid in South Africa and Namibia (and the former liberation forces fighting to topple Ian Smith in Zimbabwe) from bases inside

Mozambique. By destabilising this frontline state, the apartheid regime hopes to isolate Mozambique and retard its revolutionary transformation. Unfortunately, these nefarious, sub-imperialist ambitions of apartheid have been offered political expression by the rebels through Mozambique's internal problems, such as perceived regional inequality and slow development. Thus as the apartheid-backed assaults became more threatening to the very survival of the FRELIMO government, Mozambique was forced to sign the embarrassing Nkomati Accords (reproduced at the end of this Chapter) with South Africa on 16 March 1984. Though Mozambique has honoured the terms of the Accords by closing down the liberation movements' military bases, the apartheid regime has ignored the Accords and persisted in its support of the attacks against Mozambique. But happily, more African states, especially the other frontline states, have risen to the challenge and have been assisting in containment of these attacks.

In spite of the MNR setback, Mozambique has been consolidating its socialist revolution. Full nationalisation of the economy was completed soon after independence and the state apparatus has been transformed with the formation of the FRELIMO party of workers and peasants. Thus political and economic power have been effectively transferred to the working people who have been increasingly managing enterprises and farms directly, especially since the Fourth Party Congress in April 1983. A very strong sense of socialist internationalism has also been forged and given rise to a constant inflow of "cooperantes" from different countries to assist with the task of socialist reconstruction in various fields. The physical and social infrastructure for socialism is being laid, a literacy campaign is combating illiteracy, and the standard of living of the broad masses has been rising gradually with the increasing production of food and shelter as well as the provision of health-care, water and other facilities, especially to the rural areas.

The Fourth Party Congress in 1983 has carefully identified the other major weaknesses of the revolution besides the apartheid attacks. These problems include the organisation and relation between the state and the party, and the marginalisation of *poder popular* (people's power); the relative neglect of the peasantry and the failure of state farms created under the inspiration of *gigantismo*; popular participation and leadership as well as meeting the basic material needs of the masses with effective industrialisation. The new policies adopted by the Party Congress to cope with these weaknesses have been seen by many as a shift to the right. But this is only a temporary reform that revolves round the revitalisation of local democratic participation through the mobilisation and reinforcement of mass organs; the decentralisation of development planning for effective local self-management; and agricultural reorganisation with emphasis on cooperative farms. Famine has also undermined Mozambique's socialist construction in recent times, as the drought in the Sahel and Central Africa has spread into the country and caused a food problem there.

The "broken-back state economy" image of Mozambique from the apartheid attacks through the surrogate MNR took its greatest toll in the murder of the country's President Samora Machel inside South African territory on 19 September 1986. But in spite of the MNR siege, the country is still holding its own.

Angola: Angola's socialist experiment is similar to that of Mozambique.[31] Both are former Portuguese colonies that waged armed liberation struggle in order to make a socialist revolution. But in Angola, the liberation war was waged by the Marxist MPLA party under Dr Agostinho Neto, and the reactionary UNITA led by the renegade Jonas Savimbi, which, as independence approached, became rivals. It was the larger MPLA that the OAU and the progressive world backed to achieve independence for Angola on 11 November 1975. UNITA thereafter took to counter-revolutionary armed struggle as the USA's imperialist puppet. South Africa has since joined forces with UNITA to destabilise Angola as it similarly attempts to do in Mozambique with the MNR.

Soon after independence, the MPLA, like FRELIMO, transformed itself into a revolutionary vanguard party, the MPLA-PT (*Partido do Trabelho* or Workers' Party). It thus adopted a Marxist–Leninist ideology and established an ideological institute, the *Escola Superior do Partido*, or Higher Party School, for the political and ideological education of ministers, party officials, workers, peasants and other groups.

The Fourth Party Congress in 1983 carefully identified the other major weaknesses of the revolution besides the South African attacks. These problems include the organisation and relation between the state and the party, and the marginalisation of *poder popular*; the relative neglect of the peasantry and the failure of state farms created under the inspiration of *gigantismo*; popular participation and leadership, and effective industrialisation in order to meet the basic material needs of the masses. The new policies adopted by the Party Congress for coping with these weaknesses revolved around the revitalisation of local democratic participation through the mobilisation and reinforcement of mass organs; the decentralisation of development planning for effective local self-management; and agricultural reorganisation, with emphasis on cooperative farms.

Unfortunately, the Angolan revolution has been kept under fire from the US, South African-backed UNITA, and direct South African armed aggression under the excuse of engaging in the hot pursuit of SWAPO guerrillas operating in Namibia from bases in Angola. The defeat of UNITA in 1975 in the struggle for independence, which was a defeat for US imperialism in Africa, the principled and fraternal support for the Namibian freedom fighters, and its general role as a frontline state in the Southern African struggle, are the major reasons for reprisals against Angola, especially in southern Angola. The continuous destruction of human lives, infrastructures and productive capacity, and the diversion of national resources into defence against these imperialist and racist attacks constitute the most serious obstacle to the consolidation of the Angolan revolution and the expansion of socialist gains in that country.[32] Despite these problems, the Angolan Revolution has firmly established its basic foundations in preparation for the social transformation of the country.

Zimbabwe: The former British colony of Southern Rhodesia, renamed Zimbabwe by the nationalist leaders, achieved political independence in February 1980.[33] This was 15 years after Ian Smith's Unilateral Declaration of Independence (UDI) from

Britain in 1965 which led to a protracted armed liberation struggle, first under the Zimbabwe African People's Union (ZAPU) with the ANC (Zimbabwe) as its internal wing. Later, ideological differences led to the Zimbabwe African National Union – Patriotic Front (ZANU/PF) under President Robert Mugabe splitting from ZAPU, which remained under Joshua Nkomo. Both groups had their military wings – the Zimbabwe African National Liberation Army (ZANLA) for ZANU, and the Zimbabwe People's Revolutionary Army (ZIPRA) for ZAPU – though ZIPRA was formed originally by the front-line states from ex-ZANU and ex-ZAPU guerrillas.

The liberation war itself led to considerable radicalisation of the country with ZANLA's ZANU called "party of the people engaged in a struggle for socialism", with "fight against imperialism" emphasised, even by the nationalist leadership. But the national liberation war was not fought on an anti-capitalist basis, as the main objective of both radical wings of ZANU(PF) and ZAPU was democratisation of the existing political structure and elimination of racism. Yet, the masses supported both nationalist parties in order to achieve broad democratic rights and regain their land and country. The *petit-bourgeoisie* that supported the armed struggle in order to achieve *political* and not *social* change were, however, not opposed by the masses. Thus on the central question of land, ZANU had only vague generalisations and went to London, to the Lancaster House Conference on Zimbabwe's independence, to demand land nationalisation, but returned with mere redistribution of vacant land that was underutilised, abandoned or belonged to absentee landlords, while productive settler farms were to be left intact. For its own part, ZAPU wanted to reduce the inequality in land ownership but within the existing capitalist framework.

As the war escalated (to endanger the entire capitalist system) beyond the control of Bishop Muzorewa's reactionary Internal Settlement Government under his South Africa-backed (after the collapse of UDI in 1979) United African National Congress, Britain agreed to negotiate with the nationalist fighters at Lancaster House. This resulted in what is popularly called the "Lancaster House compromise" in which the nationalist leaders were forced by the front-line states, whose regimes were threatened by imperialist reprisals, to accept the pro-settler and imperialist concessions proposed by Lord Carrington, the British Foreign Secretary. South Africa also pressurised Ian Smith to accept the Lancaster proposals. The result was a post-Lancaster House victory for all the participants and defeat for the African masses. The transitional period between the Lancaster House Conference and the independence elections in February 1980, under Lord Soames, saw Zimbabwe as a "new colony" – as Soames went all out to weaken the anti-imperialist movement and ZANU(PF) in the elections. In spite of these manoeuvres, the election results for the 80 seats allocated for Africans in the 100-member parliament were: Mugabe's ZANU(PF) 57 seats; Nkomo's ZAPU 20; Muzorewa's UANC 3; with Ian Smith's party winning the 20 seats reserved for whites in the Lancaster House constitution. In April 1980, the Mugabe government was installed as "a British success story" – according to *The Times* of London – as the liberation seemed to have ended with a stability formula for capitalism and British imperialism.

This has led to a major controversy: that despite the revolutionary socialist commitment of the liberation, the Marxist reputation of Robert Mugabe and his promise to establish a one-party socialist state, little had changed in Zimbabwe after five years.[34] The basic economic structure of the country and the state apparatus have been alleged to be intact, virtually with tension between Mugabe's government and the African majority.[35] The settlers retained their privileges; the radical efforts of ZANLA and ZIPRA ex-guerrillas have been frustrated; the protests of African workers and peasants are being repressed; socialism is said not to be promoted while pro-imperialist ties are being strengthened. Indeed, capitalism is alleged to be seriously promoted in various ways: by Mugabe's adherence to the Lancaster House agreement; signing the EEC's Lomé Convention; joining the IMF and the World Bank; the perception of a progressive role for Britain in independent Zimbabwe, for example, the request that Britain should send troops to train a new army and give assistance; the massive Western aid with £890 million that was pledged by March 1981, as white settler farmers fondly call Mugabe "good Old Bob"; and foreign multinational capital flows into the country with keen rivalry.

Astrow rejects the common reasons adduced to rationalise this right-wing posture. These include the restrictive nature of the Lancaster House Constitution; the threats of South African sub-imperialism; the difficulty of integrating the ex-guerrillas into a national, loyal army; threat of a coup; the country's dependence on white-settler skills; and the constraints of post-war reconstruction. Rather than any right-wing shift of the nationalist leadership since independence, he argues that the current capitalist orientation of Zimbabwe is due to the class interests of the nationalist leadership and the entire political strategy of the nationalist movements. Thus while the nationalist leaders emphasised the "fight against imperialism", this was mainly for democratic rights and against Britain's bias towards the white settlers. There was thus basic agreement with British imperialism. The political programme of the left-wing members of ZANU and ZAPU is said to be similar to that of other sections of their parties.[36] All are said to be agreed on capitalist development for Zimbabwe after independence on the basis of a programme of *National Democratic Revolution* (NDR), and to disagree only on its duration and modality Thus ZANU's and ZIPRA's two-stage political programme based on Marxism–Leninism is said to require: (a) a "national democratic phase" (of NDR) fashioned after the Russian Mensheviks, and international Stalinism for an "all-class unity" of all those colonised and oppressed to fight the enemy; and (b) a second stage of socialist revolution by a movement with a post-independence proletarian ideology, whose success depends on the emergence of a working-class movement with the appropriate ideology in the first place. Yet, Astrow maintains that socialist revolution is not "the inevitable sequel to the NDR" because the working class fighting for socialism under the NDR would be seen as fighting the NDR and be repressed, and the advance to the second stage after the NDR must threaten and struggle against the *petit-bourgeois* leadership. As ZANU's electoral manifesto states:

> ZANU's ideological belief is socialism (but) in making towards the socialist transformation of Zimbabwean society, a ZANU government will nevertheless recognise historical, social and other existing practical realities of Zimbabwe.

> One of these existing practical realities is the capitalist system which cannot be transformed overnight. It is recognised that private enterprise will have to continue until circumstances are ripe for socialist change.[37]

Mugabe has elaborated this:

> . . . our Socialism must be realistic. It must never assume that in the end there won't be any private enterprise. I don't think you'll ever get to a situation where everything belongs to the state – it would be absolutely ridiculous, there must be some forms of property which continue to belong to individuals.[38]

Both the ZANU manifesto and Mugabe are correct, but they do not go far enough. With Mugabe's statement, it is clear that socialism does not abolish all individual ownership. *It abolishes only private ownership of the means of production* (distribution and exchange), so that individuals are still entitled to their dwelling homes and personal belongings in the forms of durable and non-durable consumer goods (cars, refrigerators, clothes, and so on). As for the ZANU manifesto, it is because socialist transformation takes cognisance of existing reality that it struggles against it and marks a period of transition to socialism. It is the struggle that partly creates the ripe circumstance, so while socialism will not be achieved overnight, the transition must involve concrete programmes, such as: creating a vanguard party with Marxist–Leninist ideology; nationalisation of land and enterprises; worker/peasant control of enterprises and farms; formation of cooperatives; creation of mass organisations; weakening of imperialist links and capitalist relations of production; stronger links with socialist countries and so on.

Besides the adoption of Marxism–Leninism by the party in August 1984, the promise of a one-party Marxist state (that five years later had not been realised) and the plan to end the conflict between ZANU(PF) and ZAPU through their merger, little progress had been made on this transitional programme to socialism. It is true that the USSR's mistaken support for Nkomo before the 1980 elections may have delayed the external socialist support for the transition to socialism in Zimbabwe. But that misunderstanding should be resolved quickly to speed up the socialist transition in the legitimate interest of the suffering masses in Zimbabwe. The assurance, by many Zimbabwean comrades, of intense class struggles in Zimbabwe on all fronts is important in this regard.

New Ghana:

> Fellow Ghanaians, as you will notice, we are not playing the National Anthem. In other words, this is not a coup. I ask for nothing else than a revolution – something that will transform the social and economic order of this country . . .
> J. J. Rawlings (Broadcast after 31 December Revolution, 1981.)

The slogan of the 31 December Revolution is "People – Revolution" and the Provisional National Defence Council (PNDC) maintains that the military has not taken over but wants to be part of the national decision-making process centred on the People's Defence Committees (PDCs) and the People's Army. Apart from the Marxist–Leninist ideology of the June 4 Movement that made the 31 December Revolution, the PNDC as the ruling government of the revolution has not officially and openly committed itself to Marxist–Leninist ideology or scientific socialism. As the government put it, "The PNDC remains committed to the National Democratic Revolution (NDR) and stands for a just society. This principally means for us a struggle against all forms of domination and the building of a self-reliant national economy . . ."[39] Appendix A of the CDR Guidelines elaborates the "Directive Principles of State Policy" in terms of social justice, equal opportunities, human rights, opposition to exploitation, corruption, discrimination as well as commitment to national integration, planned development and so on – but not a single word on socialism.

The political organisation of the Ghanaian revolution consists of the PNDC as the highest organ of state, the People's Defence Committees (PDCs with Workers' Defence Committees (WDCs) and a National Defence Committee) and the Committees for the Defence of the Revolution (CDRs). The workers are organised specifically into WDCs and the Ghana Trade Union Congress[40] (TUC), in addition to several loose mass organisations for students, other youths and women. But clearly there are still (as of August 1986 when I attended the Colloquium of the Journal of African Marxists held in Accra) no deliberately established revolutionary mass organisations imbued with socialist ideology and undergoing regular political education. The PDCs have been described officially as the ". . . most mass-embracing organs of popular power, organisation and struggle".[41] The objectives for their creation are to generate a mass base of popular participation for the revolution (that is, NDR), democratic rights, mobilisation for development, combat domination and exploitation and thus defend the revolution. Their functions include data collection, production and storage; education and training for manpower development; health and sanitation; housing; people's shops; afforestation; and defence and security. These PDCs are organised at community, workplace, district, regional and national levels, which are all coordinated with each having its executive committee.

Similarly, the CDRs exist in communities and workplaces with a unit comprising 500 members and open to all, except by opting out or being rejected by the majority for lack of integrity and loyalty. They are also organised at area, zonal, district, regional and up to the Political Counsellor at the national level. Their functions are mobilisation and defence, and they are self-financing from the collection of membership dues of a maximum of C20 (20 cedi) per month, together with the sale of their produce. There is thus considerable overlap between the membership, objectives and functions of the PDCs and the CDRs.

The economic programme of the "31st December Revolution" is anchored to the NDR and shaped as the Economic Recovery Programme (ERP), two editions of which were prepared in November 1984 and October 1985 for the second and third meetings of the Consultative Group for Ghana, in Paris.[42] The first statement of this ERP in December 1982 claimed that "There is hardly a single country in the world today that is unaffected by this [economic] crisis"[43] – an embarrassing statement from a revolutionary government because of the relative insulation of the socialist world from this global capitalist crisis. As the ERP is tailored for imperialist creditors and aid donors in Paris, and sees Ghana's problems as aggravated by "monetary, fiscal, foreign exchange and pricing policies", and not by domestic capitalism and foreign imperialist manipulation, its objectives are "among other things, to reform prices and restore production incentives, arrest runaway inflation, realign interest rates, cut budget deficits, rehabilitate physical infrastructure and give proper priorities for foreign exchange allocation"[44] – the objective of removing local and foreign exploitation in the ERP of 1982 has been dropped. Thus ERP was initially a four-year exercise for 1982/86, with 1983 for reconstruction and consolidation based on the incentive system, and 1984/86 for a Three-Year Medium-Term plan, which was launched in November 1983. It planned to raise the government's shareholding in retail banks, especially Barclays and Standard Banks, from 40% to 80% from 31 January 1983, and envisaged state monopoly of foreign trade with the establishment of people's cooperative shops.

The ERP for 1984/86 was, however, bedevilled by: the 1983 crisis involving about one million returnees; devastating drought in 1983/84 resulting in the loss of 174,000 tons of maize; an abortive coup early in 1983; and a 123% rate of inflation. But the programme concluded that: "Underlying Ghana's economic decline in the 1970s and early 1980s were the acute price distortions in the economy", the standard IMF–World Bank line. So the strategy was to consist of: devaluation; a cut in the budget deficit from 4.4% of GDP in 1982 to 2.2% of GDP in 1984; a reduction in the rate of inflation from 123% to 30% by 1984; price controls of 23 manufactured and imported goods; incomes policy for a 40% rise in nominal (money) wages in 1984, as real wages and salaries in 1982 were only 17% of their 1975 levels; and a fiscal drive to raise revenue and cut government spending through the removal of various subsidies – all standard IMF packages. Thus between April 1983 and August 1984, the cedi was devalued by 1,300%, and by August 1986, the cedi which, in December 1981, was C2.75 to $1 was down to C90 to $1 – and the IMF was still demanding a devaluation to C120 to the dollar – hence the adoption of foreign exchange auction or a Second-Tier Foreign Exchange Market (SFEM) on Friday, 12 September 1986, which was ended in February 1987. Then as by 1983, external debt (service) arrears stood at $601 million, debt service in 1984 was planned at $251 million or 43% of export earnings for that year, and $423 million for 1985. These programmes required external aid with an IMF loan of $539 million in SDRs (Special Drawing Rights) and Compensatory Finance Facility; $133 million from the World Bank in Reconstruction Import Credit (RIC) and Export Rehabilitation Project, and $30 million from the African Development Bank in import credit. The Third ERP for 1986/88, which was drawn for the third Paris meeting of the Consultative Group for Ghana, designed a policy framework with several items.[45] These included macro-economic management policies with improved incentives for higher production through fiscal, monetary, exchange, trade, financial and income policy measures; sectoral reforms for growth in agriculture, industry, energy, education and health; restructuring of the roles of the public and private sectors, with the public sector being pivotal; rehabilitation of human capital; financial reform; external assistance for debt management; and implementation through improved management methods. The impact of this ERP on rural poverty and development is then to be monitored.

In these circumstances, the "31 December Revolution" has several problems, the first of which is its *petit-bourgeois* reformist character centred on the National

Democratic Revolution (NDR), which is clearly a neocolonial capitalist programme whose Economic Recovery Programme is guided by the imperialist policies of the IMF and the World Bank. Even if this NDR is transitional, why is there no explicit statement of the overall socialist commitment of the revolution and any suggestion of transition to scientific socialism, as in Ethiopia? Then, of course, because of this lack of ideological clarity or commitment, there are no serious efforts at building revolutionary mass organisations to create socialist consciousness among the broad masses. Hence even the students' June 4th Movement, that pioneered the revolution and was its strongest early supporter, has been marginalised along with the older mass organisations such as Kwame Nkrumah's Revolutionary Guards and the African Youth Command. It is not enough to say that they still exist legally within the CDRs and PDCs, or were relegated because of the 1983 crisis. If the revolution still exists, these mass organisations must play active leading roles. Indeed, many serious comrades of these mass organisations have been jailed or hounded out of Ghana. There is an equally glaring absence of any preparation for launching a vanguard Marxist–Leninist Party such as exists in Mozambique and Angola.

These failures of mass mobilisation have encouraged exile groups to threaten the revolution. An example is the Exiles' Save Democracy Movement led by the banned PNP (People's National Party). Corruption,[46] called *Kalabule* in Ghana, has also been driven underground, rather than eliminated, as has the illegal foreign exchange market. These problems derive mainly from Rawlings' cosmetic and unrealistic methods, such as the incessant harassment of market mammies over food prices and the replacement of the leaders of the TUC by the Association of Local Unions (ALU). All these reformist measures cannot make a socialist revolution, especially as they are essentially guided by IMF–World Bank loan conditionalities and the approval of the imperialist Consultative Group for Ghana. The point must be underscored that, even if IMF–World Bank loans may be justified by Ghana's economic collapse during 1981/83, that crisis was over by 1986 (or should be) and imperialist credit and policies cannot be used to build a socialist revolution – not even a credible NDR as a foundation for socialist transformation. The IMF's and the World Bank's policies can only consolidate neocolonial capitalist development. But what the "31 December Revolution" requires are basic revolutionary strategies and tactics.

It is the steady and adamant application of these radical policies based on clear socialist ideology, a vanguard party and radical mass mobilisation that have advanced the socialist experiments in Cabral's Guinea and elsewhere. The absence of any internal counter-revolutionary group in Guinea-Bissau, Ghana and Zimbabwe offer them greater prospects of socialist transition than exists in Mozambique and Angola – and the opportunity should not be frittered away on the altar of reformism.

Problems and lessons of socialist experiments in Africa

The foregoing exploration of old and new socialist experiments in Africa points to some basic difficulties and common lessons, and poses the familiar question of strategy for the social transformation of the continent. The main problems centre round the relative underdevelopment of neocolonial capitalism on the continent, weak socialist consciousness, short experience of anti-capitalist class struggle, the poverty of ideology and imperialist aggression through the manipulation of internal cleavages.

Difficulties

Much has been made of the difficulty of attempting to build scientific socialism in Africa on a foundation of underdeveloped neocolonial capitalism. This poses severe problems of inadequate infrastructures and an inability to meet the basic material requirements of the population. These problems are common to all the old and new socialist experiments, with the possible exceptions of Egypt and Zimbabwe. Some socialist experiments in Africa started correctly, with an initial phase of national democratic revolution – as in Ethiopia, Zimbabwe and Ghana. The transitional nature of this arrangement, however, must not only be emphasised, but the intended transition to scientific socialism must be formulated in writing and pursued relentlessly. The success stories of scientific socialism in the USSR, China, Vietnam, for example, all eloquently demonstrate that even pre-capitalist agrarian societies can be transformed into socialist societies.

The absence of socialist consciousness among the broad masses has also been problematic for old and new socialist experiments – except in such countries as Guinea-Bissau, Angola, and so on, where armed liberation movements had to wage war to make a revolution. In such countries, the political work that went with the armed struggle developed socialist ideas and values among the masses. But in other countries where flag independence was won through nationalist struggle (and even in Zimbabwe with a settler population and a less generalised armed struggle), the masses developed nationalist anti-colonial (and not even general anti-imperialist) consciousness rather than socialist consciousness. In these majority of countries, the post-colonial comprador state, capitalism and neocolonial domination have not been systematically exposed and brought under attack by the broad masses. Hence the limited membership of communist and socialist parties or movements in these countries.

This is related to the recent history of anti-capitalist (and even anti-feudal and anti-imperialist) class struggles in Africa. Except in countries that were liberated through armed struggle, *class* has not been the basis or focus of struggle for the masses in most of Africa. Even in the old socialist experiments – Guinea, Ghana, Egypt, and so on – the preoccupation of the national leadership with the preservation of tenuous national unity under the fragile legitimacy of post-colonial regimes, has led to muted class struggle. The defensive radicalism of African Socialism, by preaching a false doctrine of classless Africa which, therefore, did not need any class struggle, also encouraged this tendency. This explains the reformism, opportunism, lack of clear, class focus and poor mass mobilisation that characterise the policies of most African socialist regimes.

Ideological mystification has also been a problem with the socialist experiments, especially the old ones. The biggest single culprit here has been the bogey of African

Socialism, followed by National Democratic Revolution as in Ghana. Both ideologies directly preclude scientific socialism and, in most countries pursuing African Socialism, they even become anti-socialist as in post-Nasser Egypt. It is this absence of clear ideological commitment to scientific socialism that has inhibited the development of its organisational requirements, such as the establishment of a vanguard Marxist–Leninist party, workers' control of enterprises, and general mass mobilisation. Conversely, it is this progressive ideological void that has encouraged social reformism, state capitalism and even neocolonial capitalism that have been advanced as socialist experiments in Africa. It is these *petit-bourgeois* programmes that breed the ethno-religious and regional cleavages that hamper development in Africa.

In these circumstances, imperialist aggression and manoeuvres have exploited the internal weaknesses of these socialist experiments in two broad ways. In scientific socialist experiments like those of Angola, Mozambique and Ethiopia, imperialism is so afraid of the snowball effects of their success that it has mounted unprovoked aggression against these countries by denying aid, funding internal conflicts and encouraging invasion through South Africa and the MNR in Mozambique, and through Eritrean secession and the Somalia problem in Ethiopia. In the moribund and defensive socialist experiments, imperialism has been content to deny "aid", abet exile invasion (as in Sekou Toure's Guinea) and destabilise them through its notorious CIA activities all within the imperialist objective of containing communist expansion in Africa – as if the continent is an imperialist estate.

Lessons of the socialist experiments

On the basis of these difficulties, *the major lessons* to be learned from the old and new socialist experiments in Africa are: (a) the danger of right-wing opportunism within a socialist experiment without class struggle; (b) the trap that African Socialism constitutes for socialist transformation; (c) the futility of nationalisation *per se* as a socialist strategy; (d) the need for the collective defence of socialist experiments in Africa.

First, as the betrayal of Kwame Nkrumah in Ghana and Nasser in Egypt, the failure of socialism in Guinea, and of African Socialism generally have abundantly demonstrated, it is impossible to build genuine socialism on the altar of national unity without committed class struggle. This, typically, leads to the isolation of the national leader and his few followers, while the bulk of the population wallows in state capitalism and internal decay. The need for systematic mass mobilisation, workers' control of enterprises, a vanguard party and a scientific socialist ideology are thus clearly emphasised.

Second, African Socialism must be clearly recognised and rejected for the *petit-bourgeois* diversionary and defensive ideology of bureaucratic state capitalism that it is. Its basic presuppositions make it an impossible vehicle for the construction of scientific socialism. In the struggle for scientific socialism in Africa, *petit-bourgeois* and romantic illusions about classless Africa, Humanism and so forth, must be firmly rejected. An uncompromising and undiluted scientific socialist ideology must be demanded by the masses as the scientific basis for the social transformation of the continent.

Third, it emerges from the socialist experiments so far that just as African Socialism is *not* socialism, in the same way, the mere nationalisation of enterprises will not yield socialism; neither will the mere proclamation of revolution or national democratic revolution lead to socialism. Nationalisation that places the nationalised enterprises in the hands of *petit-bourgeois* bureaucrats and professionals will, at best, lead to state capitalism – it often leads to the looting of such parastatals and to the fiscal crisis of the state. To be effective, nationalisation should be associated with workers' control of enterprises so that it becomes *socialisation* – and the workers and peasants should be armed to defend such nationalised enterprises against military upstarts and similar adventurers who may wish to privatise them in future (as, for example, in Ghana after Nkrumah, Chile after Allende). Similarly, any programme of national democratic revolution must give a clear time-table of its mode of transition to scientific socialism so that socialist struggle can be waged by the broad masses during the democratic revolution. This will prevent the "revolution" from relapsing into state capitalism, and even fascism.

Persistent imperialist aggression against socialist experiments also dictates the need not only to arm the broad masses to defend their revolution, but also for collective defence among African socialist states. The OAU is neocolonial and cannot be relied upon to perform this function – it has been helpless against abusive and persistent apartheid aggression against the frontline states and US aggression against Angola through UNITA. Three coordinated moves are required here. One is the collective defence of socialist states against imperialist aggression as Tanzania and Zimbabwe are doing with Mozambique against the MNR and apartheid South Africa. Imperialist aggression against any socialist state in Africa should be regarded as aggression against all the others, and it should be repelled accordingly. Then, as well as the general efforts at regional economic cooperation in Africa, the socialist states should also expand their existing mutual economic assistance in the areas of food aid, exchange of raw materials, technical assistance, exchange of industrial/technological information, and so on. This will help to neutralise or weaken the imperialist economic blackmail against them. Simultaneously, African socialist states should maintain effective socialist internationalism with the advanced socialist countries. Though these advanced socialist states have been giving enormous assistance for socialist development in Africa, they should continuously recognise the imperialist subversion against the new socialist regimes and offer their fraternal assistance even more readily. The Sino-Soviet rivalry in Africa is an obstacle here, which happily is being overcome with maturity on both sides.

The socialist question in Africa

In spite of everything that has been discussed so far, the question may be asked whether on account of the underdevelopment of neocolonial capitalism, the construction of scientific socialism can be on the agenda in Africa now. The answer is an unequivocal YES. History has answered that question since the transformation of underdeveloped capitalism into socialism in the USSR, China, and Vietnam among others. Indeed, in many African countries such as Zimbabwe, Ghana, Zambia, Nigeria, Kenya, Ivory Coast, for example, the current level of capitalist development is far higher than it was during the socialist transformation of many of the existing socialist countries. What is required is the creative application and adaptation of the principles of scientific socialism to the peculiar and concrete circumstances of each country with respect to its development of productive forces, social relations of production, the nature of the imperialist contradiction and other internal forces.

APPENDIX: Text of the Nkomati Accords[47]

The government of the People's Republic of Mozambique and the government of the Republic of SA, hereinafter referred to as the High Contracting Parties, recognising the principles of strict respect for sovereignty and territorial integrity, sovereign equality, political independence and the inviolability of the borders of all States, reaffirming the principle of non-interference in the internal affairs of other States, considering the internationally recognised principle of the right of peoples to self-determination and independence and the principle of equal rights of all peoples, considering the obligation of all States to refrain, in their international relations, from the threat or use of force against the territorial integrity or political independence of any State, considering the obligation of States to settle conflicts by peaceful means, and thus safeguard international peace and security and justice, recognising the responsibility of States not to allow their territory to be used for acts of war, aggression or violence against other States, conscious of the need to promote relations of good neighbourliness based on the principles of equality of rights and mutual advantage, convinced that relations of good neighbourliness between the High Contracting parties will contribute to peace, security, stability and progress in southern Africa, the continent and the world, have solemnly agreed to the following:

ARTICLE ONE

The High Contracting Parties undertake to respect each other's sovereignty and independence and in fulfilment of this fundamental obligation, to refrain from interfering in the internal affairs of the other.

ARTICLE TWO

1. The High Contracting Parties shall resolve differences and disputes that may arise between them and that may, or are likely to, endanger mutual peace and security or peace and security in the region, by means of negotiation, enquiry, mediation, arbitration or other peaceful means, and undertake not to resort, individually or collectively, to the threat or use of force against each other's sovereignty, territorial integrity or political independence.

2. For the purposes of this article, the use of force shall include inter alia:

a. Attacks by land, air or sea forces;

b. Sabotage;

c. Unwarranted concentration of such forces at or near the international boundaries of the High Contracting Parties;

d. Violation of the international land, air or sea boundaries of the High Contracting Parties.

3. The High Contracting Parties shall not in any way assist the armed forces of any state or group of states deployed against the territorial sovereignty or political independence of the other.

ARTICLE THREE

1. The High Contracting Parties shall not allow their respective territories, territorial waters or air space to be used as a base, thoroughfare, or in any other way by another state, government, foreign military forces, organisation or individuals which plan or prepare to commit acts of violence, terrorism or aggression against the territorial integrity or political independence of the other or may threaten the security of its inhabitants.

2. The High Contracting Parties, in order to prevent or eliminate the acts or the preparation of acts mentioned in paragraph 1. of this article, undertake in particular to:

a) Forbid and prevent in their respective territories the organisation of irregular forces or armed bands, including mercenaries, whose objective is to carry out the acts contemplated in paragraph 1. of this article;

b) Eliminate from their respective territories bases, training centres, places of shelter, accommodation and transit for elements who intend to carry out the acts contemplated in paragraph 1. of this article;

c) Eliminate from their respective territories centres or depots containing armaments of whatever nature, destined to be used by the elements contemplated in paragraph 1. of this article;

d) Eliminate from their respective territories command posts or other places for the command, direction and co-ordination of the elements contemplated in paragraph 1. of this article;

e) Eliminate from their respective territories communication and communication facilities between the command and the elements contemplated in paragraph 1. of this article;

f) Eliminate and prohibit the installation in their respective territories of radio broadcasting stations, including unofficial or clandestine broadcasts, for the elements that carry out the acts contemplated in paragraph 1. of this article;

g) Exercise strict control, in their respective territories, over elements which intend to carry out or plan the acts contemplated in paragraph 1. of this article;

h) Prevent the transit of elements who intend or plan to commit the acts contemplated in paragraph 1. of this article, from a place in the territory of either to a place in the territory of any third state which has a common boundary with the High Contracting Party against which such elements intended or plan to commit the said acts;

i) Take appropriate steps in their respective territories to prevent the recruitment of elements of whatever nationality for the purpose of carrying out the acts contemplated in paragraph 1. of this article;

j) Prevent the elements contemplated in paragraph 1. of this article from carrying out from their respective territories by any means, acts of abduction or other acts, aimed at taking citizens of any nationality hostage in the territory of the other High Contracting Party; and

k) Prohibit the provision in their respective territories of any logistic facilities for carrying out the acts contemplated in paragraph 1. of this article.

3. The High Contracting Parties will not use the territory of third states to carry

out or support the acts contemplated in paragraphs 1. and 2. of this article.

ARTICLE FOUR

The High Contracting Parties shall take steps, individually and collectively, to ensure that the international boundary between their respective territories is effectively patrolled and that the border posts are efficiently administered to prevent illegal crossing from the territory of a High Contracting Party to the territory of the other, and in particular, by elements contemplated in Article Three of this agreement.

ARTICLE FIVE

The High Contracting Parties shall prohibit within their territory acts of propaganda that incite a war of aggression against the other High Contracting Party and shall also prohibit acts of propaganda aimed at inciting acts of terrorism and civil war in the territory of the other High Contracting Party.

ARTICLE SIX

The High Contracting Parties declare that there is no conflict between their commitments in treaties and international obligations and the commitments undertaken in this agreement.

ARTICLE SEVEN

The High Contracting Parties are committed to interpreting this agreement in good faith and will maintain periodic contact to ensure the effective application of what has been agreed.

ARTICLE EIGHT

Nothing in this agreement shall be construed as detracting from the High Contracting Parties' right of self-defence in the event of armed attacks, as provided for in the Charter of the United Nations.

ARTICLE NINE

1. Each of the High Contracting Parties shall appoint high-ranking representatives to serve on a joint security commission with the aim of supervising and monitoring the application of this agreement.

2. The commission shall determine its own working procedure.

3. The commission shall meet on a regular basis and may be specially convened whenever circumstances so require.

4. The commission shall:

a) Consider all allegations of infringements of the provisions of this agreement;

b) Advise the High Contracting Parties of its conclusions; and

c) Make recommendations to the High Contracting Parties concerning measures for the effective application of this agreement and the settlement of disputes over infringements or alleged infringements.

5. The High Contracting Parties shall determine the mandate of their respective representatives in order to enable interim measures to be taken in cases of duly recognised emergency.

6. The High Contracting Parties shall make available all the facilities necessary for the effective functioning of the commission and will jointly consider its conclusions and recommendations.

ARTICLE TEN

This agreement will also be known as "The Accords of Nkomati".

ARTICLE ELEVEN

This agreement shall enter into force on the date of the signature thereof. The agreement agreed to by the High Contracting Parties shall be effected by the exchange of notes between them. In witness thereof, the signatories, in the name of their respective governments, have signed and sealed this agreement, in quadruplicate in the Portuguese and English languages, both texts being equally authentic.

Thus done and signed at the common border on the banks of the Nkomati River on this the sixteenth day of March 1984. Samora Moises Machel, Marshall of the Republic, President of the People's Republic of Mozambique, President of the Council of Ministers. For the government of the People's Republic of Mozambique. Pieter Willem Botha, Prime Minister of the Republic of S. A. For the government of the Republic of SA.

Notes

1. A. M. Babu (1981).
2. For discussions of these old and new socialist experiments in Africa, see K. N. Brutents (1977); G. Starushenko (1982); A. M. Babu (1981).
3. See A. M. Babu (1981), chs. 4, 5, 7 & 8.
4. On African socialism and Arab socialism, see A. M. Babu (1981) and Samir Amin (1982).
5. See Alavi (1972) in *New Left Review*, 74, July–August, pp. 59–82.
6. For useful information on some of these countries see A. Y. Yansane ed. (1980).
7. Ibid. and World Development Report, 1985.
8. See J. Okello (1967).
9. Emphasis here underscores the idea of socialism from the top since Tanzania had virtually no working class by 1967. Indeed, the Zanzibari revolution inspired Tanzanian socialism.
10. For detailed studies of Tanzanian socialism, see Lionel Cliffe and John Saul (eds) (1975), vols. 1 & 2.
11. See J. Nyerere (1968), p. 11.
12. He remained party chairman and *de facto* head of state.
13. See G. K. Helleiner (1973), in *Economic Journal*, March.
14. See Yansane (ed.) (1980) ch. 6.
15. Kwame Nkrumah (1964).
16. See E. M'buyinga (1982), ch. 2.
17. Nkrumah's prolific socialist writings in exile were published by Panaf in London and include the *Revolutionary Path*, *Guerrilla Warfare*, *Neocolonialism*, etc.
18. See Amin (1982), ch. 1.
19. Amin (1982) ch. 3.
20. These data are from World Development Report, (1985).
21. See Ben Turok (ed.) (1979).
22. This is the predominant consequence of puerile indigenisation in Africa. See Adebayo Adedeji (ed.) (1981).
23. World Development Report (1985).
24. See L. S. Senghor (1959).
25. On these new socialist experiments, see Barry Munslow (ed.) (1986).
26. This was during my tenure as Visiting Professor in Economics at Addis Ababa University, 1981/82.

27. For the internal class struggle in the Ethiopian Revolution, see Paul Valde's Vivo (1978); and René Lefort (1983), chs. 5–7. The abusive personal attack on Colonel Mengistu Haile Mariam in Lefort's book is unjustified and embarrassing.
28. For an account of the armed struggle for the Liberation of Mozambique, see Eduardo Mondlane (1969); B. Munslow (1986) ch. 6.
29. E. Mondlane (1969), ch. 8.
30. J. Hanlon (1984).
31. Members of the Liberation Front (1972); see also M. Wolfers and J. Bergerol (1983); and B. Munslow (1983) ch. 7.
32. The total estimated direct and indirect costs of South African war damages in Angola have been put at US$7,614 million, comprising $914 million during 1976/81 and $6,700 million during 1975/76. See B. Munslow (1986), p. 189.
33. See André Astrow (1983).
34. Indeed, Astrow maintained this position as early as 1983 when his book was published.
35. Ibid., chs. 1, 6 and 7.
36. Astrow (1983) ibid., pp. 135–44.
37. Ibid., p. 144.
38. Ibid., p. 144.
39. Committee for the Defence of the Revolution (CDR), *Guidelines 1986* (Accra), p. 1, Preamble no. 4.
40. See Government of Ghana, *A Revolutionary Journey – Selected Speeches, of J. J. Rawlings, 1981/82 Volume 1* (Accra), ch. 17.
41. See Ghana, *Power to the People – The New Guidelines for the National Defence Committee and People's Defence Committees*, April 1983 (Accra).
42. See Government of Ghana: (1) *The PNDC's Programme for Reconstruction and Development, Statement by the PNDC Secretary for Finance and Economic Planning, December 30, 1982*; (2) *Economic Recovery Programme (ERP) 1984/86*, issued November 1984; (3) *Progress of the Economic Recovery Programme*, 1984/86 and *Policy Framework*, 1986/88, issued October 1985 (Accra; Government Printer).
43. Statement from the PNDC's Secretary for Finance and Economic Planning, December 1982, p. 1.
44. See ERP, 1984/86.
45. See ERP, 1986/88.
46. On these problems, see Emmanuel Hansen (1982) in *Journal of African Marxists*, Issue 2, August, pp. 4–21.
47. *Journal of African Marxists*, Issue 6, October 1984, pp. 5–9.

12 New Masters: IMF and World Bank

Introduction

From the emergence of the African crisis in the 1970s to the 1980s, the most important function of the International Monetary Fund (IMF) and the World Bank has been to provide loans to Third World countries faced with shortages of foreign exchange. This provision of loans has offered both institutions the opportunity to prescribe policies to these countries. During 1973/79, African countries received soft credit and other financial assistance from the IMF (the Fund) to deal with balance of payments deficits, while the World Bank (the Bank) offered loans for anti-poverty projects under its rural development programme.

But since 1979, the Fund has been offering more assistance to Africa under its Stand-by Arrangements or Extended Fund Facility, with tough preconditions. Whereas African countries took only 3% of such "extended" loans during 1970/78, in 1979/80 they received 30% and they have been getting more. Since 1980, the Bank has also been shifting from its project-tied loans for poverty programmes to the provision of structural adjustment loans. Thus, since 1979, both the Fund and the Bank have been coordinating their lending policies to African and other Third World countries under increasingly similar stabilisation programmes with the imposition of pernicious preconditions on the national policies of these poor countries. These developments make it essential to explore the current status of the IMF and the World Bank as Africa's *New Masters*, their historical evolution and the relationship between their programmes and the African crisis.

The Bretton Woods system

The Bretton Woods international monetary system, established after World War II, has been in crisis since the early 1970s, and was shaped by the evolution of the international capitalist financial system up to 1944.[1] This financial evolution was the by-product of the development of the capitalist international division of labour which imposed primary production on the dominated Third World countries (TWCs) while the industrialised capitalist countries (ICCs) monopolised manufacturing, technology and finance capital. The development of this capitalist international division of labour, or imperialism, is synonymous with the expansion of the capitalist world market or trade, capital and labour force. Hence it relies on *exchange*; this international exchange requires *currency* as a numerator or measure of value, a means of payment and for reckoning credits and debits, and as an instrument of foreign reserves; these international functions of currency require an *international* institution such as the IMF to create, manage and distribute it. The international monetary system, therefore, responds to the needs and policies of world capitalism. Just as a national economy requires a currency and a Central Bank, world capitalism (both its primary-producing periphery and its industrialised centre) is organised under the hegemony of its most powerful economy – whose currency becomes the dominant or reserve currency of imperialism. After World War I, the development of the world capitalist market led to the emergence of the first real international monetary system based on gold and the pound sterling under British hegemony. But this system collapsed in the 1930s under the weight of the massive dislocations of the Great Depression (1929–32) and the events surrounding World War II (WWII), from which the US emerged as the strongest capitalist economy.

The search for a new international monetary system led to the Bretton Woods Agreement of 1944 signed under threat when the Nazis were still occupying part of Europe. The Agreements were a choice between the proposals of Keynes for Britain and of White for the US. Keynes suggested the establishment of an international monetary institution (the IMF) to create and manage an international currency called "bancor" that would eventually become the main reserve currency. The US imposed White's options under the threat of cutting credit to the European Allies' war effort; when the new Bretton Woods system emerged, its key international institutions, the IMF and the World Bank, were, therefore, both located in the US. Similarly, since the Fund could lend only what it could borrow, and the US was its only major source of credit, the new system was heavily dominated by the US, which also imposed the unequal GATT (General Agreement on Tariffs and Trade) treaties. This uncontested US hegemony lasted from 1944 to 1960 with the dollar regarded as good as gold for reserve currency – since the US held 59% of the world's gold stock in 1945 and 72% in 1948. So there was convertibility, with foreigners holding dollars as reserves being allowed to freely convert them into gold.

But with European reconstruction and recovery after WWII, their imports from the US not only declined, but their exports and those of Japan started competing with those of the US. The European Common Market and the EEC (European Economic Community) also erected barriers against US imports, and together with huge US imperialist spending abroad on military assistance and "aid" (this aid was really a subsidy for US agriculture and industry), the US recorded its first post-war balance of payments deficit in 1958, and 1960/68 saw her hegemony over world capitalism challenged by the European powers and Japan. The US imposed falling terms of trade on Third World countries (TWCs) by pitting their atomistic peasant producers against her giant multinational corporations (MNCs) and by means of "aid" and trade policies locking these poor countries into a debt trap. With the rapid expansion of the Eurodollar market in the 1960s, in addition to the other developments of the era, the US piled up increasing balance of payments deficits and had to resort to luring Europe into the Gold Pool of 1961/68, from which

France pulled out in 1967. The IMF also financed 10% of US trade deficits from 1960 to 1967. The devaluation of the pound sterling in 1967 was an indication of the American success in using European gold reserves to support the dollar, and pushing part of the burden of her foreign trade deficits on Europe.

In spite of this, on 15 August 1971, persistent US balance of payments deficits forced President Nixon to terminate the convertibility of the dollar into gold, as the US registered a net trade deficit in that year. By 1973, the US dollar had to be devalued; 1974/75 saw the recession of the capitalist world following the OPEC oil price hikes, while 1974/78 and post-1981 have witnessed deep crisis in world capitalism. Correspondingly, the Bretton Woods international monetary system, which became shaky in the 1960s, has been in serious crisis since the 1970s.

The point of this incursion into the origin of the IMF and its link with the evolution of the international capitalist system is to underscore three points. One is the nature of money as a façade, a veil, such that monetary phenomena (both national and international) essentially reflect structural changes in the economy, rather than being the mystique which bourgeois monetary theorists suggest. Another is that international monetary policies, including those of the IMF, are not merely technical issues competently devised, but calculated responses to structural forces, with such responses based on the needs and motives of their sponsors. This is why US needs in trade, investment and "aid", as stated by Douglas Dillon and President Eisenhower, have shaped IMF policies so critically. Thus, in 1964, "the Fund deliberately bent its rules, which specify which currencies could be used in repurchasing drawings, in order to provide additional finance to the US deficit."[2] The third point is that the structure and control of the international monetary system is a function of the distribution of economic power among the leading capitalist countries. The economic power of the industrialised capitalist countries (ICCs) is wielded increasingly in the control of TWCs through the IMF and the World Bank.

The New Masters: IMF and World Bank

Since 1979/80, when the deepening African crisis forced African countries to take 30% and more of the IMF's extended loans, the IMF and the World Bank have emerged as the *New Masters* of Africa – and of the Third World generally. The *Old Masters* were the colonial predators from the individual imperialist countries. The interval between the formal departure of the Old Masters around 1960 (in Africa) and the emergence of the New Masters has been dominated by the multinational corporations (MNCs). Thus the three stages of development of imperialism in Africa (and throughout the Third World), from domination by the colonialists to domination by the MNCs and now the IMF and World Bank, represent increasing multilateralism, decreasing direct visibility of imperialism and the current multilateral recolonisation of Africa.

Africa's (and the rest of the Third World's) New Masters – the IMF and the World Bank – are the dominant institutions created under the Bretton Woods system. The multilateral institutions of the system consist of GATT (General

Agreement on Tariffs and Trade), the IMF and the World Bank group, which includes the International Bank for Reconstruction and Development (IBRD) or simply the World Bank, the International Finance Corporation (IFC) and the International Development Association (IDA).[3] Both the IMF and the World Bank are housed together in Washington, share some senior staff, keep each other informed about their operations, supplement each other's activities, and membership of the Fund is a precondition for membership of the Bank. As will be shown later, they also share the same ideology and, since 1980, their programmes have been coordinated in individual countries under a common structural adjustment programme.

Official and actual objectives of the IMF and World Bank

Though both the Fund and the Bank have a common fundamental objective of constructing and consolidating the international capitalist system, the official goals of the two institutions are different. But these *official* goals are quite different from the *real* goals, as shown below. The IMF's main, official goal is contained in Article VIII of its Articles of Agreement which states:

> no member may, without the approval of the Fund, impose restrictions on the making of payments or transfers for current international transactions or engage in discriminatory currency arrangements or multiple currency practices . . .[4]

The promoted goals of the Fund are thus the maintenance of balance of payments equilibrium and the promotion of economic growth in individual member countries. The specific official objectives of the Bank are the promotion of economic reconstruction (of Western Europe and Japan after World War II) and general economic development (that is, anti-poverty).

But the objectives of these two institutions often conflict with their internal ideology and actual operations. In particular, the professed roles of both the Fund and Bank in Africa, and throughout the Third World, focus on objectives for particular countries and these are not necessarily consistent with the actual global role of both institutions.[5] The dominant objective and role of both agencies is actually the construction and maintenance of a capitalist international economic system, based on capitalist production and exchange under multilateral market forces for the accumulation of economic surplus (profit) by private capital without state restrictions. Article 1 of the Fund's Articles of Association gives it a major role "in the establishment of a multilateral system of payments [with] the elimination of foreign exchange restrictions".

The roles of the Fund and Bank with respect to the balance of payments (or debt) and growth of member states in this global context thus give them leverage over national economies, because the operations of the international system are based on the policies of individual countries. But the centrality of the balance of payments to the growth and health of national economies is controversial on two grounds.

One is on the narrow view that losses or shortages of foreign exchange should be regarded as the real constraint on African and other Third World countries; but by the IMF's conception of balance of payments equilibrium, a country may not be losing foreign exchange and be far from balance of payments equilibrium because it imposes restrictions on foreign trade and capital flows. The second ground for contesting the focus on the balance of payments is that it *exaggerates the role of the foreign trade sector and foreign exchange* in Third World countries. Why should the overall health of a national economy depend solely or mainly on its availability of foreign exchange and on its external balance, regardless of the state of the internal balance? Clearly, as structural disengagement from imperialism has shown in several countries (China, Cuba, for example) it is possible to construct and maintain a healthy national economy, regardless of the foreign exchange and balance of payments position.

Then there is the basic fact that the root of the balance of payments and external debt problems of African and other Third World countries cannot be located in trade, money and foreign exchange (or exchange rate), as the IMF and World Bank do, but in the *uneven development of production inherent in the international capitalist system*. Differences in the organisation of production with socialist and pre-capitalist relations of production in some countries also account, in part, for the balance of payments problems of the poor countries. Hence, it cannot be right for the Fund and Bank to impose uniformly capitalist rules of adjustment or stabilisation for these payments problems in poor countries.

There is also the issue of trade-off between the official objectives of balance of payments equilibrium and growth in these countries. From the global commitment to build the international capitalist system on multilateral market forces, the balance of payments objective is usually ranked higher than growth, especially by the Fund. Yet, is is quite legitimate and theoretically sound to promote development at the expense of balance of payments equilibrium, as the advanced capitalist countries have been doing for years. But the rules of the Fund and Bank forbid poor countries to do this. Moreover, the growth objective is a preoccupation of modernisation, which falls far short of the requirements for economic development. In addition to growth of income, development requires structural transformation of the economy, increase in productive capacity and ability to meet the basic needs of the majority of the national population. Hence the pervasive evidence of growth without development in the Third World.

Since the 1980s, an additional unstated but actual objective of both the Fund and Bank has been to require Third World countries to repay their debts to the imperialist countries – regardless of the dubious character of these external debts and the disastrous impact of their repayment terms on poor countries.

Control, operations and ideology of IMF and World Bank

Control: The IMF's and World Bank's controls' programmes, lending conditions and ideology underscore their status as New Masters in Africa and throughout the Third World. From their inception, the interests of the poor countries have been marginal to the official objectives and functioning of the Fund and Bank. Both are tightly controlled by their powerful members in the advanced capitalist countries with the larger quota contributions to their funds. The US, with the largest quota, has thus dominated both institutions. "Until 1956, this dominance was so absolute that decisions were made effectively by the US Secretary of the Treasury, to the point that the Fund's staff had no authority to negotiate conditions for drawing (from the Fund)."[6] No major decisions are taken against the wishes of the US, and while the President of the World Bank and the Deputy Managing Director of the IMF are always Americans, the Managing Director of the Fund is by agreement and tradition always a European. As some important decisions, including quota adjustment, require 85% voting majority, both the US and the EEC collectively have been given veto power. Table 12.1 shows the control of the Fund by its members in proportion to their quota contributions.

Table 12.1
Voting power structure of the IMF's committee of executive directors (as of April 1975)

Countries	*Member-ship*	*General account*		*Special drawing account*	
		Votes	*% of total*	*Votes*	*% of total*
Major DC's:					
US	1	67,250	21.40	67,250	21.87
UK	1	28,250	8.99	28,250	9.19
W. Germany	1	16,250	5.17	16,250	5.29
France	1	15,250	4.85	15,250	4.96
Japan	1	12,250	3.90	12,250	3.98
Sub-total	5	139,250	44.31	139,250	45.29
Other DC's	6	79,160	25.20	66,500	25.28
Total all DC's	*11*	*218,410*	*69.51*	*205,750*	*70.57*
Other LDC's*	7	76,114	24.21	82,564	23.20
African Countries†	2	19,670	6.26	19,150	6.22

DC's = Developed Countries; LDC's = Less-Developed Countries.
* Excluding Jamaica, Bahamas and Barbados, which have joint representation with Canada; and the Philippines, and Western Samoa, with joint representation with Australia.
† Excluding Egypt, Somalia, Algeria, Morocco, Tunisia and Ghana, with joint representation with countries outside Africa.

Sources: *IMF Year Book*, 1975 and *IMF International Financial Statistics*, 1975.

Programmes and operations: On the basis of their stated and unstated objectives and roles, the Fund and Bank have been operating *four main programmes* in Africa and throughout the Third World.[7] Traditionally, and before the 1980s, the Fund concentrated mainly on short-run stabilisation programmes aimed at managing balance of payments and external debt crises; the Bank was preoccupied, first with reconstruction after World War II, and subsequently with long-run anti-poverty programmes based on project-tied loans, especially under the poverty rhetoric of the Bank's former President, Robert McNamara. Since the deepening of the Third World and African crises in the 1980s, both the Fund and Bank have shifted to the construction of a common structural adjustment programme (SAP) that aims simultaneously at economic recovery, management of the external debt crisis, adjustment of balance of payments disequilibria (deficits and crises) and the promotion of rural development. While the Fund supervises the debt, trade and payments parts of the programme, the Bank concentrates on revitalising the rural areas, overall growth and debt management. The Fund's total loans under these programmes both to the advanced and the underdeveloped countries are depicted in Table 12.2.

Table 12.2
IMF loans during 1947/78 (in million SDRs)*

Region	*1947/78*	*%*	*1978*	*%*
World	44,632.1	100.0	3,744.3	93.3
Industrialised countries	26,735.1	60.0	2,473.8	66.0
Developing countries:				
Oil exporting countries	677.8	2.0	—	—
Non-oil developing countries	17,011.6	38.0	1,210.7	32.3
Africa	2,912.6	7.0	309.1	8.0
Asia	4,938.1	11.0	334.9	9.0
Europe	2,433.7	5.0	241.4	6.0
Middle East	1,198.2	3.0	147.4	4.0
Western Hemisphere	5,529.1	12.0	177.9	5.0

* SDRs = Special Drawing Rights; this is the name of the Fund's money.
Source: IMF, *International Financial Statistics*, various years (Washington).

The *lending pre-conditions or conditionality clauses* of the Fund and Bank have been discussed extensively and emotionally. These preconditions constitute the heart of the growing controversy surrounding the two multilateral institutions, and the major reason for regarding the IMF and World Bank as New Masters in Africa. Starting initially as the preconditions for obtaining IMF stabilisation loans under its Extended Fund Facility, the preconditions have also been attached less perniciously to World Bank loans (for example, being tied to projects) and since the 1980s, these conditions dominate the new structural adjustment programme of the Fund and Bank.

These preconditions, which are popularly associated with IMF conditionality are as follows:[8]

1. *trade liberalisation:* abolition of foreign exchange controls and import restrictions;

2. *devaluation:* of the exchange rate: this raises the prices of imports in domestic currency and lowers the prices of exports in terms of foreign currency;

3. *monetary anti-inflationary measures:* including control of bank lending (credit), higher interest rates and possibly higher reserve requirements for commercial banks;

4. *fiscal anti-inflationary programmes:* such as control or elimination of government's budget deficits, reduced spending, increases in taxes, higher prices to be charged by public enterprises, and withdrawal of subsidy (for example, on education, health, petrol, agriculture and so on);
5. *anti-inflationary control of wage increase;*
6. *anti-inflationary dismantling of price controls and minimum wages;*
7. *open door policy on foreign investment and multinational corporations:* including free repatriation of profits;
8. *reduction of spending on social services:* such as education, health, housing, and so on;
9. *privatisation or sale of public enterprises* (parastatals): to local and foreign capitalists. These preconditions are usually imposed in the *Letter of Intent* to lend by both the Fund and Bank.

Three untenable aspects of these harsh conditions are: their discriminatory character; uniform imposition on poor borrower-countries; and inconsistency with the prescriptions of economic theory. Thus, while the industrialised capitalist countries (ICCs) were the main borrowers from the Fund during 1947/77 (as shown in Table 12.2), little was heard of these tough preconditions. And during the chaotic monetary disorders of the 1970s in the ICCs, the IMF imposed no discipline on them; but the crises of the Third World attract maximum sanctions, even though the basic cause of these crises is the abuse of the international capitalist system. It is also popularly said that the Fund and Bank are bad doctors that prescribe the same treatment (preconditions or pill) for all patients (countries with balances of payments or external debt crises). Surely, these disequilibrium problems cannot be caused by the same factors in all countries! Moreover, these conditions contradict the solutions prescribed by economic theory for dealing with balance of payments problems – and, of course, external debts and general socio-economic crises. The standard solutions to these problems by bourgeois economic theory are:[9]

1. *import restriction:* by tariffs or import duties, quota, import licensing and the prohibition of some imports;
2. *exchange control:* to restrict imports and payments for service or invisible trade (travel, shipping, profit on foreign investment, and so on) and capital movements;
3. *multiple exchange rates:* which sub-divide imports into priority groups and attach a different exchange rate to each group;
4. *deflationary fiscal and monetary policies:* for reducing total demand;
5. *rescheduling or refinancing of foreign debts;*
6. *restrictions on profit repatriation:* by foreign investors or multinationals;
7. *debt repudiation:* or refusal to repay external debts, particularly those that were incurred unwisely or unfavourably by previous governments;
8. *new foreign loan:* (called "aid") and/or more foreign investment;
9. *devaluation of national currency:* through the official reduction of its value in terms of foreign currencies (that is, official reduction of its par value). A *floating exchange rate* in a developing country is also an effective devaluation if the market rate falls below the official rate. The use of a *second-tier foreign exchange market*

(SFEM)[10] for auctioning foreign exchange also causes a massive devaluation, as the exchange rate in this second market is often below the official rate, though both are intended to converge (as in Nigeria, Ghana and Zambia during 1986/87).

The ideology of IMF and World Bank: the myth of neutrality

Though the IMF and World Bank are promoted as neutral and technically competent multilateral institutions, they are neither detached nor neutral. From their inception, they have internally espoused the ideology of their major imperialist sponsors, and identified with their foreign policies. Thus expanded international trade, foreign investment by MNCs and "aid" have been the new programmes of the Fund and Bank to replace formal colonialism. The US, in particular, identifies her national interest and foreign policy with a world economy that is open to her trade and investment. Hence from the 1950s, C. Douglas Dillon, the US Deputy Secretary of State for Economic Affairs, devised a strategy for "sharing the aid burden" by creating an aid *consortium* or consultative group for each loan and involving the IMF as "the bellwether of Western aid programme". This was how the Fund became an instrument for creating safe lending conditions by imposing its stabilisation package on borrowers to ensure repayment of the loans. Hence, the Fund discriminates against poor borrower-countries, and never played a decisive role in the adjustment of the trade practices and exchange rates of its major sponsors.

The three basic issues in the *ideology* of the Fund and Bank thus involve their archaic philosophy of economic liberalism, their development ideology and the propagation of their ideology. The commitment to the construction of an international capitalist system based on free trade or economic liberalism, which is the core of this ideology, has been inherited by both institutions from their most powerful sponsors, especially the US. The clearest expression of this ideology is the demand for the widest possible latitude for market forces, not only in the elimination of a payments crisis, but in the overall management of the economy. This is why their *Letter of Intent*, which contains the preconditions for extending credit, is so emphatic about the removal of trade restrictions, exchange and price controls, restrictions on profit repatriation by foreign investors and the like. The idea is to integrate the poor economy more firmly into the exploitative orbit of world capitalism; for example, the July 1965 Letter of Intent issued to Ceylon (now Sri Lanka) and published by Mrs S. Bandaranaike's government of 1970 contained the following: "to review the moratorium on remittances and take steps to improve the climate for the inflow of foreign official and private capital into Ceylon".[11]

The development ideology associated with the Fund and Bank was articulated after their crude monetarist conservatism was strongly attacked by nationalist Latin American economists of the structuralist school. They have therefore had to admit that monetary stability is not an end in itself, but should be a means of achieving economic development. Thereafter, this development ideology has been foisting capitalist development as the only model for the development of Third World countries, despite the tragic failure of this neocolonial model, and its traumatic human and material consequences in the deepening crisis of underdevelopment all over the world. Nevertheless, both the Fund and Bank, in their official publications (*IMF Staff Papers* and their joint publication, *Finance and Development*), persist in imposing this archaic development model on Third World countries by wrongly conceiving underdevelopment as lack of growth; defining growth in terms of the nebulous GDP or GNP and earnings from exports of primary products, while the majority of the population of these countries languish in squalor, and their technology remains backward. Yet, the Fund and Bank congratulate themselves on the large funds that they make available for development (really for promoting the exports of their major sponsors) and the conditions under which they are extended.

This ideology is propagated not only by their powerful capitalist members, but directly through their *Staff Papers* and Training Institute. These ideological values are disseminated by their staff through articles in their official publications that promote the myth of the neutrality of their supposedly purely technical advice, generous assistance to poor countries, the championing of their development and the importance of unfettered trade and foreign exchange flows to all countries. In addition, technocrats from different countries are recruited for their Training Institute, where their ideological preferences are disseminated among them; many of whom return to their home countries to become their technocratic allies. Such people are quick to recommend IMF and World Bank intervention and aid for their countries, and strive naively to justify their pernicious credit preconditions.

Moreover, the Fund and Bank also have local allies in poor countries and, at times, discriminate between the governments of these countries. The indigenous exporters who stand to reap huge profits from currency devaluation are the core of this reactionary group – expatriate exporters are also part of this pro-imperialist lobby.

> A special sub-category of government officials are the Western-educated economists called "technocrats" who return to their native country to occupy important posts in the Ministry of Finance and Trade, and on the special commissions for economic planning and development. These technocrats have been indoctrinated with the Western liberal ideology of development, and tend to support IMF diagnoses and prescriptions.[12]

For these various reasons, IMF and World Bank policies have important implications for military coups. Popular resentment to these vicious measures has led to military coups in several countries, such as Turkey (1960), Argentina (1966), Philippines and Ghana (1972) and Chile (1973). The Fund and Bank play a critical role here (especially the Fund) by imposing exceptionally harsh credit preconditions when the opposition to the government in power is more conservative, so that the non-acceptance of its credit by the government may lead to deeper crisis and prompt a military coup, as in Chile against Allende in 1973. The crisis may also lead to the electoral defeat of a progressive regime by a pro-imperialist political party, as the defeat of Michael Manley in Jamaica in 1980 demonstrates.

Structural Adjustment Programme (SAP) and the recolonisation of Africa

The Structural Adjustment Programme (SAP) or Economic Recovery Programme (ERP, as it is called in Ghana) of the IMF and World Bank most clearly represents the extent of the stifling control of African countries exercised by the Fund and Bank, as well as the greatest threat of imperialism's recolonisation of Africa. This is with respect to the number of African countries, from the Mediterranean to the Cape, implementing one or other form of adjustment/stabilisation programme under the supervision of either or both of the New Masters (IMF and World Bank); the sweeping coverage of the preconditions for these programmes; their stated and unstated objectives, as well as their adverse consequences on these countries and on their fragile national sovereignty.

By January 1987, over 50% of all countries in Africa were implementing one or other type of programme under the supervision of the Fund or Bank, or both, as in Nigeria. The number includes such major African countries as Nigeria, Egypt, Kenya, Zaire, Senegal, Ivory Coast, and Tanzania; the serious socialist countries, such as Angola, Ethiopia, Mozambique, are the exceptions. Just as the number of countries has been increasing rapidly and threatens to rise with the deepening of the African crisis, the share of Africa in the Fund's total "extended" loans which reached 30% in 1980 also threatens to increase.[13] The damaging conditions attached to these adjustment or stabilisation programmes are so thorough and far-reaching, as discussed above, that they directly or indirectly constitute a detraction from, and an affront to, the sovereignty of the African countries. Thus in many of these countries, IMF/World Bank staff supervise the Central Bank, Ministries of Finance and Trade as well as the Budget Department. Indeed, the annual budgets of many African countries have to be approved or endorsed by IMF/World Bank affiliated Consultative Groups or Clubs in London, Paris, Washington, and so on.[14] This Fund/Bank domination has been so restrictive that early in 1987 even Mobutu in Zaire protested against the IMF. Conditions attached to these programmes range from foreign currency auction (as in Zambia, Ghana and Nigeria) with its associated massive, effective devaluation of up to 300% within one year; multiple outright devaluation; privatisation of public enterprises; trade liberalisation; free entry and profit repatriation for multinationals; and subsidy withdrawal in all sectors, among others.

These harsh conditions for recolonisation are underscored by the objectives of adjustment. Thus in Nigeria, one of the objectives of the structural adjustment programme (SAP) for the country during July 1986 to June 1988 states: "The essence of this strategy [of structural adjustment] is the restoration in the medium term of a healthier path of national economic development *as a component of an integrated world economy . . . All external support is welcomed and solicited actively . . .*" (p. 4; emphasis mine). Yet, this country is said to be pursuing a policy of national self-reliance. An absurd "link programme" is already busily constructing a model to link the exploited Third World countries with the imperialist countries for this "integrated world economy" – which is the central global objective of the IMF.

The Fund's and Bank's other proclaimed SAP objectives are, general financial discipline for the restoration of balance of payments equilibrium through export promotion; solution to the debt crisis via debt rescheduling and more loans; the revival of agriculture and the rural economy, as well as overall recovery from the economic and social crisis of the 1980s. The policy actions designed by SAP to achieve these objectives include massive devaluation; trade liberalisation; privatisation of public enterprises; drastic subsidy withdrawal and expenditure cuts in all sectors; credit and wage freeze with increase in interest rates; and relaxation of restrictions on multinational corporations, and so on. Clearly, these policy actions conflict with some of these stated objectives, for example, import liberalisation clashes with the drive to eliminate balance of payments and debt crises, which often arise from excessive imports.

More seriously, the *real and unstated objectives* of SAP derive from the first stated goal, that is, integration of borrowing countries into the international capitalist system. These unstated objectives of SAP are to: (a) ensure that the borrowing poor countries repay their debts to the imperialist creditors, which are the major sponsors of the IMF and World Bank, under a system of debt peonage; (b) intensify the foreign domination and exploitation of African and other Third World countries through unequal exchange (so-called free trade and multilateral payments) and foreign monopoly capital under the multinationals; (c) expand the accumulation of surplus (profit) by private capital through the weakening of the public sector by privatisation and through the imposition of market forces after dismantling subsidies and the welfare state; (d) undermine and weaken the working class through wage freeze and the reduction of real wages, thus redistributing income and wealth in favour of both local and multilateral capital in the construction of global capitalism; (e) foist a neocolonial capitalist model of development on Africa and the Third World in general, even where there are extant socialist experiments; (f) consolidate the global influence of imperialism over the Third World through the subjugation of its peoples in a campaign of recolonisation that is thinly disguised as neutral technical advice.

In these circumstances, the adverse effects of the structural adjustment programme (SAP) have been, and will continue to be, deeply traumatic for African and other poor countries. At best, SAP will offer only temporary respite from the current crisis by rescheduling external debts, offering more loans and marginally encouraging "local sourcing" (that is, the use of local raw materials) as devaluation raises the prices of imported inputs. But these transitory gains will merely paper over the structural cracks of the crisis, as well as prolong and intensify its hardships (it will not even postpone them) since the adverse effects of the structural adjustment, or economic recovery, programme far outweigh its gains, even in the short-run.

The major negative consequences are both internal and external to the individual African economies. *Internally*, SAP has aggravated, and will continue to do so, unemployment of all categories of workers through its massive retrenchment in the public and private sectors, privatisation, subsidy withdrawal, drastic expenditure cuts, destruction of small and indigenous capital, and import dumping. Real wages have also fallen or stagnated through wage freeze, inflation unleashed by devaluation, and the scarcity of essential commodities arising from a shift from local resource production to export promotion. The collapse of the welfare state has also created serious education, health and housing problems from the combined effects of expenditure cuts, subsidy withdrawal and the huge debt service. Privatisation of public enterprises has exacerbated structural inequalities by redistributing wealth in favour of the rich and powerful. Similarly, the crude reliance on market forces under existing inequalities and non-competitive conditions operates everywhere to intensify structural disparities, weaken industrialisation, distort resource allocation, pervert national priorities and increase existing bottle-necks, as the "Chicago boys" found in fascist Pinochet's Chile. All these will depress the economy, aggravate the contradictions of underdevelopment and the irrationality of neocolonial capitalism.

In the *external sector*, SAP's open door policy on multinational corporations and foreign investment will tighten the grip of imperialist monopoly capital over the African economies. The combined effects of massive currency devaluation, liberalised imports and withdrawal of exchange controls will undermine local industries and strengthen unequal exchange and its exploitative transfer of national surplus abroad. The high debt service of SAP, its debt rescheduling and increased foreign loans will intensify debt peonage and strangle national development by effectively diverting more resources abroad. With higher profit repatriation by multinationals (which shows up as higher "investment income" in the invisible account of the external sector), increased imports, greater debt service burden and the adverse effects of massive devaluation (like capital flight from the poor countries) balance of payments disequilibrium is almost inevitable. From these viewpoints, SAP directly detracts from the sovereignty of African and other Third World countries.

It is SAP and other IMF/World Bank programmes' negative implications for national sovereignty and adverse consequences that have provoked violent demonstrations, coups and counter-coups as well as electoral defeats in Africa and elsewhere. In 1981 and 1982, there were riots in Sudan and Morocco over the preconditions of IMF loans. In Nigeria the abortive coup of December 1985 was reported officially to be due to the Federal Government's refusal to take a $2 billion IMF loan that had been rejected in a national debate. For its adverse effects, Kenya also aborted its structural adjustment agreement with the World Bank in 1980.

These considerations raise basic questions about SAP. First, structural adjustment or stabilisation is adjusting to what norm? To adjust to an earlier position or stabilise it should imply that the earlier condition is desirable or optimal in some objective sense. So to what optimal past norm or equilibrium are African and other poor countries being returned by SAP and stabilisation? To mass poverty, disarticulation, underdevelopment, structural distortions, unemployment, inflation, prostrate extraversion or what? These are clearly undesirable and sub-optimal conditions so there should be no adjustment to restore them. Rather, there should be *further disequilibrium* away from these undesirable and sub-optimal conditions towards an optimal state. Structural adjustment and stabilisation are, therefore, undesirable and socially irrelevant.

Second, which structure is the SAP addressing? As revealed by IMF and World

Bank policies, these are the ephemeral structures of prices, trade, money and foreign exchange. Yet, these are at best *subsidiary or auxiliary structures*, and not the fundamental structures that generate crises in Africa and the rest of the Third World. The relevant *fundamental structures* that demand adjustment are those of the capitalist international division of labour, of production, consumption, accumulation, technology and dependency in the poor countries. Clearly, goods and services have first to be produced before they can be traded, priced, monetised and exported for foreign exchange. Hence SAP and related Fund and Bank Programmes operate to aggravate, rather than ameliorate, the crisis generating structures in African and other poor countries.

Third, if the basic causes of African and Third World crises lie in the structure and operations of the international capitalist system, how can adjustment in individual debtor and deficit countries solve the problem? Because in international economics the deficits and debts of some countries are the surpluses and credits of others, then clearly *both* sets of deficit/surplus and debtor/creditor countries must undergo simultaneous adjustment. Hence *the burden of adjustment must be shared by the entire international capitalist system*, both by the industrialised capitalist, and the poor countries, and not by the poor countries alone.[15]

Finally, if SAP and other Fund and Bank programmes rob African and other poor countries of their national sovereignty, then for whom is the adjustment or stabilisation? The answer to the question: *Sovereignty for whom?* must be sovereignty for the broad masses of the poor countries, not for the IMF and World Bank, or their sponsors.

In class terms, the domestic *petit-bourgeoisie* that foist SAP on African and other Third World countries and, in collaboration with imperialism, gain from it while the broad masses of workers, peasants, students, petty artisans, market women and even the "middle-class" salariat are the losers. In particular, both domestic and foreign exporters in the African countries, the local financial oligarchy (especially in banks) and industrial producers reap great benefits from SAP. Bankers gain higher profits from higher interest rates, foreign currency auction and devaluation – exporters benefit from devaluation through export incentives and the increased volume and local value of their exports. Industrial producers also benefit from higher profits due to rising commodity prices and pegged wages. These class strata, together with the technocrats, who support SAP and defend IMF/World Bank policies are traitors or *fifth columnists*. Conversely, the bulk of SAP's adverse effects fall on the poor working people who, therefore, typically oppose Fund and Bank policies. This differential class impact of SAP explains why – in common with other IMF and World Bank programmes – it is a veritable arena of class struggle.

African response to the IMF/World Bank offensive

Unfortunately, the increasing imposition of the IMF and World Bank as New Masters in the recolonisation of African countries has not been widely appreciated in Africa. Although countries such as Nigeria and Tanzania[16] have had confrontations with the Fund, both have capitulated to it (Nigeria rejected a $2 billion IMF loan in December 1985 but took a $4.28 billion World Bank loan in 1986 under a structural adjustment programme for July 1986 to June 1988). In the circumstances, more African countries have been falling under the domination of the Fund and Bank in the settlement of their external debts to imperialist creditors, which demand that before their debts can be rescheduled they must reach an accord with the IMF. Balance of payments crises and such national economic disasters as drought have also forced these countries to apply to the Fund and Bank.

Given the poor understanding of the logic of the operations of both institutions, and the weak technocratic (and even political) basis for articulating alternative recovery and adjustment programmes in many African countries, the dictation and domination of both agencies have been generally accepted in Africa, especially by the *petit-bourgeoisie*. Besides the individual national resistance put up by Kenya, Tanzania, Egypt and Nigeria, the only other serious political response to the New Masters was the 1986 OAU *request* for a moratorium of five years on the repayment of Africa's debts which, predictably, was rejected by the imperialist creditors. Since then, each country has been rationalising its acquiescence to the new multilateral domination through such spurious arguments as "debts have to be repaid", the virtue of being dependable by honouring obligations, lack of alternative to submission to the Fund and Bank, and so on.

Yet, these naive arguments miss the whole point of *organising a continental political response* to the IMF's and World Bank's threatened recolonisation of Africa. This creates an urgent need to transcend the economism that currently dominates the discussions of the Fund's and Bank's roles in Africa and the rest of the Third World. Clearly, if it is politically essential for the imperialist countries to form a creditors' cartel or consortium with the Club of Paris, Club of Rome, and so on, then the poor countries must form their own countervailing *debtors' cartel* with the Club of Caracas, Club of Lagos, for example. If negotiations with the imperialist creditor banks require prior settlement with the Fund, then African and other poor countries should also negotiate collectively through the OAU, an African Monetary Fund and similar bodies. The debt problem and negotiations with the IMF and World Bank are basically *political*. So African countries must urgently organise their national political force and link it with collective continental effort. The broad masses must mobilise and insist on this.

By now, it should also be quite clear that discussions of the roles of the IMF and World Bank in African and other poor countries must be situated squarely within the crisis of underdevelopment in these countries. Besides the systematic looting of their wealth by corrupt leaders, most of these countries are faced with balance of payments and debt crises in their efforts to liquidate underdevelopment, or to modernise. Hence SAP as well as other IMF and World Bank programmes in these countries must be tied to their national development. This will reveal a sharp and inevitable *contradiction*: the fact that if these countries accept the roles of the Fund and Bank as New Masters, and fulfil the preconditions of SAP and related stabilisation programmes, their national development will be irreparably jeopardised. There is no way in which the African and other poor countries can be faithful to their imperialist creditors, SAP, IMF and World Bank and simultaneously satisfy the legitimate demands of their national populations for development. The issue must be posed concretely in this dialectical way to underscore the need for African and other poor countries to reject the New Masters and SAP in order to pursue their national development. Brazil made this inevitable choice early in 1987 through its Finance Minister, Dilson Funaro, under the Cruzado Plan, and thus imposed a unilateral moratorium on interest payment on its staggering external debt of $108 billion. *No country can be simultaneously faithful to the IMF/World Bank and to its national population and development*. So the IMF and World Bank must be resisted – politically and collectively – and African as well as other Third World scholars must expose the bankruptcy of the Fund's and Bank's theoretical positions.

It should also be noted that both within the IMF and World Bank, there are internal divisions and reform proposals. These press the need for flexibility in the application of conditionality and adjustment periods. Within the Fund, two interest groups, placing different priority on balance of payments equilibrium and growth as the goals of the agency, have also been identified.[17] Outside the Fund and Bank, the Overseas Development Institute (ODI) under Tony Killick has proposed a "real economy approach" for the Fund that emphasises supply creation and medium-term adjustment, rather than the current preoccupation with short-run adjustment through demand management.[18] Similarly, Dell and Co. as well as Stewart and Sengupta have separately proposed Fund reforms involving low conditionality and long adjustment periods.[19] The basic inadequacy of all these reform proposals rests on their rejection of the fact that the international capitalist system is the basic generating cause of the balance of payments and debt crises of the poor countries. By implication, their faith in balance of payments adjustment and the role of individual poor countries in the process is also untenable. These issues warrant further exploration of the African crisis and the capitalist international division of labour.

The African crises and the capitalist international division of labour

The capitalist international division of labour defines the specialisation of functions within world capitalism. It is in fact a double division of labour – between the centre and periphery of world capitalism, and between the parents and subsidiaries of multinational corporations (MNCs) in the internationalisation of capital and production. In the first, predominant capitalist international division of labour, the centre of industrialised capitalist countries in North America, Western Europe and Japan, specialises in manufacturing, finance and technology, while the peripheral Third World countries of Africa, Latin America and South-East Asia have been forced by imperialism (that is past colonialism and contemporary neocolonialism) to specialise in meeting the reproductive needs of capital on a global scale, through specialisation in the production of agricultural and mineral products (primary products), and serving as markets for imperialist manufactures. The second international capitalist division of labour is anchored to the MNCs with their parent companies or headquarters in the imperialist countries, and their subsidiaries or affiliates in peripheral "host" countries. While the parent companies monopolise research and development, the production of technology and top decisions on production, marketing and surplus extraction, the subsidiaries concentrate on the extraction of raw materials, the super-exploitation of local labour and market outlets as discussed in Chapter 3.

The roles of African and other poor countries in this capitalist international division of labour are essentially two. First, to supply the material needs of imperialist capital (raw materials, markets and investment outlet); and second, to act as buffers to cushion and stabilise the crises of the global system. In this less familiar second role, the burden of adjustment to crisis in the entire system is typically passed on to the poor countries, through lower prices for their exports, higher prices for their imports, devaluation of their currency, super-exploitation of their workers, higher interest charges on their debts, depreciation of their external reserves, and so on.[20] Moreover, the crises of African and other Third World countries are generated predominantly by the unequal development promoted by world capitalism, through the structural dependence of the peripheral countries on the centre countries.

Within this imperialist division of labour, the roles of the IMF, World Bank, SAP and related multilateral stabilisation programmes are threefold. One is to firmly integrate the poor countries into world capitalism by directly supervising their socio-economic policies through the Fund and Bank, foisting a capitalist development model on them and directly linking the class interests of their *petit-bourgeoisies* to the global interests of imperialism. The second is to pin them down to primary production as much as possible. Clear evidence of this is the hostility of the Fund and Bank to capital-goods manufacturing in poor countries, yet without the local production of capital goods, all industrial efforts are superficial. Indeed, SAP is designed to give its sponsors critical leverage over the industrial policies of the poor countries – hence SAP undermines national industrial sectors as in the Philippines, Kenya, Turkey, and others.[21]

The third role of SAP and its multilateral sponsors is to attempt to ensure a constant flow of national surplus from the poor countries to the imperialist citadels; hence the priority attached to debt repayment under peonage (the Fund and Bank even directly encourage poor countries to borrow more and get into debt so that the debt can be used to control and exploit them over time). Open door policy to foreign investment, trade liberalisation under unequal exchange, reliance on market forces, and so on also operate to ensure this systematic resource transfer for stabilising and sustaining capitalist reproduction in the metropoles.

The implications of this capitalist international division of labour for the African crisis and the roles of the New Masters are graphic enough. One is to reinforce the earlier contention that, given its world capitalist setting, any programme of adjustment to the African crisis must necessarily be a global capitalist one. The current pompous posture of imposing financial discipline on the poor countries, as if they were solely or largely responsible for the crisis, must be debunked. The other critical implication is that without disengaging from the world capitalist structures that generated the crisis, African and other poor countries cannot hope to reach a solution through SAP and the New Masters. They are integral parts of the problems, so cannot constitute a solution. Individually, poor countries are too weak to confront the collective might of the imperialists. Hence the imperative of *collective self-reliance* among the African countries.

The Lagos Plan of Action and the New Masters

The 1980 *Lagos Plan of Action*[22] for the collective self-reliance of African countries seemed to have been timed to meet the challenge of the recolonisation of Africa by her New Masters. It formulated wide-ranging policies for regional and sub-regional cooperation among African countries on the basis of a planned programme of drastic reduction of Africa's external dependence. Some of the concrete objectives include the expansion of the very low level of intra-African trade; industrial development; creation of infrastructural facilities to facilitate regional cooperation; as well as linkages in technology, agriculture and related fields. The associated policy actions for this expansive integration involve the pooling of the limited capital of different countries for such joint ventures as the Trans-African Highway; exchange and collation of technological data; skilled manpower training; joint infrastructural programmes for neighbouring countries; and integrative planning at regional and sub-regional levels. In spite of the Lagos Plan's weaknesses in failing to deal effectively with the political basis for economic integration, neocolonial domination of African countries by multinationals and its pandering to external dependence through its canvassing of foreign "aid", its implementation could advance the national and collective self-reliance of African countries.

In a move calculated to subvert the Lagos Plan, the World Bank produced its own Berg Report[23] a year after the publication of the Plan. Its major thrust is the reactionary advocacy of continued specialisation in primary production and external dependence on the basis of the discredited static theory of comparative advantage. Happily, the Report was heavily attacked and the OAU rejected it in preference for its own Lagos Plan. But the Berg Report's imperialist sponsors did not give up, since it was part of the grand design for the continued domination of Africa. In the dialectics of the deepening African crisis, therefore, the neocolonialist Berg Report surfaced in a new guise in 1986 as the *UN's Priority Programme of Economic Recovery for Africa*.[24] Like the Berg Report that inspired it, the basic objectives of this UN Programme are to displace or relegate the Lagos Plan and thus push for the greater external dependence and exploitation of Africa along the lines of the IMF's and World Bank's growing initiatives towards the recolonisation of Africa.

These facts warrant the exposure of the reactionary nature and neocolonialist implications of the UN Priority Programme. The Economic Commission for Africa (ECA), OAU, other African organisations and patriots have a special duty here. The clear similarities between the Berg Report and the UN Priority Programme should be carefully articulated and disseminated as a basis for combating the role of the New Masters, which the UN Priority Programme has effectively been encouraging the IMF and World Bank to play. The policies of the structural adjustment programme (SAP) that are the instruments for the growing recolonisation of Africa – which are also advocated by the UN Priority Programme – should be resisted both through the technical (economic) exposure of their contradictions, and at the political level of mass actions in different countries, the OAU, OATUU (Organisation of African Trade Union Unity), for example. Fundamentally, the UN Priority Programme, like SAP, is an attempt to foist capitalist development on Africa.

Is there a capitalist path?

The foregoing discussions in this chapter, and the rest of this book, lead directly or indirectly to the central question: Is there a capitalist path of development for Africa (and for that matter, for the rest of the Third World)? The exclusive choice of the capitalist model of development for Africa is a central objective of the IMF and World Bank, it is the goal of the specialisation *imposed* on Africa by the international capitalist division of labour and it is the objective, or even assumption, of the discredited Berg Report and its metamorphosed form as the UN Priority Programme. The reactionary and intolerant "end of ideology" dogma of the imperialist agencies and their scholarship also attempt to foist the capitalist model as the only path of development of Africa. The ideological mutations of the *petit-bourgeoisies* in the neocolonial capitalist social formations of Africa also rest on some commitment to capitalist development. This choice of the capitalist path, as has already been noted, is frequently camouflaged as a nebulous African humanism, African or Arab socialism and even as a return to traditionalism (for example Senghor's negritude and Mobutu's authenticity).

The specific arguments advanced by the protagonists of capitalist development in Africa are as varied as the circumstances of their propagation. One of the commonest and most naive of these arguments is that in some peculiar sense, Africans are capitalist by nature – many elements of Nigeria's *petit-bourgeoisie* are very fond of this naivety. They point to low income earners that own houses as part of the proof of this assertion – as if there is anything in socialism that prohibits a worker from owning a living quarter. The basic flaw of this "capitalism by nature" is that it denies the fact that ideological commitments are not innate, but rather, that they are the results of socialisation and class struggle. People become committed to an ideology as a result of deliberate choice by themselves or their families because of their class position at birth, education and life experiences.[25] Hence, life is not determined by consciousness, but consciousness by life.

It is then suggested that capitalism has succeeded in the newly industrialised capitalist countries (NICs) so it can succeed in Africa. This is essentially the discredited Bill Warren thesis about the feasibility of capitalist industrialisation in the Third World (see Chapter 3). As argued earlier, capitalist success in the NICs is often imperialist window-dressing against socialism, as in South-East Asia. Moreover, most of these so-called new industries are multinational assets that drain the host countries through super-exploitation; in spite of this capitalist "success", the majority of the population of the NICs wallow in abject poverty as in Brazil or India, for example; the fragile capitalist show-pieces in these countries have taken over 100 years to produce, and Africa cannot accept that delay; and the international environment that permitted those industrial performances has since been growing increasingly hostile through threatened recolonisation, protectionism, debt crisis, and so on, that it offers no hope of repeating the past experiments of Japan and related countries.

The capitalist path has also been chosen on the false assertion that socialism has failed in Africa. But where is the success of capitalism? Even South Africa is not a capitalist success story on the basis of the inhuman premise of its programme. In any case, the socialism that has failed in Africa is Arab or African socialism in, for example, Egypt, Tanzania, Guinea, Zaire, not scientific socialism of the type in Angola, Mozambique, Guinea-Bissau, which are still too young to be evaluated conclusively. So scientific socialism has not failed in Africa, as has capitalism, because the former has not been given half the time of the latter, which has existed since the colonial era.[26]

A closely related argument is that imperialism is so strong that it will not allow the construction of an alternative development model to capitalism in Africa. But this is empirically false, as the Vietnamese defeat of the power of the US hegemony of imperialism clearly shows. Even in Africa, the MPLA defeated US imperialism to launch the progressive socialist experiment in Angola. It is true that imperialism is becoming more aggressive; but it is also true that despite this, more socialist experiments are being launched - and succeeding - as Burkina Faso, Angola, among others, demonstrate.

A naive notion of the growing convergence of the two contending systems has also been advanced to rationalise the capitalist path for Africa. In doing this, imperialism emphasises the trivial similarities between capitalism and socialism, and trivialises their major differences. Thus Galbraith insists on these similarities in his book *The New Industrial State*.[27] A related version of this argument states that even the advanced socialist countries are going capitalist, and so there is no point in socialist transformation in Africa.

Finally, the frivolous point has been made that capitalist countries are richer or more technologically advanced than socialist states. A frequent example is that the United States is richer than the Soviet Union. If the socialist countries refuse to enslave, colonise and impose neocolonial exploitation over Third World countries, as the imperialist states have been doing, these are reasons why they will not be so rich. To put it differently, if the US and other imperialist countries have to return their loot and plunder of centuries to the poor countries (as the Germans made reparation payments for war damages to Europe after the First World War), then the advanced capitalist countries would certainly be poorer than the advanced socialist states. This colossal, unpaid debt is one of the reasons why Africa and the rest of the Third World should refuse to pay their so-called debts to the imperialist countries. The relative duration of the existence of capitalism and socialism is also a partial explanation for differences in their technological development and wealth. Thus, while capitalism, emerging from the Industrial Revolution in Britain, was first established around 1750, socialism was not established until the Bolshevik Revolution of 1917 in the USSR. So while capitalism is 237 years old, socialism started only 70 years ago!

Then there is the appalling human degradation and relative social deprivation that go with capitalism, which Marx and Engels recognised, that help to build the wealth of the imperialist countries.[28] Thus in the US, the entire black population of about 40 million has been a heavily exploited internal colony – the same holds for other national minorities, and women, in the US and all capitalist countries. They are systematically paid lower wages for the same jobs, denied decent housing, health care, education, and so on. Surely the savings from denying these necessary payments raise total wealth? There is also a technical point about the basis of calculating Gross National Product (GNP) in the capitalist and socialist countries. Whereas the capitalist countries include goods and services, the socialist states exclude services, so their national income and income per capita tend to be lower. In any case, what should be compared between capitalist and socialist countries is ultimately *the quality of life of the average individual* and this is clearly higher in the advanced socialist states than under capitalism.

By contrast to the above, the case against the capitalist path is so obvious that because of the irrationality and social injustice of capitalism, its advocates cannot even defend it publicly in most fora. The apostles of capitalism or "market theology" thus realise the deep truth that the capitalist path has been a monstrous imposition on Africa and the rest of the Third World. From the era of colonial violence to contemporary neocolonial capitalist domination by multinationals and their domestic collaborators, capitalism has been imposed by force of arms, expropriation of the peasantry, compulsory cropping, dispossession of the masses and imperialist depredations. Even without any external intervention, the transition to capitalism in all countries has always been marked by minority imposition and class philistinism. There cannot, therefore, be any question of Africans being capitalist by nature: rather, by tradition, African communalism, extended family system and humanism dictate an underlying commitment to the socialist path.

The convergence notion in relation to capitalism and socialism is equally false. In spite of the trivial similarities, both systems differ fundamentally with respect to their crucial characteristics such as ownership of the means of production, appropriation of surplus value (profit), capital accumulation, use of hired labour (the wage system), basic social justice and the inalienable dignity of the human person. In these respects, even if the advanced socialist countries are going capitalist as alleged, African and other poor countries still need socialist construction to liquidate their underdevelopment first, become industrialised, cater to the basic needs of their mass majority and then decide what future development to pursue.

On the inequality between the two contending paths of development, some basic facts must also be remembered. One is that historically, socialism has recorded the fastest path of development in human experience in all parts of the world. What took capitalism centuries to accomplish in Western Europe, North America and Japan, has taken scientific socialism less than 30 years to achieve – between 1917 and 1945 the Soviet Union emerged as a world power, and between 1949 and 1970 China did the same.

Moreover, capitalist development in the industrialised countries has been achieved through such predatory means as slavery, colonialism and neocolonalism. So the basic question that advocates of the capitalist path must answer is: *which countries is Africa going to enslave, colonise and satellitise in order to achieve capitalist development?* There is also the obstacle of the hostile international environment with the increasing global crisis of capitalism, such that the advanced capitalist countries will simply not permit any independent capitalist development in Africa and the rest of the Third World. The fierce competition for raw materials, markets, and so on, will not allow that. The hostility of the IMF and World Bank to national industrialisation in the guise of structural adjustment programme is well known in this regard.

The illusion of capitalist industrialisation à la Warren must also be exposed and rejected. Since the introduction of import substitution in Africa, what industrialisation has occurred? The strategy has been such an abysmal failure that many are now speaking of "de-industrialisation". And, of course, the World Bank has switched from import substitution to export promotion. The illusory "transfer of technology" which is to float this capitalist industrialisation has also become so discredited as an imperialist ruse that technology has now become widely recognised as an instrument of imperialist domination and the exploitation of poor countries. Indeed, one of the major flaws in the capitalist industrialisation thesis is its failure to reckon fully with the monopoly of technology by multinationals which concentrate their research and development (R&D) activities abroad, and must inevitably strangle any serious programme of national capitalist industrialisation.

But one minor concession must be made to the advocates of the capitalist path. This is, that if Africa can wait indefinitely (Latin America and South-East Asia have been waiting for over 150 years since their flag independence in the 1830s) and accept recolonisation by the IMF, World Bank and their multinational sponsors, then capitalist transformation may occur in Africa. But this development will have to be without or against the Africans – as it has occurred in South Africa, Israel and in the US without the Indians and against the blacks. This is essentially a call for genocide, and as such is inconceivable and unacceptable. Hence the capitalist path is infeasible and untenable in Africa.

To put it differently, Africa is in a desperate hurry to develop because of the human tragedy of underdevelopment manifested by her rapidly escalating crisis. Africa demands national economic independence and self-reliance. The expropriatory bases for past capitalist development are no longer available to this continent. Imperialism through the IMF, World Bank and the multinationals will no longer permit independent (national) capitalist development in Africa or elsewhere. The resource base that can be frittered away on wasteful and grandiose capitalist development is very elusive and becoming increasingly scarce everywhere. The "technology transfer" that has been promoted as certain to catapult capitalist development in Africa has clearly become a pathetic illusion.

All these demand the urgent termination of the illusion of successful capitalist development in Africa. Indeed, the real choice before Africa now is not between capitalist and socialist development. Rather, it is a choice between the scientific socialist path of development, on the one hand, and the grim and threatening prospects of disintegration, collapse, recolonisation and barbarism, on the other.

In debunking the capitalist path, Africa must resolve three basic issues with some urgent policy actions. These are:

(1) identification of the *true priorities of the majority of Africans* in terms of food, water, functional shelter, health care, education and transport; pompous stadia, specialist hospitals, sky-scrapers, super-expressways, luxury cars, and so forth are not among these priorities;
(2) producing a *good estimate of the resource* situation in each African country together with their possible uses;

(3) elimination of the major contradiction between *producing what is not consumed and consuming what is not produced domestically*.

These dictate the imperative of effective national and collective self-reliance through the following policy actions:

1. cutting *imports and the foreign sector* drastically to about 20% of GNP;
2. drastically curtailing the exaggerated *role of foreign exchange, balance of payments and external loans*;
3. the urgent and purposeful pursuit of *counter-trade* (barter trade) with Africa and other countries, since adequate foreign exchange is not likely to be available;
4. serious development of *artisan technology* based on national needs and available resources;
5. *resource-needs industrialisation strategy* that matches the manufacturing of basic needs items with local resources;
6. *capital-goods manufacturing* through regional and sub-regional cooperation (except in the larger and richer African countries that can undertake national capital-goods projects).

To embark on this scientific socialist path of development, African countries do not need to "disconnect" deliberately from imperialism and plan to "reconnect"[29] after they have developed. Rather, they should define their priorities and strategies and relate to imperialism as much as it permits. Structural disengagement or delinking should be the strategy.

Notes

1. On the evolution of the capitalist international financial system, see Yann Fitt et al. (1980); and Cheryl Payer (1975).
2. C. Payer (1975), p. 219.
3. Ibid., ch. 2.
4. Quoted in ibid., p. 24.
5. See John Harris (1984).
6. C. Payer (1975), p. 217.
7. For the programmes of the Fund and the Bank, see C. Payer (1975) and (1982) chs. 1, 3, 5, & 8; and Peter Körner et al. (1986) chs. 2–4.
8. See C. Payer (1975) pp. 32–43, for a discussion of these preconditions.
9. Ibid., pp. 12–21.
10. This second-tier foreign exchange market (SFEM) or currency auction is usually based on free market forces of demand and supply as part of a structural adjustment programme (SAP). SFEM is now FEM (foreign exchange market) in Nigeria.
11. C. Payer (1975), p. 38.
12. Ibid., p. 44.
13. See J. B. Zulu and S. M. Nsouli (1984) in *Finance and Development*, March.
14. This imperialist endorsement was required for Ghana's 1982 and 1984 Economic Recovery Programme (they were endorsed by the Consultative Group on Ghana based in Paris) and for Nigeria's 1986 and 1987 budgets.

15. See S. Kanesa-Thasan (1981) in *Finance and Development*, September: T. Killick (ed.) (1984).

16. On the sharing of the burden of adjustment, see Peter Körner et al. (1986), chs. 4 & 5.

17. On the Tanzanian opposition to the IMF, see: "The Arusha Initiative", *Development Dialogue*, 1980; on the Nigerian rejection of the IMF loan, see Yusuf Bala Usman (1986), and B. Onimode (1987).

18. Tony Killick (ed.) (1984).

19. S. Dell and R. Lawrence (1980).

20. See Fidel Castro (1983), chs. 2, 4 & 7; E. Mandel (1980); Y. Fitt et al. (1980). See also E. A. Tarabrin (1974), and A. Gavshon (1981).

21. C. Payer (1975) pp. 152–7.

22. OAU (1980) *The Lagos Plan of Action for the Economic Development of Africa from 1980 to 2000* (Addis Ababa).

23. The Berg Report was written for the World Bank under Elliot Berg and its title is World Bank (1981) *Accelerated Programme for Sustained Development in Sub-Saharan Africa* (Washington).

24. UN (1986) *Priority Programme of Recovery for Africa* (Geneva).

25. On the origins of the formations of class consciousness, Karl Mannheim (1955), P. L. Berger and T. Luckman (1967).

26. M. Babu makes these points in M. Babu (1981).

27. See J. K. Galbraith (1978).

28. On the contradictory wealth and incredible squalor under capitalism, see K. Marx and F. Engels (1980).

29. This disconnection and reconnection was suggested by Professor Samir Amin at the conference of African Economists in Ouagadougou, Burkina Faso during April 21 to 27. The proposal has been generating lively discussion since then.

13 Ideology and Political Strategy for a Socialist Africa

> For my part, the deeper I enter into the cultures and the political circles, the surer I am that *the great danger that threatens Africa is the absence of ideology*. With the triumph of socialism in Eastern Europe, we witness a spectacular disappearance of the old rivalries, of the traditional territorial claims.
>
> In Africa, on the other hand, the countries that come to independence are as unstable as their new middle classes or their renovated prices. After a few hesitant steps in the international arena, the national middle classes, no longer feeling the threat of the traditional colonial power, suddenly develop great appetites . . . In these imperialist pseudo-states, likewise, an extreme militarist policy leads to a reduction of public investments in countries which in certain respects are still medieval. The discontented workers undergo a repression as pitiless as that of the colonial periods. Trade unions and opposition political parties are confined to a quasi-clandestine state. The people, who had given everything in the difficult moments of the struggle for national liberation wonder, with their empty hands and bellies, as to the reality of their victory.
>
> **Frantz Fanon** (1967) pp. 186–7; emphasis mine.

Introduction

Fanon's critical insight that *the great danger that threatens Africa is the absence of ideology* is even more relevant today than when he stated it two decades ago. And so is his clarion call for the *African Revolution*. These are in view of the increasingly threatening character of the deepening crisis in Africa. As the foregoing chapters have demonstrated, the African crisis is also a fundamentally ideological crisis – a crisis of the predominant capitalist model of development imposed on the African masses, and of the associated bourgeois reformism on the continent.

The exploitative social relations of production and their striking incongruence with the underdeveloped productive forces, the basic asymmetry between the profiles of production and consumption, the chronic instability of the systems of governance, the growing social decay, the universal incompetence and the conspicuous social irrelevance of anachronistic belief systems everywhere testify to this fundamental ideological crisis. The narrowly economic, political, social and intellectual dimensions of the African crisis also reflect this ideological problem in varying degrees. Hence Fanon recommended the African Revolution as a general solution to the primordial cleavages, the pervasive bankruptcy of "renovated princes" and pecuniary upstarts masquerading as African leaders, the parasitic exploitation of militarism, as well as the political repression, mass misery and universal starvation that he captured so vividly.

Yet, when Fanon referred to the absence of ideology in Africa, he did not mean a total ideological void. For even by the 1960s, Africa's ideological spectrum was already as colourful as the continental flora. There has been such a bewildering complex of pre-capitalist and reactionary ideologies such as feudalism, nationalism, Christianity, Islam, capitalism, welfarism, neocolonialism, and even utopian socialism. But being essentially reactionary ideologies, they could not be expected to cope with the urgent challenges of the material backwardness of the continent. So "the absence of ideology" refers to the pervasive lack of a progressive ideology for the rapid transformation of Africa – the absence of scientific socialism, the ideology of the African Revolution. Another way of stating all these is that the rusty underdevelopment of Africa and the intensification of this problematic are basically the collective consequences of the dynamic functioning of these reactionary ideologies. Hence, since they constitute the heart of the African crisis, these unprogressive ideologies cannot, therefore, be the solution. A progressive ideology is required to resolve the complex contradictions generated and perpetuated by these exploitative ideologies.

It is important to emphasise here that the ideological question has always to be posed in concrete historical contexts.[1] An ideology that is progressive and liberating in one historical conjuncture may become backward and exploitative in a future epoch. This is the case with all pre-capitalist and bourgeois ideologies, because they are identified with the progressive transformation of one social formation to a higher one. Thus feudalism, which was a liberating ideology relative to slavery, became a backward ideology and a barrier to social progress with the emergence of capitalism in its early state of petty commodity production. Similarly, the progressive role of capitalism, which Marx recounted so graphically in the *Communist Manifesto*[2] degenerated into an exploitative and reactionary instrument of mass enslavement to capital at a later stage in history. Thus the progressive role of Christianity and Islam in advancing knowledge (for example, through written records and literacy), and of Protestantism in advancing capitalist accumulation in its early stage, has degenerated into the reactionary role of being "the opium of the people". Only scientific socialism, which is a transitional phase in the transformation of the capitalist mode of production into communism, does not exhibit this historical duality of having progressive and reactionary phases. Hence, in Africa of the post-colonial era, the reactionary ideologies have completed their basic liberating role and become fetters to the further development of productive forces and to the liquidation of underdevelopment. This is what puts the ideological question at the top of the African agenda at this historical epoch.

The futility of bourgeois reformism

In this regard, the predominant ideological response of most African countries to the continental crisis has been bourgeois reformism. This is true of the neocolonial capitalist countries, those practising African socialism and those implementing programmes of national democratic revolution. The only exceptions are those countries seriously pursuing socialist transformation under Marxist–Leninist ideology. This bourgeois reformism has assumed different ideological streams in different countries, and the popular examples are nationalism, social welfarism, traditionalism, African socialism, Arab socialism, Christianity and Islam. In varying degrees, they contain overt and covert anti-communism, and distance themselves from scientific socialism. The state forms associated with these reformist ideologies include bourgeois parliamentary and presidential systems with multi-party and single-party arrangements, military–bureaucratic dictatorships as well as feudo-bureaucratic forms, all exhibiting complex contradictions of differing quality.

The basic objective of all these strands of bourgeois reformism is to restructure the existing social system in order to stabilise it for the continuation of domination and exploitation. The common economic reformism or programmes include mixed economy, neocolonial capitalist planning, welfarism, conservative land reforms, incomes policy, redistributive taxation, bourgeois marketing cooperatives, even nationalisation and, in the 1980s, the IMF–World Bank package of market economism called structural adjustment programme (SAP) or economic recovery programme (ERP), anchored to devaluation, trade liberalisation, subsidy withdrawal, privatisation and foreign exchange auction (the so-called Second-Tier Foreign Exchange Market, SFEM). At the political level, bourgeois reformism takes the forms of militarism, local government reforms, bourgeois party restructuring, anti-corruption crusades for accountability (both in economic management and political office holding) and now bourgeois human rights as in Nigeria during 1985/87. These are backed up by social reforms centred on facile cultural revivals featuring arts festivals, in ossified cultural symbols by a culturally rootless elite, negritude, cultural authenticity and so on.

The futility of this bourgeois reformism does not lie in the fact that uses cannot be found for some of these reformist measures. But taken individually or collectively, they fail to grapple with the basic structural generating causes of the numerous cracks in the system, pose false problems, propose bogus solutions, divert attention from the serious study and resolution of problems and thus aggravate the African crisis.

As part of its programme of defensive radicalism in the face of the rising mass radicalism on the continent, bourgeois reformism has been resorting to two ideological campaigns. One is that scientific socialism is an alien ideology and so it should not be accepted in Africa, and the other is the drive for an indigenous African ideology.

The obscurantism of socialism as a foreign ideology

As the African masses in different countries became increasingly disenchanted as the gains of independence in the 1960s were progressively denied to them, they demanded improvements from their leaders. By the 1970s and 1980s when the African crisis worsened the lot of these masses and plunged them into deprivation and misery, they responded with more militant clamour for change. In their working-class, student and radical intellectual circles, these demands crystallised increasingly into ideological polarisation as the former unity of all classes against colonialism collapsed. Radical movements grew rapidly in different African countries and led to the formation of socialist and communist parties with left-wing groups even in *petit-bourgeois* one-party states. All over Africa, this radicalisation of mass organisations demanding revolutionary change and socialist transformation compelled two broad responses from the *petit-bourgeoisie*.

One is defensive radicalism expressed in various bourgeois reformist programmes, such as African socialism, Arab socialism, bourgeois nationalism, for example, all designed to hijack and paralyse the people's revolution. The second major response to mass radicalism has been political repression, expressed either as direct repression of the masses, or as a reactionary campaign to deny the relevance of scientific socialism to the African crisis. While repression takes the fascist forms of banning students' unions, opposition parties, trade unions, and strikes, jailing rival politicians and political activists, and in extreme cases, murdering political opponents, reactionary anti-socialist propaganda is mounted by backward state-controlled media (newspapers, magazines, radio and television).

One dominant message of this reactionary campaign is that, in some diabolical sense, socialism is a foreign ideology in Africa. So *petit-bourgeois* African leaders appeal to the masses to reject it, because they claim "it can't work in Africa". They argue falsely that socialism is anti-God, Africans are capitalist by nature, socialism is alien to African culture and does not take account of African peculiarities, and so on. In the pseudo-scientific version of this propaganda, a classless Africa is proclaimed in which it is alleged that there is no exploitation and, therefore, no need for class struggle. Then the reactionaries point to a false convergence of socialism on capitalism in the advanced countries and to the so-called failure of socialism in Africa – by which they mean failure of bourgeois and social reformism[3] that go variously by the names of African socialism, Arab socialism and the national democratic revolution. In some military versions of this anti-socialist campaign, *petit-bourgeois* military leaders with manifest corporate ambition insist that "we do not want to impose an ideology on the country". As if the neocolonial capitalist and feudo-bourgeois ideologies which they implement were voted for by the people.

This reactionary campaign about socialism as a foreign ideology must be recognised for what it is and exposed in its total bankruptcy. The campaign is an integral part of *petit-bourgeois* ideology, which being essentially part of the broad capitalist–imperialist ideology, must also be rejected as a foreign ideology. After all, the Industrial Revolution that gave birth to the first full-fledged capitalist ideology was not native to Africa; neither were the major capitalist ideologues such as Adam Smith, John Maynard Keynes, John Locke, Max Weber African. At the level of primordial ideology, just as Karl Marx, Friedrich Engels, V. I. Lenin and Mao Zedong were not native Africans, neither were Christ, Prophet Mohammed and Martin Luther King. Moreover, we observe that those who insist, hypocritically, that socialism should be rejected because it is foreign, are at the same time frantically implementing other foreign ideologies such as capitalism, nationalism (which was born in pre-Hitler Germany), Christianity and Islam. Neither are these reactionary campaigners disturbed by their importation of virtually everything foreign, from educational institutions to their names, from aeroplanes, cars, watches, even to clothing and food. As for the conservative military propagators of socialism-is-a-foreign-ideology, they are foreign in their names and haughty titles, and foreign from their caps to their boots.

On socialism being anti-God, that is the preoccupation of reactionary primordialism. Even though Marx regarded religion as the opium of the people, socialism merely proclaims the secular state (as does capitalism in the USA, Britain, West Germany, and so on) and leaves the individual's relationship with God to his personal inclination. Another cultural factor that allegedly socialism does not respect is freedom. Yet, freedom is not absolute but relative. Capitalism grants elusive freedom of speech, association and movement, freedom to vote and be voted for and so forth, as bourgeois democratic rights, but *capitalism denies the means to achieve and exercise these rights*. So there is freedom of speech but there is massive illiteracy with no right to education; freedom of association goes hand in hand with the repression and banning of mass organisations and strikes; there is freedom of movement without mass transportation and there is electoral freedom to vote but not to be voted for. Labour is free but it cannot own the means of production, and so the worker must be a capitalist wage-slave. There is freedom to life and the denial of such means of livelihood as employment, housing, clothing, health-care, education and even food. So bourgeois freedom includes freedom to die of starvation and deprivation. This is the pitiful and callous fate which capitalism has been meting out to the majority of Africans since the colonial era. Hence bourgeois democratic rights and their freedom are a fraud. By contrast, scientific socialism makes human rights real[4] – by liberating the masses from capitalist and feudal bondage, domination and exploitation. It does this by granting the right to a job, to free education, free health-care, to housing, clothing and other basic necessities of life – to everybody, and not solely to a lucky, parasitic few.

The extended family system, ethnicity and humanism are the other elements of African culture which socialism is alleged not to respect because it is foreign. But it is clear that ethnicism or ethnicity (which is wrongly and derogatorily called tribalism) is a negative and reactionary *petit-bourgeois* ideology which must be rooted out of Africa through the non-discriminatory and equal-opportunity programmes of socialism. It is also clear that the ideals sought by the extended family system and African humanism can best be secured only under a generalised socialist programme in which everybody is each other's keeper. As for the myth of classless Africa that is supposed to preclude the need for class struggle, that has been thoroughly and scientifically discredited, as documented in Chapter 5.

The propaganda about socialism converging on capitalism[5] (that is, the East meeting the West) has also been used to deny the relevance of socialism to Africa. There are three basic errors in this claim. One is that it is based on under-estimating the major differences between the two systems and overestimating their trivial similarities. Among the major differences are the ownership of means of production and enterprises, the class control of the state, the democratisation of economic and political power, the right to life through access to the basic needs of the broad masses and the general moral tone of society with respect to its humaneness, and the basic integrity of the human being. The trivial similarities between socialism and capitalism are patterns of industrialisation and technology, consumption, religious worship, the use of prices and the emergence of small-scale individual enterprises in some socialist countries. Clearly, despite these minor similarities, the two systems are basically different.

Secondly, there is no question that empirically, scientific socialism has been a far greater tool for understanding the problems of backwardness and liquidating them than has capitalism, which aggravates and obscures these problems. Thus scientific socialism has not made much headway in Africa because it has been distorted as African socialism, Arab socialism and national democratic revolution. There is no question about the spectacular liquidation of backwardness in record time by socialism in China, Soviet Union, North Korea and Eastern Europe. Moreover, capitalism is now historically out-dated on a world-wide basis. In the third place, even if capitalism and socialism are converging in the advanced countries, that is not really relevant to the underdeveloped countries and Africa. This is because the alleged similarities are emerging during the mature industrialised stage of those societies. But capitalism has no prospect of developing the poor countries (on the contrary, it blocks their development and aggravates their poverty). So scientific socialism should be applied to develop them first.

The search for indigenous African ideology

As part of its broad programme of bourgeois reformism, the African *petit-bourgeoisie* has not only campaigned against socialism, and denied its relevance because it threatens their exploitative class interests and dominant political power, they have also expanded their defensive radicalism to a diversionary and futile search for an indigenous African ideology as an alternative to socialism. This mission of Africanist ideology has two main objectives. One is to divert the broad masses' struggles for scientific socialism and a revolutionary alternative which directly threatens the *petit-bourgeoisie*. So they advance safe and innocuous African socialism (or, in North Africa, Arab socialism), communalism, African humanism, African personality, negritude, and even traditionalism, among the more backward exploiting strata. These diversionary and futile ideologies are supposedly more congruent with African culture, tradition, history, temperament and philosophy. They romanticise the African past and heritage with a nostalgia designed to drug the masses into an ideological stupor. This is particularly seductive against Western racism. But the truth is that these African ideologies are preferred because they divert attention from political concerns and direct mass struggles against the abusive contradictions, injustices, super-exploitation, vicious repression and growing inequalities in capitalist society. In such ways do these so-called indigenous ideologies falsely postulate or imply (as in the case of communalism and humanism) classlessness and deny the need for class struggle to terminate mass poverty. Rather than radical class struggle to root out exploitation, these African ideologies preach national unity, national integration, one destiny and "the end of ideology" in the vain attempt to reduce politics and social debate into mere bureaucratic administration in which the basic goals of society are supposed to be settled and handed down by the *petit-bourgeoisie*.

The second main objective of this search for indigenous African ideology is to stabilise the status quo and protect capitalism from attack. Thus, all these African ideologies are notoriously and suspiciously silent on the basic economic and political questions such as who (what class) owns the means of production, appropriates economic surplus, controls the state and thus determines the distribution of political and economic power as well as social opportunities. And, of course, since these questions are swept under the carpet, so are foreign domination, the super-exploitations and the symbiotic collusion between the local and foreign exploiters.

Africanist ideologies, therefore, fail on three grounds. First is – wherever they have been applied, from North Africa to the Cape – an empirical failure to arrest the African crisis. Rather, they operate to intensify the contradictions and drive African countries towards total collapse as, for example, in Zaire, Ghana, Sudan, Senegal, and Nigeria. Secondly, while such ideologies seek to reincarnate the superstructure of the African past, they are studiously opposed to any experiment with communal ownership of the means of production, which was the economic foundation of indigenous African ideologies. This is because communal ownership would terminate the dominance of the *petit-bourgeoisie* as a class. Thirdly, seeking to solve Africa's contemporary problems by way of past, indigenous African ideologies, is basically unscientific. Every ideology is specific to a given mode of production or social formation,[6] because an ideology is the superstructural expression of the economic basis of each mode of production or social formation. Therefore, the attempt to graft a pre-capitalist ideology (that is, an African indigenous ideology which is necessarily pre-capitalist) on to a contemporary African neocolonial capitalist system is like forcing the existing capitalist mode of production or social formation, which has produced its own capitalist ideology, to replace that with a pre-capitalist ideology. And this is impossible.

First, it implies that the same neocolonial capitalist mode or formation is being required to cope with two ideologies simultaneously; this is impossible for the same mode of production. But even though it is possible for one social formation to exhibit two or more ideologies simultaneously, because a social formation is an articulation of different modes of production in which one mode is dominant, it must mean that one of the ideologies is dominant. The dominant ideology in the social formation will, therefore, correspond to the dominant mode in the social formation. So, in an African neocolonial social formation in which the capitalist mode is dominant, if a pre-capitalist indigenous ideology is to be admitted or observed in it, that pre-capitalist indigenous ideology must be subordinate because the mode of production that generated it is a subordinate mode of production in the social formation. Therefore, the pre-capitalist indigenous ideology cannot be a national ideology in any African capitalist social formation – neocolonial or not. Secondly, the attempt to make a pre-capitalist indigenous ideology dominant in a neocolonial capitalist mode of production or social formation must also imply an attempt to replace the economic basis of capitalist ideology with the economic basis of pre-capitalism. So the economic basis of the communal, slave or feudal mode of production must displace the economic foundation of neocolonial capitalism. And this is impossible. One reason is that the social relations of production of the backward pre-capitalist mode or formation will be incompatible with the level of development of the productive forces in the neocolonial capitalist mode or formation. Dialectically, the conflict that will arise from the juxtaposition will lead to the overthrow of the backward pre-capitalist economic basis and the emergence or restoration of the capitalist economic basis. This capitalist economic basis will also generate or restore the capitalist ideology as the dominant ideology. Moreover, an attempt to make a pre-capitalist ideology dominant within a neocolonial capitalist social formation also represents an attempt at retrogression, turning back the hands of the clock, which is scientifically impossible.

There is also the argument that, at the purely political level, the African *petit-bourgeoisie* that advocate the historical amnesia of grafting a pre-capitalist indigenous African ideology on to Africa's contemporary neocolonial capitalism will not accept the corresponding grafting of the pre-capitalist social relations of production or pre-capitalist form of property ownership on to their neocolonial capitalist system. This is because in the pre-capitalist, indigenous African system the commonest form of property ownership was communal, and its application in contemporary Africa would wipe out Africa's *petit-bourgeoisie*'s often corrupt private ownership and eliminate their bankrupt and repressive class dominance. Yet, in the past, African indigenous ideologies of communalism, humanism, traditionalism, and so on, were also associated with the communal ownership of the means of production, and the absence of class domination and exploitation.

For these reasons, the capitalist cultural crusaders' clamour for the adoption of a pre-capitalist, indigenous African ideology must be rejected. It is a cultural–ideological obscurantism designed primarily to diffuse mass radicalism and divert attention from the unmitigated disaster of neocolonial capitalist ideology in Africa and to protect peripheral capitalism and sustain the bankrupt and vicious class rule of the *petit-bourgeoisie*.

Bourgeois reformism, utopia and the opium of Africanity

The foregoing discussions demonstrate the patently utopian character of bourgeois reformism and the opiate property of its perverse obsession with Africanity. These features of reformism in Africa demonstrate its tendency towards the *creation of an African social utopian tradition*, similar to that in the USA.[7] This utopian tradition is a phenomenon of consciousness and culture, that disregards the laws of reality and social necessity and substitutes arbitrary speculative logic. Thus the utopian consciousness sees the world and social reality not as a system, but as a multitude of disjointed parts. In essence, therefore, African utopian tradition of bourgeois reformism is neither folk, literary nor theoretical utopia, but *official utopia*, erected by ruling groups and dominant classes.

This African, official utopia serves two major functions. One is the deception and manipulation of the masses in order to consolidate the domination of the *petit-bourgeoisie*. The other is to express the conception of the goals and prospects of society from the perspective of the dominant class, a perspective that preserves the pre-eminence of the bourgeoisie and is, therefore, partisan and arbitrary.

The main burden of bourgeois reformism and its futile search for an indigenous African ideology amounts to the creation of this official utopian tradition. This is played out on a cultural, as much as on an ideological plane, in which a seductive appeal to Africa's historical tradition and cultural values is wielded as a legitimising weapon. In the process, the utopian project sees all those opposed to it as unpatriotic Africans, or as traitors to African culture. So we are enjoined to embrace this bourgeois reformism and its indigenous ideology simply because it is *African* culture – regardless of its arbitrary logic, unjust social implications and exploitative political mission. This is what constitutes bourgeois reformism and its utopian tradition into the opium of Africanity. It is discernible in the propaganda about classless Africa, African humanism, African socialism, and so on, all of which are basically irrelevant to the resolution of the African crisis. It contributes to the aggravation of the crisis through the ravages of the neocolonial capitalist status quo, which the utopian tradition seeks to protect in Africa, as the American utopian tradition does for capitalism in the USA.

Scientific socialism for resolving the African crisis

The manifest failure of bourgeois reformism to resolve the African crisis and instead its intensification of the contradictions involved in it demand the application of *scientific socialist ideology*. It should be emphasised that this is both a *scientific* logical requirement and a *political* necessity. These interconnected aspects of the urgency for *scientific socialism* in Africa in order to eliminate Fanon's "lack of ideology" that threatens the continent, will be elaborated in this and the next sections of this chapter.

The scientific character of socialist ideology

In the serious discussion of scientific socialism, it is relevant to refer to Karl Mannheim's distinction between ideology and utopia.[8] Though both are forms of consciousness and are regarded by Mannheim as transcendental, utopia represents an image of the desired social state that is postulated arbitrarily. It is alien to reality or "incongruous with the state of reality within which it occurs". By contrast, though ideology is also a form of consciousness, it is not just a "dream", or a purely speculative method in pursuit of a dream. Rather, ideology is determined by observable social reality which shapes human consciousness according to an individual's social place in society. Hence the distinction from ideology as a mask or façade, which is used by a class to conceal its true class interest, especially in the case of the ideology of the dominant class. This is the character of the dominant *petit-bourgeois* ideology in Africa. But ideology is also simply the system of beliefs, the goals and social vision which a class or society articulates on the basis of its collective historical experience to deal with its pressing problems. This gives the sense of social reality and objective necessity in ideology.

Hence, ideology is part of the superstructural expression of the economic basis of any society. As stated earlier, every social formation has a corresponding ideological structure represented by the world-view of the dominant class in that society. This ideology thus emerges from interaction between the productive forces and the social relations of production. Every social crisis must, therefore, represent some form of conflict between the development of these productive forces and their social relations of production. Such a crisis, especially when it is as deep as that in Africa, must also be an ideological crisis, which demands the transcendence of that extant ideology.

It is in this sense that an ideology is both a social reality and a historical necessity. Its reality derives from the material mode of production, the economic foundation of society that gives rise to it. Its historical necessity arises in a double sense. One, in the sense of the need for the expression of consciousness by the members of the society in which the mode of production that generates an ideology exists. Since the members of the society of necessity enter into definite social relations of production that structure their existence, they also necessarily articulate ideologies or forms of consciousness corresponding to those relations of production. This explains why different social classes articulate different ideologies dictated by the differing places they occupy in the social relations of production. The second is that ideology is also a historical necessity because it is the social weapon that societies articulate for resolving the crises of their social formations. Thus, when the productive forces and the social relations of production in a particular mode of production come into conflict, this is a signal that an alternative ideology to that extant is needed to resolve the crisis of the existing mode of production or social formation. It is in this pertinent sense that the African crisis demands a progressive ideology for its resolution.

Capitalism, crisis and scientific socialism

When capitalism, whether neocolonial, peripheral or mature, enters a phase of generalised crisis (like the general crisis of any mode of production or social formation), this is a signal that the extant ideology is no longer an adequate expression of the interaction between the productive forces and the social relations of that mode or formation. This contradiction may be antagonistic or non-antagonistic, depending on the character of the crisis. When the crisis is general and deep, it affects all aspects of social relations and, therefore, its contradictions tend to be antagonistic. This means that the extant mode of production or social formation and its dominant ideology (or superstructure) have become outmoded. There is then a revolutionary moment for the compulsive overthrow (violently or otherwise) of the existing social formation and its dominant ideology. The overthrow of an existing social formation or mode must mean the establishment of a higher social formation or mode of production.

By implication, when a pervasive crisis of capitalism warrants or leads to its collapse, it must necessarily be replaced by the next higher mode or social formation.[9] This is the sense in which historically and scientifically, socialism is the only logical ideology for resolving the crisis of capitalism. This is because the crisis expresses the conflict and incongruence between the development of productive forces and the corresponding social relations of production. Since the existing ideological mould or social formation cannot constitute its own overthrow or replace itself, and a lower social formation cannot be installed (because its own lower social relations will conflict with the higher development of productive forces in the higher capitalist formation), this means that of necessity, a higher social formation must be installed.

In this sense the capitalist crisis heralds the obsolescence of capitalism and the necessity for socialism. Thus socialism is in the womb of the crisis of capitalism. Hence, as neocolonial capitalist accumulation everywhere has a built-in tendency to degenerate into crisis, due to its inherent antagonistic contradictions led by the implacable conflict between labour and capital, the accumulation of capital under capitalism necessarily tends to manifest the need for socialist development. It is in this sense that the African crisis has been intensified rather than resolved by the application of bourgeois reformism. Scientific socialism is thus the historically necessary ideological basis for the resolution of the continental crisis. What can be argued and varied is not the necessity or the relevance of scientific socialism to contemporary Africa (hence arguments and antics about African socialism are futile), but the character of the creative application of scientific socialism in the peculiar circumstances and forms in which the African crisis manifests itself in different countries.

Political strategy for scientific socialist Africa

After two decades of socialist experimentation in Africa, and 70 years since the first socialist revolution in the world, it is now abundantly clear that the mere assertion of the necessity for *scientific socialism*, or even its declaration in an African country, is not enough. It may lead nowhere, and even be a mere subterfuge, a defensive strategy for protecting neocolonial capitalism as in many African countries. Indeed, to say "socialism" by itself is also not enough since we have masquerading African, Arab and pragmatic socialism.[10] We should now insist first on the unambiguous adoption of scientific socialism or the adoption of a Marxist–Leninist ideology. The mere proclamation of a revolution or even of socialism is likewise not enough, since that can be used to implement a reactionary capitalist programme as in many African countries. No equivocation or innocuous synonym for scientific socialism should be accepted by the African masses – such strategies have been used to deceive and betray them in different parts of Africa. Then the specific details of the social programme for the realisation of scientific socialism must be insisted upon by the masses – and such radical programmes must be implemented dutifully. This raises several issues.

Scientific socialist revolution not national democratic revolution

First, when a revolution is proclaimed in any African country, this must be clearly declared as a *scientific socialist revolution*, not merely African revolution, national democratic revolution (NDR), bourgeois democratic revolution (BDR), or any other kind of revolution. The African masses must reject any such alternative and diversionary proclamations, because they are ambiguous and may be deceitful. While it is true that any of these non-scientific socialist revolutions may lead to scientific socialism through its transitional stages, it is equally true that in Africa, such alternative proclamations have been only a façade to deceive the masses and protect neocolonial capitalist relations. Thus Sergeant Doe's 1980 revolution in Liberia has since become a fascist, anti-socialist nightmare.

The two specific reasons for rejecting these alternative revolutionary proclamations are, first, that they do not point unambiguously to an alternative ideology to capitalism. Thus the national or bourgeois democratic revolution does not project an ideology distinct from bourgeois ideology – in spite of its radical slogans. Though, as indicated above, the NDR or BDR may lead to the construction of scientific socialism, it may also prevent it, as in Ghana (1986). The democratic revolution, national or bourgeois, has an uncanny tendency of remaining a perpetual transitional state in which capitalist relations are consolidated against the legitimate aspirations of the masses.

Indeed, these NDR and BDR constitute a trap for mass struggles: because they are proclaimed as transitions to socialism, any socialist struggles by the masses while the NDR/BDR exists is considered subversive and unpatriotic. Moreover, there is no guarantee that the *petit-bourgeois* leadership that directs the NDR/BDR will willingly give way to a more radical leadership to build the socialist phase, or that this *petit-bourgeois* leadership will transform itself qualitatively and radically in order to undertake the task of socialist construction.

Secondly, it is quite clear that the modes of production or social formations of the NDR or BDR – and even pragmatic, African or Arab socialism – are neither distinct from, nor alternatives to, the neocolonial capitalist modes. Since the object of the revolution is to replace the capitalist formation with a higher social formation, and these democratic revolutions do not constitute such higher social formations, they should be discouraged and rejected – except as specifically transitional phases of socialist struggle. If the leadership is sincere in that these other ideologies constitute programmes of transition to scientific socialism, it should directly proclaim scientific socialism. This will have the effect of announcing that the country involved is outside the imperialist orbit and, therefore, of forcing the anti-imperialist struggle to start immediately – without an interim phase of further collaboration with imperialism. Thus in Ethiopia, the BDR was proclaimed after a scientific socialist revolution and its programme had been announced.

Class alliance for scientific socialist Africa

After the scientic socialist proclamation has been made (and indeed, before it can be made with confidence), the class alliance that will develop the scientific socialist transformation must be formed, and consolidated as socialist construction proceeds. Because this class alliance is the heart of socialist strategy, it is important to be very clear about its nature. There are three main aspects to this. First, such an alliance should include two broad radical forces: the different social strata and groups fighting for *democracy and anti-imperialism*, and the more radical forces fighting for scientific socialism.[11] The objective of this broad class alliance is to present a formidable united front against the machinations of domestic reaction and its imperialist ally. This is because various reactionary forces and branches of capital – traditional rulers, landlords, merchants, politicians, reactionary professionals and imperialists – will oppose the socialist transformation. Hence all class forces with grievances against the status quo should be mobilised to fight it; careful study of all national and local grievances is necessary here. Narrow ideological sectarianism that may open the flanks of the radical forces to reactionary attacks must, therefore, be firmly discouraged.

Second, the specific class composition of this radical class alliance should be based on the careful study of the local situation suggested above. Hence this class alliance should necessarily include a vanguard group or organisation and a flank of other mass organisations. While the core will consist of the most radical members of the communist or Marxist–Leninist party – working class, peasants, students, members of the armed forces, radical intellectuals, and national democrats – the flank membership should include such class strata as petty-artisans, petty-traders (men and women who are held hostage by big commercial, industrial and financial capital), patriotic, and especially anti-imperialist, professionals and even politicians. The alliance should also extend into the exploiting classes and strata.

Third, the terms of the democratic, anti-imperialist programme of the class alliance should be dutifully explained to all the class strata involved. These objectives are: (a) the control of economic and political power to run enterprises and all state organs; (b) mass mobilisation for radical political consciousness; (c) collective defence of the alliance of all working people. These must be explained at all levels of the organisations of the class alliance and at all times.

Independent working people's organisations

> Without a guiding organisation, the energy of the masses would dissipate like steam not enclosed in a piston box. But nonetheless what moves things is not the piston, or the box, but the steam.[12]

In order for working people's energies to be effectively enclosed in this organisational piston box and generate the required steam, some specific issues should be addressed. These are: (1) vanguard or core organisation; (2) front organisations; (3) political education for mass organisations; (4) independence of working people's organisations; (5) the role of the military; (6) the mobilisation of the peasantry.

The overall organisation of the class alliance is like an onion. The core is the *vanguard Marxist–Leninist party*, with, if one exists, the communist party in alliance. Its task is to design the programme of the class alliance, the general socialist strategy and give guidelines to the mass organisations. The *front organisations* constitute the democratic and anti-imperialist mass organisations such as trade unions, peasant, artisan, traders (market women and men) and progressive professional and tenants' associations as well as other organised progressive groups. Their duty is to mount class struggle around specific democratic and anti-imperialist grievances or issues, such as industrial democracy, illiteracy, free education, health-care delivery, housing and rent, foreign domination, excessive pricing, profit repatriation, expatriate quota, market stalls, partisan legislation, land reforms, and so on.

Political education of these members of mass organisations is crucial.[13] This is central to political work among the masses and the development of their political consciousness. It requires well-trained and disciplined cadres, party schools, educational classes for mass organisations and a mass literacy campaign. This is necessary for the clearer articulation of grievances, clear communication and effective organisation through the use of meetings, committees, records and simple book-keeping.

The *independence of these organisations of the working people* should also be very resolutely maintained against infiltration and cooptation by the *petit-bourgeoisie* in work places and in politics generally. This is central to the unity of action in working people's parties and mass organisations. The policy should be firm so that the vanguard party can maintain an independent class role. It should dissociate itself from the positions of ruling class groups and pro-bourgeois class forces, and maintain a running controversy with them. This is to make its *identity* clear to the masses – and thus more graphically expose the bankruptcy of the *petit-bourgeoisie*. The radicals should thus propagate their alternative programmes to those of the *petit-bourgeoisie*. There should also be a unity of action between the masses of the urban and rural areas, higher rural/urban alliance, and a strengthening of the independent class positions of the peasants. In all these, it should be realised that there is an inseparable link between the formation of a left-wing alliance, and the struggle for the democratic unity of all anti-imperialist forces in each African country and on the entire continent.

The role of the military in the class alliance should also be addressed. Basically, so far, most coups staged by the *officer corps of the African military* have been to advance the exploitative interests of the *petit-bourgeoisie*, of which they are objective members. In the few cases where these middle-class coups were proclaimed as revolutions, as, for example, in Liberia, Ghana, Benin, most of them quickly degenerated into, at best, bourgeois reformist regimes, and, in some cases, into fascist dictatorship (Liberia). This scenario makes it essential to penetrate the *rank and file military*, who have definite grievances against the status quo, and to politicise such grievances. This requires the careful and imaginative filtering of radical literature to these rank-and-file military members, exposing them to radical ideas through newspaper and magazine articles, radio and television programmes, and so on. Such military converts can become an underground wing of the radical class alliance.

Mobilisation of the peasantry

The political strategy and class alliance for the scientific socialist transformation of Africa must deal decisively with the mobilisation of the peasantry. Even though peasants are not the only revolutionary force in Africa (and the rest of the Third World), the radical transformation of African countries is inconceivable without the active role of the peasantry who constitute the majority of the population of these countries. This is particularly necessary in spite of Marx's alleged disdain for the peasantry as a "sack of potatoes", suffering from "rural idiocy" and the passive pawns of landlords and officials, who are isolated, submerged in a "culture of silence" and thus demobilised.[14] But after the support of peasants in the revolutionary transformation of China, Vietnam and the former Portuguese colonies in Africa, the peasantry's revolutionary role has been so firmly established that many now entertain romantic illusions about their infinite revolutionary potential.

Peasant characteristics

Perhaps, the first task in the mobilisation of the peasantry and the formation of meaningful class alliance with them is a close study and understanding of them: their localisation, class structure, particular grievances, aspirations and differing levels of consciousness. In this regard, it has been fairly established that there is not just one homogeneous peasantry in any African country, but different peasantries, according to locality, type of cultivation, class differentiation, for example. This means that it is difficult to elicit a common consciousness and common response from the peasantry. From the analysis in Chapter 5, peasants are often regarded as a transitional class between primitive cultivators in communal villages and their restratification by capitalism into capitalist farmers and proletarians.[15] But this view must recognise the permanence and basic coherence of the peasantry as a working stratum. In terms of class composition and revolutionary consciousness, the middle peasants and not the poorest ones, have been identified as initially the most militant. They may, however, desert the struggle at the revolutionary stage because their social outlook is constrained by their transitory status (between capitalist farmers and poor peasants), and the poorest peasants then become the ultimate force to execute the revolution. This implies the need to avoid romantic illusions about the peasantry's unconditional and spontaneous revolutionary role.

The specific grievances of the peasantry and the social targets of peasant anger are also important for their characterisation, and partly explain why the peasantry have no common consciousness and common revolutionary response. While some strata of the peasantry are oppressed by landlords, others are repressed by state and local officials. Their particular grievances may include land shortage, exorbitant rent or tribute-paying, oppressive taxation, poor prices, denial of credit, lack of access to modern farm inputs and infrastructure (for example, isolation due to lack of feeder roads or bridges). So a common policy of "land to the tillers" may not elicit the same revolutionary response from the different groups of peasants in a country. This also implies the need to identify the specific targets of peasant anger in order to mobilise the peasants along the lines of their peculiar grievances and against their particular targets.[16] In many parts of Africa these specific targets of peasant anger are such national elites, as landlords, *petit-bourgeois* politicians and state officials, (for example, marketing boards), their representatives in rural areas, and the multinational corporations which now increasingly alienate peasant land for agribusiness (for example, Taxagric in Nigeria) and cause landlessness.

Barriers and potentials of peasant mobilisation

These characteristics of the peasantry imply that there are both barriers against, and potentials for, their revolutionary mobilisation. Frequently encountered barriers include mass illiteracy and parochialism with the regional and ethnic assertiveness of rural populations; the distance of the exploitative system which is not easily perceived by the peasants (marketing boards, tax system, for example); the possibility that peasant political action and revolt may be uncoordinated, localised and isolated unlike the collective and centralised experiences of workers; the tendency for peasants to resolve the contradictions confronting them by resignation and apathy, seeking *petit-bourgeois* solutions, and even by rehabilitating the oppressive traditional system (for example, of chieftaincy) as a mistaken bulwark against national oppression; the manipulative electoral and reformist rural activities of *petit-bourgeois* politicians and the comprador state itself (for example, formation of symbolic marketing cooperatives and peasant associations, electoral bribery, false propaganda that radical cadres want to steal peasant land, and so on).[17]

Political work among the peasantry also reveals other problems. Thus Cabral reports that peasants are a great physical force but a reluctant revolutionary force: "We know from experience what trouble we had convincing the peasantry to fight".[18] In Kenya, this was also reported: ". . . it generally requires a rare combination of tyranny and misery to produce a peasant revolt, let alone a peasant revolution".[19]

Rural cultivators are said to be doubly peasantised – by feudalism and by feudal subordination to the colonial–international capitalist system, but the absence of landlords and feudal relations at the point of direct production implies that exploitation and subordination become imperceptible by being distanced and depersonalised, thus diffusing peasant grievances. In Africa and in many other parts of the Third World, population pressure or landlessness is not yet acute enough to drive peasants into last-ditch revolutionary fight. This is related to the recent, uneven and incomplete peasantisation in Africa which preserves pre-capitalist social networks to cushion the effects of exploitation and subordination (for example, by ethnic, kinship and extended family ties). There are also the rural dwellers disturbing "burgeoning petty-capitalist aspirations" which make the new elites in power *seem* to be their natural allies.This is associated with the post-colonial state's deliberate diffusion of peasant class consciousness via the use of intermediaries between urban and rural areas under the rubric of the politics of patronage, of patron–client relations, with its associated reward-and-punishment. In these processes, "ethnicity is teased into life" from the dormant subconsciousness of the populace – first by the colonial divide and rule policy, and subsequently by *petit-bourgeois* politicians during the colonial and post-colonial periods. To overcome these barriers to peasant mobilisation, careful study and hard political work based on the methods of Cabral and Mao Zedong are critical.

Thus despite these difficulties, there are enormous potentials for the radical mobilisation of the peasantry in Africa and elsewhere. This is due to the intensification of the contradictions of the mindless oppression of the peasantry. In the process, peasants have repeatedly demonstrated their capacity for spontaneous revolutionary action.

Under colonialism, peasant discontent often flared into overt action in support of the nationalist movement – even though this was often uncoordinated so that there tended to be parallel, rather than united, urban and rural anti-colonial movements. In the post-colonial era, we have the peasant actions reported in the Congo of the mid-1960s around "Pierre Mulele's activities in the Kwilu and in the People's Republic of the Eastern Congo", and "the Mobutist denouement" in Zaire, though such movements tended to lose focus easily. There are also the revolutionary activities of the *Agbekoya* revolt in Western Nigeria in 1969, involving the sacking of police posts, storming of a state prison and protracted battles with combined army and police units.[20] In the former Portuguese colonies, the liberation movements relied heavily on the revolutionary support of peasants, while Tanzania has been attempting to build *Ujamaa* or rural socialism through peasant mobilisation.

Hard political work is required to achieve these levels of peasant radicalism. Revolutionary cadres are needed as the initial "external vanguard" for peasants, and later some of the peasants become part of the "internal vanguard" for the struggle. This requires the establishment of deep political roots among the peasantry through sound knowledge of the grievances, stresses and strains in each local community. This knowledge includes the fact that peasant revolutionary potentials differ – it is highest among the labour-exporting peasantry (that supply labour to the mines, for example, from the frontline states to South Africa) and lowest among cash-cropping peasants, with subsistence-cropping peasants occupying an intermediate position. Hence intense political education is needed for the class alliance of radical forces and peasants in order to articulate grievances, organise them, teach basic political skills, popularise the objectives of socialist transformation and thus raise the socialist consciousness of the peasantry.

The transition to scientific socialism in Africa

The socialist experiments in Africa (both old and new) can be regarded as forms of "transition to socialism" but that category has a more specific meaning. It is this specialised meaning of the transition to socialism in terms of the concrete processes of socialist construction between the proclamation of socialism and the actual emergence of socialist society that is intended here.[21] It involves the tasks of building socialist infrastructure (both social and physical), socialist economy, state and consciousness after capturing state power from the *petit-bourgeoisie* and the revolutionary overthrow of capitalism – even though this liquidation of capitalism is itself incomplete until some of the stages of socialist transition have been executed. The abortion of all the old socialist experiments and the mutation of many of the new ones thus compel an urgent review of the programmes of transition to socialism in Africa.

Experiences of socialist transition in Africa

In this regard, it is possible to identify three broad forms of socialist transition – two in actual practice in Africa and one recommended by theory and the experiences of socialist transition outside Africa – especially in Cuba, Cambodia, Vietnam, China and the other advanced socialist countries. The transition to socialism *in the old socialist experiments under African or Arab socialism* is by implication a false transition, because the old socialist experiments were themselves fake and bogus. The two dominant planks of this alleged transition under these experiments consisted of defensive sloganising and the creation of an enlarged public sector of state bureaucratic capitalism derived from the nationalisation of enterprises, as in Nkrumah's Ghana, Sekou Toure's Guinea, Zambia, Egypt, Benin and even in Tanzania.[22] Though the depth of these programmes and related reforms (especially land redistribution and the provision of such social welfare services as education and health) varied among these countries, they all basically omitted any serious commitment to class struggle, mass mobilisation, especially of the rural majority, the establishment of a vanguard party guided by Marxist–Leninist ideology and the radical transformation of the inherited bourgeois state apparatus.

By contrast, *socialist transition in the new socialist experiments* in Africa under revolutionary banners have typically comprised two broad varieties. The less serious, and even cynical, consists mainly of programmes of National Democratic Revolution (NDR) centred mainly on bourgeois (not even social) reformism for the expansion of capitalism, as in Zimbabwe and Ghana.[23] Although these transitions lay claim to future socialist orientation as in Zimbabwe (Ghana under Rawlings is not even pretending to that future socialist commitment), they elaborate no concrete programmes for this socialist construction and present no timetable for such eventual transition. Thus this NDR really amounts to neocolonial capitalist expansion under the domination of imperialist capital so that there is often not even a serious commitment to state bureaucratic capitalism (SBC), much less to socialism. Hence, this transition is more likely to entrench peripheral capitalism under foreign monopoly capital and may, therefore, be no transition to any kind of socialism. On account of its revolutionary rhetoric and ambiguous character, this form of transition may even be worse than that encountered under African or Arab socialism. But in Zimbabwe, the scenario of intense class struggle, within ZANU-PF, the state and the economy gives some hope that the NDR could usher in socialism.

The second form of socialist transition under the new socialist experiments in Africa is that exhibited by countries such as Ethiopia and the former Portuguese colonies. The programme of transition to socialism in these countries consists essentially of a bourgeois democratic revolution (BDR as in Ethiopia) – even though this may not be stated explicitly in other countries – and some socialist-oriented programmes. The BDR consists basically of measures to eradicate the remnants of feudal and feudo-bourgeois relations, especially in land, housing, culture and politics as in Ethiopia, in order to establish basic bourgeois rationality (for example "land to the tiller", establishment of universal franchise and other democratic rights). The necessity for this BDR depends on whether or not bourgeois democratic rights, essential capitalist relations of production and a sizeable proletariat have emerged. The socialist-oriented programmes in these new socialist experiments then consist of the establishment of Marxist–Leninist ideology (possibly with an ideological school), a vanguard party of working people (and the progressive military), extensive nationalisation of foreign capital and other means of production, workers' control of enterprises and putative attempts at mass mobilisation (for example, through the establishment of urban and peasant associations, cooperatives, and so on). But even in such countries as Ethiopia, Guinea-Bissau, Mozambique and Angola, where such socialist-oriented programmes are pursued vigorously, mass organisations, especially of the rural majority, the development of socialist consciousness among the broad masses and a socialist economic infrastructure (not even socialist technology) are usually at too low a level to ensure a robust and durable transition to socialism. In Angola and Mozambique, even modest socialist programmes are systematically sabotaged by fascist imperialism through the use of local reactionary forces (UNITA in Angola and the MNR in Mozambique) by the USA and South Africa.

These examples of transition to socialism in Africa highlight two major weaknesses. One relates to the point that, in order for such transition to have any chance of success, the initial socialist declaration itself must be unambiguously one of scientific socialism. The proclamation of diversionary ideological euphemisms such as African or Arab socialism, humanism and even mere revolution, typically offer a convenient political subterfuge for hijacking popular revolutionary struggles and perverting them into puerile bourgeois reformism and expansion of neocolonial capitalism. This kind of "transition" is deceptive, diversionary and basically reactionary, and should, therefore, be exposed and combated for its *petit-bourgeois* bankruptcy. Its defensive radicalism is a clear barrier to the scientific socialist transformation of Africa and the rest of the Third World. The absence of effective class struggle and mass mobilisation is the basic source of this weakness.

The other serious defect of socialist transition in Africa is its uncritical attitude towards nationalisation. All too often, the erroneous impression is created that once a regime embarks on a programme of *nationalisation* (in some cases, even on less radical *indigenisation* of foreign enterprises), it is building socialism. While it is true that some nationalisation programmes may be part of the transition to socialism, they can also serve merely to rationalise neocolonial capitalism. This can then give rise to underdeveloped state capitalism (USC) or state bureaucratic capitalism (SBC), and even to private-enterprise capitalism. This can happen when the nationalised enterprises are placed under bureaucratic capitalist management, or privatised in the future under the slogans of parastatal inefficiency and the fiscal crisis of the state.

Basic requirements for a transition to scientific socialism in Africa

Though specific details of the programme of transition to socialism vary among countries with respect to their level of capitalist development, the pressing contradictions of the particular country, the nature of the revolution, and so on, certain broad features are, however, identifiable. These are derivable from the varied experiences of successful socialist transition in such diverse historical contexts as Cuba, China, Cambodia and Vietnam in the Third World as well as in the Soviet Union and Eastern Europe. Given the changing character of the global class struggle, by far the more relevant experiences to Africa are those of socialist transformations in the Third World. This is because they are more recent and undertaken in circumstances similar to those of African and other Third World countries.

These transitions usually involve *simultaneous* transformations in the economic basis of society and in the superstructure. Some speak of economic, political (state), cultural and even technological revolutions (though the development of socialist technology is still problematic even for the advanced socialist countries).[24] They involve democratic (anti-feudal and anti-fascist) struggles, anti-imperialist and domestic anti-capitalist class struggles. The objectives are to establish permanent (or at least durable, and possibly irreversible) structural changes in the economy, the state and society; that is, to radically change the entire social formation.

There are five broad planks in this programme of transition to socialism: (a) ideological shift; (b) political transformation of the state; (c) economic transformation; (d) cultural reorientation or revolution; (e) socialist internationalism for global anti-imperialist solidarity. First, the ideological shift consists of the firm establishment of Marxism–Leninism as the guiding ideology for the transformation to scientific socialism; mere proclamation of socialism, revolution and similar slogans is not enough. There should also be an *ideological school* for the political education of the national leadership, state and party officials and cadres in this ideology. This is to ensure the correct ideological line and sound theory as the basis for effective praxis.

Second, the political struggle has at least three thrusts. One is the establishment of a revolutionary vanguard party as the basic organisational core of the progressive social formation. Mass mobilisation for the inculcation of socialist consciousness among the toiling majority both in urban and rural areas with basic political education is also important; and so is the need for class struggle to weed out reactionary forces and heighten the revolutionary momentum of the nation. This is basically domestic anti-feudal and anti-capitalist class struggle as well as an anti-imperialist offensive to liberate the nation from foreign domination.

Third, the economic transformation should also include at least three basic elements. The nationalisation or public ownership of the means of production is the first. Initially, this should exclude sole proprietorships, such as taxis, minor retail trade and the like, because the goals of nationalisation are the elimination of foreign domination and all forms of exploitation, centralisation of national economic surplus and so facilitate comprehensive planning. There should be workers' control of enterprises (this plus nationalisation equals the *socialisation* of the means of production), and *workers should be armed to defend those enterprises and trained to manage them effectively by themselves*. Comprehensive planned development of the national economy should then provide physical and social infrastructure; proportional development of agriculture and industry, as well as other branches of national economy with a basic capital-goods sub-sector; and develop people's self-management in living and working places. The elaboration of annual, medium- (3 to 5 years) and long-term (10 to 25 years) or perspective plans are very useful for these purposes under a high-powered National Planning Commission.

Fourth, the cultural reorientation or revolution should aim at eliminating the decadent and pecuniary values of capitalism, and replacing them with more humane values and socialist consciousness.[21] This requires the teaching of the rights and duties of socialist citizenship, respect for public property, the need to be each other's keeper, the dignity of labour, the superiority of collective/cooperative work and living over bourgeois individualism, the scientific and technological outlook, and so on. This demands the total overhaul of the entire educational system, reorientation of all the mass media, the introduction of socialist management methods in bureaucracies and enterprises, separation of religion from the state (that is, creation of the secular state) and discouragement of religious syncretism and fanaticism. This cultural programme should be an integral component of ideological and political education for everybody, including the national and party leadership at all levels. The evident consumerism and tendencies towards revisionism even in some of the advanced socialist countries is partly the result of the failure of this cultural reorientation.

Finally, socialist internationalism must be strengthened. This requires delinking with imperialism (though these days, even advanced socialist countries are pushing for greater nationalism and increased trade links with imperialist countries for such diverse reasons as the settlement of the external debts of countries like Poland, the acquisition or exchange of technology and what is termed increasing global interdependence), and establishing close political, diplomatic, economic and other ties with the socialist world. The idea is to whittle down the imperialist orbit in the world and thus accelerate global liberation from imperialist domination and exploitation.

Notes

1. On the changing character of ideology, see D. J. Manning (ed.) (1980), and George Novak (1979).
2. K. Marx and F. Engels (1970).
3. While bourgeois reformism is designed to maintain the status quo, social reformism seeks to build a socialist utopia or the foundations of socialism without class struggle. So while bourgeois reformism is identified with neocolonial capitalist regimes, social reformism prevails under African and Arab socialism, and the national democratic revolution.
4. On the cold-war propaganda of the USA and other imperialist countries over human rights, see USSR (1982) *Where Human Rights Are Real.*
5. This is the bourgeois myth celebrated in K. Galbraith (1978).
6. On the relationship between ideology, mode of production and social formation, see B. Onimode (1983); and G. Taylor (1979).
7. See Edward Batalov (1985), Chs. 1 and 3; also A. L. Morton (1952).
8. Karl Mannheim (1968).
9. On this historical succession of modes of production or social formations, see K. Marx and F. Engels (1980).
10. See M. Babu (1981).
11. On this question of class strategy, see Regis Debray (1971).

12. Quoted in D. Singer (1970), p. 1.

13. For this successful political education in liberation struggle, see Amilcar Cabral (1971).

14. On this characterisation of the peasantry, see D. L. Cohen and J. Daniel (1981), ch. 19; and P. Friere (1975); also Don Barnet (1973).

15. See Cohen and Daniel (1981) pp. 267–70.

16. On the grievances and targets of peasant anger, see Amilcar Cabral (1971); Tunde Adeniran (1974) in *Journal of Black Studies*, vol. 4, no. 4, June, and C. E. F. Beer (1975).

17. These barriers to peasant mobilisation are discussed in Cohen and Daniel (1981).

18. Amilcar Cabral (1971), p. 50.

19. Quoted in Cohen and Daniel (1981) pp. 270–1.

20. See Tunde Adeniran (1974).

21. On the transition to socialism, see Bettelheim (1978); and E. Boorstein (1968).

22. See M. Babu (1981) chs. 3, 5 & 9.

23. See A. Astrow (1983).

24. This concern over the development of socialist technology was a major issue in the 1986 Congress of the Soviet Communist Party (CPSU). See M. Gorbachev (1986), pp. 32–9.

25. On the need for cultural reorientation under socialism, see S. Amin (1977) chs. 8–10.

Bibliography

Adedeji Adebayo (1981) "Background Notes on Africa's Food Situation and Policies and Strategies", Paper presented at the North–South Food Roundtable, Washington D.C.

Adediran, Tunde (1974) "The Dynamics of Peasant Revolt – A Conceptual Analysis of the Agbekoya Parapo Uprising in the Western State of Nigeria", *Journal of Black Studies*, Vol. 4, No. 4 June.

Adelmann, I., & Chenery H. B. (1966) "Foreign Aid and Economic Development – The Case of Greece", *Review of Economics and Statistics*, XLVIII, February, pp. 1–19.

African Centre for Monetary Studies (1982) "Implementation of the *Lagos Plan of Action* – Working Notes on the Aspects of Trade and Finance", Paper presented at the Seminar organised by the ECA, CODESRIA and IDEP, Addis Ababa, 1–4 March.

Ahmed, I. (1976) "The Green Revolution and Tractorisation", *International Labour Review*, July–August.

Ake, Claude (1979) *Social Science as Imperialism – The Theory of Political Development* (Ibadan University Press).

Akeredolu-Ale, E. O. (1975) *The Underdevelopment of Indigenous Entrepreneurship in Nigeria* (Ibadan University Press).

Alavi, H. (1972) "The Post-Colonial State", *New Left Review*, 74, July–August, pp. 59–82.

Amin, Samir (1974) *Accumulation on a World Scale* (New York, Monthly Review Press).

——— (1974) *Imperialism and Unequal Development* (New York, Monthly Review Press).

——— et al. (1978) "Social Sciences and the Development Crisis in Africa – Problems and Prospects", *Africa Development*, Vol. 3, No. 2.

——— (1981) "Underdevelopment and Dependence in Black Africa: Origins and Contemporary Forms" in D. L. Cohen & J. Daniel (eds), *Political Economy of Africa – Selected Readings* (London, Longman).

——— (1982) *The Arab Economy Today* (London, Zed Press).

——— & Cohen R. (1977) *Classes and Class Struggle in Africa* (Lagos, Afrografika Publishers).

Apple M. W. (1979) *Ideology and Curriculum* (London, Routledge and Kegan Paul).

Astrow, André (1983) *Zimbabwe: A Revolution that Lost its Way?* (London, Zed Press).

Babu, M. (1981) *African Socialism or Socialist Africa?* (London, Zed Press).

Baran, Paul (1957) *The Political Economy of Growth* (New York, Monthly Review Press).
Barnet, Don (1973) *Peasant Type and Revolutionary Potential in Colonial Africa* (Richmond Publishers).
Barongo, Yolamu (ed.) (1982) *Political Science in Africa: A Radical Critique* (London, Zed Press).
Batalor, Edward (1985) *The American Utopia* (Moscow, Progress Publishers).
Bentham, Jeremy (1973) *Emancipate Your Colonies* (London).
Berger, P. L., & Luckman, T. (1967), *The Social Construction of Reality* (New York, Doubleday & Co.).
Berry, L. Ya (ed.) (1977) *Planning a Socialist Economy*, Vol. I (Moscow, Progress Publishers).
Biersteker, T. J. (1978), *Distortion or Development? Contending Perspectives on the Multinational Corporation* (Cambridge, Mass., MIT Press).
Boeke, J. H. (1953) *Economics and Economic Policy of Dual Societies* (New York, Institute of Pacific Relations).
Bowker, Richard, in S. Fine (1964), *Laissez Faire and the Welfare State* (Ann Arbor, University of Michigan Press).
Broody, A. (1970) *Proportions, Prices and Planning* (Budapest).
Brutents, K. N. (1977) *National Liberation Revolutions Today* (Moscow, Progress Publishers).
Cabral, H. A. (1969) *Revolution in Guiné* (London, Stagel).
Cabral, A. (1973) *Return to the Source* (New York, Africa Information Service).
Cairncross, A. K. (1953) *Home and Foreign Investment, 1870/1913* (Cambridge).
Castro, Fidel (1983) *The World Economic and Social Crisis* (Havana, Publishing Office).
——— (1985) *Mexico Daily Excelsior*, 21 March.
Chayanov, A. V. (1966) *The Theory of Peasant Economy* (Chicago, Aldine).
——— (1971) *Peasants and Peasant Societies* (Penguin).
Chomsky N. (1969) *American Power and the New Mandarins* (New York, Vintage Books).
Cimade, Inodep, & Min, K. (1986) *Africa's Refugee Crisis – What's to be done?* (London, Zed Books).
Clarkson, S. (1979) *The Soviet Theory of Development – India and the Third World in Marxist–Leninist Scholarship* (London, Macmillan).
Cliffe, L., & Saul, J. S. (eds) (1975) *Socialism in Tanzania*, Vol. 1 and Vol. 2 (Dar es Salaam, East Africa Publishing House).
Cohen, D. L., & Daniel, J. (1981) *The Political Economy of Africa* (London, Longman Publishers).
Connor, J. O. (1973) *The Fiscal Crisis of the State* (New York, St. Martins Press).
Constantinoh, R. (1978) *Neocolonial Identity and Counter-Consciousness – Essays on Cultural Decolonisation* (London, Merlin Press).
Curtin, P. D. (1969) *The Atlantic Slave Trade* (London).
Davidson, Basil (1974) *Can Africa Survive? Arguments Against Growth Without Development* (Toronto, Little Brown & Co.).
Dean, Edwin (1972) *Plan Implementation in Nigeria, 1962/66* (Ibadan, Oxford University Press).
Debray, Regis (1971) *Strategy for Revolution* (New York, Monthly Review Press).
Derry, T. K. & Jarman, T. L. (1956) *The Making of Modern Britain* (Plymouth Press).

Diejomaoh, V. P. (1983) "The Economic Integration Process in Africa: Experience, Problems and Prospects", paper presented at the 7th World Congress of the International Economic Association, 5–9 September, Madrid, Spain.

—— & Iyoha, M. A. (eds) (1980) *Industrialization in ECOWAS* (Ibadan, Heinemann).

Dike, K. O. (1960) *Trade and Politics in the Niger Delta* (Lagos, Federal Ministry of Information).

Dinham, B., & Hines, C. (1983) *Agribusiness in Africa* (London, Earth Research).

Domar, E. (1946) "Capital Expansion, Rate of Growth and Employment", *Econometrica*, 14, pp. 137–147.

—— (1972) "A Soviet Model of Growth" in Nove, A., & Nati, D. M. (1972) *Socialist Economics* (Penguin).

Durand, J. O. (1967) *The Modern Expansion of World Population*, Proceedings of the America Philosophical Association.

ECA (1975) *African Economic Indicators*, Economic Commission for Africa (ECA), Statistics Division, Addis Ababa.

Edwards, R. C. et al. (eds) (1972) *The Capitalist System – A Radical Analysis of American Society* (Englewood Cliffs, Prentice-Hall).

Emmanuel, A. (1972) *Unequal Exchange and the Imperialism of Trade* (New York, Monthly Review Press).

Esman, M. J. (1978) *Landlessness and Near Landlessness in Developing Countries* (Cornell University Press).

Falola, T., & Ihonvbere, I. (1985) *The Fall of the Second Republic of Nigeria* (London, Zed Books).

Fanon, Frantz (1967) *The Wretched of the Earth* (Harmondsworth, Penguin).

—— (1967) *Toward the African Revolution* (New York, Grove Press).

Fine, Ben (1980) *Economic Theory and Ideology* (London, Edward Arnold).

Fitt, Y. et al. (1980) *The World Economic Crisis – US Imperialism at Bay* (London, Zed Press).

Frank, A. G. (1970) *Latin America – Underdevelopment or Revolution* (New York, Monthly Review Press).

—— (1972) *Lumpen-Bourgeoisie and Lumpen-Development* (New York, Monthly Review Press).

—— (1980) *Crisis in the Third World* (New York).

Friedman, J. (1979) "Basic Needs Approach to Agropolitical Development and Planning from Below", *World Development*, Vol. 7.

Freire, Paulo (1975) *The Pedagogy of the Oppressed* (Harmondsworth, Penguin).

Galbraith, K. (1978) *The New Industrial State* (Harmondsworth, Penguin).

Gamble, A. & Watson, P. (1976), *Capitalism in Crisis-Inflation and the State* (London, Macmillan).

George, Susan (1976) *How the Other Half Dies* (Harmondsworth, Penguin).

Geteano, E. (1974) *Open Veins of Latin America: Five Countries of the Pillage of a Continent* (New York, Monthly Review Press).

Gibson, B. (1980) "Unequal Exchange – Theoretical Issues and Empirical Findings", *Review of Radical Political Economics*, Vol. 12, No. 3.

Girvan, N. (1977) "Technology – A New White Magic for Africa", *Africa Development*, Vol. 2, No. 2.

Gorbachev, M. (1986) *Political Report of the CPSU Central Committee to the 27th Party Congress* (Moscow, Novosti Press Agency Publishing House).

Gouldner, Alvin (1972) *The Coming Crisis of Western Sociology* (New York).

Green, R. H., & Seidman, A. (1968) *Unity or Poverty? The Economics of Pan-Africanism* (Baltimore, Penguin).

Griffen, K. (1979) *The Political Economy of Agrarian Change – An Essay on the Green Revolution* (London, Macmillan).

Gutheridge, W. F. (1976) *Military Regimes in Africa* (London, Methuen & Co.).

Gutkind, P. C. W., & Wallerstein, I. (eds) (1976) *The Political Economy of Contemporary Africa* (Sage Publications).

Harrod, R. F. (1939) "An Essay in Dynamic Theory", *Economic Journal*, 49, pp. 14–33.

Hazlewood, A. (1975), *Economic Integration – The East African Experience* (London, Heinemann).

Helleiner, G. K. (1964) "The Fiscal Role of the Marketing Board in Nigerian Economic Development, 1947/61", *Economic Journal*, Vol. 74, No. 295, September.

Herskovits, M. (1962) *The Human Factor in Changing Africa* (New York, Vintage Books).

Hirschman, A. (1958) *The Strategy of Economic Development* (New Haven, Connecticut).

Holland, Stuart (ed.) (1979) *Beyond Capitalist Planning* (Oxford, Blackwell).

Holslitz, B. F. (1960) *Sociological Factors in Economic Development* (Glencoe, The Free Press).

Hunt, E. K. (1975) *Property and Prophets – the Evolution of Economic Institutions and Ideologies* (London, Harper & Row).

IMF, *World Economic Outlook*, 1980 (Washington).

IMF, *World Economic Outlook*, 1982 (Washington).

Joseph, J. J. (1982) "Foreign Investment and Profits in Developing Countries", Paper presented at the AAPSO Second International on the "Role of TNC's and Economic Development Strategies", 28 April–4 May, Addis Ababa, Ethiopia.

Kaplinsky, R. (ed.) (1978) *Multinational Corporations in Kenya* (Nairobi, Oxford University Press).

Kirichenko, V. N. (1980) *Socialist Long-Term Planning* (Moscow, Progress Publishers).

Klein, R. W. (1973) "A Dynamic Theory of Comparative Advantage", *American Economic Review*, Vol. LXIII, No. 1, March.

Knight, M. M. et al. (1928) *Economic History of Europe* (London).

Körner, P., et al. (1986) *The IMF and the Debt Crisis* (London, Zed Books).

Kuper, L., & Smith M. G. (1969) *Pluralism in Africa* (Los Angeles, The University of California Press).

Kuznets, Simon (1946) *The National Product Since 1869* (New York).

Lenin, V. I. (1948) *Imperialism – The Highest Stage of Capitalism* (Moscow, Progress Publishers).

——— (1964) *The Development of Capitalism in Russia* (Moscow, Progress Publishers).

Lipsey, R. G. (1971) *An Introduction to Positive Economics* (London, Weidenfield & Nicolson).

Magdoff, Harry (1968) *The Age of Imperialism* (New York, Monthly Review Press).

Magubane, B. (1976) "The Evolution of the Class Structure in Africa" in P. C. W. Gutkind & I. Wallerstein (eds) *The Political Economy of Contemporary Africa* (London, Sage).

Mamdani, M. (1983) *Imperialism and Fascism in Uganda* (Dar es Salaam, Tanzania

Publishing House; Ibadan and Nairobi, Heinemann).
Mannheim, Karl (1968) *Ideology and Utopia – An Introduction to the Sociology of Knowledge* (London, Routledge Publishers).
Manning, D. J. (1980) *The Form of Ideology* (London, Allen and Unwin Publishers).
Marcussen, H. S. & Torp, J. E. (1982) *Internationalisation of Capital – Prospects for the Third World* (London, Zed Press).
Marx, Karl (1977) *Capital*, Vol. 1 (Moscow, Progress Publishers).
——— & Engels F. (1978) *On Colonialism* (Moscow, Progress Publishers).
——— (1980) *Collected Works* (Moscow, Progress Publishers).
Mattick, Paul (1980) *Marx and Keynes – The Limits of the Mixed Economy* (London, Merlin Press).
McClelland, D. (1964) "A Psychological Approach to Economic Development", *Economic Development and Cultural Change*, Vol. 12, No. 3.
Monroe, J. F. (1976) *Africa and the International Economy, 1800–1960* (London, Dent and Sons).
Morton, A. L. (1952) *The English Utopia* (London, Lawrence & Wishart).
Nabudere, Dan (1978) *The Political Economy of Imperialism* (London, Zed Press).
——— (1981) *Imperialism in East Africa*, Vol. 1 (London, Zed Press).
——— (1982) *Imperialism in East Africa*, Vol. 2 (London, Zed Press).
Nigeria (1945) *A Ten-Year Plan for Development and Welfare in Nigeria*, Sessional Paper No. 24.
Nigeria (1974) *Progress Reports on the Second National Development Plan, 1970/74* (Lagos).
Nkrumah, Kwame (1973) *Class Struggle in Africa* (London, Panaf/Zed Books).
——— (1974) *Neocolonialism – The Highest Stage of Capitalism* (London, Panaf/Zed Books).
——— (1964) *Consciencism* (London, Panaf/Zed Books).
Novak, George (1971) *Empiricism and its Evolution – A Marxist View* (New York, Pathfinder Press).
Novak, George (1979) *The Origins of Materialism* (New York, Pathfinder Press).
Ntalaja, N. (ed.) (1986) *The Crisis of Zaire – Myths and Realities* (African World Press).
Nzula A. T. et. al. (1979) *Forced Labour in Colonial Africa* (London, Zed Press).
Okello, J. (1967) *Revolution in Zanzibar* (Nairobi, East Africa Publishing House).
Onimode, Bade (1987) *The Crisis of Neocolonial Capitalism in Nigeria* (Oguta, Zims Pan-African Publishers).
——— (1982) *Imperialism and Underdevelopment in Nigeria – The Dialectics of Mass Poverty* (London, Zed Press).
——— et al. (1983) *Multinational Corporations in Nigeria* (Ibadan, Les Shyraden).
OAU (1981) *The Lagos Plan of Action for the Economic Development of Africa, 1980–2000* (Addis Ababa).
OECD (1967) *The Level and Structure of Research Development Efforts in OECD Member Countries* (Paris, OECD, 1967).
Osagie, E., & E. C. Edozien (1982) *Economic Integration in West Africa* (Ibadan, Ibadan University Press).
Palmberg, Mai (ed.) (1983) *The Struggle for Africa* (London, Zed Press).
Panter-Brick, K. (ed.) (1978) *Soldiers and Oil* (London, Frank Cass).
Parson, Talcott (1960) *Structure and Process in Modern Societies* (Glencoe, The Free Press).
Payer, Cheryl (1982) *The World Bank – A Critical Analysis* (New York, Monthly Review Press).

——— (1974) *The Debt Trap – The International Monetary Fund and the Third World* (New York, Monthly Review Press).

Poulantzas, Nicos (1975) *Classes in Contemporary Capitalism* (London, New Left Books).

Rawlings, J. J. (1981) *A Revolutionary Journey – Selected Speeches* Vol. 1 (Accra).

Ray, K. N. (1967) *The Role of the Machine-Tool Sector* (n.p./nd.)

Robinson, Joan (1971) *Economic Heresies* (London, Macmillan).

Robson, P. (1968) *Economic Integration in Africa* (London, Allen and Unwin).

Robson, F., & Lury, D. (eds) (1969) *The Economy of Africa* (London, George Allen & Unwin).

Rodney, Walter (1972) *How Europe Underdeveloped Africa* (Dar es Salaam, Tanzania Publishing House).

Rostow, W. W. (1962) *The States of Economic Growth – A Non-Communist Manifesto* (Cambridge University Press).

Rowthorn, Bob (1980) *Capitalism, Conflict and Inflation* (London, Lawrence and Wishart).

Rweyemanu, J. F. (1980) *Industrialization and Income Distribution in Africa* (CODESRIA, Dakar and Zed Press, London).

Sandbook, R., & Cohen, R. (eds) (1975) *The Development of an African Working Class – Studies in Class Formation and Action* (London, Longman).

Saul, J. S. (1974) "African Peasants and Revolution", *Review of African Political Economy*, August–November, pp. 41–68.

——— (1981) "African Peasants and Revolution" in D. L. Cohen & J. Daniel (eds) (1981) *Political Economy of Africa – Selected Readings* (London, Longman).

Schatz, S. P. (1977) *Nigerian Capitalism* (Berkeley, University of California Press).

Seidman, A. & Makgetla, N. S. (1980) *Outposts of Monopoly Capitalism – Southern Africa in the Changing Global Economy* (London, Zed Press).

Senghor, L. S. (1959) *African Socialism* (New York, Society of African Culture).

Shivji, Issa (197?) *Class Struggle in Tanzania* (Dar es Salaam, Tanzania Publishing House).

——— (1973) *The Silent Class Struggle in Tanzania* (Dar es Salaam, Tanzania Publishing House).

Stahl, M. (1974) *Ethiopia – Political Contradictions in Agricultural Development* (Stockholm, Ruben and Sjogren).

Staruskenko, G. (1982) *Why More Countries are Opting for Socialism in Africa and the World Today* (Moscow, Novosti Publishing House).

Sutton, K. (1974) "Agrarian Reform in Algeria – The Conversion of Projects into Action", *Afrika Spectrum*, 77 (1), pp. 50–68.

Sweezy, P. M. (1972) *Modern Capitalism and Other Essays* (New York, Monthly Review Press), Ch. 4.

Tandon, Yash (ed.) (1982) *Debate on Class, State and Imperialism* (Dar es Salaam, Tanzania Publishing House).

Temu, A., & Swai, B. (1981) *Historians and Africanist History – A Critique* (London, Zed Press).

Teriba, O., & Kayode, M. O. (eds) (1977) *Industrial Development in Nigeria: Patterns, Problems and Prospects* (Ibadan University Press).

Thomas, D. S. (1976) *Importing Technology into Africa: Foreign Investment and the Supply of Technological Innovations* (New York, Praeger).

U.N. (1983) *Twenty-Five Years of Service to African Development and Integration* (Addis Ababa, ECA).

UNCTAD Secretariat (1977) "Technological Dependence, Its Nature, Consequences and Policy Implications", *Africa Development*, Vol. 2, No. 2.

UNESCO (1979) "Declarations and Recommendations" of the Expert Meeting on the Formulation of Social Science Policies in Africa South of the Sahara, Kinshasa, Zaire, 8–12 October.

UNIDO: "The Changing Role of Manufacturing in African Economic Development: Trends, Prospects and Issues", *African Development*, Vol. VII, No. 1/2, 1982.

United States Department of Commerce, *Survey of Current Business*, December 1973.

USSR (1982) *Where Human Rights are Real* (Moscow, Progress Publishers).

Vaitsos, C. (1970) "Transfer of Resources and Preservation of Monopoly Rents", *Economic Development Report*, No. 168, Centre of International Affairs, Harvard University.

Van den Berghe (1965) "Toward a Sociology of Africa", *Africa – Social Problems of Change and Conflict* (San Francisco, Chandler).

Widstrand, C. (1975) *Multinational Firms in Africa* (Uppsala, Scandinavian Institute of African Studies).

Williams, Eric (1972) *Capitalism and Slavery* (London, Deutsch).

Wolde, Haile Michel (1981) "Issues in Social and Economic Development of Africa" (mimeo).

World Bank *World Development Report 1980, 1982, 1984, 1985, 1986, 1987* (Washington).

World Bank (1981) *World Bank Accelerated Development in Sub-Saharan Africa* (Washington).

World Bank (1983), *Sub-Saharan Africa – Progress Report on Development Prospects and Programmes* (Washington).

World Bank (1984) *Toward Sustained Development in Sub-Saharan Africa – A Joint Program of Action* (Washington).

Yachir, F. (ed.) (1981) *Technology and Industrialisation in Africa* (Dakar, CODESRIA).

Yansane, A. Y. (ed.) (1980) *Decolonisation and Dependency* (Sage Publications).

Zahar, R. (1974) *Colonialism and Alienation – Political Thought of Frantz Fanon* (Benin, Ethiope Publishing Corporation).

Zakine D. (1968) "Classes and Class Struggle in Developing Countries", *International Affairs*, No. 4.

Zeilinski, J. G. (1968) *Lectures on the Theory of Socialist Planning* (Ibadan & London, Oxford University Press).

Index

Institute for African Alternatives

The Institute for African Alternatives was established in 1986 to encourage research and discussion on contemporary problems in Africa. The Institute is located in London (UK) and consists of a suite of offices, a lecture hall, a common room and study rooms.

IFAA is headed by a Council consisting of the following:

Activities

Research and Debate: The Institute facilitates research on African problems and encourages debate around current issues.

Conferences, Workshops, Seminars: A major annual conference is held at IFAA with invited speakers from across Africa, as well as a special annual conference on African women. Workshops are also held on a specialist basis and seminars on particular topics. Where possible proceedings are recorded and published.

Lectures and Classes: From time to time a lecture series is arranged. Classes are also run on such topics as History of Africa, Development problems, Neocolonialism, History of African Women, Southern Africa etc. A residential 3 months course on "Policy Making, Development Policy and African Women" is under preparation.

Publishing: An important role is the publication of conference proceedings at IFAA, books by associates of IFAA, occasional lectures and other materials.

An African Women Development Newsletter is underway which will appear quarterly and be distributed in at least six countries in the first instance.

Documentation Centre

A start has been made to create a specialist documentation library and it is hoped to expand this greatly in due course.

Address: IFAA
23 Bevenden Street
London N1 6BH
UK

Telephone: 01-251 1503
Telex: 923753 Ref W6019